Alternatives Within the Mainstream

Alternatives Within the Mainstream British Black and Asian Theatres

Edited by

Dimple Godiwala

CAMBRIDGE SCHOLARS PRESS

Alternatives Within the Mainstream: British Black and Asian Theatres, edited by Dimple Godiwala

This book first published 2006 by

Cambridge Scholars Press

15 Angerton Gardens, Newcastle, NE5 2JA, UK

British Library Cataloguing in Publication Data
A catalogue record for this book is available from the British Library

ISBN 1904303668

TABLE OF CONTENTS

ACKNOWLEDGEMENTS:

I am grateful to Rukhsana Ahmad, Yvonne Brewster, Nizwar Karanj, Valerie Mason-John, Sol B. River, Bapsi Sidhwa and Jatinder Verma for their support of this project. I appreciate the generosity of Rukhsana Ahmad, Anu Kumar, Bapsi Sidhwa and *Kali* Theatre Company for lending me unpublished playscripts. Grateful thanks are due to Colin Chambers for his excellent advice on the MS and to Peter Thomson for his constructive comments on the chapters which made up the special issue of *Studies for Theatre and Performance*. I owe thanks to my husband Stephen Michael McGowan for his helpful comments on my writing and the warm support and encouragement he unfailingly provides. For the help they extended, my thanks to all the librarians and staff at York St John College Fountains Learning Centre, in particular, Lottie Alexander, Claire McCluskey, Adriana Lombari, Fiona Ware and Linda West. Thanks also to *Kali*, Yvonne Brewster, Valerie Mason-John, Sol B. River, the Royal National Theatre, *Talawa, Tara* Arts and *Tamasha* for the photographs in this book.

This book is dedicated to Nizwar Karanj and also to my parents, Kaushalya and Prabodh Godiwala.

Other acknowledgements follow the chapters.

PERMISSIONS:

I am grateful to Peter Lang for permission to reproduce some of the critical material on *Chiaroscuro* which was first published in my monograph *Breaking the Bounds: British Feminist Dramatists Writing in the Mainstream since c. 1980*, New York & Oxford: Peter Lang, 2003.

Abridged versions of my Introduction 'Alternatives Within the Mainstream: British Black and Asian Theatres' and my chapters 'Genealogies, Archaeologies, Histories: The Revolutionary "Interculturalism" of Asian Theatre in Britain' and '*Kali*: Providing a Forum for British-Asian Women Playwrights' first appeared in the special issue on Black and Asian theatre, *Studies in Theatre and Performance*, Vol. 26.1 (2006). Deirdre Osborne's 'Writing Black Back: An Overview of Black Theatre and Performance in Britain'; Kathleen Starck's 'Black and Female is Some of Who I Am and I Want to Explore it: Black Women's Plays of the 1980s and 1990s'; Jatinder Verma's 'The Shape of a Heart' and a slightly different version of Sol B. River's 'Serious Business' also first appeared in the same issue.

Some material from Deirdre Osborne's 'The State of the Nation: Voicing the Margins in the Staging of the UK', first appeared in 'Proceedings of the

Thirteenth Annual Conference of the German Society for Contemporary Theatre and Drama in English', 3-6 June. Published in Christoph Houswitschka and Anja Muller-Muth (eds.), *Staging Displacement, Exile and Diaspora*, University of Bamberg, 2005.

Some material from Zodwa Motsa's 'A Scourge of the Empire: Wole Soyinka's Notorious Theatre at the Royal Court' first appeared in her introduction to *Wole Soyinka: The Invention & The Detainee* (ed.) Zodwa Motsa, Tshwane: University of South Africa Press, 2005.

WEBSITES:

All the websites used by contributors in this book were functioning when they were accessed. The editor and contributors take no responsibility for the subsequent dismantling or malfunctioning of websites.

I. INTRODUCTION

ALTERNATIVES WITHIN THE MAINSTREAM: BRITISH BLACK AND ASIAN THEATRES

AN INTRODUCTION

[*2001: A Ramayana Odyssey*: Tara Arts]

Reading Pierre Bourdieu's *Outline of a Theory of Practice* recently, I noticed, amongst the many excellent sociological uses he has put Michel Foucault's theories in *An Archaeology of Knowledge* to, an extension of the latter's definition of the ideal cultural analyst or anthropologist.[1] For Bourdieu, because agents of society are possessed by their *habitus* more than they possess it, because they take for granted the values, norms, practices and ideologies of their particular group, the unthinkable and the unnameable schema which are implicit in and make possible the *doxa experience* can only be partially identified or articulated by the native informant.[2] It takes an *outsider-*

---

[1] 'It is not possible for us to describe our own archive. Constituted and formed within it, it delimits us as we speak from within its very rules. It is that which gives to what we can say its modes of appearance, its forms of existence and co-existence, its system of accumulation, historicity, and disappearance. Who then can hold the mirror up to us? Who can describe us as we are, in the mode of our becoming, even as we transform ourselves? Is it not one who is interstitial—inside enough to understand fully our boundaries and delimitation, at once close to us, and yet different from our present existence, someone on the border of our time and our presence, someone who can indicate yet its otherness and our possibilities, one who is a presence in the gap between our own discursive practices?' Michel Foucault, *The Archaeology of Knowledge*, p.130–1; translation modified.

[2] Pierre Bourdieu explains *doxa* as the experience of the *misrecognition* (and therefore, recognition) of the social practices of one's own group as 'natural', indisputable or taken for

oriented discourse to analyze and theorize the social practices of groups which exist as lacunae in the native's conscious mind (Bourdieu [1972] 1977: 18, 20, 164 ff). As an *interstitial-outsider* in British society, by virtue of being a permanent British Resident rather than a national, I hope 'to speak', as Bourdieu puts it, rather than '*be spoken*' in my introduction to contemporary forms of British theatre (Bourdieu [1984] 1993:3). In this book, these are Black and Asian theatres.[3]

Mapping the terrain

A publisher told me he did not approve of separatism when I proposed a critical anthology on Black and Asian drama; an admirable sentiment perhaps, as an attitude towards inclusion is always laudable.

However, locating the histories of subject-agents who belonged to previously colonized territories within the logic of western trajectories, defines Black by what it is not, by what it does not resemble. Black and Asian identity in Britain, therefore, is generally perceived as being located in a difference from, and not within the constructed ethnic identity (Englishness) of the mainstream. The latter may be defined as contemporary *White* writing which seldom represents the racial Other. It is only by locating themselves in an identity space which reflects the material of their histories, the forms of their own performance, their values and ideologies, their social practices, can dramatists of colour begin to write their identities and experience as subjects-in-the-world.

I hesitate to define this space yet again as 'post-colonial' drama. To use this now-tired term is to continue to locate the west in the centre of a discourse which has been more or less ignored by the (White, western) mainstream. As Anne McClintock puts it, the term postcolonial 'confers on colonialism the prestige of history proper'; it implies that it is colonialism which is 'the determining marker of history'. It further implies that '[o]ther cultures share only a chronological, prepositional relation to a Euro-centred epoch that is over [as implied in 'post'], or not yet begun [as implied in the prefix 'pre']. In other words, the world's multitudinous cultures are marked, not positively by what distinguishes them, but

---

granted. The native informant therefore displays a practice and a discourse partially ignorant of its own truth. ([1972] 1977: 164 ff, 18-20).

[3] We have not, in the main, contested the terms 'Black' and 'Asian', taking them to denote those of Afro-Caribbean origins (Black) and those whose ancestors hail from the Indian sub-continent, which includes modern day Pakistan and Bangla Desh (Asian). We have taken those of mixed ethnic origins to belong to the category they identify with. However, we sometimes subsume those of colour under the monolithic rubric 'Black' to denote a common purpose and solidarity. For more on biological-hybrid identities see Dimple Godiwala, 'Postcolonial Desire: Mimicry, Hegemony, Identity', (in Kuortti & Nyman 2006).

by a subordinate, retrospective relation to [Europe]' (McClintock [1992] 2000: 84-97, 177).

In this respect, John Liu, analyzing race and ethnic relations in the west, contends that race and ethnic minorities have been relegated to a position of underdevelopment and dependency in a socio-economic structure similar to that of a classical colony. Thus the situation of the country is that of an 'internal colony'. The policies and structures which arose in the classical colonial situation continue to exist in an internal colonial situation (Liu 2000: 1347-1348).

In a country such as Britain which is riven by the hierarchy of class, race then represents another kind of barrier. The institutionalization of racism allows for tokenism, by which a certain kind of liberal from the dominant classes can reassure himself of his multicultural inclusiveness whilst continuing to exclude his racial/economic others in very large part.

Tanika Gupta's observation that Asian dramatists 'don't get nominated for mainstream awards. It still feels very much as if the theatre industry and TV and film really take only their own work seriously – meaning White work.' (Marlowe, 2003) combined with the fact that a separate casting file exists for Black and Asian actors, confirms the simultaneous tokenization and ghettoization experienced by Blacks and Asians in the theatre.

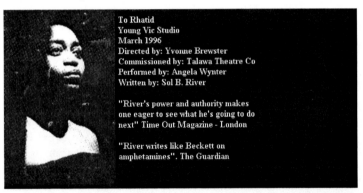

To Rhatid
Young Vic Studio
March 1996
Directed by: Yvonne Brewster
Commissioned by: Talawa Theatre Co
Performed by: Angela Wynter
Written by: Sol B. River

"River's power and authority makes one eager to see what he's going to do next" Time Out Magazine - London

"River writes like Beckett on amphetamines". The Guardian

[Sol B. River and Talawa's *To Rahtid*. Photo courtesy: Sol B. River]

To return to my argument for a separate anthology: many British mainstream critical anthologies of drama were nothing but representations of White male writing, and, since Christopher Innes' hesitant and naïve analysis of contemporary women's plays in the short end-chapter to the otherwise excellent *Modern Drama* published by Routledge in 1992, White women's writing. In relation to the writing of Black and Asian dramatists, the work of White writers represents the very impulse that the former are resisting, as the portrayal of English society as fixed by whiteness is implicit in the dramatic and production texts of almost every White English dramatist and director, in their collective neglect to portray Britain as multicultural

(See Godiwala 2003; 2004; 2006a). Richard Eyre and Nicholas Wright's wide-ranging survey, *Changing Stages: A View of British Theatre in the Twentieth Century,* which was also a television series in 2000, does not even pretend to include British Black and Asian theatres as part of Britain's changing stages (Eyre & Wright 2000). These self-conscious makers of a continued fixity of 'Englishness' in theatre write by means of an anachronistic authorized discourse in their particular *doxic field* which operates by means of exclusion.[4] Perhaps it is this tendency which constitutes the impossibility of the notion of an intercultural theatre which Patrice Pavis speaks of. He opines that it may be 'more productive to speak of *intercultural exchanges* within theatre practice rather than of the constitution of a new genre emerging for the synthesis of heterogeneous traditions (Pavis 1996: 1). However, the racial heterogeneity of contemporary Britain seems to be a subject tackled largely (and excellently) by the strangers in diaspora rather than the indigenous or 'ethnic English' dramatist or director. Furthermore, it is these very theatres which function as sites of genuine interculturalism within the changing structures of British stages. There is thus a very real need at this moment in the early years of the twenty-first century, when many scholars are engaged with writing about and analyzing Black and Asian theatre, to record these theatre histories and the work of the many dramatists and theatre companies, as well as make generally known the identities of those responsible for some of the best work on the British stage.

Enacting identity through performance

Contemporary Black and Asian dramaturgy is born of immigrant lineage. The makers of this theatre (playwrights, directors and actors) are mainly first and second generation British nationals and citizens; but they may also include *expatriate* writers who choose to live and work in Britain for personal reasons but are not British. Identity may well be a much theorized postmodern issue; but for Black and Asian writers of diaspora, located in a culture quite different from their familial and/ or geographic originary culture/s, identity and its construction becomes an urgent, often fraught, issue. Necessarily hybridized by the geographical and cultural locus of their productions which can often be at odds with the culture (or imagined culture) they feel they belong to, Black and Asian

---

[4] Colonial ideology has reified the ideas of English superiority which are then infused through the exclusions of discourses such as the one within which the idea of Eyre & Wright's English theatre is constituted. For an analysis of the patriarchal, colonial and capitalist impulses which substrate western culture and drama, see *Breaking the Bounds* (Godiwala 2003: 3-36).

theatremakers inscribe within British drama a space which is informed by a dual history of belonging.

[*The Gods are not to Blame,* Talawa Theatre Company and Yvonne Brewster's adaptation of Ola Rotimi's *Oedipus.* Photo courtesy: Yvonne Brewster]

Black and Asian producers of theatre *enact performance* differently as they have their own systems of significations. An audience of a Caribbean-Black or Indian or Pakistani play has different expectations from the performance. Often, they expect to see their own group's cultural and social codes, in the verbal and non-verbal elements of the performance text: language (and if this is English, an enaction of, for example, Indian or Caribbean forms of English); gesture; performance forms such as music or dance and other non-verbal elements.

Culturally – or by means of rigorous training – programmed, an actor's *disposition* is inscribed in schemes of thought, perceptions, mental dispositions and, at a deeper level, in the form of body schema: bodily postures and stances, ways of standing, sitting, looking, speaking, walking. The cultivated disposition enables each agent (actor) to convey modes of social practice and ideology which are inherently cultural (cf. Bourdieu [1972]1977: 15).

This sets Afro-Caribbean-Black apart from 'Indian' or 'Pakistani', and further distinguishes the subtleties of a Muslim play from a Hindustani or Parsi one. Especially, it also distinguishes Black and Asian theatre from the British mainstream. For the critic of these theatres, it often calls for an assessment and analysis of twin histories: those indigenous to English theatre and culture, which may be employed often as the play, many a time employing a multicultural cast, and playing to mixed-audiences, borrows freely of the practices and forms from the locus of its existence; and those indigenous to the culture the play originates in, either in the imagination or lived experience of social practices of its producers and performers. Black and Asian theatres are (formalistically and stylistically) ideally a marriage of minds of the best of the performance forms of both cultures they represent; at their most provocative, and in terms of content, they flag up the indignities suffered by the strangers in Western society and induce a change in attitudes in the host culture/s by producing what Pierre Bourdieu calls *a genuine counterculture*: one which is capable of distancing and analyzing the practices and ideology of the dominant culture rather than

> inverting it or, rather, imposing an inverted form of it. [...A] genuine counterculture is able to supply weapons for use against the soft forms of domination, the advanced forms of mobilization, the gentle violence of the new professional ideologists, who often rely on a kind of quasi-scientific rationalization of the dominant ideology; against the political uses of science, not to mention the biology or sociology of the advanced (and highly euphemized) forms of racism. [...It] would mean proliferating the weapons of defence against symbolic domination. (Bourdieu [1984] 1993: 3 my emphasis)

The Blacks in Britain

The Afro-Caribbean Black presence in Britain goes back several centuries, rather than, as popularly believed, their mass arrival on *Empire Windrush*. The Black presence on the stage, though not very well documented, goes back to the tournament of the wild knight and the black lady, Renaissance representations in Ben Jonson's *The Masque of Blacknesse,* John Marston's *The Wonder of Women* and, of course, *Othello* (Gundara & Duffield 1992; MacDonald 2002: 1-11).

Since the Lumière brothers captured on film blackface minstrels on a London street in 1896, the Blacks have been

[Bert Williams, before and after blacking up]

represented in film and later, in television drama (Bourne 2001). The act of Blacks blacking up emphasized their difference to the 'notion of a fixed English identity [which] was doubtless a product of, and reaction to, the rapid change and transformation of both metropolitan and colonial societies which meant that, as with nationalism[s], such identities needed to be constructed to counter schisms, friction and dissent. [...] Fixity of identity is only sought in situations of instability and disruption, of conflict and change' (Young 1995: 3-4).

In a narrative which resembles blacked-up blacks, the expatriate Parsi-Indian actor Nizwar Karanj was forced to 'brown up' for his role as sacrificial victim in Steven Spielberg's 1984 film *Indiana Jones and the Temple of Doom* and his role as servant in the 80s BBC production *The Jewel in the Crown* as he was 'not quite brown enough' (Godiwala 1995). On the other hand, the Indo-English actor, Karan Kapoor, who played an English public school-boy in the same series was not required to use brown make-up. Homi Bhabha's theory that the not-quite-whiteness of colonized subjects poses a 'threat' to White culture seems contested by the experience of the minstrels and Indian actors *who might be far too light-skinned to conform to received stereotyped images of blackness or brownness of the colonised represented in performance.*[5] What is performed – blacked-up blackness – conceals and disavows 'what remains, opaque, unconscious, unperformable', (Butler via Lacan, 1993: 234) i.e. the arbitrariness of colour. The materiality of the racialized body is abstracted into 'Blackface' impersonation which remains purely representational, to convey certain racial ideologies which are embodied in blackness; it becomes an allusion to what race embodies, an appropriation and control, a displacement and an abstraction (cf. MacDonald 2002: 4-5) in white cultures, such as 'the savage other' in *Temple of Doom*, and the hierarchies of the colonized in *The Jewel in the Crown*.[6]

Blacks have been historically represented on the English stage with the curious ambivalence found famously in Shakespeare's Othello. The continuing fixities that determine the construction of Black identity in the rigid White space of the British

---

[5] For a response to Homi Bhabha's theory of *mimicry* (Bhabha 1994). and an analysis of the arbitrariness of the binarily opposed colour divide between coloniser and colonised, see Dimple Godiwala, 'Postcolonial Desire: Mimicry, Hegemony, Identity', (in Kuortti & Nyman 2006).

[6] Originally, slaves mocked their masters by performing slapstick imitations called 'puttin' on ole massa'. Whites, assuming these were representations of authentic black culture, blacked up as minstrels to imitate African Americans. Blacks blacking up is the irony of blacks imitating whites imitating blacks who were mocking whites in the first place (Hill 2003: 8).

stage often means that although the host culture is often represented in plays by
writers of colour, White dramatists seldom represent Black or Asian British
cultures or social practices in their work, even though Britain has seen the
heterogeneity of the racial presence for several centuries.

There is thus a need for the contemporary Black presence on the British stage.
Deirdre Osborne opines in 'The State of the Nation': 'The importance of including
and perpetuating indigenous Black British drama in the mainstream theatrescape

[*Urban Afro Saxons*, photo courtesy: Talawa Theatre Company]

can be neither under-estimated nor over-emphasised [...] Black drama exposes
mainstream (predominantly White) theatre-goers to aspects of Black British
cultural input that is *as* indigenous to contemporary British cultural identity as that
provided by White playwrights. It provides Black audiences with authentically
rendered cultural representations which have not as yet been able to develop a
flourishing continuum in Britain's cultural psyche' (Osborne in this anthology).
Kathleen Starck points out that 'The emergence of plays by Black women writers
in Britain is a later phenomenon. Although there have been male Black playwrights
such as Errol John, Wole Soyinka, and Derek Walcott whose plays had been
produced by the end of the 1960s, and later those such as Caryl Phillips and
Mustapha Matura, women remained largely invisible until the late 1970s/early
1980s.' Furthermore, 'Black women often did not feel represented by their White

sisters' writings. In addition to White women's oppression based on gender and class, Black women's experience not only included but often placed at the centre the category of race. Coinciding with the theorising of issues of national, cultural, sexual and ethnic identities in cultural, literary, lesbian and feminist studies, Black women started finding 'stage voices' of their own only from the 1980s' (Starck in this anthology).

The need for a separate space for Black writing *arises from the neglect of Black and Asian theatre and culture by White female and male playwrights alike*. The urgent need for radical societal change felt by Black dramatist, novelist and poet Jackie Kay led her to write *Chiaroscuro* which dealt with issues that Blacks in Britain found most difficult to confront and deal with: the total erasure of their identities, histories, names. In identifying wholly with a host culture which constantly rejects them, Kay's play reveals characters with misshapen ideas of their own self-worth, their appearance, their tastes, their practices (Godiwala 2003: 16-23). Examples of the latest work in Black theatre by women are the late Dona Daley and Debbie Tucker Green's texts.

The Asians in Britain

The Asian presence in Britain goes back to the 1630s (Visram 1995: 4). Visram narrates how Indian sailors (lascars) who journeyed to England during the Raj were poor and suffered 'ill-treatment, sickness and long waits in British ports. Pay and conditions were very poor.' Although there were some rich Indians in Britain in the 19th century, and some professionals, the majority were working class and desperately poor. Most wealthy Asians, such as Prince Ranjitsinji and Maharajah Duleep Singh were royal. Wealthy Indian women (the *Bourgeoisie Noire*) such as the Oxford-educated Cornelia Sohrabji (the first woman law student in Britain) and Sophia Duleep Singh (suffragette) were educated and politically active. There were a number of Indian MPs in England: Dadabhai Naoroji (MP in 1892), Sir Mancherjee Bhownaggree (1895), Shapurji Saklatvala (1922) (Visram 1995: 13-25).[7] In the 50s many rural poor from India emigrated to Britain. Visram's narrates the history of one man which typifies most Asian origins in Britain:

---

[7] *La Bourgeoisie Noire* was a phrase coined by E. Franklin Frazier, to describe the business class of Harlem. These were the people who escaped the white man's kitchen and dining room; families of professional and upper class men. (Hill 2003: 84). I think the phrase particularly apt here to describe the upwardly mobile Indians who were facilitated in their upward social and economic progress by the hierarchical British caste system which, like India, also operated on the basis of *varna*.

My father had come here in 1956, one of the first Pakistanis to come. He came to improve his standard of living, to earn some money and go back home. (Visram 1995: 41).

Meanwhile the Kenyan and Ugandan Asians were admitted into Britain as refugees in 1967 and 1972.

For the most part, Indians in England have been poor and from the lower classes. Denied an economic and social mobility in the caste-ridden, and, after the British presence, *class*-ridden subcontinent, Indians came to Britain as servants to the East India Company officers and royalty during the British Raj in the 17th to 19th centuries. The subsequent mid-20th century migrations from Africa and India consisted of the poor labourers who had no (or low) caste and had crossed *kala pani* to emigrate to Africa and elsewhere as they had 'no caste to lose' and everything to gain from the British system which afforded economic mobility to those who worked hard and practiced a discrimination similar to the caste system.[8] Caste which was originally determined on the basis of *varna* (colour) placed the Indians in Africa in a hierarchical order with the British on top and the Africans beneath them, enabling them to progress socially in a manner denied them in India.

[Members of the community and cast. Tara Arts' *Exodus*, Battersea Arts Centre, 1998]

British-Asian culture has needed to have a diasporic obsession with all traditions and rituals 'authentically' Indian, and, in the pursuit of the preservation

---

[8] *Kala pani*, literally 'the black waters', signified the oceans which no person of caste could cross without putting themselves in jeopardy of self-pollution, thereby losing caste. It was only those who were poor or of no caste, those that had 'no caste to lose' who would make the journey as servants and labourers to lands as distant as Africa, Malaysia and England.

of these, fossilizes them.[9] As Nissim Ezekiel put it: this is 'a kind of sterile continuity' of the migrant, 'a continuity without cultivation' (1965). The identity of the British-Asian is contingent on the particular Indian-ness of his sacraments, as he 'carrie[s] his village with him'. As Sartre put it in his preface to Fanon's *The Wretched of the Earth*, the sacred is turned into a weapon against despair and humiliation, 'in other words, the colonized defend themselves against colonial alienation by taking religious alienation to greater lengths'.[10] Originating in the need for the formation and preservation of identity as a collective resistance to the hostile exclusivity of the host culture, this collective longing to be constituted within the discursive matrix of the subcontinent, bizarrely – but also perhaps appropriately – extends to the mass commercial Bollywood film. Merged with this collective fantasmatic is the tradition and ritual carried so long and so rigidly by the diaspora, as to become ossified and almost meaningless except to the still – through all the generations – displaced subject to whom it offers the comforts of solidity and the connectedness and rootedness which was never offered by England.

Born and bred in England these subjects constituted in an almost forcible and forced difference are denied any definitions which would confer on them an English-ness through the long generations of their residence and citizenship. Thus the simulacra of customs past are a necessary fixation bestowing identity in a schizophrenic existence which offered social and economic mobility to so many but withheld any sense of belonging. These subjects are then, for the most part, structurally – and schizophrenically – constituted by the very terms of doxic English exclusion[11] to create and remain in the Indias of the mind whilst they

---

[9] Radio presenter Saadia Nasiri 'was surprised to find that in Pakistan [...] women had more freedom. 'Our parents are more strict [...] When we are in Pakistan my cousins [...] say, 'We are going to the disco tonight...' I think, 'Oh my God! Discos in Karachi!'' This 'time-warp' the British-Asians live in is explained by Sita Narasimhan. '[We Asians in Britain] perpetuate outworn customs, habits, languages and attitudes from twice-dispaced communities' (See Gifford 1990: 73-74).

[10] Sartre conflates sacrality with religion which is appropriate in this context (Sartre 2001: 146).

[11] Cf. Robert Young speaks of Englishness as a becoming, 'a fluidity' and a '*need* for otherness'. Yet this Kojèvian-Hegelian otherness he speaks of is in terms of a sexual need and desire for a *genderized* other which is *also* a racial other, a difference which almost always fulfils the need to define what English is *not*. Although his portrait of the contemporary London landscape is inclusive, imaginative and multicultural, much as Young would like to establish that the fluidity of Englishness is all embracing it cannot be ignored that Oscar Wilde and George Bernard Shaw are part of the White (washed?) English canon, but Salman Rushdie and Tanika Gupta will never be *English*. Englishness, however

partake of and contribute to the economy of their country of migrancy (Godiwala 2001).

This is the exclusionary matrix within which the Blacks and Asians are constituted, denying both the ability or opportunity to 'participate equally of the culture/s they inhabit', just as Beth in *Chiaroscuro* has to reject 'Dostoevsky, Dire Straits and Simon and Garfunkel' in order to accept and come to terms with her blackness by '[rushing out to buy] the black records that had never sat on [her] shelves, the blues, funk, jazz and soul I'd been missing' (Godiwala 2003: 22).

Nomadic acts

David Williams has reminded us that Peter Brook's vision of theatre is one of a space made provisionally homogeneous by the act of mixed groups comprised of performers and audience coming together in a shared space. He notes that this is especially important to the notion of a multicultural theatre, where the provoking of an audience to individual and collective action beyond the space of the theatre, and the rewriting of histories and performances induce what may be called a reformative action within communities making multicultural theatres (such as that of the British Blacks and Asians), performance acts of perpetual crisis, causing British society to re-write its racial exclusions in the social, economic and political context (Williams in Pavis 1996: 68).

These theatres may also be named *nomadic acts* by way of Deleuze and Guattari's conceptualization of the *nomad's deterritorialization and reterritorialization* ([1972] 1984). What I call 'nomadic acts' are contemporary acts (of theatre) which break the bounds of the exclusions and delimitations of the codes of White mainstream theatre and society, acts which cross and re-cross economic, political and social boundaries thereby transforming them, freeing individuals and communities by inspiring and provoking change in attitudes and behaviour to an acceptance of strangers in society.

∇

This book seeks to promote an awareness of the other cultures and theatre forms and styles that make today's British theatre the heterogeneous and dynamic space it is. Although this volume contains a substantial amount of new critical writing on Britain's Black and Asian theatres, it has not been possible to attempt a

---

inclusive it may have been in its formation, has always excluded the racialized *black* other. (1995: 2).

full history, as this would be at the cost of close or deep readings of individual plays. This book is fairly comprehensive as a collection of writing on and analysis of Black and Asian British theatres. It does not claim, however, to be a record of the entirety of their theatrical production, however recent those origins may seem in the early years of the twenty-first century.

It is generally supposed that there is not and has not been much work by the producers and makers of Black and Asian theatres in Britain; nothing can be further from the truth. It is not so much that there is not enough of this kind of work than there is not enough critical attention focused on it. A case in point was when box-office takings during the Black Theatre Seasons contradicted the critics' lukewarm response (see Alda Terracciano's survey of the Black Theatre Seasons at the West End in the 80s and 90s). This critical anthology aims to bridge the gap caused by the paucity of serious critical attention to Black and Asian British theatres by presenting a wide-ranging series of chapters which address not only histories and the work of leading theatre companies and groups, but also the dramatic works of individual dramatists both female as well as male. The book includes chapters which are overarching surveys of the plays, the companies, the venues, and also contains detailed, focused critical studies. The autobiographical voices of a handful of seminal theatremakers closes the book.

It has not been intended to present a specific point of view in this volume. It is a collection of often divergent points of view, from a list of contributors who are a motley assortment of critics and historians. The one crucial thing in which we all believe is the importance of documenting, recording and analyzing the histories and dramaturgy of Britain's Black and Asian alternatives within the theatrical mainstream.

Jatinder Verma, director of Tara Arts, Yvonne Brewster, noted for her directorial work especially with Talawa Theatre, Rukhsana Ahmad, playwright and author who has been responsible for the setting up of Kali Theatre Company, Valerie Mason-John, actor, director, writer, Sol B. River, the famed Yorkshire playwright and Bapsi Sidhwa, author of the play *Sock 'Em With Honey* but perhaps better known as a leading novelist, have all supported this project with enthusiasm, some contributing essays which describe their work in British theatre.

This critical anthology is in six parts:

Part II (*Histories and Trajectories*) follows the *Introduction* and contains chapters which survey the work of the Black Theatre Forum, which in the 80s and 90s was an umbrella term for Black and Asian theatrical work ('Mainstreaming African, Asian and Caribbean Theatre' by Alda Terracciano); other chapters trace the histories of Black ('Writing Black Back' and 'State of the Nation' by Deirdre Osborne) and Asian ('Genealogies, Archaeologies, Histories' by Dimple Godiwala) theatres in Britain.

Part III (*Histories of Theatre Companies and Arts Venues*) charts brief histories of the major theatre companies, Talawa (by Victor Ukaegbu), Tara and Tamasha (by Dominic Hingorani) and contains a survey of Birmingham's changing arts venues (by Claire Cochrane).

Part IV called simply *Controversies* analyzes what is, at the time of writing, a recent example of how art can sometimes shock or offend orthodox sensibilities. I can vividly recall the staging of the adaptation of Salman Rushdie's *Haroun and the Sea of Stories* at the Royal National Theatre in October 1998. The heavy security which consisted of infra-red metal detectors and guards inside and outside the London theatre was not on offer for Gurpreet Kaur Bhatti or her audiences in 2004. This section contains one chapter ('Drama in the Age of *Kalyug*' by Anthony Frost) which documents the Sikh diaspora's uproar over *Behzti* and issues of censorship.

Part V (*The Dramatists*) critically explores the work of several dramatists. Kathleen Starck's survey of Black women dramatists ('Black and Female is Some of Who I Am') focuses on some of the plays by Killion M. Gideon, Liselle Kayla, Roselia John Baptiste, Trish Cooke and Zindika whilst plays by Jackie Kay and Valerie Mason-John are examined in the light of a 'search for identity' and 'the claim for Englishness' (Dimple Godiwala). Wole Soyinka's 'The Invention' is critically evaluated by the editor of the play's first publication (University of South Africa Press, 2005) as she examines the marginalized role that Soyinka played at the Royal Court in the 50s ('A Scourge of the Empire' by Zodwa Motsa). Ashley Tellis looks at the best and worst of Sol B. River's theatrical strategies ('Theatre as Edutainment'); Roy Williams' work comes up for critical review as Elizabeth Barry and William Boles explore 'agency and identity' and Samuel Kasule explores 'madness and theatricality' in the work of Kwame Kwei-Armah. My chapter on Kali theatre company ('Providing a Forum for British-Asian Women Playwrights') focuses on its early productions, reading closely plays by Anu Kumar, Rukhsana Ahmad, Bettina Gracias and Bapsi Sidhwa. Kathleen Starck focuses on some of Tanika Gupta's plays analyzing how the playwright breaks the bounds of being solely a writer of race and Valerie Kaneko Lucas analyzes 'Women, Sexuality and Violence' in the plays of (the male playwright) Deepak Verma and (the women playwrights) Gurpreet Kaur Bhatti and Yasmin Whittaker Khan. An author's synopsis precedes each chapter.

Part V (*Theatre Voices*) contains autobiographical essays by some of Britain's theatremakers. Jatinder Verma traces the histories of his emigration to England and the setting up of Tara Arts, both of which are inextricably intertwined; Yvonne Brewster's narrative tells us that she is more than just Talawa's leading director; Sol B. River ruminates on theatre as being more of a 'serious business' than he imagined; prize-winning novelist Bapsi Sidhwa describes her first experience of writing for and being produced in the theatre; and Valerie Mason-John reveals herself as prolific in several modes of writing.

The British stage has been changing through the twentieth century to accommodate sites of radical and vital difference, from class and gender to sexuality, but it is Black and Asian theatres – England's theatres of race – which acknowledge the plurality and heterogeneity of Britishness more than any other kind of theatre in Britain today.[12]

Dimple Godiwala
Summer 2005
York

Photo credit: The photographs of Egbert 'Bert' Williams (1875-1922) are from Laban Carrick Hill's *Harlem Stomp! A Cultural History of the Harlem Renaissance*, Little Brown and Company, 2003. p.108.

Works cited

Bhabha, Homi (1994), *The Location of Culture*, London: Routledge.

Bourdieu, Pierre (1977), *Outline of a Theory of Practice* [*Esquisse d'une théorie de la pratique, précédé de trois études d'ethnologie kabyle*, 1972], trans. Richard Nice, Cambridge: Cambridge University Press.

Bourdieu, Pierre (1993), *Sociology in Question* [*Questions de sociologie*, 1984], trans. Richard Nice, London: Sage.

Bourne, Stephen (2001), *Black in the British Frame: The Black Experience in British Film and Television*, London: Continuum.

Butler, Judith (1993), *Bodies that Matter: On the Discursive Limits of 'Sex'*, London: Routledge.

---

[12] The Gunpowder Season opened at the Swan as this book was going to press in summer 2005. With a diverse cast which had an almost equal number of black actors as white, plays such as the anonymously scripted *Thomas More* and Massinger's reworked and re-named *Believe What You Will* had blacks play some parts which would normally have been played by white actors. With directorial decisions such as these made within mainstream theatre the future of English theatre looks plural as the concept of Englishness is made to include those born and brought up in England regardless of race. The 21st century Englishman may be black or white, on or off the English stage. (For other examples of multicultural casts in white mainstream theatre, see Deirdre Osborne, 'Writing Black Back: An Overview of Black Theatre and Performance in Britain' and Claire Cochrane, '"A Local Habitation and a Name": The Development of Black and Asian Theatre in Birmingham in the 1970s' in this volume).

Deleuze, Gilles and Félix Guattari (1984), *Anti-Oedipus: Capitalism and Schizophrenia* Vol. 1 [*L'Anti-Oedipe,* 1972], trans. Robert Hurley, Mark Seem, and Helen R. Lane, London: Athlone Press.

Deleuze, Gilles and Félix Guattari (1988), *A Thousand Plateaus: Capitalism and Schizophrenia* Vol. 2 [*Mille Plateaux: Capitalisme et Schizophrénie,* 1980], trans. Brian Massumi, London:Athlone Press.

Eyre, Richard and Nicholas Wright (2000), *Changing Stages: A View of British Theatre in the Twentieth Century,* London: Bloomsbury.

Ezekiel, Nissim (1974), 'Naipaul's India and Mine', [*Imprint,* 1965], *New Writing in India* (ed.) Adil Jussawalla, India: Penguin.

Foucault, Michel (1997), *The Archaeology of Knowledge* [*L' Archéologie du savoir,* 1969], trans. A. M. Sheridan Smith [1972], London: Routledge.

Gifford, Zerbanoo, *The Golden Thread: Asian Experience of Post-Raj Britain,* London: Pandora, 1990.

Godiwala, Dimple (2001), 'Hybridity/Invention/Identity: British-Asian Culture and its Postcolonial Theatres', *Journal for the Study of British Cultures,* 8, 1.

Godiwala, Dimple (2003), *Breaking the Bounds: British Feminist Dramatists Writing in the Mainstream since c. 1980,* New York & Oxford: Peter Lang.

Godiwala, Dimple (2004), '"The performativity of the dramatic text": domestic colonialism and Caryl Churchill's *Cloud Nine',* *Studies in Theatre and Performance,* 24: 1.

Godiwala, Dimple (2006a), 'Our Country's Good' (Timberlake Wertenbaker), *Encyclopaedia of Modern Drama,* Scholastic Library Publishing.

Godiwala, Dimple (2006b), 'Postcolonial Desire: Mimicry, Hegemony, Identity', in *Reconstructing Hybridity,* (eds.) Joel Kuortti and Jopi Nyman, Amsterdam and New York: Rodopi.

Gundara, Jagdish S.and Ian Duffield (eds.) (1992), *Essays on the History of Blacks in Britain From Roman Times to the Mid-Twentieth Century,* Aldershot: Avebury.

Hill, Laban Carrick (2003), *Harlem Stomp! A Cultural History of the Harlem Renaissance,* New York: Little Brown and Company.

Innes, Christopher (1992), *Modern Drama: 1890-1990,* Cambridge: Cambridge University Press.

Liu, John (2000), 'Towards an understanding of the internal colonial model', in Diana Brydon (ed.), *Postcolonialism: Critical Concepts* Vol.4, London: Routledge.

MacDonald, Joyce Green (2002), *Women and Race in Early Modern Texts,* Cambridge: Cambridge University Press.

McClintock, Anne (1992), 'The Angel of Progress: pitfalls of the term "post-colonialism"', *Social Text,* 31/32 (Spring), 84-97. Also in Brydon (ed.), *Postcolonialism: Critical Concepts.*

Osborne, Deirdre (2004), 'The State of the Nation: Voicing the Margins in the Staging of the UK', Proceedings of the Thirteenth Annual Conference of the German Society for Contemporary Theatre and Drama in English, 3-6 June. Published in Christoph Houswitschka and Anja Muller-Muth (eds.), *Staging Displacement, Exile and Diaspora*, University of Bamberg, 2005. A longer version of the conference paper is in this book, 'The State of the Nation: Contemporary Black British Theatre and the Staging of the UK.'

Pavis, Patrice (ed.) (1996), *The Intercultural Performance Reader*, London: Routledge.

Sartre, Jean-Paul (2001), *Colonialism and Neo-Colonialism* [1964], trans. Azzedine Haddour, Steve Brewer and Terry McWilliams, London: Routledge.

Starck, Kathleen (2006), 'Black and female is some of whom I am and I want to explore it: Black Women's Plays of the 1980s and 1990s', in this book.

Visram, Rozina (1995), *The History of the Asian Community in Britain,* Sussex: Wayland.

Williams, David (1996), '"Remembering the others that are us": Transculturalism and Myth in the theatre of Peter Brook', in Patrice Pavis (ed.), *The Intercultural Performance Reader*, London: Routledge.

Young, Robert (1995), *Colonial Desire: Hybridity in Theory, Culture and Race*, London: Routledge.

Newspapers
Marlowe, Sam (2003), 'Gupta's Choice,' in the *Independent*, 26 June.

Interviews
Godiwala, Dimple (1995), Interview with actor Nizwar Karanj, Oxford.

II. Histories and Trajectories

CHAPTER ONE

MAINSTREAMING AFRICAN, ASIAN AND CARIBBEAN THEATRE: THE EXPERIMENTS OF THE BLACK THEATRE FORUM

ALDA TERRACCIANO

Synopsis:
The chapter explores the activities of the Black Theatre Forum, an umbrella organisation of African Caribbean and Asian theatre companies active in London during the 1980s and 1990s. Set against the wider context of state funding to the arts and the cultural diversity policies of the time, the analysis focuses on the dynamics of production and reception of the Black Theatre Seasons - the first festival of black theatre produced by a black led organisation in mainstream London venues. The unique intercultural stance expressed by artists of the African and Asian diaspora and their search for a 'black' theatre aesthetics emerge as points of critical debate within the field of theatre and cultural studies.

The chapter will explore the process of mainstreaming artistic aesthetics and traditions of African and Asian descent in British theatre and relevant negotiations with the public funding system. It will do so through a close analysis of the activities of the Black Theatre Forum (BTF), an umbrella organisation of seventeen African, Caribbean and Asian theatre companies based in London. In particular, it will look at the dynamics of production and fruition of the Black Theatre Seasons, a series of six festivals produced by the Forum in the London West End during the 1980s, which presented plays all written, directed and interpreted by artists of African and Asian descent. In an attempt to take black theatre outside the limited confines of fringe and community venues, the various Seasons aimed at de-marginalising the contribution of black artists, while offering them a unique arena where theatre aesthetics and politics could be creatively explored, pointing to new directions in the life of black performance.

The use of the term 'black' in the chapter refers to the political banner that, from the late 1960s to the 1980s, unified the fight by communities of people of African and Asian descent in Britain for equal opportunities and greater visibility. Indeed, this terminology implied solidarity with political and civil rights struggles that went well beyond the geographical boundaries of Britain and came to identify the artistic expression of people of African and Asian origins in the theatre and other art forms. Hence, the social and political climate of the time was emblematically reflected in the development of the Forum during the 1980s to its decline towards the end of the 1990s.

The Beginning of the Black Theatre Seasons

The first seeds of the Forum were sown in 1983 with talks between Parminder Vir, Ethnic Arts Adviser at the Greater London Council (GLC), and Anton Phillips with the aim to put forward a policy for the development of black theatre to the GLC. A strategy was needed to underpin the achievements of the GLC, one of the main supporters of black theatre companies in London, and make more resources available for future developments. With this in mind, Anton Phillips, Director of Carib Theatre Productions (a company he co-founded in 1981 with Yvonne Brewster, the later co-founder and Director of Talawa Theatre Company) submitted, in 1983, an application to the GLC for the production of a season of black plays at the Arts Theatre in the London West End.

From the very onset of his artistic career, Phillips advocated an independent development of black theatre in Britain that 'would celebrate Blackness and would show Black people as they really are' (*Plays and Players* 1972). His idea of producing the Season was in line with such views, whilst the time seemed right to put forward a plan of action. In fact, as a result of the 1981 inner city riots, a new generation of black militants developed a so-called 'entryst strategy' to support their communities by entering institutions and occupying places with decisional and advisory powers. Meanwhile, funds had started to be directed towards the so-called 'race relations industry', and local authorities in addition to the GLC became more responsive to the demands for equal access to resources raised by people of African and Asian descent[13]. The phenomenon is accurately described in Anthias and Yuval-Davis' study where they pointed out:

---

[13] Noticeably, since David Pitt, a Labour candidate originally from Trinidad later knighted, became the first black chairman of the GLC in 1975, the number of black Labour

The very existence and definition as 'community' projects reflected, however, their marginality on the one hand and the growing use of 'community' as a euphemism for Blacks and ethnic minorities on the other hand. It is through the funding process that central government was able to pass the dilemma of drawing up a clear policy on handling racial tension on the local authorities, who were then able to pass it on to whoever was prepared to take it on in the local population by way of setting up grant-aided projects (Anthias & Yuval-Davis 1996: 181).

In this respect, the 'popular planning' advocated by Ken Livingstone, then member of the Labour Party and head of the GLC from the early to the mid 1980s was indicative of the trend. It celebrated the work of the 'community' – however problematic the meaning and use of the term – and by allocating funds at a grassroots level gave rise to a renaissance of the arts especially for those of African and Asian backgrounds. However, it also created a dependency of these groups on state funds as mainstream arts institutions did not follow in its footsteps, with disruptive consequences at the time when funds were curtailed.

It is against this political backdrop that Phillips' efforts to fundraise and produce the first Black Theatre Season were set. His strategy, as emerges from his correspondence with Rekha Prashar, the administrator of Tara Arts Company, was to capitalise on the favourability of current governmental policies and use the potentially successful outcomes of the Season to attract support for a permanent theatre venue dedicated to black theatre.

In the meantime the only venue in central London which was available to host the Season was the Arts Theatre, where the Unicorn Theatre Company was already booked with its children plays during the day[14]. This was not an insignificant detail, as it restricted both the set and light designs of the shows which were going to be presented during the evening. Moreover, after paying his first visit to the theatre, Phillips realised that the sum which he was likely to be granted by the funding body would have only covered the core costs for the Season. Therefore, in order to keep within the budget, he had to limit his choices and invite on board companies that already had plays in rehearsal and which were prepared to re-schedule their tours in order to fit in with the Season's programme at the Arts Theatre. Regardless

---

councillors in the public body grew steadily over the years. At the same time, the politicisation of sectors of the black population in conjunction with the riots in 1981 and 1985, supported black Labour candidates, including Bernie Grant, previously Labour councillor in Haringey, Diane Abbot and Paul Boateng, to win their seats in Westminster.

[14] Interestingly, the Arts Theatre had a long track record of presenting unconventional productions and companies. In 1955 it was the first theatre in London to show a Eugene Ionesco's play, *The Lesson*, directed by Peter Hall while in the 1970s it hosted alternative groups and theatre companies.

of all these limitations, Phillips pursued his plans and submitted an application to the GLC requesting an estimated amount of £32,434. As stated in the document:

> The Season of Black Plays at the Arts Theatre is designed to give Black actors and actresses, writers, directors, designers, stage managers, etc. the opportunity to practise their skills in a kind of theatre in which they rarely perform. (…) Our objectives are to present plays of a high professional standard to as wide an audience as possible. Also to assert that Black Theatre has a right to be seen in the best venues (GLC Appendix A 1983).

With a final amount of £26,000 granted on the basis that the Season represented 'a first step towards establishing black theatre alongside other arts forms in the London art scene', the programme of this pioneering first season included *Nevis Mountain Dew,* by Steve Carter (USA) directed by Rufus Collins for Black Theatre Co-operative, *Two Can Play*, by Trevor Rhone (Jamaica) directed by Anton Phillips for Inventory Productions, *The Outlaw* by Michael Abbensetts (originally from Guyana) directed by Robert Gillespie for Carib Theatre Productions and *Fishing* by Paulette Randall (UK) directed by Yvonne Brewster for Black Woman Time Theatre. The playbill offered a cross section of works from artists of the African diaspora and aimed at attracting both black audiences and those white theatregoers who would not ordinarily have attended performances in fringe venues or community centres. For this reason, a significant part of the grant was spent on advertising, as the question of attracting audiences to the Season was a rather complex matter. On the one hand, it was a case of subverting the expectations of the public as the plays neither followed in the footsteps of light comedy and musicals, as is usually the case on the West End stage, nor the 'highbrow' choices of theatres like the Royal Court. Additionally, the Season presented a programme which offered white audiences the opportunity to see the sort of plays rarely performed in mainstream theatres, reflecting, as they did, the interests and concerns of the communities to whom the plays referred. In this respect, Yvonne Brewster's production of Randall's first play, *Fishing* echoed the feminist concerns of the time. It also represented one of the early attempts to portray black British women's life on stage from a black woman's perspective, revealing, in the words of the reviewer Nicholas de Jongh, 'the gulf between black women of two generations, and their angry, despairing submission to men' (de Jongh, 1983). Certainly the play offered the cast an interesting opportunity to experiment with different modalities of acting and the variety of experiences within black communities in Britain. As Yvonne Brewster recalled:

> The play presented different kinds of women: there was the African actress, Ellen Thomas, interpreting the character of Jean, who is really English, although sounds West Indian, and is sexy, tall and elegant. And then there was Peggy Phango from South Africa

interpreting the role of Aunt May, who couldn't have had a more different figure, as she is very dark, short and round; Ingrid played by Yvonne Gidden looking so much like a West Indian, Caribbean woman, and finally Corinne Skinner-Carter, with her Caribbean look, in the role of Ingrid's Mum. So the production presented all these different cultures within black femininity [...] That was unheard in the West End in those days. (Brewster 1999).

Considering the kind of venues where black theatre companies usually performed, it was also a question of regrouping black audiences, enticing them to travel to the city centre and to purchase tickets at higher prices than they were accustomed to. All this required a rather skilled approach. Although all the plays included in the programme had very strong casts and were positively received by the press, the box office takings were unsatisfactory. However, this was perhaps an inevitable stage for any new groundbreaking venture, and sales did indeed increase during the course of the Season.

The disappointing overall box office result was offset by the enthusiastic reception of the first Season by the artists involved and the critical success of Trevor Rhone's *Two Can Play* which transferred to the Theatre Royal Stratford East and attracted the interest of producers in New York[15]. These outcomes encouraged Phillips to prepare for a second season of plays, this time with a marketing strategy that would combine 'word of mouth' with a more widespread distribution of publicity material in community centres and areas with high density of black population. Moreover, considering that for the first Season Phillips' attempts to recruit a theatre press officer from the so called 'ethnic communities' had been frustrated for lack of suitable candidates, he had decided to establish a traineeship that promoted access to the profession for people of African and Asian origins. Unsurprisingly, the trainee who was engaged for the first Season 'was later employed by the Theatre Royal, Stratford, and the Tricycle Theatre, to assist with the publicity of black plays being staged by those theatres' as Phillips noted later in an interview.

The Black Theatre Season 1985 and the establishment of the Black Theatre Forum

Around the same time, news broke of a new decentralising strategy for the arts, introduced by the Arts Council (ACGB) in March 1984 that would divert funds to

---

[15] Trevor Rhone (1940) is an accomplished Jamaican writer. Amongst his more successful plays are *Smile Orange,* later transferred on the screen, and *School Out. Two Can Play* was first performed in 1982.

the Regional Arts Associations (RAAs). The move, welcomed by those advocating the development of artistic activities in the regions, was detailed in a document entitled *The Glory of the Garden-Strategy for a Decade* in which the Chairman of the Arts Council, Sir William Rees-Mogg explained how the Council wanted 'to encourage and respond to local initiative in helping to create new institutions or strengthening old ones' (Rees-Mogg 1984: v). The Council planned to cut funds to existing clients, devolving them to the Regional Arts Associations, and 'encouraging the growth in business sponsorship' (Rees-Mogg 1984:12). The report maintained that the policy would benefit 'Black and Asian drama' although it contained no specific indications of the ways in which this would be achieved. Moreover, while the strategy seemed to reflect the Tory government ideology, the introduction of business sponsorship for the arts was feared by companies with an overt political or campaigning profile, as it would invariably make it difficult for them to attract sponsorship from the generally conservative private sector more inclined to protect the status quo.

It is also quite striking that two out of three black and Asian theatre companies (viz., Temba and Tara Arts Company) funded by the council were going to be devolved to regional bodies. As a result, touring activities of London based companies like Temba would have been reduced, with fewer opportunities for indigenous white people in the regions to be exposed to national black theatre, a privilege not open to many other European countries at the time. Indeed, black companies could not depend exclusively on regional budgets for their funding, as the impact of their work was to be judged on a national basis. In fact, not only they were introducing mainstream British audiences to non-European art forms from a unique black British perspective, but helping to enlarge British culture from within

Moreover, while in the document it is mentioned that 'clients devolved to the Associations carry with them the subsidies which they were receiving directly from the Arts Council' it later states that 'where the Council withdraws all or part of its current support from individual revenue clients, it will not normally expect that support to be replaced out of the development funds which it will be providing for the Regional Arts Associations' (Rees-Mogg 1984: 20, 24). This was leaving the companies threatened with cuts vulnerable to an evaluative process that inevitably reflected a new set of priorities. Additionally, the significant under-representation of black people on the management and executive boards of these bodies, together with the modicum of black people in some regions, would have made the case for black arts seem less relevant for some Regional Arts Associations (RAAs). As the paper made no mention of the changes which were necessary within Local Authorities and Regional Arts Association to democratise their policies and reflect their multicultural constituencies, it is understandable that the plan provoked strong reactions within the sector.

whilst enhancing its perception by the outside world[16]. It therefore seems particularly short-sighted that while the paper made exceptions for companies 'which tour throughout the country' or 'have an essentially experimental function' or 'a minority appeal which is not located in any particular region', it failed to specify the unique position occupied by black theatre companies in Britain (Rees-Mogg 1984: 36).

This said, by October 1984 Phillips submitted his application for a second Season to the GLC and in January 1985 he called a meeting at Temba Theatre Company's premises with the representatives of other London-based black theatre companies to formulate a policy and present it for consideration to the GLC Ethnic Arts Sub-committee. Artists invited to the meeting included Yvonne Brewster (Talawa Theatre Company), Beverly Randall (Black Theatre Co-operative), Jatinder Verma (Tara Arts Company), Alby James (Temba Theatre Company), Don Kinch (Staunch Poets and Players), and Parminder Vir (GLC). The meeting laid the foundations for the establishment of the Black Theatre Alliance (BTA – as the Forum was initially called) with the aim of promoting the creation of an intercultural programme within the Greater London Arts Association (GLAA). Following this first meeting, more members were invited to join in, including Joseph Marcell (theatre representative on the Roundhouse/Black Art Centre Steering Committee with the task of bringing the Forum up to date with developments at the Roundhouse and attune its artistic policy with that of the Forum), Harmage Kalirai (Asian Theatre Co-operative), Dhirendra (British Asian Theatre Company), and Gloria Hamilton (Umoja Theatre Company). During the following years, representatives of other groups joined the Forum, which eventually became the co-ordinating body of seventeen theatre companies in the interest of promoting African and Asian British heritage as a vehicle to stimulate the renaissance of black theatre in Britain[17].

While the Forum was officially established, a separate organisation, Second Season Production was set up by Phillips to administer the core costs of the season. This opened at the Arts Theatre in January 1985 with *Scrape off the Black* by Tunde Ikoli, presented by Temba Theatre Company, followed by Farrukh Dhondhy's *Vigilantes*, presented by Asian Co-operative Theatre, and *The New Hardware Store* by Earl Lovelace, presented by Carib Theatre. This last play aimed to attract diverse audiences by balancing the need for representing

---

[16] It is noteworthy that while the Notting Hill Carnival had expanded into a national and international mass event over the previous thirty years, proposals were put forward to devolve its funding to the RAA.

[17] For a more detailed analysis of the discussions taking place amongst members of the Forum see Terracciano, Alda *Crossing Lines: An Analysis of Integration and Separatism Within Black Theatre In Britain*, PhD Thesis, IUO (Naples: 2002)

contemporary British life with the 'back home' reality of post-independence Trinidad.

The Season was presented once again at the Arts Theatre to capitalise on the advance made with the previous one[18]. Yet, audience figures for the first play did not mirror the positive response of mainstream theatre critics. Regretting the failure of a Friday night performance of *Scrape off the Black* to attract more than the '...30 people, most of them white', the reviewer of the *Sunday Times* (January 13, 1985) suggested that if the play was staged at the Royal Court Upstairs, the Tricycle or the Bush it would have received a better audience response. However, the point of producing black plays in the West End was precisely to stimulate the emergence of new theatregoers within both white and black communities, while opening the mainstream to black theatre themes and aesthetics. As Alby James noticed in an interview:

> I remember that I worked with Tunde to expand the original script that had been produced at the Riverside. He was enormously proud of what we had achieved. That was the kind of statement that the Seasons wanted to make as well, about the fact that we deserved to be in the West End, we could put on worthy works that could attract black audiences and white ones, so that they would sit together and enjoy what they were seeing. This was the way I wanted to go forward (James 2000).

The play directed by James, who shared with Ikoli the experience of being a 'second generation' black Briton, dealt with the dilemmas of a young 'mixed race' son and his white Cornish mother confined within the four walls of a council flat in East London[19]. It opened on 9 January and included in its cast Catherine Terris in the role of Rose, the mother, Carole Harrison as her friend Mary, Ben Onwukwe and Stephen Persaud respectively in the roles of Trevor and Andy, Rose's two sons[20]. The action develops in four scenes sharply cut with dimming lights and blackouts, mirroring in their structure the incisiveness of the dialogue. The opening stage direction sets the scene:

---

[18] This year apart from *Time Out* and *City Limits* most of the publicity campaign was channelled through the black press, including *The Voice*, *West Indian World*, *Caribbean Times*, *Asian Times*, *Garavi Gujarat* and *Root* with tickets for the season in part sold through the fringe box office of Capital Radio to allow a more widespread campaign all over London. (See A. Phillips 1984 and the GLC 1984)

[19] The expression 'second generation' refers to people born to parents who immigrated to Britain in the two decades following World War II. *Scrape off the Black* was first commissioned in 1980 by the Royal Court. It was then produced at the Theatre Royal Stratford East in 1987 and 1998 under the direction of Philip Hedley.

[20] After the opening at the Arts Theatre the play went on tour in theatres and small venues including the Albany Empire in Deptford. See file *Scrape off the Black*, Temba Theatre Company Collection, Theatre Museum Archive.

Early morning, the sun streaks through the closed curtains of Mrs B's council flat. A telephone rings. The sitting room door opens and in comes Rose in a night-dress, hair dishevelled, she coughs, lights a fag and picks up the phone ...the pips go. The caller rings off'. Rose: Hello bastard. 'She slams the receiver down, tidies up a little and settles down on the settee. There's a knock at the door. She struggles to get herself off from the settee and goes off to open the front door. She is followed back by her son Trevor...
(Ikoli 1985: 1)

Not much happens in this concise, ninety-minute play. The action is triggered by Trevor's disruption in his mother's everyday life. He hopes to catch his brother Andy who always comes to see her every time he is out of prison. As the 'bastard' son of an African father, Trevor will hint at his struggle as a black man in London, whose 'half-caste' status seriously circumscribes his chances in life. Impotent to prevent Rose's decline, Trevor is the recipient of his mother's resentment. Yet he is reluctant to admit racism within his own family and struggles to rationalise his mother's sourness and lack of affection. Locked in a circle from which nobody in the family can escape, the theme of miscegenation in the play is not observed through the experiences of the couple, but interestingly from that of family relations. The focus on the relationship between parents and children not only signals a new interest in the concerns of the second generation, but also permits a wider view on the effects of external pressure on individuals. The dialogue between the two main characters, Rose and Trevor, defines a complicated and contradictory territory. On the one hand, the strain of being a single white mother in a racist society leaves its mark on Rose, which she is not able to shrug off. As she bitterly remarks: 'What Englishman would have looked at me with you two darkie children...trailing behind me?' (Ikoli 1985: 22). And later on:

Rosy: When I went for a decent place the landlord would take one look at you kids and shake his head. You were a mark. Even ordinary people walking along the street would turn their noses up at me when they saw me pushing you along the pram, treating me like I was some kind of vermin or something. That's what London was like in them days.
(Ikoli 1985: 63)

On the other hand, the same preconceptions of which she is a victim are projected against her Pakistani neighbours:

We'll soon be havin' sewing machines goin' day and night. I don't know where they find the time to have so many kids. All they seem to do is work. And the Council don't help. If you happen to live there that's your hard luck. They let the place get turned into a dump. (Ikoli 1985: 16)

In such a scenario, Trevor is left alone to find his own identity, craving for his mother's love, while moving around the country. As his brother Andy remembers in one of his brief appearances on stage:

We've been a contradiction since the day we were born: African father, Cornish mother; black skins, cockney accents. Shifted from foster homes to children homes...a tour round the South of England (...) Do you know your trouble. You attach too much importance to belonging to or being part of something: a family, a race, when in reality you're better off on your own, answering to no one but yourself for your own actions... (Ikoli 1985: 50)

It seems that the semi-autobiographical situation described by Ikoli in *Scrape off the Black* echoed the experiences of many theatregoers as 'racial differences do not dissolve and disappear into the melting pot; instead they simmer to produce a ghastly brew' as Mary Solanke suggested in *Black London*. At the same time, Ikoli's appropriation of the genre of 'domestic drama' was coloured by a symbolism well-captured by the director in the staging of the play.

The feeling of oppression and claustrophobia conveyed in Ikoli's play echoed other plays by Caribbean writers like *Trinity* by Edgar White, *Sweet Talk* by Michael Abbensetts, or *11 Josephine House* by Alfred Fagon. In all these plays, the 'room' represented as much the reality of the accommodations occupied by African-Caribbean migrants when they first moved to Britain as their existential condition described in George Lamming's novel *In the Castle of my Skin* (1953). The colour black, that entrapped individuals in superimposed sets of preconceptions and expectations, was mirrored in the furnished rooms where domestic dramas were set. These 'interior' spaces, often conveying a sense of claustrophobia, functioned as arenas for emotional retreat for the characters as well as reflecting the socio-cultural confinement imposed on them by racism. In the case of James' *mise-en-scène*, Nicholas de Jongh noted that 'Ellen Cairn's slightly expressionistic stage set, with its sombre-hued domestic furniture contributes to this effect' (de Jongh 1985).

Interestingly, the same feeling of oppressiveness caused by superimposed labels was experienced by many theatre practitioners during the 1980s. As Farrukh Dhondy argued:

The injunction is still upon us to be black and political. Why? Principally because the black arts or interest in them from funding and producing and patronising bodies, is an off-shoot of the political phenomenon of immigrant settlement (Dhondy 1985).

While a number of black artists started to make a point of freeing themselves from the 'burden' of representing their communities for the benefit of their artistic freedom, some theatre directors advocated the need for integrated casts as a sign of the progressive inclusion of black theatre within mainstream British culture[21]. For

---

[21] Kobena Mercer has argued at length on the burden laid on black artists in the film industry in his 'Black Art and the Burden of Representation', *Third Text,* No. 10 (Spring 1990).

Alby James, this was a way to oppose the 'separate development' of black theatre from the rest of British theatre, if such separation was intended as cultural apartheid rather than as the creation of a space to develop a theatre of research[22]. But mainstreaming the arts also meant to create spaces where different audiences could meet. According to Brian Bovell:

> Doing a Black play at the Royal Court for instance. You get the regular Time Out reader, you know what I mean, they come from Islington. And it's a quite night. At the end of the evening they go. Basically I believe their reactions come off of guilt. The next day if you are doing the play for a black audience, I like to say a colourful richness, the play becomes a different play. It is live. You are getting response and participation. Vocalisation (Rees 1992: 122).

To facilitate the encounter between different sections of the audience was a main objective of the Seasons. And the work of young writers like Ikoli at the beginning of the decade was indeed pivotal in raising questions about the diversification of theatre audience reception, something that reviewers did not always fully embrace preoccupied, as they were, with the 'colour' of theatre makers. While Mary Bryce from the *Tribune* asked 'how constructive is it *now* to label as 'black theatre' that which has a wider appeal?' it is true that plays like Ikoli's were indicative of a transformation within British audiences as they challenged the mono-cultural fixation of sectors of the establishment and media (Bryce 1985).

Another crucial element to consider in looking at the programme of the Season is the gap between older and younger generations of black artists. Once again, the gap reflected external political forces as much as intergenerational conflicts. The introduction in 1981 of a new Nationality Act under the Conservative leadership of Margaret Thatcher narrowed the definition of British citizenship, threatening the rights of many black people born in Britain. In the past, as a result of the British Empire, the concept of British nationality had expanded to reflect the enlarged geographical boundaries of the country. However, since the 1960s, immigration to Britain started to become a more problematic issue, especially for people of dark skin colour (see the Commonwealth Immigration Act of 1962 establishing a system of employment vouchers and the Commonwealth Immigrants Act of 1968 introducing exclusionary measures for those people who had received their British passport outside Britain). Now, the 1981 legislation established that even people who were born in Britain could not become citizens or have the right to permanently settle in the country unless they were born from parents with British citizenship or parents who had legally settled in Britain. While the law created a set

---

[22] On the question of integrated casting see James 1988 and articles in *Plays and Players* in July, September and October 1986.

of problematic perceptions towards young black people not always 'perceived by other citizens and by the authorities as a legitimate part of the national collectivity and of the civil society', black Britons born in the country found themselves in need of carving their own space within society that reflected their rights and ownership of Britain and its culture (Anthias & Yuval-Davis 1996: 49). In this respect, the points Laird raised in his conversation with Rees can offer an interesting point of reference in evaluating the programme of the Season, in which *Scrape off the Black* was presented next to *The New Hardware Store,* a play set against the backdrop of post-independence Trinidad dealing with the legacy of British colonialism both in economic and cultural terms. As Laird noted:

> There is a division. This is it. Their black experience is the experience of the Caribbean or Africa. To us the experience is of black people here. It is also a black experience. But different. Black is just a colour of skin. Their experience coming from the outside, the way they see things, they see they have to impress something on people. The way we see it, we play it – like Tunde writes we want to show the universe inside rather than conquer the one outside (Rees 1992: 125).

Laird's comments point at the struggle in which every new generation in search of its own distinctive and original voice engages. However, it also suggests the research for an artistic format that could mirror the cultural hybridity of the younger generations and the efforts to affirm their rights of British citizens.

Vigilantes, by Farrukh Dhondy presented by the Asian Co-operative Company under the direction of Penny Cherns threw the audiences precisely in this new territory. This time the story revolved around a group of young Asians struggling to protect their community from racist attacks and the erasure of links with tradition while dealing with complex family relationships and prejudice in the community. The play received a good response from the audience and more generally box office figures doubled the income of the previous season, rising from £6,895 to £13,413. Interestingly, the programme had been successful in attracting young audiences and people of Asian origins, making it apparent that higher investment of resources in the marketing campaign together with a programme in tune with the interests of the communities and concerns of the time were the best tools to promote black theatre outside its usual confines. Therefore the Forum made a point of investing resources in audience development for the production of the third season, whose success would help raise the profile of the organisation and attract new funds – an important step in light of the forthcoming closure of its main sponsor, the GLC, in March 1986.

Challenges to internal cohesiveness and the re-interpretation of classics: the Black Theatre Season 1986

The production of the third season saw the active involvement of more members of the Black Theatre Forum in drafting the programme, making grant applications, arranging press and marketing and securing a theatre in the West End. At the same time lobbying activities for the acquisition of a theatre building increased, following the negative response from Lord Birkett, Director of Recreation and the Arts at the GLC, to a request of capital funds for £2 millions for the purchase of the Arts Theatre (Meadows 1985). As the Arts Council required two or more years of 'artistic excellence' before considering project funding, the Forum needed to capitalise on the GLC contribution to 'mainstreaming' black theatre and promote the access of black artists to theatre institutions. This was crucial not only because such institutions received the bulk of public funding for the arts and should have reflected the pluricultural character of British society in their programmes, but because they were considered 'arbiters of taste' and therefore conductors of new trends and aesthetics in British arts. In this respect, the impact of the GLC went beyond its role of public funding agency and has to be seen in more ideological terms[23].

Having said that, consensus within the Forum about the strategy to follow proved to be difficult to reach. Firstly, not all members prioritised the acquisition of a theatre building, as some feared it would have prevented individual companies from acquiring their own spaces. At the same time, different positions emerged in relation to a potential collaboration with the Roundhouse for its autumn season, an idea eventually dismissed for lack of a common artistic vision with the Roundhouse committee. In order to appreciate the terms of the relationship between the Forum and the Roundhouse committee, it might be useful to briefly look at the way in which the project for the housing of black theatre in Camden Town had developed during the previous two years. In mid-1983, there had been talks about the possible conversion of the vast building, once the base of Wesker's Centre 42, in a centre for the black arts. In accordance with the policy inaugurated

---

[23] Before its dismissal the GLC produced a Black Arts Programme, *The Black Experience* from February 24 to March 24, 1986. It featured a number of well-attended activities, including a photographic exhibition, seminars, concerts, training days, film scripts competition, screening of films, an oral history project and the production of C.L.R. James *The Black Jacobins*. The play, directed by Yvonne Brewster, included a cast of twenty-four actors, featuring Norman Beaton in the role of Toussaint. See Michael Coveney, 'The Black Jacobins', *Financial Times* (February 27, 1986); Martin Cropper, 'The Black Jacobins', *The Times* (March 5, 1986); Nicholas de Jongh, 'Slaves to Fortune', *The Guardian* (February 28, 1986).

at the GLC by its Labour administration, which came into power at about the time of the inner city riots in 1981, the idea was that the Camden Council would buy the building (one of the early figures was £330,000) while the running costs (estimated at around £400,000) would be covered by the GLC with a small contribution by the Arts Council. The place was planned to host not only black British theatre and music companies, but international tours, art exhibitions and conferences. Tony Banks, the new Labour MP for Newham North West and GLC arts chairman, had been pivotal to strike the deal and assure that the process of acquisition was in place by the end of the following year. The centre would have been managed by a 'supreme' artistic director who would co-ordinate the activities programmed by the single artistic directors of the various disciplines.

Although many black practitioners had been advocating for a home for the black arts, the programme of rehabilitation of the derelict building in north London actually split the black community in two. Many disagreed with the idea of sharing the same space, of vast proportions and bad acoustics, with companies producing very different work. They resented the lack of a policy to sustain the acquisition of small theatres for individual theatre companies. As Anton Kumalo, at the time director of Temba Theatre Company, pointed out:

> Trevor Nunn and Peter Hall would not be expected to operate their companies under one roof, not because of personal differences but simply because they could not accommodate each other's artistic ideas and methods. The RSC does not share with the National Theatre, Riverside does not share with the Lyric, Hammersmith and the Royal Court does not share with the Half Moon. Why does everyone think the blacks can do it? (Jehu 1983)

Crucial differences of style, aesthetic method and cultural backgrounds that existed within the black theatre movement represented one of its most valuable assets. However this risked being overlooked for the benefit of a political manoeuvre unable to respond to such a variety of positions. The saga of the Roundhouse, as it was later named, provoked a plethora of articles and public statements from black artists which would require a more detailed analysis. It might suffice to say that eventually the project collapsed as a result of financial difficulties as much as resistance from some sections of the black theatre movement to the homogenising attitude of British institutions. The use of a common 'black' banner by artists of African and Asian descent was an act of resistance towards discriminating racial practises within the British system, rather than a way to level differences of histories, traditions and personal aesthetic researches amongst the communities forced together in the multicultural 'melting pot'.

Similar differences emerged during the planning phase of the 1986 Black Theatre Season. According to Yvonne Brewster 'the Season was not the place for experimentation, but more West End orientated material was necessary', while others looked at the Season as an opportunity to try out new methodologies of work and present audiences with unconventional plays (Minutes of Black Theatre Forum 1985). For this reason, initial plans of moving the Season to the Royal Court Theatre were put aside on the basis that the theatre 'would not release its right to decide what plays were put on there and would retain ultimate artistic control'. At the same time, the members of the Forum had to respond to the establishment of an Asian Theatre Forum (composed by Tara Arts, British Asian Theatre and Asian Co-operative Theatre) created to discuss policy, funding practises and artistic development for Asian theatre in Britain. In order to facilitate internal cohesiveness and external effectiveness, the Forum planned to function as the main lobbying body, offering 'a political stance of unity'. It tried to reflect all of its constituents, while adopting a unified strategy in its policy. At the same time, an artistic committee equally representing artists of Caribbean and Asian origins was set up to direct the Season and manage the funds, this time covering not only core costs but also the theatre productions whose costs had been so far sustained by the invited companies[24]. Finally, the Forum agreed to an extended touring policy in a joint effort with the GLC to reach more audiences and stimulate black theatre in other parts of the country.

The programme for the Seasons 1986 was based on the idea of presenting West End and black audiences with the traditions of theatre from India and the Caribbean. The plays selected were *The Little Clay Cart*, a classic of Indian theatre by Shudraka presented by Tara Arts, *Rākshasa's Ring* a Sanskrit drama by Visakhadatta, and *The Pirate Princess*, a pantomime by the contemporary Jamaican writer, Barbara Gloudon presented by Temba. A grant application of £154,840 was submitted to the GLC as the only sponsor of the Season. The substantial increase in the budget was a consequence of the use of bigger casts for the two Indian classics, while the pantomime involved the engagement of a live music band and a choreographer. Also a 30% audience increase the previous year – the result of increased expenditure on advertising – suggested an expanded advertising campaign for this one and ticket prices were kept at low range (£4, £3 and £1.50 concession) to attract members of the public either unemployed or on low income.

The most interesting feature of this Season however, was the cross-cultural exchange between artists of African, Caribbean and Asian origins and their take on classical non-European theatre traditions. In this respect the Forum could pave the way to a new understanding of interculturalism and transnationalism in the theatre practised by artists of non-Western origins. Dislocated from their original cultural pools and exposed, as they were, to the influence of life in the West, their

---

[24] Initial members of the committee were Anton Phillips, Yvonne Brewster, Jatinder Verma and Raj Patel.

exploration of African, Caribbean and Asian arts and aesthetics reflected a sensibility sharpened by common experiences of migration and cultural hybridity. The challenge was to re-evaluate those traditions and make them respondent to urban black and white audiences. For this reason the committee decided to approach Rufus Collins, who had then moved to Amsterdam, to direct *Rākshasa's Ring*. Not only would his knowledge of Indian classical stagecraft techniques have been valuable in the production, but his political awareness would have added an interesting angle to the play based on an ancient treatise on the art of government[25]. The programme was then completed by Jatinder Verma who directed his company Tara Arts in *The Little Clay Cart* with Alby James and Paulette Randall directing Temba in *The Pirate Princess*.

Whereas the West End was home to musicals and light comedies in which the British colonial past had been romantically interpreted by white directors and producers and where Indian or African characters had been traditionally represented as the 'exotic', the Season represented a bold attempt to revert such dynamics and look at British contemporary culture through the lens of the histories and traditions of the colonised.

In this respect, Jatinder Verma's production was particularly interesting as it came at a moment in Tara Arts history of great ferment and transformation. Since the acquisition of a building base in 1983, the company had established a professional wing and was then charting new territories in the experimentation of Indian theatre techniques and popular and classical traditions. Anuradha Kapur's visit to London in 1985 to direct the company in *This Story's Not For Telling* (a play devised by the actors making minimalist use of props and scenery in a style fusing circus, dance, melodrama, acrobatics and masks), was instrumental in opening up a new scenario in the production of Asian theatre in Britain[26].

In an attempt to win South Asian audiences and, at the same time, creatively explore their tastes for the phantasmagoria of Bollywood movies, Verma started to investigate the anti-realism of Indian theatre traditions which he had witnessed during flying visits of artists from the subcontinent[27]. The *mise-en-scène* of *The Little Clay Cart,* using Indian stagecraft, costumes, make-up, movement, music and speech patterns, would have disappointed anybody in search of an authentic

---

[25] Interestingly, in his proposal for the staging of this long play, Rufus Collins envisaged the use of Indian shadow play or screens to represent the scenes taking place off stage and give to the audience the necessary background information to the main action.

[26] Professor Kapur was at the time member of the Theatre Union, one of the most talented street theatre groups in New Delhi. See Pandya 1985.

[27] For a more detailed analysis of the development of Tara Arts see Terracciano, Alda, 'Il Teatro Black. L'Esperiemento del Tara Arts Group', *Drammaturgia,* IV (Roma: Salerno Editrice, 1997) 174-195.

Indian play and represented a form of cultural appropriation with far-reaching consequences for the company.

The play, presented for the first time in the West End of London, opened on January 9, 1986 and included in its cast Yogesh Bhatt in the role of Sansthanaka, Naushaba Khan in the role of Vasantasena, Ayub Khan Din in the role of Charudatta, while the others (Nizwar Karanj, Bhaskar, Paul Bhattarjee, Sudha Bhuchar and Mala Sikka) doubled the various roles of courtier, masseuse, storyteller, judge and executioner[28]. The original five hours-long play was adapted by Verma, choreographed by Shobana Jeyasingh and accompanied by the music compositions played live by Baluji Srivastav and Yousuf Ali Khan. This epic play, originally written in Sanskrit by Shudraka around 8th Century A.D., was unique within the repertory of classical Indian theatre, it not being based on a religious or legendary subject but elaborating on the themes of romance and revolution. A rich courtesan, Vasantasena, falls in love with an impoverished merchant, Charudatta, and therefore incurs disapproval from the King's brother in law, Sansthanaka. At the same time, thieves, gamblers, servants and monks who populated the background of the play, show their increasing resentment against the King. This eventually results in a revolution which not only overthrows him but, destitute of power, his brother-in-law as well and eventually allows the two lovers to be reunited.

Interestingly, the majority of critics either did not respond to the parallels raised in the play with the episodes of racial intolerance taking place in Britain at the time, or they openly circumvented them. A case in point is John Peter who wrote in the *Sunday Times*: 'someone has added bits of framing commentary to the text, including a passage about present-day racism in London, which sticks out like a sore thumb. The play has a different message, and like all classics it doesn't like being molested' (Peter 1986). In general, the critics concentrated their attention on the English translation of the text, the beautiful choreography and the actors' interpretations, 'their versatility, their grasp of total theatre and their split second timing' (Hall 1986). Kenneth Rea pointed out that the style adopted by Verma, halfway between stylisation and realism was indeed a very good choice for an audience not used to the traditional aesthetics of 'rasa'[29] – clearly referring here to

---

[28] *The Little Clay Cart* had been produced by Tara Arts in December 1984 under the original title of *Miti Ki Gadi* at the Institute of Indian Culture.
[29] [**Rasa refers to the eight, later nine, classical aesthetic modes such as joy, desire, sorrow which, to meet the strict demands of classical theory, must be balanced in a skilled work of art. See the *Natya Shastra*. Ed.]**

white British audiences rather than the South Asian ones whose familiarity with Asian theatre techniques was clearly overlooked[30].

The same success was not registered by the production of *Rākshasa's Ring*. Written by Visakhadatta around the 8th Century A.D., the play included an integrated cast of Asian and African Caribbean actors. It was based on the *Artha-Shastra*, the classical Indian treatise on the art of government that predated Machiavelli's *The Prince,* and explored the dynamics between Kautilya, the Emperor's Chief Minister, and the newly appointed minister Rākshasa, faithful to the overthrown dynasty and planning to restore its power. Unfortunately, Rufus Collins' unexpected unavailability to direct the play just a week before rehearsals were due to start left the Artistic Committee in the difficult position to find a suitable substitute. Eventually, as Anton Phillips was the only one to have read the play, he took on Collins' role. However, as he did not have Collins' experience in cross-cultural theatre and lacked the necessary time for a thorough research of the play, the final production lacked the edge that had been initially envisaged. Phillips recalled:

> I had only a week before going into production. During that week I never slept, I just researched and read and cast. Eventually it was a sumptuous production and beautifully designed. But the critics, oh my god, they assassinated me. Strangely enough, I must admit that I quite liked it and a lot of people who saw the production enjoyed it, but the critics, well they hated it and blamed me for everything. It was a huge shock, which left me depressed for months (Phillips 1999).

A different kind of challenge was faced by the directors of *The Pirate Princess,* the final play in the programme. Co-directed by Alby James and Paulette Randall with the music of Felix Cross, the play offered a unique platform to these second-generation black Caribbean British artists. As the tradition of the Jamaican Pantomime had its own rules and stylistic format, the production offered the directors and music composer the opportunity to appropriate the culture of their parents and infuse it with their new, hybridised cultural identities.

In Jamaica, the production of annual pantomime started in 1941 under the auspices of the Little Theatre Movement of Jamaica. Originally, it centred on the cycle of stories in which Ananse, a sort of Everyman character imported with the slave trade from Ghana, uses all his abilities to acquire wealth and success and is regularly defeated by his own greed and over-ambition. Interestingly, the underlying moral common both to the Ghanaian tradition and to the Victorian pantomime was re-formulated within the Caribbean context, making 'Anancy' a more subversive character. Transformed as a trickster, his adventures served to

---

[30] (Kenneth Rea 1986). The play received a good response from the audience with a final net box office income of £4,337.

undermine the hegemonic power of the colonialist culture and social apparatus and relate them to current political events in Jamaican society.[31] Elaborated by the poetess Louise Bennett in the *Anancy Tales,* these stories were then adapted in the Jamaican pantomime until new themes and characters were introduced by writers like Barbara Gloudon[32].

While Alby James was producing the revival of *Mamma Decemba* for Temba, Paulette Randall, who had just come back from her first visit to Jamaica, took responsibility for the first phase of rehearsals in consultation with James and Yvonne Brewster. In fact, James and the set designer, Carinda Salanday, had visited Jamaica together before starting the rehearsals to research the subject and witness one of the pantomimes staged by the Little Theatre Movement. On the other hand, Randall's journey to Jamaica had introduced her to the spiritual qualities of the culture on the island. Now the challenge for her was to figure out how to stage a Jamaican pantomime starting from the only examples she knew: the British pantomime and musical[33]. Moreover, having been trained as a director at the Royal Court Theatre, she could not avoid engaging with the emotional quality of the play and an inclination to realism. As she noticed:

> I think that at the end The Pirate Princess became a musical. We had a lot of underscore, so that, for example, rather than breaking the dialogues with songs, we tried to find a way to progress them into the songs. On the other hand, because the play was still a drama it needed to be real. Even if it was a pantomime the characters would still go through an emotional journey, so I had to find a way to allow that to happen. (Randall 2000).

A similar attitude towards the genre was manifested by Felix Cross. Initially employed to arrange the original music score of the play, he eventually composed all the 21 songs for the production in great haste[34]. As the pantomime was going to

---

[31] [Anansi the mythical spider's transformation into a subversive trickster occurs well before the Jamaican pantos. The oral history of slaves in the region bears testimony to the subversive and anarchic aspect of Anansi who provided an almost political tool for the slaves to resist the dominance of the colonisers. Ed.]

[32] The list of Gloudon's pantomimes includes *Jack and the Gungoo Tree,* which won her the 1984 Jamaican Drama Critics Award as Best Production for Children, *Moonshine Anancy, The Witch,* the hugely popular *Ginneral B* critical of the American takeover both in the commerce and culturally and *Johnny Reggae* a play that, being about a young man exploited by the record industry, exposed the downfalls of the music business and won her many enemies.

[33] Brewster had already staged a successful pantomime in Britain in 1972 for the Dark and Light theatre company and directed *The Witch* by Barbara Gloudon at the Little Theatre Movement in Kingston in 1975.

[34] The production of *Pirate Princess* by the Little Theatre Movement featured the music by the Jamaican artist Conroy Cooper. But the original scores never arrived and so Cross had to

be performed in London and not in Jamaica, he felt free to explore its music heritage and re-work the genre. As he remembered:

I wrote the music for Pirates Princess according to what I assumed it would be in Jamaica: a mix of R & B reggae, Mento music, Jamaican soul and some other rhythms from Jamaican folk music. I based it on that, as I knew quite a lot about those styles. But then, when I went to Jamaica I realized that in the pantomime there are a lot of choruses, like the Gilbert and Sullivan high choruses. It is very English. What makes it Jamaican is the subject matter, the costumes, the scenery, something to do with the spiritual element which enters the play. It has to do with the words, the dialect in the speeches and the instrumentation, not so much the notes, the harmonies and the tunes (Cross 2000).

What became soon apparent was that the real cross-reference between this production and the Jamaican genre was the audience. While Felix Cross noticed a presence of both white and black people throughout the run, Randall's remarks about the effects of black audiences on the performance is revealing of a specific performative style[35]. As she pointed out:

The audience was raucous; they were shouting at the stage, it was fantastic. Some of the actors had never done anything like that before, so I had to warn them that people could have talked to them during the show and they had to learn how not to step out of their roles. This kind of theatre forces the performers to become an ensemble and work with one another and with the audience. Nothing like the theatre I have sadly witnessed here, where I might as well sit and watch a film because the actors would play without any regard to us whatsoever (Randall 2000).

In this respect, it seems that the words of Malcolm Hay from *Time Out* captured the spirit of the production: 'the play sends you out into the world with a lighter step and a keener sense of the sheer pleasure of being alive' (Theatre Museum Archive). This bold re-invention of the Jamaican tradition, certainly gave confidence to the artists involved in the production to continue along the path they seem to have accidentally found. Together with the other artists involved in the Season, their re-interpretation of histories and theatre traditions outside the geographical boundaries of Africa, Asia and the Caribbean had attracted varied audiences and helped to make sense with them of the new hybridised condition of post-colonial Britain. A new trend in black British theatre had been successfully established.

---

compose the music himself. See 'Pirate Princess Script Goes to London', *Sunday Gleaner* (January 19, 1986) and Felix Cross, private interview with the author.
[35] The play had a good box office return with a net figure of £4,903.

The enlarged base of the Forum and the Seasons 1987, 1989 and 1990

In light of the internal tensions mounted during the production of the Black Theatre Season 1986, the members of the Forum decided to engage in a wider process of consultation for the selection of future plays short listed by the Artistic Sub-committee for the Seasons. The discussions that took place in the following years about the quality of the plays, their political and theatrical references, the state of black arts and their position within the British cultural industry represented a vehicle for expanding knowledge and professionalism, while soothing interracial tensions. At the same time, the cohesiveness of the Forum started to increasingly deteriorate as the divide between the Asian and Caribbean sections of the Forum increased.

As a matter of fact, the situation only reflected the wider context of cultural policies in the country. Looking at the fragmentation that hit the black theatre movement as the 1980s drew to an end might help to gauge the extent of the difficulties faced by these practitioners in holding the Forum together. To defuse internal and external confrontations, Yvonne Brewster reiterated her proposal for an enlargement of the Forum membership to include smaller, active companies and help them raising their profiles creating a stronger front against reactionary policies. As a result Sass Theatre Company, Double Edge, Afro-Sax and L'Ouverture became members in 1987, while Theatre of Black Women, African Players and Tenne Theatre Company entered the Forum the following year.

Another bone of contention undermining the unity of the Forum was the artistic policy established in the previous years. Gloria Hamilton and Don Kinch were particularly critical of the mainstreaming attempts of the organisation, which seemed to overlook the lack of representation of smaller members and their lack of exposure in the production of the Seasons. According to James, this represented an insurmountable impasse, as the *raison d'être* of the Season was to abide by the rules of excellence in order to attract mainstream audiences and consequently enhance visibility and opportunities for the whole sector (Terraciano 2000)[36].

Internal differences continued to brew while the Forum started to re-shape its organisational structure. Firstly, it was decided that each play presented in the 1987 Season would be marketed as a Black Theatre Forum Production and that the Forum would employ a producer to plan the season together with the members of the Artistic Committee. A director would be employed for each production, supported by the committee both for casting and production. The Artistic

---

[36] After a substitution of *11 Josephine House* suggested by Umoja Theatre Company, with *Moon Dance Night*, Gloria Hamilton resigned from the organization to then re-enter it at a later stage as an external collaborator.

Committee, operating for the duration of the whole Season, would comprise of five people: one representative from each of the three companies submitting the script, plus one member of the executive and one member of the Forum. With regards to the funding, new sources had to be sought following the abolition of the GLC. A series of meetings were held with representatives of the Greater London Arts Association and the Arts Council and eventually the GLAA accepted to provide financial support for a fourth Season with a grant of £165,000, while contributing to the activities of the organisation with an annual revenue grant of £22,000 for the following five years. During such time, the Forum was expected to enlarge the scope of its activities forging international links, co-ordinating a registry of black practitioners for outreach work, establishing a centre to facilitate the development of black artists, and setting up a Building Fund Appeal. The publication of an independent journal was also planned.[37] Malcolm Frederick was elected Chairperson and it was agreed that trainee directors would be employed for the Season to foster the cultural exchange between different groups in the Forum: Yogesh Bhatt from Tara Arts to assist Carmen Munroe, William Jorite from Double Edge to assist Yvonne Brewster; and Derek Blackwood to assist Jatinder Verma.

With regards to the venue to host the Season, problems were far from being resolved and, after a series of discussions, the dates were moved from September to November to accommodate other engagements of the Arts Theatre. The programme for the 1987 Season was as ambitious as the others. It included *Remembrance*, by Derek Walcott directed by Carmen Munroe, at her second directorial experience, *Moon Dance Night* by Edgar White, directed by Yvonne Brewster and *Tewodros*, by Ato Tsegaye Gabre Medhin directed by Jatinder Verma. While the Season opened with the work of one of the most distinguished Caribbean playwrights, an interesting challenge was met by Yvonne Brewster with the production of *Moon Dance Night*. Set on a Caribbean island, the play explores the relationship between Felix, a young hotel worker who longs to move to London to become a famous musician and Dwen Ellis, a newscaster on holiday on the island after many years of absence who eventually returns to London after undergoing a ceremony which changes her life. This was a text with complex cultural references in which the central role played by the ritual offered the director an opportunity to engage with elements of African culture rarely represented on stage. As Brewster noticed:

The play is based on the redundancy of the black man; in fact, 'Redundant' is the name of one of the characters. The play is ritualistically, culturally and conceptually very

---

[37] In November 1995 the Forum started to publish *Frontseat,* a quarterly magazine on black arts.

important to people of African descent. Ritual is a complex issue because African culture has never been acknowledged for its ancient history and ritual has come to identify it tout court. (Brewster 1999).

The production, which was positively received both by the audiences and the press, was followed by the Ethiopian classic *Tewodros* dealing with the rule of Kassa, Emperor of Ethiopia between 1855 and 1868, whose visionary policy changed the face of the country while the British colonial power was making its entry. The opportunity to work with an African-Caribbean cast was welcomed by Verma, as it allowed him to explore new directions in back British identity and draw from different artistic sources in search of his artistic vocabulary.

The audience did not follow the experiment with his same enthusiasm experienced by the director and his company[38]. This said, the Season closed with a relatively good audience attendance, partially boosted by the organisation of a Royal Gala Performance of Edgar White's *Moon Dance Night* on October 21, 1987 in the presence of HRH, Prince Edward[39]. The event had been organised with the aim of fundraising for the purchase of a theatre in the London's West End. Leading political personalities and celebrities were invited to the event to promote the value of the Season as 'a professional spotlight in the world of live visual arts' (Phillips 1987).

In contrast with such forms of publicity, some new members pressured the Forum to take its activities back to the communities. Artists like Derek Blackwood from Double Edge Theatre Company began to question the need for staging plays in the West End while black arts centres were closer to the audiences that the Forum wanted to reach. Uninterested in mainstreaming black art at the expense of blunting its edge, Blackwood touched a raw nerve as the issue had already been raised by Gloria Hamilton and other members of the Forum. In order to reduce disagreement and to facilitate the decision making process, in June 1988 the majority of the members voted an executive structure that would meet regularly every month and report to the board of directors during their annual meetings. Moreover, in the attempt to engage with the communities, the Forum started

---

[38] In the Publicity/Marketing Report for the Season 1987 it appears that this 'most serious, sophisticated Black Theatre Season' had targeted 'young and trendy arty types, Black/Asian theatre goers, Regular theatre goers, London residents'. See Networking Public Relations, *Report for the Season*, 1987.

[39] The total expenditure for the Season was £160,221, coupled by a total income of £183,755, which left a projected surplus of £23,534. Total income from box office for *Remembrance* was £5,341, for *Moon Dance Night* was £6,706 and for *Tewodros* was £3,714. Including the £1,399 income from the Gala Night of *Moon Dance Night* the total income from the box office for the Season was £17,500 with an attendance of 6,909 people of which £4,398 paying.

organising a series of master classes and seminars. However, nothing was done to change the format of the Season 1989 apart from the choice of the venue. As the Arts Theatre could not be a viable option any longer, the Donmar Warehouse in the West End, the Almeida and the Shaw Theatre were considered, with the latter being eventually earmarked for its capacity of 500 seats and its location in Euston Road, making it within easy reach of areas with a significant black population.

The GLAA offered again the same grant of £165,000, this time with the requirement of stimulating the emergence of young theatre practitioners. As the activities of the Forum had progressively moved towards the training of younger generations, the Season served as a privileged space to test the abilities of emerging theatre directors. Paulette Randall and John Matshikiza were approached as potential directors of the African-Caribbean plays in the programme, while the actor Renu Setna proposed to direct a double bill of Middle Eastern plays using integrated casting as part of the Forum commitment to Asian work.

The Season was eventually scheduled for the period between January and April 1989 and the programme included *Dog*, by Dennis Scott, directed by Randall, a semi-allegorical, poetic play representing civil turmoil in Jamaica in 1974 and the clash between affluent middle class life and that of the underclass; a double bill directed by Renu Setna including *Lazarus and his Beloved* written by the Lebanese Kahlil Gibran and *The Song of the Death* by Tewfif El-Hakim; and *Beef, No Chicken* by Derek Walcott, directed by Matshikiza, whose 'lightness' aimed at balancing the density of the previous two plays and attract more audiences[40]. Indeed, in terms of box office income, this resulted in being the most successful production in the history of the Black Theatre Seasons[41]. The play is a farce set in Trinidad revolving around the attempts of a restaurateur to save his premises where the corrupted council wants to build a highway. The sharp division between the lukewarm response of the press and the box office income seemed to reinforce the point made by some members of the Forum more interested in plays that could resound within the black community that in those that would attract the interest of white critics.

Interestingly, both *Dog* and the *Double Bill* registered low audiences whilst receiving positive comments from the press. In particular the inclusion of Arab plays in the programme of a Black Theatre Season surprised the Arab media,

---

[40] The production was a British premiere. The play had been produced for the first time in New Haven, Connecticut in 1982.

[41] The total income at the box office for *Beef, No Chicken* was £15, 625 with an attendance of 4,036. For the double bill the box office registered a total income of £4,461 and an audience of 1,419 while *Dog* registered a total box office income of £6,570 and an audience of 2,041. A proper audience survey would be started only later for the Black Theatre Season 1990.

stimulating its interest and appreciation in the enterprise, particularly in light of the negative image that the Salman Rushdie affair had cast over the Arab world. Both *Lazarus* and *Song of the Death* offered a different view on its cultural palimpsests: the first focussed on the poetic rumination about the biblical character and his lamentation of the loss of the divine communication discovered beyond the grave; the second, a drama concerning a centuries-old family feud in a dusty peasant village in Egypt, revealed the clash between tradition and modernisation in the North African society.

All this said, the very low attendance of Asian audiences to the Season revealed the opening of a gap between the Forum and its audience base. A possible explanation was that the programme did not include plays attractive to Asian audiences. Another possibility was that Asian audiences did not wish to see themselves in the context of a Black Theatre Season and that the political banner promoted by the Forum no longer reflected the way people defined themselves or established their political affiliations. Moreover, the absence of women and new British writing were raised in the discussions that followed the production of the Season and convinced the Forum to set up a 'New Writer's Project' to stimulate new writing by black writers to be included in the programme of the next Season. It was also agreed to promote courses to counteract the shortage of black people in set, lighting, sound and costume design, set building, painting and the whole range of theatre crafts, where black people were still under-represented. The need to redress the balance not only on stage but also backstage suggested the promotion of a 'Technical Theatre Training for Black People' in collaboration with the GLAA in 1989.

For the Season 1990, Yvonne Brewster proposed the inclusion of a play that could be of interest to black communities but also serious enough to attract the attention of the critics. *Blood, Sweat and Fears* by Maria Oshodi, a young, visually impaired playwright, was therefore selected under the direction of Yvonne Brewster. The programme then included *Say Hallelujah*, by Jimi Rand directed by Malcolm Fredrick (the play is set in D'Coursey's corner store where a series of characters portraying various aspects of black life in London pass through); and *Eden* by the African American playwright Steve Carter, directed by Alby James. Set in Harlem in 1927 in the aftermath of Marcus Garvey's campaign for black nationalism, the play explores the animosities and mutual suspicion that bedevilled relations between American blacks and West Indian immigrants[42]. As the Season

---

[42] *Say Hallelujah* had been already produced in 1989 at the Young Vic Studio by the Lambeth Ensemble Theatre Company under the direction of Jimi Rand. For an account of the production see Glen Noble, 'Larger than Life', Black Theatre Forum Collection, Future Histories Archive. The play had been originally copyrighted by the author in 1976 and was revised in 1988.

seemed to shift its focus to the African-Caribbean experience, it is not a surprise that the breakdown of audience attendance revealed 70% African-Caribbean, 24% Europeans, 2% Asians and 4% others. Interestingly, the majority of the audience comprised of people between 22 and 35 years-old (56%) and professionals (63%). With regards to the high percentage of young audiences, this was probably a result of the change of venue, as the Season moved this year to the Riverside Studios a venue with a long tradition of presenting unconventional work.

Again, a Gala Night performance was organised for *Blood, Sweat and Fears* on April 26, 1990 at the Riverside Studios, this time not to fundraise for a building but in aid of research on Sickle Cell, a disease more common amongst people of African Caribbean descent which was the focus of the play. Brewster's proposal to include the play in the programme of the Season was a response to those members of the Forum asking for closer links with the community and raising awareness of its concerns.

As the Season came to a close, plans to establish a centre where black theatre could be produced and experimented returned to the table. At that time, news of the collapse of the Roundhouse project in Camden Town had started to appear in the media. As reported in the *Daily Telegraph,* 'the limited company set up to run the project is to go into voluntary liquidation after the Arts Council refused to release £900,000 allocated for the scheme, deeming it unrealistic' (Daily Telegraph 1990). Phillips, who had produced the last Season for the Forum, suggested that time was ripe to present the GLA with a plan for the acquisition of a theatre building. The space earmarked by Phillips and Malcolm Frederick was located in Brixton, an area with high density of people of African and Caribbean descent. Distancing itself from the initial ideas of a theatre in the West End, the focus of the Forum had been increasingly shifting towards this community, and the proposal for a 'C.L.R. James Arts and Media Centre' in Brixton was proof of this shift[43]. Having being deeply involved in the project, neither Phillips nor Frederick paid attention to the deadline set up by the GLA for submitting a new programme for the Season. When the plan for the Centre was turned down, they had only few days for devising the programme which eventually was not submitted (Phillips 1999). In the meantime, the structure of the GLA had been re-organised and the body was renamed London Arts Board (LAB). As part of its new strategy, LAB singled out new areas of

---

[43] The C.L.R. James foundation was a registered Charity named after the Caribbean writer with the aim to continue the work pursued in the past by journals like *Race Today* and *Creation for Liberation*. Phillips saw the possibility of joining the foundation to fundraise for a multi-level building which would contain a theatre, an art gallery, an educational institute and a café bar, reminding of what had been the Keskidee Art Centre in Islington in 1970s.

development for the black theatre movement and decided to re-distribute the funds that had not been employed for the Season to other projects and companies.

Widening perspectives

Activities included in the five-year plan for which the Forum had received funds concretised in a number of training courses, seminars, workshops and arts events. 'Masterclasses for Black Voices', a training seminar for black actors, was organised in March 1992; 'React to', a twelve week drama project in collaboration with Crown Ten Production was produced by the Forum in April 1992 to tackle social exclusion and raise drug awareness among young people. The project culminated in a final performance at the Tricycle Theatre with the support of Felix Cross, Malcolm Frederick and Maureen Hibbert as workshop/performance directors and Trish Cooke as script editor/writer. These activities notwithstanding, the impact once achieved with the Seasons in the West End was never repeated. As members of the Forum struggled to maintain the level of funding previously dispensed by the GLC to their companies, they decided that the Forum should invest more to help strengthen the sector. Its vocation to be a connector within the black arts world led to the production of a registry of black practitioners for outreach work, and creation of databases to facilitate the employment of directors, writers and actors. Finally, during the 1990s, resources were invested in audience development, while attempts continued over the years to establish a black theatre centre as testified by Oscar Watson's project proposal for a National Black and Asian Theatre Development Centre produced in 1996. At the same time Writers' Workshops were organised every year from 1992 to 1995. In particular, the workshop 'Accents and Interpretation' (1995) represented a significant attempt to explore the creative use of Caribbean accents in performance, following on from a number of master classes and voice classes produced in previous years.

During the 1990s, a number of conferences were also organised to address both the history and the future of black theatre and art management in Britain, including 'Yes! It Can Be Fun: Working in Black Arts Administration/Art Management' (1994) and 'Future Histories' (1995), a conference organised at the South Bank Centre in November 1995, which represented an important attempt to create a platform for academics, theatre practitioners, critics, education workers, consultants and representatives of funding bodies to discuss the past, present and future of black theatre and develop a strategy for the sector.

Towards the end of the 1990s, priorities at the London Arts Board changed, the grant to the Forum was cut and funds were allocated to wind down its activities. While the board of Directors continued to work and advocate for the establishment of a development agency, the already meagre funds eventually dried up and the activities of the Black Theatre Forum officially ended in 2001.

Conclusions

As discussed in the chapter, efforts of the Black Theatre Forum to create a common platform where artists of different cultural backgrounds and artistic visions could debate their views and channel them in creative ways did not happen within a vacuum. On the contrary, they reflected the state of black arts and their position within the British cultural industry during one of the most prolific decades for black British theatre in the 20th century. The positive impact of the Seasons in the artistic landscape of London contributed to the inclusiveness of black plays in the repertoire of established theatre houses while the West End also started to see an increase of productions or transfers of plays by writers of African and Asian descent. These included *Black Heroes in the Hall of Fame* a 'choreodrama black musical in seven acts rounding up centuries of black heroes and heroines' written by Flip Fraser and J.D. Douglas and presented at the Astoria Theatre in 1987 under the music direction of Ken Kendricks received very positive reviews and audience response; *Mother Poem* by Eddie Kamau Braithwaite presented at the Drill Hall in 1989 and *Fences* by August Wilson presented at the Garrick Theatre in 1990 both directed by Alby James; *Glory* by Felix Cross presented at the Lyric Theatre Hammersmith in 1990 with the direction of Earl Warner[44]. A number of plays also started to be produced or presented at the Royal National Theatre including *The Little Clay Cart*, by Shudraka directed by Jatinder Verma in 1991, *The Coup* by Mustapha Matura directed by Roger Michell in 1991, and *The Waiting Room* by Tanika Gupta directed by Indhu Rubasingham in 2000.

Similarly the importance of attracting more black audiences to the theatre was also picked up in a number of reports by public funding institutions, and public debates were promoted around the issue of inclusiveness of people of African and Asian descent in various areas of the cultural industry of the country.

The legacy of the Forum is also tangible in the work of Future Histories, the first national repository for African, Asian and Caribbean performing arts in Britain, which bodes well for future dissemination of British African and Asian art history worldwide.

However, up to the time of writing, no arts centre or theatre or research space for the experimentation on African and Asian performance has been acquired by any theatre group or other organisations in London. This could well be the Black Theatre Forum's final legacy to black theatre in Britain.

---

[44] *Black Heroes in the Hall of Fame* toured the USA and was later revived in 1992 at the Hackney Empire. See Terracciano, Alda, *Key African, Caribbean and Asian Productions from 1975*, in S. Croft (ed) *Black And Asian Performance at the Theatre Museum, a Users' Guide* (London: 2003)

Acknowledgements: Alda Terraciano thanks Errol Lloyd, Anton Phillips, Yvonne Brewster, Alby James, Felix Cross, Jatinder Verma, Paulette Randall and Ameena McConnell.

Works cited

Anon. (1997), 'Re-Inventing Britain, Identity, Transnationalism and the Arts', *British Studies Now*, No. 9, London: The British Council, April.

Anthias, Floya & Nira Yuval-Davis (1996), *Racialized Boundaries. Race, Nation, Gender, Colour and Class and the Anti-Racist Struggle*, London and New York: Routledge.

Barker, Walker V. (1985), *The Arts of Ethnic Minorities. Status and Founding*, London: Commission for Racial Equality.

Battram, A. & Segal, Clare, (eds.) (1985), *Arts and Unemployment*, The Community Arts Support Agency.

Bennett, Susan (1997), *Theatre Audiences*, London and New York: Routledge.

Callow, Simon (1997), *The National (1963-1997)*, London: Royal National Theatre.

Cork, Kenneth (1986), *Report on English Theatre*, London: Arts Council of Great Britain.

Crosbie, K. (1984), *Theatre in the Caribbean*, London: Hodder and Stoughton.

Donnell, Alison, (ed.) (2002), *Companion to Contemporary Black British Culture*, London and New York: Routledge.

Francis, Jenny (1990), *Attitudes among Britain's Black Communities Towards Attendance at Arts, Cultural and Entertainment Events*, London: Arts Council of Great Britain.

Gilbert, Helen and Joanne Tompkins (1996), *Post-colonial drama: Theory, practice, politics*, London and New York: Routledge.

Goodman, Lizbeth (1993), *Contemporary Feminist Theatres*, London: Routledge.

Goodwin, Tim (1988), *Britain's Royal National Theatre*, London: National Theatre and Nick Hern Books.

Hall, Stuart and Paul du Gay (1997), *Questions of Cultural Identity*, London: Sage Publications.

Hill, Errol (1997), *The Trinidad Carnival*, London: New Beacon Books.

Hutchinson, Robert (1982), *The Politics of the Arts Council*, London: Sinclair Brown.

James, Winston and Clive Harris, (eds.) (1993), *Inside Babylon: The Caribbean Diaspora in Britain*, London: Verso.

Kapo, Remi (1981), *A Savage Culture, Racism - A Black British View*, London: Quartet.

Khan, Naseem (1976), *The Arts Britain Ignores,* London: Commission for Racial Equality.

Lebel, Jean-Jacques (1969), *Entretiens avec le Living Théatre,* Paris: Pierre Belfond.

Lewis, J., D. Morley, & R. Southwood (1986), *Arts - Who needs it? The Audience for Community Arts,* London: Comedia

Mercer, Kobena (1990), 'Black Art and the Burden of Representation', *Third Text,* No. 10.

Owusu, Kwesi (1986), *The Struggle for Black Arts in Britain,* London: Comedia.

Pavis, Patrice (1992), *Theatre at the Cross-roads of Culture,* London and New York: Routledge.

Rees, Ronald (1992), *Fringe First: Pioneers of Fringe Theatre on Record,* London: Oberon Books.

Rees-Mogg, William (1984), *The Glory of The Garden,* London: Arts Council of Great Britain.

Rees-Mogg, William (1989), *Towards Cultural Diversity,* London: Arts Council of Great Britain.

Rugg, A. (1984), *Brickbats and Bouquets,* London: Race Today Publication.

Selvon, Sam (1998), *The Lonely Londoners,* New York: Longman.

Shellard, Dominic (1999), *British Theatre since the War,* New Haven and London: Yale University Press.

Sivanandan (1982), *A Different Hunger,* London: Pluto Press.

Terracciano, Alda (1997), 'Il Teatro Black. L'Esperiemento del Tara Arts Group', *Drammaturgia,* IV, Roma: Salerno Editrice.

Terracciano, Alda (2002), *Crossing Lines: An Analysis of Integration and Separatism within Black Theatre in Britain,* PhD Thesis, IUO, Naples.

Terracciano, Alda (2003), Key African, Caribbean and Asian Productions from 1975, in S. Croft (ed.) Black And Asian Performance at the Theatre Museum, a Users' Guide, London.

Verma, Jatinder (1989), 'Transformations in Culture: the Asian in Britain', *RSA Journal,* Vol. 137 no. 5400, November.

Theatre Files and Reports, Theatre Archives

Annual Report: Tara Arts Group (1989), London.

Appendix A of *Application for Grant Towards Running Costs* (1983), Greater London Council, Carib Theatre Private Collection.

Scrape off the Black, File: n.d. Temba Theatre Company Collection, Theatre Museum Archive.

Ikoli, Tunde (1985), *Scrape off the Black,* manuscript, Temba Theatre Company Collection, Theatre Museum Archive.

Meadows, Agnes (December 20, 1985), *Black Theatre Forum Progress Report*.
Minutes of Black Theatre Forum Board Meeting (May 8, 1985).
Networking Public Relations, *Report for the Season* (1987).
Phillips, Anton (December 11, 1984), correspondence with Capital Radio, Carib
    Theatre Private Collection.
Phillips, Anton Forum (October 1, 1987), correspondence with Black Theatre,
    Black Theatre Forum Collection, Future Histories Archive.
Plays and Players (July, September and October 1986).
Report from the Director of Recreation and the Arts (17 October 1984), Greater
    London Council, Carib Theatre Private Collection.
Report on the Arts of the (Immigrant) Ethnic Minorities in Scotland (1982),
    London: Arts Council of Great Britain.
Tara Arts Group, Brochure of the company's history from 1977 to 1983, Tara Arts
    Archive.
Temba Theatre Company, Pamphlet of the company, 1986, Temba Theatre
    Collection, Theatre Museum Archive.

Newspaper reviews
Anon. (October 1972), 'The Black Actor in Britain', *Plays and Players*.
Anon. (16 February 1990), 'Roundhouse', *Daily Telegraph*.
Calder, John (18 October 1985), 'The Experience of Blackness', *New Society*.
Coveney, Michael (27 February 1986), 'The Black Jacobins', *Financial Times*.
Cropper, Martin (5 March 1986), 'The Black Jacobins', *Times*.
Dhondy, Farrukh (May 1985), 'Black is Political', *Art Express*.
Hall, Fernau (11 January 1986), 'Tara Arts Group', *Daily Telegraph*.
James, Alby (31 January 1988), 'Taking a Black Stage View', *Independent*.
Jehu, Jeremy (6 October 1983), 'Roundhouse Discrimination', *Stage*.
de Jongh, Nicholas (28 February 1986), 'Slaves to Fortune', *Guardian*.
Pandya, Amrit (10 November 1985), 'Dead for Dowry', *Observer*.
Peter, John (12 January 1986), 'Theatre', *Sunday Times*.

Interviews
Phillips, Anton (12 March 1999), interview with Alda Terracciano.
Brewster, Yvonne (15 December 1999), interview with Alda Terracciano.
Cross, Felix (9 February 2000), interview with Alda Terracciano.
James, Alby (26 Febraury 2000), interview with Alda Terracciano, London.
Randall, Paulette (21 February 2000), interview with Alda Terracciano.

Extended bibliography: Black Theatre Seasons articles and reviews

Season 1983
Anon. (October 1983), 'Theatre' *London Log.*
Anon. (1983), 'Black Theatre Festival 'First', Black Theatre Forum Collection, Future Histories Archive.
Nevis Mountain Dew
Anon. (1983),'Black Theatre Season', *The Sniper*, p. 16-17, Black Theatre Forum Collection, Future Histories Archive.
Christopher, Hudson (10 October 1983), 'A Rum Party', *Standard.*
Grant, Steve (13 October 1983), 'Nevis Mountain Dew', *Time out.*
Irving, Wardle (7 October 1983), 'Not Such a Good Party', *Times.*
Martin, Hoyle (8 October 1983), 'Black Theatre Season opens', *Financial Times.*
Michael, Billington (11 October 1983), 'Nevis Mountain Dew', *Guardian.*
R.S. (9 October 1983), 'Life Supported', *Sunday Telegraph.*
Two Can Play
Brown, Mick (27 October 1983), 'Two Can Play', *Guardian.*
Connor, John (4-10 November 1983), 'Two Can Play', *City Limits.*
Diaz, Herma (9 November 1983), 'Excellent Jamaican comedy', *Jamaican Weekly Gleaner.*
Marriott, R.B. (15 March 1983), 'Brisk comedy farce', *Stage and Television Today.*
Masters, Anthony (28 October 1983), 'Two Can Play', *Times.*
Moore, Oscar (3-9 November 1983), 'Theatre: Fringe Shows', *Time Out.*
Tappin, Janet (11 November 1983), 'Two Can Play', *Caribbean Times.*
The Outlaw
Anon. (17 November 1983), 'Outlaw', *Standard.*
Anon. (20 November 1983), 'Outlaw', *Observer.*
Anon. (21 November 1983), 'Outlaw', *Sunday Telegraph.*
Billington, Michael (17 November 1983), 'The Outlaw', *Guardian.*
Choen, Phil (24 November 1983), 'Clashes of colour', *Islington News.*
Cossou, Egon (10 December 1983), 'The Outlaw', *The Voice.*
Hay, Malcom (17-23 November 1983), 'The Outlaw', *Time Out.*
Hoyle, Martin (17 November 1983), 'Outlaw/Arts', *Financial Times.*
Hudson, Christopher (17 November 1983), 'Theatre', *Standard.*
Marriott, R.B. (1 December 1983), 'Originally alien race living a new life', *Stage and Television Today.*
Nathan, David (1983), 'Rare Talent', *Jewish Chronicle*, Black Theatre Forum Archive.
Tappin, Janet (25 November 1983), 'Outlaw', *Caribbean Times.*
Wardle, Irving (18 November 1983), 'Warmly Anti-racist', *Times.*

Woddis, Carole (25 November-1 December 1983), 'The Outlaw', *City Limits.*
Fishing
Anon. (11 December 1983), 'Fishing', *Sunday Telegraph.*
Anon. (11 December 1983), 'Fishing', *Sunday Times.*
Hoyle, Martin (8 December 1983), 'Black Theatre season opens', *Financial Times.*
Hoyle, Martin (8 December 1983), 'Fishing/Arts', *Financial Times.*
de Jongh, Nicholas (9 December 1983), 'Fishing', *Guardian.*
Masters, Anthony (8 December 1983), 'Better than lovers', *Times.*
Season 1985
Anon. (December 1985), 'New theatre season opening', *Jamaican Gleaner.*
Geyer, Anne (3 September 1985), 'New roles for blacks in Britain', *Los Angeles Times.*
Jones, Jennifer (7 December 1985), 'Black theatre moves centre stage', *Community News.*
McKenley, Jan and Scafe, Suzanne (11-17 January 1985), 'Real Times', *City Limits.*
Shearman, Colin, 'Stage stuck', Temba Theatre Company Archive, Theatre Museum.
Smurthwaite, Nick (10 April 1986), 'Young, gifted, black and plunging new depths', *Stage and Television Today.*
Vigilantes
Ali, Tariq (14 February 1985), *Time Out.*
Anon. (February 10, 1985), 'Vigilantes', *Sunday Times.*
Chatterjee, Bobby (1 March 1985), 'Shelly – 'a lovely person'', *New Life.*
Kingston, Jeremy (8 February 1985), 'Culture clash', *Times.*
Shorter, Eric (12 February 1985), 'Black Theatre's unsettled Cockneys', *Daily Telegraph.*
Truss, Lynne (March 1985), 'Vigilantes', *Plays and Players.*
Young, B.A. (11 February 1985), 'Vigilantes/Arts', *Financial Times.*
The New Hardware Store
Anon. (28 February 1985), 'The New Hardware Store', *What's On.*
Anon. (March 1985), 'The New Hardware Shop', *Cosmopolitan.*
Anon. (1 March 1985), 'A Brent black theatre in West End', *The Chronicle.*
Anon. (1 March 1985), *Brent black theatre in West End*, 'Kilburn Times'.
Anon. (5 April 1985), *City Limits.*
Asquith, Ros (24 March 1985), 'Paving the road to hell', *Observer.*
Carne, Rosalind (8 March 1985), 'The New Hardware Store', *Guardian.*
Cropper, Martin (12 March 1985), 'The New Hardware Store', *Times.*
Haslam, Janet (15 March 1985), 'New Hardware Store', *Caribbean Times.*
Hay, Malcolm (14-20 March 1985), 'The New Hardware Store', *Time Out.*
Hoyle, Martin (11 March 1985), 'The New Hardware Store', *Financial Times.*

KW (18 March 1985), 'Events. A parable of Trinidad', *West Africa*.
Marriott, R.B. (11 April 1985), 'Raw reflection of Trinidad turmoil', *The Stage*.
Peter, John (10 March 1985), 'The New Hardware Store', *Sunday Times*.
Shorter, Eric (8 March 1985), 'The New Hardware Store', *Daily Telegraph*.
Steward, Ian (21 March 1985), 'Two-timing, twice over', *Country Life*.
Woddis, Carole (15-21 March 1985), 'The New Hardware Store', *City Limits*.
Wright, Charles (22 March 1985), 'Symbolic clash in Trinidad', *Ham and High*.
Scrape off the Black
Anon. (13 January 1985), 'Scrape off the Black', *Sunday Times*.
Asquith, Ros (13 January 1985), 'Black brothers', *Observer*.
Bryce, Mary (15 February 1985), 'Scrape off the Black', *Tribune*.
Connor, John (18-24 January 1985), 'Scrape off the Black', *City Limits*.
Hoyle, Martin (15 January1985), 'Scrape off the Black', *Financial Times*.
de Jongh, Nicholas (12 January 1985), 'Scrape off the Black', *Guardian*.
Peter, John (13 January 1985), 'Debasing the currency of drama', *Sunday Times*.
Shorter, Eric (12 January 1985), 'Scraped problem', *Daily Telegraph*.
Solanke, Mary, 'Scrape off the Black', *Black London*, Temba Collection, Theatre
    Museum Archive.
Wardle, Irving (12 January 1985), 'Scrape off the Black', *Times*.
Season 1986
Anon. (7 February 1986), 'Curtains for Black Theatre Season?', *Willesden & Brent
    Chronicle*.
Rakshasa's Ring
Anon. (7 February 1986), 'Black epic with a powerful ring', *Hampstead &
    Highgate Express*.
Billington, Michael (8 February 1985), 'Ring of discord', *Guardian*.
McKenley, Jan (14 February 1986), 'Rakshasha's Ring', *City Limits*.
Newcombe, Morris (16 February 1986), 'Rakshasa's Ring', *Sunday Telegraph*.
The Little Clay Cart
Deo, Shashi, 'The stage arts of Asia', *Ilea Contact*, Tara Arts Archive.
Dickson, Andrew (17-23 January 1986), 'The Little Clay Cart', *City Limits*.
Eccles, Christina (16-22 January 1986), 'The Little Clay Cart', *Time Out*.
Emmanus, Brenda (January 1986), 'Interval Theatre', *Chic*.
Hall, Fernau (11 January 1986), 'Tara Arts Group', *Daily Telegraph*.
Hay, Malcolm, 'Miti Ki Gadi', *Time Out*, Tara Arts Archive.
Hepple, Peter (23 January 1986), 'Tara Arts set the black cart rolling', *Stage and
    Television Today*.
Kalsi, Barinder, 'A Little Clay Cart', *City Limits*, n.d. Tara Arts Archive.
King, Jane (17 January 1986), 'Cutting out the dance', Tara Arts Archive.
Kingstone, Jeremy (10 January 1986), 'The Little Clay Cart', *Times*.
Murdin, Lynda (13 January 1986), 'Doing the Delhi glide...', *London Standard*.

Nayager, Tony, 'A courtesan comes to grief', n.d. Tara Arts Archive.

Peter, John (12 January 1986), 'Theatre', *Sunday Times.*

Rea, Kenneth (14 January 1986), 'The Little Clay Cart', *Guardian.*

The Pirate Princess

Amrit, Pandya (24 January 1986), 'A challenge to white theatre', *Tribune.*

Anon. (19 January 1986), 'Pirate Princess Script Goes to London', *Sunday Gleaner.*

Connor, John (1 January 1987), 'Flash trash', *City Limits.*

Gardom, Timothy (21 March 1986), 'Lots of Fun, but There's a Serious Message, Too', *The Weekly Gleaner.*

Hay, Malcolm, 'The Pirate Princess', *Time Out,* n.d. Temba Theatre Collection, Theatre Museum Archive.

Season 1987

Ali, Naqi (28 August 1987), 'Fourth black theatre season comes to the West End', *Asian Times.*

Anon. (August-September 1987), 'Black Theatre Season', *Artswork.*

Anon. (28 August - 3 September 1987), 'Hansib presents 4th Black Theatre', *Asian Times.*

Anon. (September 1987), 'Black Theatre Season '87', *Root.*

Anon. (September 1987), 'Black Theatre Season '87', *Westindian Digest.*

Clive, Davis (3 September 1987), 'Black theatre: The next stage', *The Listener.*

Woddis, Carole (3-10 September 1987), 'Black action', *City Limits.*

Remembrance

Anon. (27 August 1987), 'Jimmy goes on show...', *Hornsey Journal.*

Anon. (4 September 1987), 'A first TV's Corinne', *Islington Gazette.*

Bishop, Maria (25 August 1987), 'Black Theatre Season '87', *The Voice.*

Chand, Paul (17 September 1987), 'Remembrance', *Stage.*

Conway, Lydia (22 January 1987), 'Out of the darkness', *What's On & Where To Go.*

Edwardes, Jane (9 September 1987), 'Remembrance', *Time Out.*

Foster, Edward (8 September 1987), 'Remembrance', *Independent.*

de Jongh, Nicholas (8 September 1987), 'Remembrance', *Guardian.*

Leech, Michael (3 September 1987), 'Seeking the truth', *What's On.*

Radin, Victoria (18 September 1987), 'Poetic license', *New Statesman.*

Reid, Tricia (28 August 1987), 'Black Theatre Season and a new direction for Carmen', *Caribbean Times.*

Smurthwaite, Nick (3 September 1987), 'Enter black girl', *Guardian.*

Taylor, Paul (7 September 1987), 'A colonized mind', *Independent.*

Woddis, Carole (9 September 1987), 'Remembrance', *City Limits.*

Tewodros

Allan, Teresa (5 November 1987), 'Tewodros', *City Limits.*

Anon. (1 September 1987), 'Seasoned objection', *The Voice*.
Anon. (2 November 1987), 'Mistress and Merchants', *Times*.
Anon. (5-9 November 1987), 'Tewodros', *The Voice*.
Gardner, Lyn (5-12 November 1987), 'Tewodros', *City Limits*.
Griffiths, Lorraine, 'Honouring our heroes', *The Buzz*, n.d. Black Theatre Forum Archive.
James, John, 'Mad, funny or both', n.d. Black Theatre Forum Archive.
Kingston, Jeremy (2 November 1987), 'Tewodros', *Times*.
Leech, Michael (14 November 1987), 'Strong folk tale for Arts Theatre', *What's On*.
Rose, Helen (11 November 1987), 'Tewodros', *Time Out*.
Taylor, Paul (2 November 1987), 'Empire states', *Independent*.
Moon Dance Night
Absalom, Steve (8 October 1987), 'News girl Moira in storm over play', *Daily Mail*.
Anon.,'Hampton's lunchtime treats', *Independent*, n.d. Black Theatre Forum Collection, Future Histories Archive.
Anon. (2 October 1987), 'Wurly gig', *Evening Standard*.
Anon. (1-5 October 1987), 'Moon Dance Night', *Weekend Choice*.
Anon. (15-19 October 1987), 'Moondance Night', *The Voice*.
Anon. (22 October 1987), 'Thespian Edward on fringe', *Evening Standard*.
Anon. (27 October 1987), 'Royal flush', *The Voice*.
Armitstead, Claire (9 October 1987), 'Black Theatre/Drill Hall', *Financial Times*.
Buss, Robin (5 October 1987), 'Tugging at the roots...', *The London Evening Standard*.
Chand, Paul (15 October 1987), 'Moondance Night', *Stage and Television Today*.
Grant, Steve (7 October 1987), 'Moondance Night', *Time Out*.
Griffiths, Lorraine (29 October – 2 November 1987), 'A princely performance', *Weekend Voice*.
Hay, Malcolm (30 September – 7 October 1987), 'Brewster's millions', *Time Out*.
James, John (23 October 1987), 'Frustrated passion', *Times Educational Supplement*.
Kellaway, Kate (11 October 1987), 'Stress cure', *Observer*.
King, Francis (11 October 1987), 'No little niggers', *Sunday Telegraph*.
M.L. (14 October 1987), 'Another Country', *What's On*.
Peter, John (11 October 1987), 'Committing murder by cliché', *Sunday Times*.
Reid, Tricia, 'Sylvester's shining', *Caribbean Times*, n.d.
Rissik, Andrew, 'Now the news from home', n.d. Black Theatre Forum Collection, Future Histories Archive.
Theatre news, Black Theatre Forum Collection, Future Histories Archive.
Vidal, John (9 October 1987), 'Moondance Night', *Guardian*.

Season 1989

Anon. (10 January 1989), 'The Shaw makes it big for black theatre', *The Voice.*

Anon. (19 January 1989), 'Black Theatre Season opens', *Camden & St. Pancras Chronicle.*

Anon. (27 January 1989), 'A new stage in black direction', *Hampstead & Highgate Express.*

Anon. (23 February 1989), 'Black Theatre Season ticket offer', *City Limits.*

Anon. (March 1989), 'Black Theatre Season', *Plays and Players.*

Griffiths, Lorraine (20 December 1988), 'Black Theatre Season 1989', *The Voice.*

Griffiths, Monique (11 April 1989), 'The Black Theatre Season - stuck in a rut?', *The Voice*

Dog

Anon., 'Dog opens Black Theatre Season', *The Bleaner*, n.d. Black Theatre Forum Collection, Future Histories Archive.

Anon. (24 January 1989), 'Dog', *Listings.*

Anon. (26 January 1989), 'Dog', *Stage and Television Today.*

Anon. (27 January 1989), 'The Black Theatre Season', *Asian Times.*

Anon. (27 January – 2 February 1989), 'Barking up the right tree', *Caribbean Times.*

Anon. (9 February 1989), 'Dog', *City Limits.*

Anon. (8 February 1989), 'Shaw Theatre', *Time Out.*

Christopher, James (1 February 1989), 'Great Scott', *Time Out.*

Marmion, Patrick (1 February 1989), 'A sorry tail', *What's On & Where To Go.*

Stumpfl, Claudia (23 January 1989), 'Black theatre', *Guardian.*

Lazarus and his Beloved/Song of the Dead

Anon. (25 January 1989), 'Black Theatre Season', *What's On & Where To Go.*

Anon. (6 February1989), 'Lazarus and his Beloved', *Observer.*

Anon. (9 February 1989), 'Wednesday, Feb. 15', *Stage and Television Today.*

Anon. (16 February 1989), 'Rare chance to see Middle East dramas', *Willesden & Brent Chronicle.*

Anon. (22 February 1989), 'Black Theatre Season', *Time Out.*

Arro, Isabel (8 February 1989), 'Cross casting', *What's on & Where to Go.*

Jones, D.A.N. (19 February 1989), 'Cocktails with old Crookback', *Sunday Telegraph.*

Porter, Cedric (17 February 1989), 'Plays with a touch of Eastern flavour', *South London Press.*

Renton, Alex (1 March 1989), 'Lazarus and his Beloved and Song of the Dead', *Independent.*

Solanke, Adeola (22 January 1989), 'Raising the dead', *What's On & Where To Go.*

Beef, No Chicken

Anon. (10 March 1989), 'Beefy role', *Coulsdon & Purley Advertiser.*
Anon. (22 March 1989), 'Black Theatre Season: Beef, No Chicken', *City Limits.*
Anon. (22 March 1989), 'Black Theatre Season: Beef, No Chickens', *Time Out.*
Anon. (22 March 1989), 'Black Theatre Season: Beef, No Chickens', *What's On & Where To Go.*
Armitstead, Claire (24 March 1989), *Hampstead & Highgate Express.*
Fisher, Paul (30 March 1989), 'Beef, No Chicken', *Guardian.*
Gray, Dominic (22 March 1989), 'The open road', *What's On.*
Hay, Malcom (15 March 1989), 'Beef, No Chicken', *Time Out.*
Hoyle, Martin (14 March 1989), 'Beef, No Chicken', *Financial Times.*
James, John (31 March 1989), 'Ghostly plots', *Times Educational Supplement.*
Woddis, Carole (18 March 1989), 'Beef, No Chickens by Derek Walcott (Show)', *City Limits.*

Season 1990
Christopher, James, 'On the Black Theatre Season', n.d. Temba Theatre Collection, Theatre Museum Archive.
Griffiths, Lorraine (13 February 1990), 'Hitting theatre goers for six', *The Voice.*
McFerran, Ann (2 March 1990), 'Black boards', *Times Educational Supplement.*
Onwordi, Sylvester, 'Black to the future', n.d. Black Theatre Forum Archive.
Pinnock, Monica (23 February 1990), 'Our write', *Tribune.*
St. Hill, Dionne, 'The dreamer and the man: Anton Phillips', n.d. Black Theatre Forum Collection, Future Histories Archive.

Say Hallelujah
Anon. (2 March 1990), 'Black boards', *Times Educational Supplement.*
Anon. (4 March 1990), 'Say Hallelujah', *Sunday Correspondent.*
Anon. (4 March 1990), 'Say Hallelujah', *Independent on Sunday.*
Anon. (4 March 1990), 'Say Hallelujah', *Observer.*
Anon. (4 March 1990), 'Say Hallelujah', *Sunday Telegraph.*
Anon. (4 March 1990), 'Say Hallelujah', *Sunday Times.*
Anon. (14 March 1990), 'Say Halleleujah', *Time Out.*
Anon. (15 March 1990), 'Say Hallelujah', *City Limits.*
Anon. (4 April 1990), 'Say Halleleujah', *Daily Telegraph.*
Billington, Michael (22 February 1990), 'Curtain up on the early Ibsen', *Guardian.*
Billington, Michael (28 February 1990), 'Cultural counter attack', *Guardian.*
Coveney, Michael, 'Arts Theatre Archive', n.d. Theatre Museum Archive.
Edwardes, Jane (7-14 March 1990), 'Say Hallelujah', Black Theatre Forum Collection, Future Histories Archive.
Gardner, Lyn, 'Seasoned populism', n.d. Temba Theatre Collection, Theatre Museum Archive.
Kingston, Jeremy (23 February 1990), 'Prayers for a grocer', *Times.*
Macaulay, Alastair (28 February 1990), 'Say Hallelujah', *Financial Times.*

McDonagh, Melanie (27 February 1990), 'Inglorious Hallelujah', *Evening Standard.*

Nightingale, Benedict (27 February 1990), 'Exuberant good humour in store', *Times.*

Paton, Maureen (15 March 1990), 'Say Hallelujah', *Stage and Television Today.*

Pinnock, Monica (23 February 1990), 'Outwrite', *Tribune.*

Renton, Alex (28 February 1990), 'Closed for stock-taking', *Independent.*

Smith, Mari, 'Say Hallelujah', n.d Black Theatre Forum Archive.

Spencer, Charles (1 March 1990), 'Bible bashing', *Daily Telegraph.*

Way, Katharine (8 March 1990), 'Say Hallelujah', *City Limits.*

Blood, Sweat and Fears

Anon. (21 April 1990), 'Blood, Sweat, and Fears', *Guardian.*

Anon. (1 May 1990), 'Biting humour out of Sickle Cell', *Caribbean Times.*

Anon. (11 May 1990), 'Star Trek's a burger chain', *Hammersmith & Fulham Guardian.*

Anon. (3 October 1990), 'Blood, Sweat and Fears', *City Limits.*

Anon. (30 October 1990), 'Blindness is no handicap', *The Voice.*

Brown, Georgina (26 April 1990), 'Life, but not as we know it', *Times.*

Cohen, Norma (6 May 1990), 'Cell Crisis', *Times Educational Supplement.*

Eyres, Harry (25 April 1990), 'Blood, Sweat and Fears', *Times.*

Macaulay, Alastair (25 April 1990), 'Blood, Sweat and Fears', *Financial Times.*

Paton, Maureen (10 May 1990), 'Sick minds', *Stage.*

Rose, Helen (2 May 1990), 'Blood, Sweat and Fears', *Time Out.*

Eden

Anon., 'Eden', *The Voice*, n.d. Black Theatre Forum Collection, Future Histories Archive.

Anon. (27 March 1990), 'Eden', *Times.*

Armitstead, Claire (3 April 1990), 'Eden', *Financial Times.*

Asquith, Ros (29 March – 5 April 1990) Black Theatre Forum Collection, Future Histories Archive.

Forbes, Deidre (27 March 1990), 'Thinking freedom', *Now.*

de Jongh, Nicholas (12 April 1990), 'Eden', *The Guardian.*

Kingston, Jeremy (3 April 1990), 'The Bartons of 63rd Street', *Times.*

Onwordi, Sylvester (18 April 1990), 'West of Eden', *What's On.*

Reade Simon (12-19 April 1990), 'Eden', *City Limits.*

Robertson, Nicola (11-18 April 1990), 'Eden', *Time Out.*

Taylor, Paul (4 April 1990), 'Poor relations', *Independent.*

CHAPTER TWO

WRITING BLACK BACK: AN OVERVIEW OF BLACK THEATRE AND PERFORMANCE IN BRITAIN

DEIRDRE OSBORNE

Synopsis:

Black people have lived in Britain longer than they have in the USA and yet, until the closing decade of the twentieth century, their contribution to British theatre has received limited and short-lived attention. In this chapter I trace a trajectory of representation of black people in theatre from the early modern through to the pre-Windrush period to recognize that which has paved the way to the increasing visibility of contemporary black British playwrights of African descent in theatre of the new millennium.

Food for thought

The frameworks of socio-cultural derogation, namely imperialism and its major consequence, racism, have historically either suffocated or distorted the existence of sustainable and autonomous black theatre in Britain. Retrieving the presence of black people working in theatre prior to the late twentieth century foregrounds not only bigotry and marginalization regarding the contributions of black practitioners, but also draws attention to the protean qualities of the delimiting term 'black' and its specific adaptations by dominant ideologies. As there is no extant evidence of any drama being penned or devised by black people in Britain until the twentieth century, the first stage of surveying the presence of black people in British theatre history resides imperfectly in exploring how black characters are represented in the plays of white writers from the sixteenth to nineteenth centuries. Not until the mid-nineteenth century, with the presence of Ira Aldridge, a black American actor (who adopted British nationality) interpreting black and white roles in classical plays to international acclaim, can we locate the initiatory step of a black performer gaining a limited autonomy over representing a black character in mainstream theatre.

Black women and men in the British Isles have offered both a literal and representational presence which has been habitually consigned to the footnotes of history yet exerted as Niebrzydowski identifies, through 'their representation in language and in a variety of artistic media' (Niebrzydowski 2001: 188). As is often noted in historical accounts of the presence of black people in Britain, Septimus Severus (the famous Libyan-born Roman general) came to Britain circa 210 A.D.. However, Niebrzydowski reminds us, 'it is salutary to note that black women had arrived in the British Isles by the beginning of the first...[millennium]...The remains of a young African girl were found in a burial dated c.1000 A.D.'(187). The foregrounding of male subjectivity in discourses relating to black identity in Britain has occurred not only in the scarce historical documentation that exists but also, as Joseph argues, until the late twentieth century in theatre, where 'the absence of Black women as subjects with agency' was marked (Joseph 1998: 198).

In mediaeval morality plays, the type of the black-faced devils (signified by actors painting themselves black or by wearing black costumes) drew upon the visual representations in Christian iconography of black faces symbolizing the fall from grace. The allegorical association of blackness with evil and sin and the corresponding attaching of whiteness to purity have a long history not only in European Christianity and culture but also on the English stage.

As twentieth-century scholarship has demonstrated,[45] European racializing discourses (that developed from the first manifestations of colonization and its subsequent transporting of people enslaved for economic reasons, cast black people into a generalized category of debasement and villainy on the English stage. As early as 1510 Moors were represented in masques and are recorded as performing in street pageants in 1522, and both Henry VII and Henry VIII

---

[45] Barthelemy, Anthony Gerard (1987), *Black Face Maligned Race: The Representation of Blacks in English Drama from Shakespeare to Southerne*, Baton Rouge and London: Louisiana State University Press, Evans, K.W. (1969), 'The racial factor in *Othello*', *Shakespeare Studies*: 124-140, Faggett, Harry L. (1970), *Black et al. Minorities in Shakespeare's England*, Houston, Texas: Prairie View Press, Gottesman, Lillian (1970), 'English voyages and accounts: impact on dramatic presentation of the African', in William F. Grayburn (ed.), *Studies in Humanities*, Indian University of Pa: 26-32, Jones, Eldred D. (1962), 'Africans in Elizabethan England', *Notes and Queries* 8: 302, Jones, Eldred D. (1962), 'The Physical Representation of African Characters on the English Stage During the 16th and 17th Centuries', *Theatre Notebook* 17 (Autumn): 17-21, Miller, W.E. (1962), 'Negroes in Elizabethan London', *Notes and Queries* 8: 138 and Tokson, Elliott. H. (1982), *The Popular Image of the Black Man in English Drama, 1550-1688* Boston Mass.: G.K.Hall and Co.

employed a black trumpeter, John Blanke, at their courts[46]. Traders had brought five black men from Guinea to London in 1550 and the increase in trading vessels going to and from Africa throughout the 1570s and 80s meant that encounters between white Englishmen and black people became more frequent. This produced an edict from Queen Elizabeth by 1596 that decreed how the 'sundry' blackamoors were to be deported, a paradoxical move it seems as she employed an African entertainer and page at her own court (File and Power 1995: 6).

White courtiers appeared as Moors in masques throughout the sixteenth century in English and Scottish courts. 'The maskers usually wore Moorish garb, black stockings, gloves, and a black mask' (Bartelemy 1987: 19-20). This served a permissive and carnivalesque purpose. Risqué and indecorous behaviour was possible amongst maskers who could temporarily operate outside expected protocol in the celebration of the masque. Ben Jonson's *The Masque of Blackness* (1605) was one in which royal maskers darkened their skin and was devised in response to Queen Anne's request to play a 'black-more' (Barthelemy 1987).

The earliest substantial treatment of a Moor in a play occurs in George Peele's *The Battle of Alcazar* (1588/9?) where the evil genius, Muly Mahamet, constituted the prototype for black Moors on the English stage for the next century or so. Clearly, as Barthelemy points out, 'Moor' for seventeenth-century audiences and readers was an appellation which included 'Asians, Native Americans, Africans, Arabs and all Muslims regardless of ethnicity'(x). The extension of knowledge of people beyond Christendom gained via travel writing and exploration endowed this category with increasing specificity in terms of geography and culture - something that was not matched in the imaginative renderings of non-white people for, as Barthelemy observes, 'It is no exaggeration to say that the overwhelming majority of black Moors who appeared on the popular English stage between 1589 and 1695 endorsed, represented, or were evil' (72).

The most famous playwright of the English renaissance, Shakespeare, had a familiarity with late Elizabethan court circles which would have given him direct experience of at least one black performer. Lucy Negro was one of the players featured in the Gray's Inn Christmas revels of 1594. It has even been suggested that she might be the inspiration for his Dark Lady of the sonnets. In many ways, Shakespeare continued the grim legacy of Muly Mahamet with *Titus Andronicus*. Aaron represents unbridled evil that equates his skin colour with abomination. He taints all who associate with him. Yet as Barthelemy demonstrates, Aaron is also devotedly paternal, defends his blackness and separates it from his choice to be evil so that he symbolizes villainy *per se* rather than simply embodying a place within a preordained allegory of blackness. Together with Shakespeare's other Moor protagonist Othello, the Moor stereotypes are manipulated in varying degrees to

---

[46] 'Before the Black Victorians', http://www.mckenziehpa.com/bv/before.html

discomfort audience expectations through reversals of roles and characteristics aligned with sex and the projection of venery onto blacks (see Barthelemy: 150-1). It should be noted, however, that this feasibly transpired for experimental reasons rather than Shakespeare's ability to transcend contemporary ideology.

Other renaissance writers who produced images of black people in their plays include Jonson, Dekker, Heywood, Webster, Middleton and Chapman. In addition, early imaginative treatments of the 'Negro' are captured in dialogue poems by Herbert, Rainolds, King and Cleveland across the seventeenth century.[47]

However, the colonising and commercial interests of the English renaissance and its fledgling imperialist forays into the New World overwhelmingly shaped the imaginative response to black people and their representation by white English playwrights. Tokson accounts for the racial encounters this produced as 'fresh and perplexing' (Tokson 1982: 9) for the indigenous white English population. David Davis asks if the literary imagination helped to bridge the gap between the races as the world was bifurcated into Old and New (Davis 1966: 9).

Yet this idea of a 'gap' as worth bridging becomes problematic. Rather, it is the tension between articulating possible common ground (usually demonstrated in emotions and actions) and its subsequent effacing by a resurgent core of demonized, intrinsic evil housed invariably in the alien (black) races that consolidates the trope of 'blackness' in plays of this period. The iconography that denoted black people was specifically played out in representations that removed them from inhabiting the identity of 'person'. The black man as an incarnation of pagan devilry and representative of superstition and concupiscent savagery was a familiar trope for European writers and audiences alike. Only through Christianising and the adoption of white associative customs, speech and manners could the staged black race be redeemed. Without this the slide into bestiality and brutality was easily managed by playwrights and received as a confirmation of type. Through embodying some characteristics of credible people, type characters thus served to represent a group identified by sex, race, religion or nationality.

There were few plays which dramatized black characters during the Renaissance or the later Restoration, despite the fact that black people comprised a significant percentage of the London population (albeit overwhelmingly as servants and sailors) living in a parallel world, 'working and living alongside the

---

[47] Characters in some of the plays sampled include Nigir in Jonson's *Masque of Blackness*(1605), Zarack in Dekker's *Lust's Dominion* (1599), Toto in Heywood's *The Fair Maid of the West* (1600-03?), Zanche in Webster's *The White Devil* (1611), Porus in Chapman's *The Blind Beggar of Alexandria* (1598). The dialogue poems Tokson explores are George Herbert's 'A Negro maid woos Cestus', Henry Rainolds's 'A Black-moor Maid wooing a fair Boy', Henry King's 'The Boyes answer to the Blackmoor' and John Cleveland's 'A Fair Nymph Scorning a Black Boy Courting Her'.

English...as familiar a sight to Shakespeare as they were to Garrick, and almost as familiar to both as they are to Londoners today' (Gerzina 1995). However, whilst Thomas Southerne's *Oroonoko* (1695), derived from Aphra Behn's novella, offers a sympathetic portrayal of a Moor who is betrayed by white duplicity, and establishes the notion of the 'noble savage', Oroonoko still displays many of the hindrances of a racist representational legacy. As black characters were not played by black actors in Shakespeare's day, so was this continued over subsequent centuries in productions of his plays. The only reference to any possibility occurs in the example of eminent black Londoner Ignatius Sancho, a friend of Garrick's, being considered for a role at Drury Lane but prevented by a speech impediment from appearing upon the stage. Adaptation of older works was a feature and with this came some revisions through form and content.

Throughout the eighteenth century, there was an expansion of the black population in Britain as plantation owners relocated their households from the colonies or sea-captains and colonial administrators returned home, bringing their servants with them. Paintings, historical records and literature of the eighteenth century reveal evidence of the black servant class and their social presence. Intermarriage with the white working-class poor produced a form of social integration which, at the beginning of the nineteenth-century, also included the destitute and political voicelessness that characterized this sector.[48]

It was in the Victorian era that black people in Britain would become largely invisible in representations of cultural life. Without exception they were marked out as separate from the civilized and superior Anglo-Saxon race and this suffuses the dramatization of black characters in British theatre right up until the late twentieth century when plays by black writers began to be more frequently staged.

A View from Abroad: Black Performers (1830-1930)

As the MacKenzie Heritage Picture Archive notes, 'The most visible Black people in Victorian society were performers of the various kinds: prize-fighters, actors, musicians and singers' ('Black Victorians' resource page). The fact that movements towards the abolition of slavery were more established and faster moving in Europe and Britain than in the United States produced an opportunity for someone like the African-American actor Ira Aldridge to attain prominence on English and European stages. He was the first black man to play white roles in

---

[48] See Nigel File and Chris Power, *Black Settlers in Britain*, Peter Fryer, *Staying Power: the History of Black People in Britain*, Douglas Lorimer, *Colour, Class and the Victorians*, S.I. Martin, *Britain's Slave Trade,* Susan Okokon, *Black Londoners, 1880-1990*, Ron Ramdin, *The Making of the Black Working Class in Britain*, Folarin Shyllon, *Black People in Britain, 1555-1833*, James Walvin, *Black and White: The Negro and English Society, 1555-1943*.

Shakespeare's plays which were considered the ultimate test of performance virtuosity.[49] Aldridge initially arrived in Scotland in 1824 to study at Glasgow University which did not operate the colour bar of American colleges. He left America ostensibly to pursue acting and developed a truly international reputation. Acclaimed throughout the UK and Ireland he furthermore embraced a kind of multiculturalism by performing in bilingual productions when he toured non-English-speaking countries. One example of critical reception notes that,

> Curiosity led us last night to see the black tragedian…[had he appeared]…merely as a provincial performer and an Englishman, he would have merited considerable applause, but considering he has attained his eminence under all the disadvantages of the present state of American society, his claims must belong to a much higher grade. (The Globe, 11 October, 1825, quoted in Marshall and Stock 1958: 63)

Although Aldridge's early repertoire included the expected 'black' roles in *Othello, Oroonoko, The Slave, The Castle Spectre, The Padlock* and *The Revenge*, he had exhausted the number of black characters he could play by the late 1820s and turned to playing white roles including King Lear and Macbeth whilst also writing his own melodramas and doggerel verses with political overtones. As his provincial and continental touring reputation was consolidated, London critics revealed racist antipathies to his performance and their unilateral vitriol succeeded in closing one of his early West End seasons. The customary lack of engagement with, and cultural alienation from, the experiential uniqueness black drama and performances offer has been characteristic of the critical arena of reception, wherein the rigid parameters of evaluation are frequently testimony to a reassertion of traditional theatrical hegemonies.[50]

Aldridge's example confirms how the history of politics and the right to freedom became intrinsic to black cultural enterprise and continue to be so up to the first years of the second millennium. After Aldridge's precedent, another African-American, Samuel Morgan Smith (c.1833–82) travelled to England in 1866 and became the actor-manager of the Theatre Royal in Gravesend. He played Othello, Hamlet, Richard III, Macbeth and Shylock there and on tour to critical acclaim.(Hill: 29-31). In 1866 he reprised these roles in a short season at the Royal Olympic Theatre, London and up to his death engaged in a rigorous circuit of provincial touring. The third example of an African-American actor coming to

---

[49] Errol Hill notes that the African-American Shakespearean actor, James Hewlett travelled to England in 1825 to 'to fulfil an engagement at the Coburg Theatre in London…but there is no record of his appearance there' (Hill 1984: 15).
[50] 'Fleet Street commentators find black actors easiest to appreciate in socio-dramas, while the alternative press patronises black plays by raving over them all. Both are inhibiting to experiment', writes Jim Hiley (1985: n.p., Miscellaneous Black Theatre Archive).

England for the opportunity to act in Shakespeare (as he was unable to do in the United States) is Paul Molyneaux Hewlett (1856-91). However, despite receiving positive reviews for his portrayals of Othello, 'details of his appearances have not been traced. The novelty of another authentic black like Aldridge or Morgan Smith was apparently wearing thin. With emancipation in England and America no longer issues to rally a following, Molyneaux found life very difficult indeed' (Hill 1984: 39). In 1889 he returned to America, dying two years later. Tellingly it was not until 1930 that another black actor played Othello on the London West End stage, and it would be another American, Paul Robeson, who actually studied diction with Aldridge's daughter, Amanda Ira Aldridge, to prepare for the role.

Ira Aldridge was a lone but influential example of a successful black theatre performer in Britain in the first half of the century. As John M. Turner outlines, in other areas of entertainment such as the circus, hippodromatic shows, menageries and travelling fairs, black people as performers were not an unusual sight. In particular William Darby (1796-1871), an indigenous black Briton known professionally as 'Pablo Fanque' performed to national acclaim in circuses and was proprietor of many until his death (Turner 2003: 20-38) There are indications in the Victorian press of the presence of other black performers appearing in London theatres such as 'The Black Malibran', Dona Maria Loreto, who appeared at Her Majesty's theatre on 13 July 1850. It is noted that, 'Flushed with her reception in *La Belle France*, Maria Martinez crossed the channel, to appeal to a London public for a ratification of the favourable verdict pronounced by the music-lovers of Paris and Madrid'. And 'as a mark of social progress in the 'black race'…The novelty of the 'coloured lady' songstress to appear to-night has created quite a sensation in musical circles…the Parisian press was eloquent in her favour' (untitled newspaper cutting in 'Miscellaneous Black theatre File' in the Theatre Museum).

The vigorous expansion of the British empire from the second-half of the nineteenth century saw an accompanying refinement of racist ideology as a key component to maintaining and justifying territorial acquisitions in both political and socio-cultural contexts. Whilst minstrel theatre and its fundamental premise of debasing the black body in performance became consolidated in American popular culture long after the Civil War and Reconstruction, there is no parallel documentation of the legacy of black performers in Britain over the same period. However, as Michael Pickering points out, the racist impersonating of black people by white performers in blackface minstrelsy was 'one of the most pervasive forms of popular entertainment in England and the rest of Britain during the Victorian period' (Pickering 2003: 159). The 'nigger minstrel' lost sustainability from mid-century onwards as black performers began to participate in minstrel shows. Groups such as the Fisk Jubilee Singers, Black American students who toured in Britain (1874-5) at the invitation of an aide to Queen Victoria, introducing the Queen to gospel music, presented the authenticity that blackface minstrelsy mocked through gross mimicry. Les Black offers a quotation from the Earl of Shaftesbury's response to a concert in 1875:

> I am delighted to see so large a congregation of the citizens of London come to offer a renewal of their hospitality to these noble brethren and sisters of ours…They have returned here, not for anything in their own behalf, but to advance the interests of the coloured race in America…coming here with such a spirit I don't want them to become white, but I have a strong disposition myself to become black. (Black 2000: 146)

Shaftesbury's 'strong disposition to become black' does not exactly anticipate the sustained popularity of BBC television's Black and White Minstrel Show which was (disturbingly) televised to large viewing audiences up until the 1970s.[51] Michael Macmillan[52] notes the extensive lack of documentation regarding the theatre histories of black people in Britain up to the 1920s when 'major cultural icons such as Paul Robeson' (Macmillan 2004: 55) came to Britain. There was still a long way to go until it could be said that black British people had developed a validated and autonomous cultural identity, what May Joseph identifies in her reading of Paul Gilroy as 'a tangible and permeating presence within the British state' (Joseph 1998: 197) In fact the presence of black people on the British stage into the early twentieth century remained by and large that of touring African-American individuals and groups.

This was not, however, without opposition within the acting profession. In 1923, Harper, Banks and Co. faced the antagonism of the English Variety Artists Federation when they toured *Plantation Days* for the Empire Theatre Revue. The show's season was reduced from ten weeks to six despite taking up only fifteen minutes in the revue and being a commercial success ($8,000 in one week), proving that audiences 'care for American entertainment and especially colored performers' (*The Afro-American South's Biggest and Best Weekly* 1923: n.p.) The opposition to their performing was exemplified in a campaign based upon the slogan 'British theatres for the British', launched in protest by the English Variety Artists Federation. Their chairman Albert Voyce was keen to point out that acting was the white person's province rather than stating concerns for black members of

---

[51] Michael Macmillan notes, 'It wasn't until the mid-1970s that the BBC, bastion of 'balanced' broadcasting decided it was time to take *The Black and White Minstrel Show* off the air' (Macmillan 2004: 54).

[52] He incorrectly dates *The Blinkards*, the first play by a black writer to be published in Britain, to 1907. It was in fact written in 1915 (first staged by members of the Cosmopolitan Club in Cape Coast, Ghana) and first published in Britain in 1974. The playwright, William Esuman-Gwira Sekyi (1892-1956), better known as Kobina Sekyi, had received his education in England and was a resident there. Using the well-made-play form, Sekyi's play has been described as 'a light comedy of the Shavian type…written in both English and Fante…its central ideas on the dangers of Europeanism' (Sekyi 1974: 11).

the Federation (if there were any) being denied work. Customary racializing terms reveal Voyce's anxiety regarding any social integration of black and white people in the performing arts context and the assumption that black people automatically occupy an inferior position. 'There are also in England Negro turns, most respectable and most decent, who behave themselves and keep their place. But we view with the greatest apprehension a cabaret where black artists actually mix with white folks at tables' (*New York Tribune*, 4 July 1923).[53] Even though segregation was associated overwhelmingly with the US, and Britain represented a possible sphere for performance for black American artists from Aldridge onwards, racializing and judgemental codes are obviously applied to a touring black company in the UK at this time.

This extract furthermore refers to a production of *In Dahomey* in 1903 at the Shaftesbury Theatre, an all-black musical which had been a great success theatrically,[54] noting an interval of twenty years until this was repeated with *Plantation Days*. This appears to have transpired 'for the reason that while the principal members of the company behaved themselves perfectly as much could not be said of some of the Negro chorus men. It is also recalled that the staging here at Earl's Court of an exhibition called 'Savage South Africa' was productive of a good deal of the same sort of trouble'. Such recorded viewpoints indicate the racist overlay that tempers the opportunities apparently afforded to nineteenth-century black American actors who rejected contexts of segregation to pursue their art in Britain.

The centrality of African-American men was not all-pervasive, as women too gained recognition, albeit primarily in musical roles. Revues titled *Dover Street to Dixie* and *Blackbirds* starred the African-American singer Florence Mills in 1923 and 1926, a woman who it was recorded 'thought much of the status of coloured people, and fought hard to establish them as men and women with the same claims on the world as the whites...Somewhere one sensed the sad dignity of a race which the world had treated unjustly – a kind of sensibility which made all our memories of nigger-minstrel buffoonery seem shabby and dull...The memories of London playgoers, at all events, are not likely to disappoint the faith that she held.'[55]

Together with musicals such as *Show Boat* and *Porgy and Bess* in West End theatres, the revue was the primary performing context for black performers throughout the 1920s and 30s. Elisabeth Welch was another African-American who settled in Britain to pursue opportunities in a performing career that the

---

[53] Extract from newspaper cutting in Miscellaneous Black Theatre File Theatre Museum.
[54] The Theatre Museum in Covent Garden, London holds programmes, reviews and publicity regarding this production (Croft 2002: 15 and 31).
[55] No author, no date, no publication. 'Florence Mills: An Impression of her Art'. Biographical File, Theatre Museum, London.

segregation of her birthplace prohibited and was 'so accepted as an ornament of the British Stage that many do not know that she was, in fact, born in New York'.[56] Her first appearance in England was in the revue *Dark Doings* at the Leicester Square Theatre in 1933 followed by success in *Nymph Errant* at the Adelphi theatre in the same year. An obituary notes that 'Perhaps unfairly, it is as a black artist that she will be principally remembered, though her appeal and her style were strictly international...Her racial mix, however, did a great deal to help promote race relations in an age when such a notion was not at all popular' (Freedland 2003: 27). Welch herself told an interviewer, 'I call myself the beginning of the United Nations. Mother's people came from Leith ...[Scotland]...Father was the son of a Negro who had married an American Indian woman' (Robinson 1983: n.p.). Adelaide Hall too moved to London in 1938 and enjoyed the longevity of her contemporary, Welch, as not only a legendary jazz singer but also a cabaret artist and actor. She appeared in *The Sun Never Sets* at Drury Lane in 1938, apparently untroubled by what is described as 'the imperialist racism'[57] of the piece despite being outspoken about racism in the United States.

In terms of drama, black actors featured in productions of Eugene O'Neill's *All God's Chillun' Got Wings*, first staged in England at the Royal Court with Jim Harris, Emma Williams and Henry Brown in 1929 and revived with Paul Robeson in 1933. Robert Adams and Ida Shipley were the only two black actors in London Unity Theatre's 1946 production of the play, the rest of the cast being white people blacked up. In an overlooked aspect of black theatre history, Delia Jarrett-Macauley notes that black Jamaican feminist Una Marson directed her play *At What a Price* (1932) performed by members of the League of Coloured Peoples 'at the YMCA hostel Central Club...23 November 1933' and that 'the play transferred for a three-night run, beginning on January 15, at the Scala Theatre, central London', receiving favourable reviews and making history as 'the first black colonial production in the West End' (Jarrett-Macauley 1998: 53-4). Paul Robeson starred in O'Neill's *The Emperor Jones* at the Ambassadors Theatre in 1925 and in 1930, was the first professional black actor to play Othello since the 1880s. Drama productions in mainstream theatres which cast black actors throughout the 1930s ostensibly featured him and were penned by white writers.[58] The one exception to this is C. L. R. James's *Toussaint L'Ouverture* (1936) for the Stage Society, which also included other black actors, Robert Adams, Orlando Martins, R.E. Fennell, John Ahuma and Lawrence Brown. What these examples reveal is that there was a

---

[56] Unsourced programme notes (1959).Elisabeth Welch Biographical File, Theatre Museum, London.

[57] No author noted. *The Times* Obituaries, 8 November 8, 1993.

[58] *Basalisk* (1935) by Peter Garland, *Stevedore* (1935) by Paul Peters and George Sklar and *Plant in the Sun* (1938) by Ben Bengal.

cultural presence of black people in the context of theatre and performance which drew upon many strands of the African diaspora and its trans-Atlantic and colonial manifestations. It was the asserting of indigenous black British identity that would add to this diasporic legacy throughout the second half of the twentieth century.[59]

From Unity to Foco Novo: Black (and White) Power (1936-1988)

Arising out of the flux that World War II had wrought demographically upon British society's cultural make-up (concentrated primarily within London), companies comprising black actors briefly flourished in the form of Robert Adams's wartime London Negro Repertory Theatre (co-founded with Peter Noble), the West Indian Drama Group, founded by Joan Clarke in 1956 and based at the West Indian Students' Union and the Ira Aldridge Players, set up by Herbert Marshall in 1961 as a permanent black theatre company.[60] Clarke was a Unity activist and in charge of training for the theatre. She specialised in directing shows with all-black casts. Her all-black Caribbean production of O'Neill's *Anna Christie* in 1959 'may have been a world first' (Chambers 1989: 358). For the British Council she directed *The Insect Play* and *Thunder Rock* with all-black casts. The prominence of a woman director such as Clarke forms a powerful but primarily unrecognized antecedent for women like Joan-Ann Maynard, Yvonne Brewster, Paulette Randall and Josette Bushell-Mingo later in the century.

Concurrent with these groups, the Unity Theatre continued the pre-war links it had established with black actors such as Robeson and Adams to produce post-war plays that addressed issues of racism. It used black actors in black roles or deliberately cast black actors in productions that had no black roles, encouraging actors such as Frank Singuineau and Errol Hill in the 1950s (*Camden New Journal*

---

[59] See my chapter 'State of the Nation: contemporary Black British theatre and the staging of the UK' in this book.

[60] The Players presented 'an all-black musical at the Theatre Royal Stratford East called *Do Somethin' Addy Man!*'. This was a re-working of the Alcestis story, Chambers tells us, set in contemporary Camden Town, London. The group seems to have discontinued after this (Chambers: 359). However, the inconsistencies in titles and lack of archived material points to problems in gaining a clear idea of the groups which were operating in this period. In unsourced programme notes, George Browne is recorded as composing the musical *Do Something Addy Man* from the straight play by Jack Russell for the Negro Theatre Group started by Herbert Marshal (Cy Grant Biographical File, Theatre Museum). Bruce King states that 'Lloyd Reckford tried to establish the first black theatre company in London. His New Day Theatre Company began in 1960 with two short plays by Derek Walcott...Edric and Pearl Connor then formed the Negro Theatre Workshop (1963) which rehearsed plays at the West Indian Students Centre and Africa Centre' (King 2004:76-7).

1999: 8-19). Significant productions included Ben Bengal's *Plant in the Sun* (1939) in which Robeson played a 'white' character (revived 1949), the short-lived Unity Repertory Company's 1946 professional revival of Geoffrey Trease's *Colony* (1939), which used black actors in a play about racism as did *Dragnet* (1947) by Joe MacColum[61] and *Longitude 49* (1950) by Herb Tank, in which Adams, Shipley, Singuineau and Hill appeared. A new generation of actors Carmen Munroe, Rudolph Walker, Mark Heath and Anton Phillips, who were to be seminal to black theatre's taking root in Britain decades later, all performed for Unity.

Writing in *New Theatre* (1946), Peter Noble refers to the new internationalism that followed the war years debunking the fallacy that had previously prevented the formation of an all-black theatre company in Britain – that there are no black actors in the country – as 'there are a number of talented coloured players in England, from Africa, America, and the West Indies' (Noble 1946: n.p). As Noble points out, many black actors at this time chose not to act in preference to the demeaning roles on offer: 'stupid, servile roles of Negro retainers, servants and general comic relief'. Both Noble and his interviewee, Adams, dismiss the claim that there are no plays suitable for black actors to conclude with,

> A theatre, such as Mr Adams is determined to form, giving regular performances in London and the provinces of intelligent plays acted by Negro **and** white actors, would be of unlimited value towards the creation of a wider understanding of the Negro problem. Such a theatre would indeed be a power for dispelling colour prejudice and there are indeed immense possibilities in a progressive Negro Theatre which would be an important liberal weapon for the uprooting of basic inhibitions and the sowing of seeds of tolerance. (Noble 1946: n.p.)

However, the existence of 'Negro Theatre' outside America was tenuous. Noble notes that, as the Bantu Theatre of Johannesburg no longer operates, Adams's proposed theatre will be the only black theatre within the British Empire. Integrated casting is advocated as the expectation and the theatre as a site for dismantling racism. Although, as Chambers notes, 'Unity had always taken a stand on racism, particularly against anti-semitism' and 'during the war had refused membership on the grounds of racial attitude', their seeming progressiveness regarding racial inclusiveness was not all- pervasive, for '[l]ater when Britain had become more multi-ethnic after recruiting Commonwealth labour, Unity, like most of the left, remained overwhelmingly white though it continued to be staunchly anti-imperialist' (Chambers 1989: 400).

---

[61] Colin Chambers points out that authorship of *Dragnet* in the Unity programme is credited to Roger Woddis and only credited to its director Joe MacColum in the Lord Chamberlain's Collection where it is called *Dragnet for Demos*.

Post-war immigration was impelled by many factors that created a mutual supply and demand dynamic between Britain and its colonized (or decolonizing) people. Reconstruction of war-ravaged Europe, refuge from political and social tyranny, the impetus to seek employment, the reassurance of state welfare systems, educational opportunities and recruitment of a workforce were some of the key factors which produced a trans-global movement of people. The island of Britain began to attract an influx of non-Anglo-Saxon people in numbers not previously experienced. Whilst ex-colonies such as the United States, Australia and Canada had relied upon European immigration to initially construct white-dominant societies to the detriment of the existing indigenous populations, Britain was now caught in the global slipstream of what King describes as 'an immense movement of peoples brought about by racial, political, and economic liberalization and the lowering of protective barriers' (King 2004: 2). The ethnic majority's use of a western measuring stick as an indicator of quality produced a dynamic of paternalism and discrimination against black arts organisations and artists which was as inhibiting of creative endeavour as the limits imposed by racializing immigration legislation from the 1960s onwards. In this, drama can be seen to have constituted a barometer of socio-cultural shifts of people and their access to citizenship.

It was not until Trinidadian writer Errol John's *Moon on a Rainbow Shawl* (1956) was staged at the Royal Court (and won the *Observer* play competition) that a play by a black writer was performed in Britain. John's use of what has been termed 'nation language'[62] challenged the notion of standard English as the necessary vehicle for drama. Staged in 1958, this year also marked the outbreak of race riots in Nottingham and Notting Hill in London. Further to this, Jamaican playwright Barry Reckord had three plays produced at the Royal Court. *Flesh to a Tiger* (1958) was a drama set in the Caribbean and starred indigenous black British actor and singer, Cleo Laine with Tamba Allen, Pearl Prescod, James Clarke, Lloyd Reckford, Johnny Sekka, Nadia Cattouse and Connie Smith. *You in Your Small Corner* (1960) followed and then *Skyvers* (1963), staged with white actors as the Royal Court could not find any black actors! Other notable productions during the period included Wole Soyinka's *The Invention* (1958), *The Lion and the Jewel* (1966) at the Royal Court and *The Road* at the Theatre Royal, Stratford East in 1965. In the West End, the dominance of African-American writers in terms of the

---

[62] The term Nation Language is an established means of referring to language that has emerged from the Caribbean and was adopted by the Caribbean Arts Movement. The term has been employed in academia and beyond for a couple of decades and is a staple term of reference in any post-colonial literary context. See Edward Kamau Brathwaite through to Kwame Dawes and numerous other writers regarding its usage politically, theoretically and in literature.

staging of black plays was consolidated with Langston Hughes's musical *Simply Heavenly* directed by Laurence Harvey at the Adelphi in 1958, followed by Lorraine Hansberry's *A Raisin in the Sun* at the same theatre in 1959.

In the 1960s the New Negro Theatre Company at the Theatre Royal, Stratford East staged white writer Paul Green's *No Count Boy* with a black cast including Tamba Allen, Mark Heath, Johnny Sekka, Neville Munroe, Clifton Jones, Gloria Higdon and Carmen Munroe and Clifton Jones's *La Mere/The S Bend*, both directed by Jones. Errol Hill's *Man Better Man* (1965) was staged by the Trinidad Theatre Company for the Commonwealth Arts Festival. King notes that the beginning of West Indian drama in England 'is intertwined with the beginnings of the new West Indian theatre in the Caribbean' (King 2004:71), negating Una Marson's work of the 1930s in Jamaica (she established the Kingston Dramatic Club in 1937) and her subsequent influences upon West Indian expatriate culture during her time at the BBC in London throughout the 1940s.

A significant development towards 'home-grown' plays emerged in Ed Berman's InterAction lunchtime plays staged at the Ambience café in Queensway. *Black Pieces* by Mustapha Matura was staged at the Ambience and for the Black and White Power' season at the ICA in 1970 and marked the beginning of a new direction of 'first-wave' black male playwrights who had been heralded by Barry Reckford, Wole Soyinka and Derek Walcott in the 1950s. Two members of the cast, Alfred Fagon[63] and T-Bone Wilson, went on to write their own plays. Matura's early works are structured as comedies of manners and show a link between a black world and a white middle-class bohemian one. However, the content is laced with Trinidadian culture and heritage and 'allowed an English audience to experience a world hidden from their view' (Rees 1992: 25). Roland Rees recounts Alfred Fagon's reaction to reading Matura's first play: 'He looked at the script and said: 'I cannot read this.' I said: 'Why?' He said: 'I dare not read it.' Alfred explained he had never seen anything written down in the way he spoke...To him it was a momentous occasion. And indeed those early plays by Mustapha broke that ground' (Rees 1992: 106). Matura was the first black playwright living in Britain to take up the mantle of nation language. Together with Michael Abbensetts, Matura represents West Indian dramatists who wrote from within the belly of the (imperial) beast producing dramatizations of a male-

---

[63] Fagon's *11 Josephine House,* is about a 'writer in search of a form from within his own culture, but muddled by the models of his inherited culture'(King 2004:24), *Death of a Blackman*(1975) dramatises the life of Jamaican musician Joe Harriot who died early, and *Four Hundred Pounds* tells of two male pool players and gamblers, the four hundred symbolising the Middle Passage and the money bet on not potting the black ball because it symbolised slavery.

dominated, Caribbean-related world wherein white characters are marginal and two-dimensional.[64]

The immigrant plays 'othered' the English in ways which later indigenous black Britons moved away from. Matura's *Welcome Home Jacko* (1979), written for the Black Theatre Co-op (re-named Nitro in 1999), was even 'translated' from its original Trinidadian swing beat into black London English when it played off-Broadway in 1983. Actor Brian Bovell attests to the challenges to New York audiences: 'Black Americans came and they had never seen a play like that. Lee Strasberg students came and couldn't believe it. They had never seen anything like this from England. They expected Noel Coward or the RSC' (Rees 1992: 128).

Rees's Foco Novo company employed mixed casting, staged many black writers' works and was instrumental in providing opportunities for writers such as Tunde Ikoli who was mixed-race and born in Limehouse.[65] British-born Michael Ellis in his play *Chameleon* (1985), like Ikoli in *Scrape off the Black* (1983), is concerned, as King notes, with 'black separatism versus some form of assimilation, or the in-betweenness of those of mixed race' (King 2004: 212), a theme which a play from the current generation, Kwame Kwei-Armah's *Fix Up* (2004) explores in the context of black education and self-knowledge. The generation of British-born dramatists to which Ikoli belonged were also aware of their dual theatrical heritage and its intersections with the pin-wheel of politics and social representation: 'All of this comes back to language – how to say verse, the Peter Hall European view of theatre. Whatever we thought when we started off, the theatre is a middle-class playground' (Rees 1992: 123). Their impetus as writers was to write for black actors and to stage experiences marginalized in the 'middle-class playground.' The argument of there being not enough black actors to merit all-black companies or productions had resonated well beyond the immediate increased post-war presence of immigrants from the Commonwealth. Calls for an all-black national theatre company were revisited in the press over subsequent decades. This was highlighted most significantly in the debates around casting in the late 1970s up to the early 1990s when it became clear that social demographic reality was not being matched by the actors who were appearing on mainstream stages. The demand for more integrated casting and a reversal of whites 'blacking up' to play Othello intensified after reports commissioned by Actors' Equity in response to the low employment

---

[64] Abbensetts stated that, 'I suppose I find it easier to write about people who are born in the Caribbean...I think if you're born in the Caribbean, and in my case if you're Guyanese, you have certain way of looking at life.'(Stoby 2002:4)

[65] Foco Novo produced Ikoli's *On the Out* (1978), *Sink or Swim* (1982), *Sleeping Policeman* (1983) with Howard Brenton, *Week in Week out* (1985) *The Lower Depths* and *Banged Up* (both 1986).

rates of its black union members.[66] The formation of all-black companies such as TEMBA by Alton Kualo (1970), Black Theatre Co-operative by Mustapha Matura and Charlie Hanson (1978), Theatre of Black Women by Patricia Hilarie, Paulette Randall and Bernadine Evaristo (1982), Imani-Faith by Jacqueline Rudet (1983), Black Mime Theatre by Denise Wong (1984) and Talawa by Yvonne Brewster, Carmen Munroe, Mona Hammond and Inigo Espejel (1985) attempted to redress the inequality. By 1991 theatre critic Benedict Nightingale, commenting on the proliferation of societal or non-traditional casting (black casts performing white cultural classics) as impelled by the need for talented black actors to work and to demonstrate their expertise, asks, 'If we can believe the wooden O is now England, now France, why cannot we agree that emotional truth is more than skin deep?' Obviously different sets of goal posts exist for the imagination.

The inter-relationship between black theatre and politics in terms of survival has been intimate and precarious for the companies and practitioners involved. This has been never more clearly demonstrated than in the racial politics of subsidy (Ponnuswami 2000: 221) of the mid-1980s and the fate of TEMBA when (as I identified earlier in the chapter), like the cast of *Plantation Days* in 1923, it refused to 'know its place' and attempted to expand beyond its ascribed identity of ethnically separate theatre, which resulted in the Arts Council withdrawing its funding and the company's dissolution. Alby James, the company's final Artistic Director and whose professional trajectory charts the white theatrical establishment (the Royal Court, Royal Shakespeare Company, BBC and Glyndebourne), was

---

[66]The prejudice against black performers began with training. In the results of her survey on race and British top-league drama schools, Khan found that out of 675 students, fifteen were black and five of these were from abroad. Furthermore, 'for years at least one institution, the Central School of Speech and Drama, has been taking on its few Afro-Asian protégés on the understanding that they'll only stay for a term in their third year – the showcase year when students get their chance to shine – because frankly, there just aren't enough black parts to go round' (Khan 1975: n.p). In the same year the theatre correspondent for the *Daily Telegraph* reported that only four out of 210 actors at the RSC and RNT were 'Afro-Asian', and in the West End these artists comprised 2.3%. The Race Relations Act 1976 offered exemptions from employment on the grounds of race if it was necessary for 'authenticity'. Thus actors who were refused work because of their race had no recourse to the law. Mr Archie Pool, leader of the Radical Alliance of Poets and Players outlined the position: 'Black performers face the same discrimination as black workers. We get no funds and no facilities…There is a closed-door policy by theatre managers – official and on the fringe'. In a letter to the *Guardian* Rosamund Caines describes how 'Directors seem to be under the impression that all black faces must be making a significant social comment to justify their appearance in a play, they are never to be seen as members of conventional British Society' (13 November 1980) A year later this is echoed at the annual Equity meeting where Miriam Karlin denounces the fact that 'even now there is a feeling that only certain roles are suitable for black actors'.

quoted as stating that 'not enough of us had been given the opportunity to acquire the skills to improve the quality and variety of our work. I wanted TEMBA to gain national status. I didn't want to stand around in community halls. I didn't want to work on minimum finances. There had to be somewhere where black actors could go to earn a good salary' (Taylor 1990: 6). Other casualties had mounted up, too. The Camden Black Theatre Seasons in 1987 and 1988 showcased work of the Theatre of Black Women, Black Theatre Co-operative and Foco Novo amongst others, but the Munirah Theatre Company had to withdraw 'due to substantial cuts in annual revenue funding' in the 1988 season.[67] Similarly, playwright Tunde Ikoli describes the demise of Foco Novo:

> At first I thought it was the new Thatcherite dogma where you had to prove yourself. We went through all kinds of stages…of discussing and looking for ways to find sponsorship…We were told all these appraisals…[by the Arts Council]…were really for our own benefit, and if we did what we were supposed to, we would find ourselves leaner and more efficient in the future…Then we disappeared overnight (Rees 1992: 133-4).

Of the twenty or so black theatre companies that existed in Britain in the 1980s, only two survived by the late 1990s. Ponnuswami quotes Yvonne Brewster's lamentation, 'Black Mime is no more, Carib Theatre Company is no more, Yaa Asantewa Centre is under terminal threat and so it goes on. There are so few black companies with regular grants left' (Ponnuswami 2000: 231).

Onwards and Upwards: The Nineties and beyond

In the face of the cuts to funding it was clear that traditional hegemonies were still locked in place in the closing decade of the last century. However, it is not simply funding cuts which have erased the contributions of many black dramatists and performers from British theatre histories but, as Ponnuswami identifies, also key to this legacy of disappearance is 'the absence of a critical infrastructure' (Ponnuswami 2000: 221). The archiving and recording of black people's drama and performance is in a fledgling state of operation, and this is something that needs the attention of the organizations and practitioners themselves. The theorization which has developed in relation to music and, to a certain extent, popular culture, film, television and literature needs parallel application to the circumstances of theatre and performance. There are changing definitions of blackness in relation to dramatic literature and theatre in Britain which require separate consideration from that of prose and poetry. Substantial determining factors such as funding, policy, prejudice and tradition are at work in shaping

---

[67] Programme notes. Miscellaneous Black Theatre File

Black British Theatre, but these are not the only determinants. In 1991 Jatinder Verma stated, 'If there is going to be any point in using the term 'black theatre', it has to find a theatrical form for itself. It has to be more than a question of equal opportunities or all-black productions. It's not enough just to have a black or Asian cast doing a Chekhov play, you must dig deeper to get at the truth' (Smurthwaite 1991: n.p.). Felix Cross believes that 'it is only when black theatre develops something white theatre doesn't have that it will have the power and influence to move forward' (*Independent*, 1 April 1998: 14).

One important area of retrieval has been that of contemporary women's theatre. Corresponding to the male-dominated worlds created by Matura, Ikoli and others was the emergence of black women's theatre and performance, and most particularly the work of playwrights such as Jacqueline Rudet, Winsome Pinnock, Trish Cooke, Jenny McLeod, Maria Oshodi and Jackie Kay, who entered the mainstream with varying degrees of longevity, as well as the staging of plays by less established writers: Grace Dayley's *Rose's Story* (1985), Killian M. Gideon's *England is De Place for Me* (1987) Sandra Yew's *Zerri's* Choice(1989), Lisselle Kayla's *Don't Chat Me Business* (1990) and Valerie Mason-John's *Brown Girl in the Ring* (1999).

As has been noted (King 2004: 120-1, Ponnuswami 2000: 218-21), the publishing of plays and their anchoring in cultural consciousness has proven to be as difficult for black dramatists in the late twentieth century as fighting to have work staged in non-community settings has been. In this the work of women editors has proven invaluable in consolidating the legacy of black women playwrights as sampled in *Plays by Women* Vol. IV. (1985) *Plays by Women* (1986, 1990) *Black Plays* (1987, 1989, 1995), *Lesbian Plays* (1987), *First Run: New Plays by New Writers* (1989) and *Six Plays by Black and Asian Women Writers* (1993). Polemically, the articles by Helen Kolawole in the mainstream press and academic texts such as Gabriele Griffin's *Contemporary Black and Asian Women Playwrights in Britain* (2003) presage a sustained commentary upon the work of black theatre practitioners as has not hitherto been the case. Yet, as I have analyzed in the chapter 'The State of the Nation: Contemporary Black British Theatre' elsewhere in this volume, the year 2003 saw a unique situation develop in mainstream London theatres (although not the West End) through the staging of a number of high profile plays by Black British dramatists, a phenomenon which has continued into 2004.

Fusions of form and subject matter which collapse the mould of mainstream theatre identities are still promised by the work from the new contenders. Playwrights such as Debbie Tucker Green employ techniques of dialogue which draw upon both Caryl Churchill and Suzan Lori Parks and, together with the work of Kwame Kwei-Armah, experiment with constructing a black aesthetic. In *Born Bad* (2003) the characters pared down to their basic biological connections as

Dawta, her sisters, brother, Mum and Dad are remorselessly sucked into the vortex that leads to the heart of their family in a conversation from which there is no escape, a domestic purgatory. The complications of victimhood, complicity and betrayal in acts of abuse reveal the subjectivity of each person's truth. Roy Williams creates social-realist drama in which young black people are centralized, contending with geographies of urban and economic alienation, and the impediment of a lack of nurturing adult guidance. Sol B. River, a Leeds-based playwright, embraces both patois and the choreo-poem techniques of Ntozake Shange in work such as *To Rahtid* (1996) which, like the lyricism of Tucker Green, hammers naturalistic language usage into a malleability that celebrates black-centred experience despite oppressive socio-historical determinants. Later work such as *Two Tracks and Text Me* (2003) overlaps poetry, dance, music and video in a 'live action/electronic hybrid' (Hickling 2003: 30), juxtaposing telecommunications media and a three-stranded narrative about child abuse.[68]

Such subjectivities staged in the range of work of the new millennium indicate how 'colonized cultures are sliding into the space of the colonizer and in doing so, they are re-defining its borders and culture' (Macmillan 2004: 60). This is saliently illustrated by an anecdote from the actor and writer Lennie James who recalls his 'shock of inclusion' in the legacy of the British theatrescape when working in New Zealand in 2001. 'In New Zealand I became an Englishman…in New Zealand, all the history of England was my history. When people interviewing me spoke of the long history of British theatre, it was all mine. I was allowed to own it…I can't tell you how strange that sensation was' (James 2004: 12).

Acknowledgements: Deirdre Osborne acknowledges the staff of the Theatre Museum study room, Kwame Kwei-Armah, Talawa Theatre Company, Roy Williams and Kadija Sesay George.

Works cited

Barthelemy, Anthony Gerard (1987), *Black Face Maligned Race: The Representation of Blacks in English Drama from Shakespeare to Southerne*, Baton Rouge and London: Louisiana State University Press.

Black, Les (2000), 'Voices of hate, sounds of hybridity: Black music and the complexities of racism', *Black Music Research Journal*, 20.2.

---

[68] River notes that 'I strive to bring exuberance to the stage that encompasses equality, diversity, ingenuity and fresh representation' (River et al. 2004: 12). For more on Sol B. River see Ashley Tellis' critical analysis, 'Theatre as Edutainment: Sol B. River's Dramatic Burden' and River's essay 'Serious Business' elsewhere in this volume.

Camden New Journal (4 November 1999), Miscellaneous Black Theatre File Theatre Museum, Covent Garden, London.

Chambers, Colin (1989), *The Story of Unity Theatre*, London: Lawrence and Wishart.

Croft, Susan (2002), *Black and Asian Performance at the Theatre Museum: A User's Guide*, London: Theatre Museum.

Davis, David Brion (1966), *The Problem of Slavery in Western Culture*, Ithaca NY: Cornell University Press.

File, Nigel and Chris Power (1981), *Black Settlers in Britain: 1555-1958*, London: Heinemann.

Gerzina, Gretchen (1995), *Black England: Life before Emancipation*, London: John Murray.

---- (ed.) (2003), *Black Victorians: Black Victoriana*, New Brunswick: Holbrook.

Hill, Errol (1984), *Shakespeare in Sable*, Amherst: University of Massachusetts Press.

Jarrett-Macauley, Delia (1998), *The Life of Una Marson: 1905-65*, Manchester: Manchester University Press.

Joseph, May (1998), 'Bodies outside the State: Black British women playwrights and the limits of citizenship', in Peggy Phelan and Jill Lane (eds.), *The Ends of Performance*, New York and London: New York University Press.

King, Bruce (2004), *The Internationalization of English Literature: The Oxford Literary History. Vol.13: 1948-2000*, Oxford: Oxford University Press.

Marshall, Herbert and Mildred Stock (1958), *Ira Aldridge: The Negro Tragedian*, London: Rockliff.

Macmillan, Michael (2004), 'Re-baptizing the world in our own terms: Black theatre and live arts in Britain', *Canadian Theatre Review* 118.

Niebrzydowski, Sue (2001), 'The Sultana and her sisters: Black women in the British Isles before 1530', *Women's History Review*, 10: 2.

Noble, Peter (1946), 'Robert Adams plans a negro theatre' (excerpted from *New Theatre* and held in Black Actors/ Black Actors in Shakespeare File, Theatre Museum.

Osborne, Deirdre (2005), 'The state of the nation: voicing the margins in the staging of the UK', in Christoph Houswitschka and Anja Muller-Muth (eds.), *Staging Displacement, Exile and Diaspora: Proceedings of the Thirteenth Annual Conference of the German Society for Contemporary Theatre and Drama in English*, University of Bamberg, Germany. A longer version of the conference paper is in this book, 'The State of the Nation'.

Pickering, Michael (2003). 'The blackface clown', in Gretchen Gerzina (ed.), *Black Victorians: Black Victoriana*, New Brunswick: Holbrook.

Ponnuswami, Meenakshi (2000), 'Small island people: black British women playwrights', in Elaine Aston and Janelle Reinelt (eds.), *The Cambridge*

Companion to Modern British Women Playwrights, Cambridge: Cambridge University Press.

Rees, Roland (1992), *Fringe First: Pioneers of Fringe Theatre on Record*, London: Oberon Books.

Stoby, Michelle (2002), 'Black British drama after *Empire Road*', *Wasafiri* 35.

Sekyi, Kobina (1974), *The Blinkards*, London: Heinemann.

Tokson, Elliott. H. (1982), *The Popular Image of the Black Man in English Drama, 1550-1688*, Boston, Mass: G.K.Hall and Co.

Turner, John M. (2003), 'Pablo Fanque, black circus performer', in Gretchen Gerzina (ed.), *Black Victorians: Black Victoriana*, New Brunswick: Holbrook.

Newspaper reviews

Anon. (15 June 1923), *The Afro-American South's Biggest and Best Weekly*, Baltimore, Miscellaneous Black Theatre File, Theatre Museum.

Anon. (1 April 1977), *The Times,* Miscellaneous Black Theatre File, Theatre Museum.

Anon (3 April 1981), *The Daily Telegraph,* Miscellaneous Black Theatre File, Theatre Museum.

Anon. (18 May 1991), 'Casting couched in a colour code', *The Times Sunday Review*.

Anon. (1 April 1998), 'Missing in action: our black stars', *Independent*. Miscellaneous Black Theatre File, Theatre Museum.

Caines, Rosamund (13 November 1980), *Guardian* n.p. Miscellaneous Black Theatre File, Theatre Museum.

Freedland, Michael (17 July 2003), *Guardian*.

Hickling, Alfred (23 October 2003), 'Two tracks and text me', *Guardian*.

Hiley, Jim (14 October 1985), *Guardian* n.p. Miscellaneous Black Theatre File, Theatre Museum.

James, Lennie (11 February 2004), 'Who do you think you are?' *Guardian*.

Khan, Naseem (29 April 1975), *Guardian* n.p. Miscellaneous Black Theatre File, Theatre Museum.

River, Sol B. et al. (7 January 2004), 'Ditch the mumbling smackheads', *Guardian*.

Robinson, David (18 June 1983), *The Times*. Elisabeth Welch Biographical File, Theatre Museum.

Smurthwaite, Nick (21 April 1991), 'It's a classic answer for black theatre', *Observer*. Miscellaneous Black Theatre File, Theatre Museum.

Taylor, Sean (26 April-3 May 1990). 'Black to Black', *City Limits*.

Websites

'Before the Black Victorians', http://www.mckenziehpa.com/bv/before.html

CHAPTER THREE

THE STATE OF THE NATION: CONTEMPORARY BLACK BRITISH THEATRE AND THE STAGING OF THE UK[69]

DEIRDRE OSBORNE

Synopsis:

The unprecedented mainstream programming and staging of plays by Black British dramatists characterises London's theatrescape of the new millennium. In contrasting ways, the plays of Kwei-Armah, Williams and Daley expose general issues and themes through the centrality of Black British experiences. These writers represent a new generation of indigenous Black British cultural assertion, demanding perpetual inclusion in the British cultural psyche where white-dominated theatrical hegemonies remain evident.

The year 2003 saw a unique situation develop in mainstream London theatres (although not the West End) through the staging of a number of high profile plays by Black British dramatists, a phenomenon which has continued into 2004.[70] This

---

[69] Material in this chapter first appeared as conference paper proceedings in *CDE – Contemporary Drama in English* Vol.12. Christoph Houswitschka and Anja Muller-Muth eds. Verlag: Wissenschaftlicher Verlag Trier, 2005 and is reprinted with kind permission of Wissenschaftlicher Verlag Trier.

[70] At the time of writing, Royal Court Theatre: *crazyblackmuthaf***in'self* by DeObia Oparei (January 2003) and *Fallout* by Roy Williams (June 2003), Hamptead Theatre: *Born Bad* by Debbie Tucker Green (April 2003), Royal National Theatre: *Elmina's Kitchen* by Kwame Kwei-Armah (May 2003), Soho Theatre: *Dirty Butterfly* by Debbie Tucker Green

indicates a shift has occurred towards perceiving Black British drama as commercially viable, moving away from traditional assumptions of its genesis and production as residing primarily within community or non-mainstream theatre contexts[71]. Yet of the eleven plays staged during this period, nine were directed by white directors, primarily male. Whilst the staging of plays by Black British dramatists in mainstream London theatres might reveal an increasingly contested sense of the 'mainstream' and revisions of what has been perceived as the traditional theatre market, traditional theatrical hegemonies remain evident. White men continue to remain at the helm despite the forays into cross-cultural programming with 'new' writing.[72]

(February 2003) and *Wrong Place* by Mark Norfolk (October 2003), Theatre Royal Stratford East: *Urban Afro Saxons* by Kofi Agyemang and Patricia Elcock (November 2003). At the time of writing (June 2004) this has continued with the Royal Court Theatre staging *The Sons of Charlie Paora* by Lennie James (February 2004) and *Blest Be the Tie* by Dona Daley (April 2004), Theatre Royal Stratford East: *The Big Life* by Paul Sirett and Paul Joseph (April 2004) and Royal National Theatre: *Sing Yer Heart Out for the Lads* by Roy Williams (April 2004) and Kwei-Armah's latest play *Fix Up* due to premiere at the RNT in December. Rhashan Stone's *Two Step* premiered at the Almeida as part of the September PUSH 04 season of black-led arts. With the exception of Paulette Randall's staging of *Urban Afro Saxons* and *Blest Be the Tie* and Josette Bushell-Mingo's *Two Step*, all of these productions were directed by white directors.

[71] Roland Rees founder of Foco Novo Theatre Company (1972-88 dissolved when the Arts Council withdrew its funding) noted how, 'In the parlance of subsidy providers, community did not mean an area where there is a homogenous population. Quite the contrary. Community came to mean any place which lay outside the orbit of the community from which theatre drew its audiences.' (Rees,128)

[72] No keener example of this exists than the approach adopted by latest Artistic Director at the Royal National Theatre, Nicholas Hytner. As Maddy Costa identifies, by 2004, 'of the 16 associates Hytner last year invited to be part of his creative thinktank, only five are women and only one (the actor Adrian Lester) is black. Meanwhile, the people with whom he works most closely...are men of roughly the same generation as himself. 'I wouldn't want us to be culturally homogenous, but I don't want to be ticking boxes either,' Hytner responds. 'And it's an evolving group.' '(Costa, 2) Although Kwei-Armah's new play, *Fix Up* premieres at the RNT in December 2004, it is directed by the same white male director from *Elmina's Kitchen*. Similarly the return of Williams' *Sing Yer Heart Out for the Lads* in April 2004 was directed by a white male director.

The importance of including and perpetuating indigenous Black British drama in the mainstream theatrescape can be neither under-estimated nor over-emphasised. It provides a key cultural site wherein ethnicities and experiences who may not otherwise meet are directly exposed to each other's cultural practices. Its maintenance is a prerequisite for disabling white elitism in British theatre. Black drama exposes mainstream (predominantly white) theatre-goers to aspects of black British cultural input that is *as* indigenous to contemporary British cultural identity as that provided by white playwrights. It provides black audiences with authentically rendered cultural representations which have not as yet been able to develop a flourishing continuum in Britain's cultural psyche.

[*Urban Afro Saxons*. Photo courtesy: Talawa]

This chapter focuses on a range of contemporary plays by black British writers as main-stage theatrical works. The period marks the presence of cutting edge work which both upholds and subverts traditionally marginalised positionings (socio-politically and theatrically) to make important cultural interventions that respond to our times. The plays of DeObia Oparei, Dona Daley, Debbie Tucker Green, Mark Norfolk, Courttia Newland, Kwame Kwei-Armah, Rhashan Stone and Roy Williams can be viewed as critiques of and interventions into 'cultural citizenship' and its uneasy accommodating of black British experience as constituent of British cultural output. I employ this term as a means of indicating how the participation and acceptance of traditionally marginalised social groups in mainstream cultural contexts frequently draws in issues of race and social identity in the content and reception of these early twenty-first century plays. They exemplify the temerity, tenacity and tenuousness that can be seen to characterise the positioning of Black British artists within the censoring or censorious institution of the British theatre complex and its cacophony of critical voices.

In these plays issues of implicit marginality in theatre practice are addressed through conceptualising and working with notions of cultural citizenship and its representations via theatre and drama. Exploring cultural citizenship through its implicit and explicit representation in drama in performance enables an interrogation of those oppressions still endured by so many in actuality. Moreover it marks out a body of writing, a newly emerging genre which is correspondingly exposed to a white- dominated critical arena that has hitherto been sporadically responsive.

Thematically and generically I place the plays into three groups and closely read *a selection* of these: (i) 'incendiary plays', Roy Williams' *Fallout* (2003), Kwame Kwei-Armah's *Elmina's Kitchen* (2003) and Mark Norfolk's *Wrong Place* (2003) draw upon representations of urban working class black men and their intersections with violence and the criminal justice system and are notable for cross-generational male-male conflict and the absence of living, loving mothers, (ii) 'you have to laugh', comedies, DeObia Oparei's *crazyblackmuthaf***in'self* (2002) which parodies the idea of any stable sexual, national or racial identity – 'A journey to the soul of Africa from the heart of St. John's Wood via the groin of Peckham'(Oparei, back cover) – and Kofi Agyemang and Patricia Elcock's *Urban Afro Saxons* (2003) which debates 'What makes you British?' through an array of incisive and wittily represented multi and cross cultural experiences arising from a community under a state of siege. (iii) 'drama of family ties', their corrosion and fortification in the light of damaging forces (internal and external) in Debbie Tucker Green's *dirty butterfly* and *born bad* (2003), Courttia Newland's *B is 4 Black* (2003), Dona Daley's *Blest be the Tie* (2004) and Rhashan Stone's *Two Step* (2004).

My focus upon 'incendiary plays' and the 'drama of family ties' namely single works of Daley, Kwei-Armah and Williams results from the impetus to judiciously extract indicative texts from a larger cultural output, the systematic readings I offer creating a critical framework within which other texts may be read. As Rebecca Stott has quoted Karl Jaspers, 'What is important in phenomenology is less the study of a large number of instances than the intuitive and deep understanding of a few individual cases.'(Stott, xiv). Such a methodology aims to knock off balance the delusive certainties of generalising and to act as a counterpoint to the lack of first-hand experience of many white Britons of their black counterparts as confirmed by the Commission for Racial Equality's latest survey[73].

---

[73] *The Guardian* newspaper previewed the results of the 2004 poll which found that ninety percent of white people have few or no friends from amongst their fellow black, Asian or Muslim Britons whilst 'Three in 10 of ethnic minority people surveyed said all or most of their friends were Asian or black'. July 19 (1)

The Plays

Black writers write for black actors. Unlike white writers who tend to assume the normative of whiteness without interrogating its correspondent privilege, black writers comment upon the dominant culture's failure to acknowledge this by staging issues of race, ethnicity, and colour as an explicit accompaniment to the thematic content of their work. This is further articulated in a variety of ways in performance. Not only are there culturally specific references in the form of names, behaviour, spirituality, humour, gesture, use of patois, food, staging of the domestic environment and shared understandings of social expectations but also inhabiting a space in a surrounding society in which both writers and their black characters are cast as a minority is registered, critiqued and displayed.

The legacy of immigration and diasporic cultural forms is a recognised and underpinning influence upon contemporary Black British writing, the diaspora now including the generations of indigenous Black Britons. As Gabriele Griffin has noted in her historicising of late twentieth century British Black and Asian women's drama,

> Whereas during the 1980s plays were dominated by inter-generational conflicts as expressive of the difference between the adult subject who migrated and the child who, so to speak was migrated, and their different accommodations to that situation, by the 1990s plays tended to focus much more on how to live in Britain now, beyond the experience of the moment of migration, as part of a generation that had grown up in the UK (Griffin, 25).

The engagement with and articulation of the many strands of indigenousness is the starting point for my readings of the selected texts. The experiences and imaginative worlds represented need acknowledging and revealing. Issues of citizenship, nationality, race identities and the concept of British-ness (to name a few) reveal how current discursive categories and critical languages are insufficient and fatigued in mapping relationships to such issues in theatre practice and polemic. It becomes clear that a voicing of the margins in the 'staging of the UK' emerges. Devolution throughout the United Kingdom in the past decade has opened up micro communities to challenge the meaning of a unified sense of 'British-ness' and hence this requires a cultural platform, which voices such perspectives. It is clear that Black British identity is 'a multiple identity, one which combines national and racial subjectivities and, in doing so, contests the dualistic world order which deems blackness and British-ness to be mutually exclusive.' (Mama, 114)

Digger in *Elmina's Kitchen* is described as having come from Grenada and emigrated at fourteen with an accent that '*swings from his native Grenadian to hard-core Jamaican to authentic black London*'(Kwei-Armah, 4) He refers to

British-born Deli as 'You British blacks' (14) yet Baygee, '*the last of the West Indian door-to-door salesmen*'(13) calls Digger 'White boy'. Notably, only the characters who represent the older generation who emigrated from the Caribbean refer to the effects of colonisation. Clifton's, 'The most witchcraft is practise by the white man. How do the arse you think he managed to take Africa from we.' produces an explosive slapping down from his son, 'Don't bring none of your white this and dat in here, Clifton. I don't want to hear that.'(38) In this, Kwei-Armah unequivocally locates his British characters' identities as not being derived in relation to the colonising enterprise but from their strategic survival in a specific urban context of Hackney, London.

Likewise, Daley's protagonist Florence specifically resides in a high-rise council estate at Clapham Junction, London. The residue of Empire symbolised in cultural landmarks such as the Statue of Eros, derided by the visiting Jamaican sister Martha, evokes Sam Selvon's Lonely Londoners' revisions of London's imperial symbols. Her disdain for and implicit deconstructing of imperial cultural ideology reveals an assertion of the ex-colonised over the coloniser at source: 'Then we did go to Piccadilly Circus...the hub of the Empire dem used to tell we in school...one little statue...and plenty dirt and muck round de place.'(Daley, 44) Those who stayed behind are shown to have material advantage over those who emigrated to England, drawing attention to the fallacy of supposed economic gains to be had from emigrating in the first place.[74] It is this interrogation of the concept of British-ness, the assertion of voices that exist and represent that beyond mainstream critical vision that frequently appears in Black British drama. In the cultural output characterised as 'British' there is a changing landscape transformed by political struggle in representing identity shaping institutions of family, law and education. In the selected plays, identity as derived from country of origin, cultural antecedents and its relationship to British-ness is apparent and forms a resistance to the implicit oppression and marginalisation.[75]

---

[74] 'Martha: People pee inna de lift, fighting to keep warm. Small balcony fe a garden. Yu don't have to live like this'(Daley 30)

[75] Lennie James (who played Joe in the premiere of *Fallout*) has noted that, 'A strange thing happened to me when I got off the plane in New Zealand. My mum has a favourite saying: that she never was a black woman until she got off the boat in England. In New Zealand I became an Englishman...in New Zealand, all the history of England was my history. When people interviewing me spoke of the long history of British theatre, it was all mine. I was allowed to own it...I can't tell you how strange that sensation was.' (James, 12)

i: 'Incendiary plays'

In *The Price of the Ticket: Collected Non-fiction (1948-1985)* James Baldwin elucidates the introspection, the journey to the source that precedes the attainment of self-authenticity needed in forging one's identity, 'Go back to where you started, or as far back as you can, examine all of it, travel your road again and tell the truth about it. Sing or shout or testify or keep it to yourself: but *know whence you came.*' (Introduction, xix) From the same collection he records the painful explorations of the relationship between African diasporic experience and culture at the conference of Negro-African Writers and Artists (*Le Congres des Ecrivains et Artistes Noirs*) in Paris 1956 – words that resonate with black male experience as dramatised in the plays of Williams and Kwei-Armah nearly fifty years later and the reception of these works (arguably cultural products of the African diaspora) into the canon of contemporary British drama.

> Just what the specific relation of an artist to his culture says about that culture is a very pretty question...Is it possible to describe as a culture what may simply be, after all, a history of oppression?...is this history enough to have made of the earth's black populations anything that can be described as a culture? For what, beyond the fact that all black men at one time or another left Africa, or have remained there, do they really have in common?...What they held in common was the necessity to remake the world in their own image, to impose this image on the world, and no longer be controlled by the vision of the world, and of themselves, held by other people ('Princes and power', 49-50).

Although emerging from different circumstances, socio-cultural politics and a pre-Civil Rights context, this passage articulates the identity seeking and right to name oneself that resonates through African diasporic writing and is an identifiable motif that connects the incendiary plays.

Williams' *Fallout* creates a nightmarish odyssey through a racially related homicide investigation, which finds angry black policeman Joe (mid-thirties) up against the liberal hypocrisy of white colleagues and the gang culture glorification now flourishing in the community where he grew up. Inter- and intra- cultural differences are brought to a head in an edgy exploration of losing connections to one's cultural roots and the ever-diminishing chances of obtaining justice for a murdered African teenager.

The 'fallout' suggested by the title refers not only to the stage world ramifications of the brutal homicide but also gestures to a wider sociological context of the trans-generational sense of displacement and social disenfranchisement that the black characters are shown to experience. Although the director Ian Rickson was keen to point out that Joe is a 'prince', an epic figure, a kind of prodigal son returning to his 'kingdom' (Rickson 2004), Joe's disenfranchisement from the estate community, the police force and inability to command a smidgeon of respect from the young people he is desperate to bring to justice (and even save) becomes a portrait of a man who is anything but this. Expressed in contemporary idiom, Joe's sense of distinguishing himself from those whom he perceives as the debased black estate teenagers evokes Thomas Southerne's African character Oroonoko who, living by heroic ideals is a unique and solitary figure yet implicitly serves to endorse black people as generally inferior.

> Oroonoko: I own the Folly of my Enterprise,
> The Rashness of this Action, and must blush
> Quite thro' this Vail of Night, a whitely Shame,
> To think I cou'd design to make these free
> Who were by Nature Slaves –
> (*Oroonoko* IV. ii. ll.57-61)

> Joe: …You know what, it's fuckers like you, like that pisshead, is why I had to leave. Now it's fuckers like you that bring me back to where I started. You had to drag me down, ennit?...
> …
> Shanice: Yu go. Carryin on like we should tek after yu, why should we be like yu?
> *Exit* Joe (Williams, 109 &110).

Buffeted on all sides, Joe is reduced to slapping the teenage suspect Emile to try and force him to confess as though physical violence is the only recourse of black people – policeman and criminal suspects alike. With the white characters in the play operating in soothing, logical and restrained counterpoint to Joe's explosiveness, stereotyping seeps in. Like Oroonoko, Joe becomes a victim of white duplicity which, in twenty-first century guise is the 'rule-book' of the institution. Williams clearly does not want to present either black *or* white characters as heroes and uses Joe as the voice of recognition and acknowledgement that, while white society might stereotype black people, black people can also engage in behaviour that confirms it (conveniently) like a self-fulfilling prophecy.

However, in choosing to make the only character who does not demonstrate this as the murdered Kwame, Williams offers a limited and bleak representation of his black characters. The emotional thrust of the play oscillates between asking the audience to understand but also be repelled by the dehumanising quality of the disenfranchised lives. This was not aided by aspects of Rickson's staging. Many of the audience were positioned above the playing area on four sides, hence well situated to objectify the players like goldfish in a bowl. Although this might have served to replicate a surveillance camera to a certain extent (the means by which Kwame's killers were detected), the proxemic distancing effect can also alienate the audience from that in which the drama aims to emotionally involve them.

Whilst Joe is used to point out that there are choices apart from the assaults, thefts, continuous dishonesty and abusiveness, there is no sense of any alternative in the claustrophobic world of the estate. Recreation and survival are merged into a base need for gratification through sex, drugs, alcohol and random vengeful violence as a means of establishing an identity. For an audience which may be primarily white (the Royal Court are unable to confirm demographics of its theatre-goers) to be inserted into a familiar viewing position in relation to black experience of this dramatised kind, the dangers of perpetuating the findings of the CRE survey are obvious.

Kwame, four weeks away from starting university has been killed in the opening moments of the play and Joe's lack of self-control and leading on of a witness destroys any chance of a conviction and his own prospects in the police force. Racism is implicitly the underlying impetus for the action of the plot and is cited as a justification for black people behaving badly yet, in presenting such a dichotomy between the slightly priggish but diffident Matt, a Met career man and the volatile resentful Joe, its post-Macpherson report 'poster boy' limited in his self-knowledge, Williams effectively adds to the marginalising and generalising of the very identities he seeks to display and celebrate.

Whilst he echoes the Damilola Taylor[76] case, Williams avoids examining the fundamental tensions between African and Caribbean communities which implicitly fuel the play's action, stating that the main theme is 'the political correctness that had been the response to the exposure and acknowledgement of institutional racism'(Williams, Education Pack). The difference between the murdered Kwame and the other teenagers is constantly highlighted but never explored. Shanice shows Kwame kindness but mendaciously tells her boyfriend Emile that he tried to kiss her when in fact he turned her down, and covers her tracks in racialising terms, 'he tries to plant a kiss on me, comin out wid shit dat West Indian women are fast and loose, not as pure as African women like his mum...he loved to show how smart he was, like deh is two kinds of black, and he come from the better one...People weren't gonna tek dat.' (32) Here Williams indicates the racialising distinctions that occur within the same race based upon African and Caribbean derived 'black' identities.

Colonisation has produced deep seated trauma and dismantling of families across generations as the teaching, nurturing and protecting of children has been ruptured by children witnessing brutality and discrediting enacted upon their families, communities and via institutions. The ghettoisation Williams dramatises

---

[76] A young black teenager Damilola Taylor was murdered by teenagers in Peckham London in November 2000. The prosecution case collapsed after their prime witness, a girl from the area was shown to have been unreliable. In early 2005, four teenagers were remanded in custody awaiting trial for the homicide.

in *Fallout* reveals teenagers marooned in a context wherein any vestige of a gerontocracy is absent and they form compensatory urgent, desperate bonds bound by violence, desensitisation and lost hopes. Kwei-Armah's *Elmina's Kitchen* takes the particular experience of black Caribbean immigrants and their descendents as a basis for demonstrating the devastating effects of gun crime upon the black community. But similarly to Williams' work, it is the contestations between masculinities (black men- black men *and* meta-textually, black men-white men) that are the fuel to these incendiary plays. They present flashpoints of male violence arising from male characters feeling trapped in cul-de-sacs of circumstances which they perceive as demeaning and emasculating.

The represented male characters inhabit worlds where verbal and physical aggression enables a foothold in a grim cycle of survival. Fathers shame sons or provide woefully inadequate role models. Estate life and the consequences of poverty and social marginalisation are not only dramatised in the teenagers but also peripheral characters in *Fallout* such as Manny, the gang leader Dwayne's father who, listed as being in his late thirties in the *dramatis personae* is a down and out addict. He only appears when he is begging from his son for paltry amounts of money and takes no responsibility for the consequences his actions have upon Dwayne. The exchanges between them expose Dwayne's vulnerability in being associated with a self-gratifying, neglectful (now) vagrant father. The relationship also provides a sub-textual indication of the extreme emotional and probable socio-economic deprivation that has characterised Dwayne's life up to the point of Kwame's murder.

Manny: Yu shame me.
Dwayne: Yu want chat 'bout shame? Shame is seein yu, in the off-licence tryin to buy a can of beer wid only twenty pence in yer hand. Beggin dat Indian man to let yu have it.
Manny: So wat, yu gonna mess up yer life? (87)

The fact that Manny's decline into addiction means he confuses his children only exacerbates Dwayne's hurt and subsequent hostility. Displaced to the criminal margins of society, even his own father does not confirm his identity.

Manny: Yu my Bwoi. Good bwoi, Junior.
Dwayne: Wat?
Manny: Wat?
Dwayne: Wat yu juss call me?
...
Dwayne: Junior is yer son, who live up by Shepherd's Bush, my half-brudda, dass who Junior is. Junior live wid his two little sistas, Tasha and Caroline, yer daughters...Remember dem? Nuh, it muss be Anton yu remember, yer son who live up by Dagenham way. Or is it Stuart, my little brudda, who live two minutes away...Nuh,

nuh, it muss be the latest one, dat lickle baby wid the stupid name, Kenisha. Wass my name? (86)

Without the experience of receiving respect nor being able to respect his father, Dwayne is shown to transpose his edifice of heartlessness and aggression easily onto the surrounding world.

Likewise Ashley, the youngest in three generations of men in *Elmina's Kitchen* can only seek self-respect through embracing the drugs world of the gangsta Digger who offers him the quick fix symbols of material success and hence status that Deli, his father cannot.

Ashley *stares at* Deli *with hate in his eyes...* Ashley: He takes away your pride, then your livelihood, and all you can do is stand dere like a fish? You've lost it blood. Deli *(flash of temper)* I'm not no blood wid you. Ashley: Regrettably, that's exactly what you are. (25)

Ashley, the would be drug dealer once in Digger's crew (in an almost Oedipal moment) even goes to shoot his own father in order to not be 'the informer's boy', privileging his street credibility over blood ties he considers demeaning:

Ashley *slowly takes out his gun.* Deli *just stares at him.*
Ashley You let me down Dad...
Digger: Alright, now point the gun at your punk-arsed dad... ...*(screams at him)* Is this the type of people we need in our midst?
Ashley: No.
Digger: OK then, raise the gun, point it.
Ashley *does.*
Digger Good. Is your finger on the trigger?
Ashley: Yes.
Digger: Good.
Digger *pulls out his gun and shoots* Ashley *dead.*
...Yes. Ah so dis war run! (93-4)

Notably in both plays mothers are absent - either dead or offstage. There are two passing mentions of Ashley's mother and Anastasia the sole on-stage woman in *Elmina's Kitchen* has lost her child and tangible motherhood. Elmina is simply the dead woman, idealised by her son and complained about by his father, her ex-husband who had absconded from the marriage and child rearing responsibilities. Moreover, the sexual denigration of women takes on many forms. Kwei-Armah's stage directions at Anastasia's first entrance suppose a universal salaciousness: '*we can see that she has the kind of body that most men of colour fantasise about. Big hips and butt, slim waist and full, full breasts.*' (15) compared to Deli and Digger who are '*a happy spirit...a born struggler...slightly overweight*' (3) '*looks every bit the 'bad man' that he is. His hair is plaited in two neat sets of cane rows*' (4) whilst Clifton is '*large-built...a boastful man*' (32). Black women are the property of black men to kill over in *Fallout*. In a context where boys murder other boys, gang rape of the most desirable girl on the estate as a right is a distinct possibility.

> Shanice: Don't touch me.
> Dwayne: Yer lucky dass all I'm doin. Nuff brers round here want ride yu, yu nuh...How yu gonna fight dem all off?...The fact dat yer goin wid sum fool, mek dem want it even more. I keep telling dem nuff times, no one touches yu, but I can't hold dem off for ever, Shanice. (41)

Williams creates a context of moral lawlessness and disrespect for bodily integrity that establishes a route of implied reasons for Kwame's murder. Although Shanice represents a point of intimacy for both Emile and Dwayne, she is not immune from the threat of violation because she is female.

I'm not suggesting that theatre needs to demonstrate templates of acceptable morality but the replications of misogyny raises questions about women's perceived status in these plays by male writers and the kind of society which produces such representations. The contestations between masculinities figure bleakly as the driving impetus behind both examples of Williams and Kwei-Armah's work. If as Baldwin's words about black writers seeking to make the world in their own image is to remove them from a powerlessness of representational subjection are true, then both writers appear to have trodden a fine line between perpetuating negative typing of black people and staging aspects of black British working class experience to spark debate. The patriarchal objectification of women is relentless from the harsh sexualising of the young women in *Fallout* to black women as unfaithful or driving men away with nagging in *Elmina's Kitchen*.[77]

ii: 'Drama of family ties'

Constituting respite from the relentless damaged masculinity that haunts the work of the incendiary plays, Dona Daley provides an arena for voices not often heard in *Blest be the Tie*. Her *dramatis personae* of three people creates an intimacy by which to explore a changing society through dramatising the shifts and adaptations her women characters make in order to survive the experience of being black in Britain. Jatinder Verma has referred to the implicit 'sensibility of provocation' provided by the impact of Black and Asian immigration since the

---

[77] For more on Williams and Kwei-Armah in this volume, see Elizabeth Barry and William Boles, 'Beyond Victimhood: Agency and Identity in the Theatre of Roy Williams' and Samuel Kasule, 'Aspects of Madness and Theatricality in Kwame Kwei-Armah's Drama'.

1950s in forming 'the often 'hidden texts' of modern multi-cultural Britain.' (Verma, 195-6). Like Winsome Pinnock's plays, Dona's texts are informed by her Caribbean heritage both culturally and politically using the British metropolitan context as a crucial reference point for her characters. The linguistic distinctiveness of writing in patois (Dona's term) and the negotiations of race, nationality, community and family as indicators of belonging, exclusion and cultural adaptations form the backbone of her drama.

Blest be the Tie continues the trajectory of post war Jamaican women's experience of migration established in the earlier *Weathering the Storm*. Read in succession, they chart the aspirations fuelled by the socio-economic catalyst through to the cultural hybridity evident as a strategic response to struggle. Disillusion as blood ties are stretched to breaking point is counterbalanced by the vitality and sustenance of new connections forged in England. Daley draws us into evaluating the diasporic inheritance via dramatising the comparison between those who were left behind and those who emigrated through a female-centred perspective.

Some contemporary writers might be dismissive of writing about the migration experience saying that the new work to be created lies in the specific cultural and geographical spaces in which British born inheritors of the diaspora now reside. Daley attested that acknowledging 'the shoes that had pinched' was part of her development and heritage. Her inspiration for *Blest be the Tie* was derived from a couple, a black man and a white woman married for over fifty years who had appeared in a television documentary celebrating fifty years since the *Windrush* docked and whose photograph also features in the report of the Commission on the Future of Multi-Ethnic Britain (2000). 'Just think what they must have been

through, what they must have *survived*' were Daley's words (Daley 2001).

[*Blest be the Tie*. Photo courtesy: Talawa]

Blest be the Tie has a cast of three women in their fifties, a generation rarely seen on the British stage in central roles. It charts a reunion of the sisters Martha (who stayed in Jamaica, now re-named Cherise) and Florence who emigrated and their very differing relationship to this and to Florence's best friend, the white English woman, Eunice. Long buried conflicts explode and reconciliation is finally produced through an implied critique of the compromising choices each woman has made.

Florence's impoverished circumstances (the now affluent) Martha assesses are shown to be negligible in the face of the contentment Florence has carved out – despite them. 'Some of us don't need whole heap of tings to mek us happy. Me not lonely and me satisfy wid what me have. Me can't start again in a strange place.' which affirms the dual cultural heritage she has attained and which Martha reminds her, 'Dat strange place is yu homeland!'(30) Here Daley reveals the acute complexities of the 'ties' that bind or are severed through the migration and settling process. Martha's persuasion of the returner's incentive, a better climate and good monetary exchange rate, 'Yu pension would carry yu far',(34) erupts into an argument between the three women. Racial and cultural divisions become apparent as Eunice feels 'shut out' and in feeling so, resorts to familiar racialised defences. 'You people can close ranks when you ready' (36) and employs the racist language and thinking of her context when referring to how she married a black man, 'The 'blousey girl' from Chapeltown was having a darkie's baby.'(40) Ironically as the indigenous British woman, she is isolated and fearful, a reversal of the immigrant as an outsider.

Yet Eunice's actions and friendship with Florence redeem her from the limited and abhorrent way in which she responds to Martha's outspokenness and criticism. The dynamic of neglect and nurture engenders a debate regarding the claims to intimacy, the ties of friendship versus biological ties: 'Martha …Me and my sister is one blood Just because you live genst her and me live far don't mean seh that there isn't a tie between us!'(49) 'Eunice…A Christmas card once a year!…I was just saying when you are with people day in and day out you kind of have a different view…' (46, 49). The difference between providing love and providing materially for someone as an *act* of love provokes a series of revelations puncturing the safety of any expectations the audience may build-up of the

characters. We are wooed into a homecoming narrative in which the reference points of where 'home' is and who is 'returning', are twisted and re-turned in a subtle undermining of certainties.

[*Blest be the Tie.* Photo courtesy: Talawa]

Significantly, the motherhood of the women characters whilst integral to their lives is peripheral to their stage identities

– perhaps reflecting the separation through economic imperatives that characterised post-war Caribbean families in the immigration stream. 'I have to suck salt out of a wooden spoon to get that settee. Leave the kids them sleeping early morning gawn fe clean' (59) recalls Florence. Children are registered through answering machine messages, letters, or are abroad and do not participate in the staged action. Thus Daley unhooks her women characters from traditional moorings to identities as girlfriends, wives and mothers – something director Paulette Randall sees as her unique contribution to Black British drama – a dramatisation of the cross-race friendship of two women (rather than a woman and a man) as the primary relationship (Randall 2004). The lesbian sub-text is registered but truncated, 'Florence: If yu was a man I could really love you. Eunice; I know, I know. I love you too. Very much. Florence: If tings had been different. Eunice: Another place. Another age maybe. *They look at each other and kiss and hold each other for a while.*' (61). Structured as a series of revelations wherein the balance of power in terms of socio-economic circumstances in past and present constantly serves to alter our perceptions, the play uniquely articulates a love triangle without men and without sex.[78]

The critical voices: 'to be or not to be...'

Drama produced by indigenous Black British writers slides out of the neatness of the postcolonial framework and its reliance upon definitions of hybridity to account for indigenous populations whose antecedents were immigrants two or more generations before. Responding critically to the cultural output of indigenous Black Britons reveals the partial vision of traditional discursive arenas. It demands the forging and acknowledging of new points of reference, a scope of critical reception which in turn reveals the limitations of mainstream theatrical and academic conceptualising.[79] The voices dramatised (whilst ostensibly housed within the European realist genre) speak out and back to traditional sites of cultural legitimation not only in the audiences they attract, but also in representing experiences not unilaterally shared by residents within academia or critical circles.

Considering the reception of these plays in reviews from the mainstream press tellingly reveals the limitations of the dialogic relationship created between staged play and its critical reception. It foregrounds the impulse to regard this work as a perpetual 'pale imitation' of the existing white dominant epistemologies - made

---

[78] For more on *Blest Be the Tie* and *Urban Afro-Saxons* see Victor Ukaegbu on *Talawa* Theatre Company in this volume.

[79] See Dave Gunning's discussion of the lack of engagement with the specific locale of Britain as 'a contained entity unto itself' with its own explanatory power concurrent to its global significances.(Gunning, 31)

palatable for white audiences through locating blackness within familiar contexts. Plays that stray from the favoured areas ascribed to representations of black experience appear to receive a critical reprimand – despite their obvious audience appeal.[80] However, when the content of plays corresponds to the media 'comfort zone' in accounting for the Black British community: broken families, unemployment, drugs, violence, abuse, housing estates and 'gangstas', then the entrance to the mainstream becomes an issue too, of cultural responsibility.

The writers I have profiled were commissioned by mainstream theatres which seek to promote new work, have thriving education sections producing study packs and foster the work of young people. This suggests that there is an investment in registering the voices dramatised as, constituents of contemporary writing. Winsome Pinnock 'the godmother of black British playwrights' has identified the extreme importance of this, 'Theatre is a sort of moral conscience of a society, an arena where a society can examine itself. If some voices are missing, I don't think that it's honestly fulfilling that role and is, in fact, practising a subtle form of censorship.'(Kolawole, 2003)

In 1991 Yvonne Brewster, the co-founder of Talawa Theatre Company revealed her determination for matter-of-fact inclusion into the British theatrescape, 'My ultimate aim is never to have to say 'black theatre' again. It would mean that I had come full circle, as I never had occasion to use the term when I started out in Jamaica.' By 2002, the editor of *Wasafiri* Shusheila Nasta asks, 'Should we still in 2002 be highlighting our focus on 'black writing in Britain?...or should we be getting ahead and out of these tired old debates?' The naming of oneself, 'to be or not to be' Black British appears only to be possible from the safe embrace of the mainstream and the academy. Upon interviewing Roy Williams and Courttia Newland, it was clear that they *do* want to claim being titled Black British Writers. Newland further supported this by referring to parity; once black writers are on an equal footing in publishing and performance opportunities with non-black writers who continue to dominate the mainstream, *then* it will be possible to accept the title British writing. For, as he pointed out, we still refer to 'African American' writing (Newland 2004; Williams 2004). The contentiousness of the separation of black theatre as a term to denote an autonomous staged identity and experience and the simultaneous segregating of black from 'standard' theatre continues to be a double-edged sword. As Winsome Pinnock has argued, 'it reflects and articulates the reality of a division within theatrical institutions in which black or 'other' performers are viewed solely in relation to their supposed difference' (Pinnock, 'Breaking Down the Door' 29-30).

---

[80] See bibliography for indicative reviews of *Blest be the Tie* and *Two Step* which exemplify critical limitations and shortcomings.

Much of the neglectful reception of new black writing appears to stem from the lack of knowledge of the cultural networks and writing worlds in which these playwrights circulate and from whence they draw their inspiration. Their specificity and individuality is too easily generalised into transience and mediocrity as though the black presence in Britain will somehow go away or eventually become assimilated into a monolithic cultural greyness. Such a dynamic clearly has implications for the anchoring of contemporary black writing (in all its forms) within British cultural psyche. Black British writing may have been taken up by the mainstream at the moment, but there is no indication that it has a stable and permanent place in it.

Although strategies towards the black arts have evolved, inevitable negotiations are still made with the forces of compromise engendered by white male cultural hegemony in its collaborations with black British dramatists. Felix Cross of Nitro believes 'it is only when black theatre develops something that white theatre doesn't have that it will have the power and influence to move forward.'(14) To forge a permanent foothold it well might be that the experiential rather than experimental dimension brought to British culture by the plays of Black British dramatists creates the uniqueness and difference that is demanded for perpetual inclusion.

Acknowledgements: Deirdre Osborne's acknowledgements and thanks extend to Kwame Kwei-Armah, Roy Williams, Mrs F. Daley, Paulette Randall, Kadija Sesay, Talawa Theatre Company, Josette Bushell-Mingo, Lennie James, Paul Morris, Ian Rickson, Dominic Cooke and Courttia Newland who all gave their time in valuable conversations about theatre and drama.

Works Cited:

Agyemang, Kofi and Patricia Elcock (2003), *Urban Afro-Saxons*, unpublished ms. Courtesy of Talawa Theatre Company.

Baldwin, James (1985), *The Price of the Ticket: Collected Non-fiction (1948-1985)* London: Michael Joseph Ltd.

Campbell, Patrick (ed.) (1996), *Analyzing Performance: A critical Reader* Manchester: Manchester University Press.

Daley, Dona (2004), *Blest Be the Tie,* London: Royal Court Theatre.

Gottlieb, Vera and Colin Chambers (eds.) (1999), *Theatre in a Cool Climate* Oxford: Amber Lane Press.

Green, Debbie Tucker (2003), *Born Bad,* London: Nick Hern Books.

Griffin, Gabriele (2003), *Contemporary Black and Asian Women Playwrights in Britain,* Cambridge: Cambridge University Press.

Gunning, Dave (2004), 'Anti-Racism, the Nation-State and Contemporary Black British Literature' *The Journal of Commonwealth Studies* Vol.39 No.2.

Kwei-Armah, Kwame (2003), *Elmina's Kitchen,* London: Methuen.

Mama, Amina (1995), *Beyond the Masks: Race, Gender and Subjectivity* London and New York: Routledge.

Nasta, Shusheila (2002), 'Editorial' *Wasafiri* Issue 36.

Newland, Courttia (2003), *B is 4 Black,* unpublished ms. Courtesy of the playwright.

Norfolk, Mark (2003), *Wrong Place,* London: Oberon Books.

Oparei, DeObia (2002), *crazyblackmuthaf***in'self,* London: Royal Court Theatre.

Pinnock, Winsome (1999), 'Breaking Down the Door' in Vera Gottlieb and Colin Chambers (eds.), *Theatre in a Cool Climate* Oxford: Amber Lane Press.

Rees, Roland (ed.) (1992), *Fringe First: Pioneers of Fringe Theatre on Record London*: Oberon Books.

Southerne, Thomas (1696) *Oroonoko*, in Robert Jordan and Harold Love, (eds.) (1988), *The Works of Thomas Southerne Vol.II*, Oxford: Clarendon Press.

Stone, Rhashan (2004), *Two Step,* London: Oberon Books.

Stott, Rebecca (1992), *The Fabrication of the late Victorian Femme Fatale* London: Macmillan Press Ltd.

Tompsett, A. Ruth (1996), 'Changing Perspectives' in Patrick Campbell (ed.) *Analyzing Performance: A critical Reader* Manchester: Manchester University Press.

Verma, Jatinder (1996), 'The Challenge of Binglish': Analyzing Multi-Cultural Productions' in Patrick Campbell (ed.) *Analyzing Performance: A critical Reader* Manchester: Manchester University Press.

Williams, Roy (2003), *Fallout* Education Pack, London: Royal Court Theatre.

Williams, Roy (2003), *Fallout,* London: Methuen.

Newspapers
Anon. (19 July 2004), '90% of whites have few or no black friends' *The Guardian.*

Cavendish, Dominic (31 October 2003), 'Heat on the Street Confounds Expectations' *The Daily Telegraph.*

Costa, Maddy (22 March 2004), 'Saint Nick' *The Guardian* Manchester (UK).

Cross, Felix (1 April 1998), 'Missing in Action: our black stars' *The Independent,* Black Theatre Miscellaneous File. Theatre Museum, London.

Hiley, Jim (14 October 1985) *The Guardian* n.p. Black Theatre Miscellaneous File. Theatre Museum, London.

James, Lennie (11 February 2004), 'Who Do You Think You Are?' *The Guardian.*

Kolawole, Helen (26 July 2003), *The Guardian*.

Smurthwaite, Nick (21 April 1991), 'It's a classic answer for black theatre' *The Observer* n.p. Black theatre Miscellaneous File. Theatre Museum, London.

Bassett, Kate (5 September 2004), *Two Step* by Rhashan Stone, *The Independent on Sunday*.

Billington, Michael (3 September 2004), *Two Step* by Rhashan Stone, *The Guardian*.

Cavendish, Dominic (24 April 2004), *Blest Be the Tie* by Dona Daley, *The Daily Telegraph: News; Review on Saturday*.

Clapp, Susannah (5 September 2004), *Two Step* by Rhashan Stone, *The Observer*.

Gardner, Lyn (23 April 2004), *Blest Be the Tie* by Dona Daley, *The Guardian*.

Koenig, Rhoda (3 May 2004), *Blest Be the Tie* by Dona Daley, *The Independent*.

Mountford, Fiona (20 April 2004), *Blest Be the Tie* by Dona Daley, *Evening Standard*.

Nightingale, Benedict (3 September 2004), *Two Step* by Rhashan Stone, *The Times*.

Peter, John (5 September 2004), *Two Step* by Rhashan Stone, *Sunday Times*.

Shuttleworth, Ian (21 April 2004), *Blest Be the Tie* by Dona Daley, *Financial Times*.

Shore, Robert (28 April-5 May 2004), *Blest Be the Tie* by Dona Daley, *Time Out*.

Spencer, Charles (8 September 2004), *Two Step* by Rhashan Stone, *The Daily Telegraph*.

Taylor, Paul (6 September 2004), *Two Step* by Rhashan Stone, *The Independent*.

Interviews

Daley, Dona (2001), interview with Deirdre Osborne.

Newland, Courttia (February 2004), interview with Deirdre Osborne.

Randall, Paulette (2004), interview with Deirdre Osborne.

Rickson, Ian (22 March 2004), interview with Deirdre Osborne.

Williams, Roy (March 2004), interview with Deirdre Osborne.

CHAPTER FOUR

GENEALOGIES, ARCHAEOLOGIES, HISTORIES: THE REVOLUTIONARY 'INTERCULTURALISM' OF ASIAN THEATRE IN BRITAIN[81]

DIMPLE GODIWALA

Synopsis:
This chapter traces a genealogy of British-Asian theatre locating it within the practice of interculturalism. Tracing the origins of a revolutionary and hybrid theatre form, it is archaeologically excavated to reveal the political and aesthetic strategies it deploys in its commitment to its form which may be said, often, to be a **becoming-in-difference***: a dis-play of a happy marriage rather than a confrontation of western and eastern artistic practices.*

'For the theatre, Asia is a constant!' (Ariane Mnouchkine)

'From Asia comes what is specific to theatre, which is the perpetual metaphor which the actors produce – when they are capable of producing it.' (Ariane Mnouchkine)

---

[81] This article contains some material previously published in my articles 'Hybridity/ invention/ identity: British Asian culture and its postcolonial theatres', *Journal for the Study of British Cultures*, Vol.8, No.1, 2001 and 'Hybridized identity as counterdiscursive strategy: a genealogy of British Asian culture and its postcolonial theatres', *Journal of South Asian Popular Culture*, Vol.1, No.1, 2003.

[*Revelations,* Tara Arts 2001]

Although Asian theatre has been an explicit influence on European directors such as Copeau, Brecht, Artaud, Brook, Barba and Mnouchkine since the end of the nineteenth century (see Kiernander in Pavis 1996: 93), this chapter focuses on those forms of Asian theatre practised in Britain by the British-Asians whose ancestors hail from the Indian subcontinent. [82]

British-Asian theatre comes into being mainly when the generation of the Indian-East African diaspora, whose fathers have moved to middle-class status in Africa, emigrates to England. The 70s and 80s saw emerge the talent of individual dramatists as well as theatre groups; the major theatre companies being Tara Arts and then Tamasha and Kali. 1977 saw the inception of the first theatre company, Jatinder Verma's Tara Arts, which began as a community group staging the literature and drama of the Indian subcontinent.

However, the particular *lineage* of British-Asian theatre is more complex: it encompasses ancient and contemporary India *as well as* England, the latter mediated through the classical, the modern and the historical. It is the unsettling

---

[82] 'India' and 'the Indian subcontinent' includes India, Pakistan and Bangla Desh for the purposes of this chapter.

fusion of the multiple texts of the classical *Natya Shastra* and kitsch-y Bollywood, as well as the history of (verbal and non-verbal) western and Indian theatre morphologies, each text valorized individually and collectively in the contemporary British-Asian psyche which is constructed in artistic and aesthetic alterity. Indian classical and fusion-music and song generate a host of cultural meanings which are a code through which to reach the Asian audiences.

Yet, British-Asian theatre is not Indian by the standards of the latter's pressures and needs to adhere to classical Sanskrit practice.[83] Nor is it part of classical or contemporary English theatre traditions in Britain. British-Asian theatre is constructed through the difference of acculturation as it is modified through intercultural exchange and socialization, avoiding the false representation produced by rigidly antithetical and binary categories which lead to the need for 'authenticity' and 'elitism' that India and England currently seek in their individual and divorced calls for a living theatre. Perhaps the poor atrophying state of contemporary English theatre that Eyre laments (Eyre 2000) is caused by the rigid adherence to the mimetic mode, which the contemporary *neo-naturalist minimalism* of English theatre achieves only to compete with the ubiquitous and ultimately more accessible mode of entertainment: film.

Critical discourse upon which the transient and ephemeral performance texts are predicated to legitimately enter historical theatrical discourse must pause to take stock of the lineages which result in this difference of British-Asian

---

[83] In India, theatre/s and performance styles are under constant pressure from scholars and critics to maintain the traditional lineage of the originary high-language Sanskrit and the classical text of the *Natya Shastra*, whilst demonstrating a fluidity and innovative change which is a sign of a living theatre. The 1999 *Natyotsav* at C[entre for]A[sian]T[heatre] in Dhaka revealed the need for Indian theatre and its practitioners to demonstrate an 'aliveness' in a performance culture continually fossilized at home and abroad by the need of the Central Government apparatus to export 'Indian arts and culture' and have it serve as a 'tourist attraction'. As Rustom Bharucha puts it, 'the 'Orient' can be manufactured in India itself and then transported abroad to validate earlier modes of 'Orientalism' which are in the process of being dismantled elsewhere' (Pavis 1996: 210). Compare Peter Brook's arguments for a holy theatre and his definition of a deadly theatre (Brook 1968) to the arguments of Syed Jamil Ahmed, 'Contemporaneity of tradition: the case of Pala Gan and Kamala Ranir Sagar Dighi'; K.N. Panikkar, 'Sanskrit theatre style modernity'; Ataur Rahman, 'Tradition and contemporary theatre'; Nripendra Saha, 'The Bengali theatre and the heritage of Sanskrit drama'; and Kapila Vatsyayan, 'Dance or movement techniques of Sanskrit theatre' (*Natyotsav* 1999) for a comparative view of critiques of English theatre and Indian theatre in the context of their individual heritage by scholars and practitioners of each theatre tradition. Cf. Richard Eyre, 'Why British culture needs a healthy dose of elitism', (2000: 3), as the 'deadly' theatres of two ancient cultures are juxtaposed with the vitality and invention of neo-discursive theatres of today.

performative texts. Post-war 60s Labour-England was a time of openness to the working classes on the English stage, even as their texts and performances conformed to middle-class aesthetics and theatrical conventions. Just as class was then an exotic difference, now it is the 'ethnic' subject whose stages and performances infuse vitality on the London stages. Critical dramatic discourse often flounders, unable to judge this excess of neo-discourse and practice, as, in spite of at least a century of the interculturality of European theatre, English theatre has been mired in its divorce from the east. Eugenio Barba may have been right to call for what he defined as a 'Eurasian theatre', which, far from being a superficial 'supermarket of cultures', would enrich western theatre in enabling an overcoming of its ethnocentricity by 'discovering one's own centre in the 'tradition of traditions''. Rather than an Occidentalism or what Edward Said defined as Orientalism, Barba endorses the capacity to locate 'one's individual or collective tradition into a context which connects it with other, different traditions' (Barba in Pavis 1996: 217-222). This is not an answer to British directors such as Richard Eyre and Nicholas Wright who, far from seeing Asian theatre as an example of a revolutionary or hybrid form which contributes to the changing stages of Britain, fail to acknowledge even its existence in the book and TV series *Changing Stages: A View of British Theatre in the Twentieth Century* (2000a). Their rigid adherence to a fixed notion of Englishness can be noted in their anachronistic insistence that '[t]o stage a Shakespeare play is [...] to toy with *our genetic make-up*' (2000a: 22. My emphasis).

It is the *doxa* experience so peculiar to the English stage which accounts for its particular inability to recognize other forms of performance as valid or equal in importance. Shakespeare has been, for centuries, the core of the experience of English theatre, but the texts themselves have been internationally produced using performance styles native to Japan as well as Bombay. It is not, then, Shakespeare's texts but the adherence to very western, nay, *English* styles of performance which has contributed to the English *doxic* experience of misrecognizing the naturalization of certain (western) performance styles, and thereby considering them normative. The colonial ideology which still runs fluidly through the structures of English theatremaking has made the normative styles of re-presenting Shakespeare, not merely natural but *superior*.

The idea of a truly intercultural theatre can exist perhaps only when English theatremakers learn thoroughly not only the most strictly ritualized exchanges of the east, in which all moments of the action and its unfolding are not merely *executed* because rigorously foreseen, but excelled in by having room for strategies within that ritualized discourse ('invention within limits'). The actors must be able to remain in command of the *interval* between obligatory moments, and can therefore act on their co-actors by playing with the *tempo* of their exchange in an ability to improvise with mastery and excellence within that other tradition of practice (cf. Bourdieu [1972] 1977: 15). This cultural excess of practice is always already inscribed within the space-of-difference of British-Asian theatre where we are able to locate Deleuze and Guattari's tenets of what constitutes a *revolutionary* artistic practice, thereby locating it 'in the heart of great or established [theatre].' These are: 'deterritorialization of language, the connection of the individual [theatre production] to a political immediacy, and the collective assemblage of enunciation' ([1975]1986: 18). This, in British-Asian theatre, is a result of a proliferation of fractured discourses and texts (theatre texts, languages, acting styles and so on) which are familiar to the English and/ or the Indian, but re-presented in a stage-of-difference; i.e., a fluid stage of transformation-in-process. This *becoming* is a process of 'reconstructing the past [which] usually heralds the emergence of new voices and new tools for understanding that past' (Gilbert & Tompkins 1996). It is not possible to re-enact or recover intact performance styles, methods, ideologies or texts of a period or an age which may be lost to the contemporary theatremaker (as indeed it is impossible to resurrect an authentic Elizabethan Shakespearean performance, especially in terms of reception), living, as the British-Asian does, in cultures of difference. British-Asian theatres are – at the level of artistic practice – a marriage of minds and cultures which allows for a birthing of the strange and monstrous morphologies that Deleuze and Guattari speak of in *Kafka* (Deleuze and Guattari 1975) – morphologies which in turn dazzle and entrance but may, at worst, be horrifying to culturally sanctioned orthodox aesthetic tastes. But this is the risk of a *becoming-in-difference*, the risk of experiment, the risk that the hybridity set into motion on the stage may not conform to either set of received aesthetic judgements. At its best moments, the identity of British-Asian theatre moves fluidly between east and west as '[t]he past continues to speak [...] but it no longer addresses us as a simple, factual 'past', since our relation to it [...] is always-already 'after the break'' (Hall 1994: 395) even as it is mindful of interculturalism, not merely in terms of its locus, but in the consistent employment of White actors and, eclectically, western performance methods.

Is British-Asian theatre a post-colonial theatre? History, critics have noted, inevitably manoeuvres a strategic presentation of certain views and a repression of others. The introduction has foregrounded that the phrase locates the west in the centre of the discourse and practice. Western history in the imperial episteme is said to have erased Other histories with violence, valorizing western knowledges and, in theatre, western styles, forms, sounds, and gestures. The languages of theatre, both verbal and non-verbal, were western as other theatre languages were suppressed, erased or became subjugated and acquired a negative valence in the face of imperial morphologies. The re-presentation of othered performance texts and the de-centring of imperial texts by appropriation into othered performative strategies then becomes central to hybrid theatres. The very presence of the Other theatres in Britain necessitates a restructuring of English theatre from within, displacing authoritative versions of 'English' theatre and in this case, of importing Indian-ness and inventing an indigenous theatre which throws into relief much of current English theatre which is 'deadly' and stultified in practice.[84]

A sign of the widespread acceptance of British-Asian theatre was seen in the 2002 Andrew Lloyd-Webber—A.R. Rahman—Meera Syal West End production of a musical based on kitschy Bollywood antics so beloved by the Asians in Britain. Notwithstanding the severally bad reviews by critics, *Bombay Dreams* was an event in British theatre as it marked a boundary line that Asian theatremakers were able to cross. The West End, after all, although not home to serious theatre of

any kind, lures a popular audience, and the production of a wholly Asian piece by a major West End producer marks the entry of the Asians into the kind of 'theatre' liked by England's mass audiences.[85] (A year later, Nina Wadia and Pravesh Kumar wrote another Bollywood spoof, *Bollywood: Yet Another Love Story*, proving how close this source of fantasy is to the British-Asian heart).

[Nizwar Karanj in *Hayavadana*, Tara Arts 1987]

The translation into Indian languages, music, songs, gestures, tonal inflexions, dance, movement

---

[84] Richard Eyre (2000: 3) doxically notes that 'one has to be a very wilful optimist to believe that the dying body of British theatre is going to make a miraculous recovery.' It is an 'atrophying' body of 'poor work' and 'poor audiences'.

[85] Although Black Theatre Seasons had, in the 80s, produced two Asian plays at the West End: the ancient Sanskrit classics, Shudraka's *Miti Ki Gadi* and Visakhadutta's *Rakshasa's Ring,* this was the first play produced by a white mainstream producer on the West End proper. For more on Black Theatre Seasons productions see, in this volume, Alda Terracciano's 'Mainstreaming African, Asian and Caribbean Theatre: The Experiments of the Black Theatre Forum'.

destabilizes the political position of the English language and English drama in England, thereby decentring the imperial hegemony underlying English culture. British-Asian drama is one of hybridity as it fractures temporality and rehistoricizes, remapping spatial epistemologies and interrogating notions of linearity which are part of the conventions of realism even as it conveys entire audiences – via the theatrical spaces of imagination – into unviolated 'pre-contact' spaces, in strategies of de-construction which implode dominant western theatre practice. British-Asian theatre can be seen as a marriage of theatre forms of east and west as it is a hybrid and heady mix of two heterogeneous cultures.

Most Asian theatre in Britain is political and serious as it uses several intercultural-postcolonial strategies to construct its forms and styles. *Re-citing the classics* is one strategy by which British-Asian theatre destabilizes and re-locates authority and authenticity by altering power structures via revisionist performance. This results in what Helen Tiffin calls 'canonical counter-discourse' by which she means the localization and indigenization of canonical texts in order to divest them of their apparent authoritative status. 'Rewriting the characters, the narrative, the context and/ or the genre [is] a means of interrogating the cultural legacy of imperialism and offers renewed opportunities for performative intervention. [...] Counter-discourse seeks to de-construct significations of authority and power exercised in the canonical text, to release its stranglehold on representation and, by implication, to intervene in social conditioning' (in Gilbert & Tompkins 1996: 16). Thus the power structures in the originary text are destabilized and reallocated.

[Naseeruddin Shah in *Cyrano* at the National Theatre 1995]

Tara Arts brought many an ancient Indian classic to England. *Bhavni Bhavai,* the 14th-century Gujarati folk play (Asit Thakore) is ancient India melded with western music and performance conventions in a necessary overlap of morphologies as the oedipal tale of a prince-hero brought up by untouchables allegorizes racism in the host culture. *Hayavadana,* Girish Karnad's post-independence play, indirectly derived from the 8th-century *Katha-Sarit-Sagar* via *Die vertauschten Köpfe* ('Transposed Heads') by Thomas Mann is a trope for the interstitial

position of midnight's children. The derivations are an acknowledgement to the intellectual traditions of Indo-Germanic culture and an acceptance of the post-independence Indian-English identity interstice. Tara Arts' storyteller negotiates the space between the stories of Hayavadana, a progeny of miscegenation and Padmini's love for the intelligence and poetry of Devadutta and the beauty of Kapila in a confusing allegiance to two men, two texts, two cultures.

Although Tara Arts began as a company which imported classical Indian theatre texts in a bid for theatrical authenticity, the company has also proved ace at *dis-playing and dis-placing the authority of the classics of Empire* as it has re-cited Western texts making them work for the interstitial diasporic communities of the Asians in Britain. Jatinder Verma has directed Molière's *Tartuffe*, Shakespeare's *A Midsummer Night's Dream* and *Troilus and Cressida*, Rostand's *Cyrano*, and Gogol's *The Government Inspector* among other western classics. Verma and his company dismantle the authenticity of Englishness in performing the canonical classics by the act of simple transposition of the dialogue into rich regional Asian accents and inflexions. Tone and gesture, voice and stance dis-locate the canon transposing the text into Indian theatrical spaces signified by the richly colourful

Indian sets and costumes, music and dance. Using an array of meta-theatrical devices from storytelling to Indian song which often reflect on the self-consciousness of post-war theatre in England, Verma re-works, re-en-acts, re-visions and dis-places the imperial authority latent within.

Farrukh Dhondy's *Film, Film, Film* (1986) was a spirited attempt to fuse a re-appropriation of *King Lear* with Bollywood cinema serving well the appetite of his Asian audiences for classics and kitsch. The Shakespearean narrative is transposed into the corrupt and fecund-pop machine of Bollywood: source and sustenance of Indian fantasy, norm and value-system, predicated in Dhondy's play on coded satirical asides accessible to the Asian audience in a gleeful exclusion of the English.

Tanika Gupta's Indianization of *Hobson's Choice* successfully transposed the patriarchal Victorian characters into the matrix of contemporary Indian capitalist patriarchy, setting it in the Salford of the textile industry. This play, thrice-invented, takes us schizophrenically from *King Lear* through the 1915 Harold Brighouse play to a stunning contemporary rendition of a British-Asian patriarch's power and control of his three quick-thinking, rebellious daughters. Critics unanimously agreed that the transposition was an effective one in what was 'a glorious production' which combined a 'life affirming vitality' (Spencer 2003) with a successful re-invention which 'never strains credibility in its new setting' (Coveney 2003). Carole Woddis saw the play as symptomatic of 'Britain's changing face'; a 'moment of change-over in English social structure' (2003). In an innovative production at the Young Vic, which remarkably had the audience, mid-performance, cross the street to attend an Indian wedding, Gupta managed to weave the themes of British-Asian interstitial identity, romantic love, emancipation and patriarchal domination in a drama which cross-fertilized English and Asian cultures in terms of production and performance as well as themes.

Storytelling as a performative strategy challenges stasis and fixity of performance as its revisionist improvisational approach and lack of regard for naturalistic conventions such as the fourth wall are ways of interrogating received western models. Additionally, storytelling valorizes oral cultures which have been violently superimposed upon and negated by colonial cultures which considered themselves as repositories of knowledge, power and status as a result of carefully documented histories. The storyteller re-visions history and is a tool which aids and facilitates audience imagination, transporting it into remote areas of experience and geographies. The active-imagination's engagement with the oral/verbal challenges the increasingly passive audience-receptivity of a visual culture/ medium/ discourse/ text. This already theatrical tradition transfers easily onto the stage and was well utilized in Verma's *Genesis* to distinguish between African and Indian culture. Vayu Naidu's storytelling in *South* (2003) through dance, an ancient Indian practice, is transformed as it is has Everyman as well as Everywoman (Everyman transformed). The fusion of Bharat Natyam, jazz and robotic movements from dancers belonging to different cultural performance forms (Black, Indian, European) keeps to her aim of '[building] bridges of understanding between the science of self and the shorelines of culture' (Thaxter 2003).

The hybrid stages of Asian Britain are the principal arena for the destabilizing of imperial authority with regard to *the English language*. Although the use of English as a language is not necessarily an endorsement of British authority, 'choosing [a different language] in which to express one's dramatic art is, in itself, a political act' (Gilbert & Tompkins 1996: 168). Asian Co-operative Theatre's trilingual *Jawaani* [Youth] (1988) was a double-bill: *Heartgame* and *Prem* [Romantic Love] explored the tensions of young Asians as they are regulated to make traditionally arranged marriages with spouses from the sub-continent who are removed from them by language and culture. Juxtaposing a young Indian wife with a British-Asian husband reveals the hybridized cultural position of the latter culture. The clash between western romantic love which spells freedom and the traditional arranged marriage is explored using Gujarati, Bengali and Indian-English languages. Choosing to perform in Indian languages is 'a refusal to submit to the dominance of the standard language and to subscribe to the 'reality' it sustains' (Gilbert & Tompkins 1996: 185). The norm is destabilized by the act of incorporating Indian languages, but more dramatically so when English is eschewed completely on 'English' stages. As Jatinder Verma puts it in his comments on Mehtaab, the first company to receive support for non-English work, the Punjabi language *Kali Shalwar* went 'beyond the flirtation with Indian languages into another text which would exclude some and include others [thus seeming to fulfil] the same need that Bollywood cinema offers the British Asian' (Verma 1997).[86] Apart from this diasporic need to indulge in splendid nostalgia, it points subtly to the need to accept that *English is itself a dialect language*, variously derived; 'it can claim no more authenticity than the linguistic forms it helped to spawn' (Gilbert & Tompkins 1996: 169).

The practice of British-Asian theatre is comparatively nascent: it has seen three decades of individuals and groups trying to find a voice. *Autobiographical narration* becomes, at times, a necessary strategy as the voices indulge in a necessary expression in order to find valorization in cross-cultural identification. Two excellent examples of semi-autobiography marrying theatrical magic are Ayub Khan-Din's *East is East* which, although set in Salford, cut across race and culture to give the audiences a British cultural universal in the portrayal of a working-class mixed-race couple and their travails. Another is Jatinder Verma and Tara Arts' millennial trilogy, *Journey to the West*, which speaks of the displacement of the Indian labouring classes to imperial Kenya and their subsequent social mobility in Africa and then Britain as the last of the series (*Revelations*) depicts a contemporary young, upwardly mobile generation to whom invention in music, lifestyle, language is natural as they create a new England in the heart of old Empire. *Genesis, Exodus* and *Revelations* are, as titles, an acknowledgement to classical western discourse and an acceptance of links made and ties forged between Western and Asian modalities of thought. In the making, which has involved a thorough research of the Indian-Kenyan-British-Asian diaspora and involved every counter-strategy available, *Journey to the West* is an epic which represents the hybrid culture of the British-Asian. A marriage of Other theatre forms and styles and bringing them onto the British stage in a hybrid identity, this is an example of a neo-discourse's indebtedness to a global heritage as inspiration is derived from the *Odyssey*, the *Ramayana* and the *Mahabharata*, the *Hsi-yu ChiXiYou Ji* and the *Bible* – classical epics and traditional texts of the oldest cultures on earth. This was a watershed event in the history of British-Asian culture, as a neo-cultural performative discourse traverses pre-colonial geographies in a search for its classical literatures, displaying a living theatre as it marries the oldest skills of aesthetics in a celebratory epic which negates the several critiques of colonialism and empire as violent practices which suppressed or subjugated native knowledges. Each ancient culture which was part of the British Empire – India, China, Africa – is revealed as having been able to both sustain and preserve itself and *incorporate* England as part of its intellectual, aesthetic, and literary practice.

---

[86] Mehtaab Theatre Company's *Kali Shalwar* was a different production from Kali Theatre Company's play of the same title.

An unusual but equally celebratory strategy used by British-Asian writers and directors deploying racial hybridity is the *use of western 'slice of life' to dis-play counter-discursive histories* in a narcissistic marriage of form and content. So Ayub Khan-Din's *Last Dance at Dum-Dum* tells the tale of the twice-displaced Anglo-Indian community in India – a text of dissonance and alterity – wherein we witness a slice of life in the history of a group forced into being by a promiscuous Empire's miscegnation, hybridity and exclusion. A unique and counter-discursive slice-of-life, also produced by Tamasha theatre, *A Tainted Dawn* (1997) was able to dismantle the hierarchy of white domination by ostensibly ignoring the cause and historical context of the Partition of the Indian subcontinent. In effect, the history and moment of Partition was rewritten to erase any references or representations of the British in India, thereby giving us a whitewashed/tarred Indian history.[87] However, it performed within a theatrical space[88] which extends into the diasporic audience imagination, and carries the living memory of the violence of displacement. This performance strategy, where real lived performance mingles with a collective memory, offers the possibility - eventuality even - of the signifiers of performance merging with the signifiers embedded in memory. This is a conjoining which addresses not just the pain and futility of cultural and geographical displacement of populations but also the violence of an imperial power which surfaces in the performance text only in fragments. For example, the performance has a few lines of Jawaharlal Nehru's speech of freedom at midnight resounding over speakers, and a lighting design which intermittently displays blood-streaked cracks in the very foundations of the set.

Most of Tamasha's plays have been in the tradition of *le tranche de vie. House of the Sun* (1991) based on Meira Chand's novel, charts the lives of wealthy and not-so-wealthy Sindhis displaced after Partition to Bombay; the adaptation of Mulk Raj Anand's *Untouchable* (1989) which was the company's inaugural piece and the two plays scripted by Ruth Carter, *A Yearning* (1995 – adapted from Garcia

---

[87] Writing in a language ossified and hyperbolically valorized during Empire's brief moment is difficult enough with every reference to black/dark/night being fraught with an excess of negativity. Cf. the Chinese parallel *gwailo*. (*Gwai*=white ghost + *lo*=male person, or, *po*=female person). In one century of occupation the imperial dominating culture had appropriated the pejorative *gwailo* in every European language spoken by those who lived and worked in the island colony of Hong Kong and turned it into a self-congratulatory compliment in a counter-discursive revisionist linguistic strategy. It would be interesting to see if the British Black (a political category which includes anybody who is non-White) could reverse every 'dark reference' in the English language.

[88] 'Theatrical space' refers to the spaces of audience imagination which a living theatre is able to reach. A 'theatre space', by reductive contrast, is the literal architectural space in which the performance takes place.

Lorca's *Yerma*) and *Women of the Dust* (1992) were in this tradition of grim and detailed documentation of lives narrowly lived in the sub-continent. Tamasha's slices of Indian life are based mostly in the villages where the ancestors of the British-Asians hail from. When set in a city (such as *House of the Sun* set in Bombay) the plays relate lives riven with prejudice, arranged marriages, a superstitious over-reliance on horoscopes, gossip and other details which serve to reassure the British-Asian that India, rural or metropolitan, is backward, economically and socially. Whilst this strategy is put to effective use in Ayub Khan-Din's *East is East* and *A Tainted Dawn* which is a series of images of Partition, Tamasha's plays cater to the need of the British-Asian to feel s/he has left behind a land of inopportunity and economic decline.[89]

Ninaz Khodaiji's *Insomnia* is a foreign play rather than a British-Asian one. Her writing was praised by critics as she set the lives of four privileged young Bombayites (now known as *Mumbaikars*) against a backdrop of the early 90s communal riots. The wasted privilege which oozed from every pore of the quartet who drink, dance and date their lives away (Gibbs 2004) reflects accurately the lives of wealthy Bombay folk of any age.

Enacting *pre-colonial history* is important as a strategy demonstrating that Indian culture was rich in terms of art, literature, music, painting and other aspects of a superior cultural production prior to its modernization and anglicization. The 2003 production of Jatinder Verma's *A Taste for Mangoes* has at its centre the colonial David Ochterlony who engages with and appreciates the lush difference that India provides him in terms of social customs. Like Richard Burton, the 19th-century cross-cultural impersonator, Ochterlony was able to fluently display an Indian *cultural performative* in dress, manners, language and sexuality. Unlike Burton, who was a spy, Ochterlony was entirely caught up in a genuine appreciation of things Indian, displaying an *ideological performative* as well.[90] Known to Indian historians as Nasir-ud-Daula, Ochterlony had a long ascendancy in a country which has seen, variously, Persian, Mongol and Turki rule in an ancient culture which is a heady mix of multiple customs. Verma's production attracted good press, as when Benedict Nightingale lamented: '[W]hat a pity imperialism, power and Victorian prejudice combined to end cross-cultural affairs like this' (2003).

Pre-colonial history in Shelley Silas's *Calcutta Kosher* attempts to document the history of the Jews in India through the slice of life of a mother and her daughters. The Jewish presence in India dates back to the 18th century, and despite

---

[89]For more on Tamasha and Tara, see in this volume, Dominic Hingorani, '*Tara Arts* and *Tamasha*: Producing Asian Performance – Two Approaches'.
[90]For a detailed exposition of linguistic, cultural and ideological performatives, see Godiwala (in Kuortti & Nyman 2006).

their acceptance in the very plural society of ancient India, few survive today, mainly due to their traditional insistence on marrying within the community. Silas's play examines the themes of tradition, harmony, kinship and preservation of racial identity. John Peter called it 'a wise, compassionate, moving play', 'a gem that glows in the dark' (2004).

Clive Bradley's *The Maharaja's Daughters* for Mehtaab Theatre Company (2002) was an historical play based on the lives of two Indian princesses brought up in England within a foreign matrix of gentility, Christianity, the suffrage movement whilst 'the Empire dies, and the world goes to war, all in a single well-appointed sitting room' (Gibbs 2002).

Writing about the Other is accomplished by a handful of Asian playwrights adept at the social and cultural codes of mainstream English culture, dis-playing a mastery of linguistic and cultural performatives. Dipak Chowdhury's *The Play* was compared to absurdism in the vein of Jean Genet (Adams 2002) whilst Thaxter called it a Pirandellian comedy about pretence and reality (2002). Ayub Khan Din's semi-autobiographical *Notes on Falling Leaves* is a stream-of-consciousness two-hander played by 'a very ordinary, working-class woman' and her cruel son who, taking advantage of her half-paralyzed senile state, relates sexual and other details which he would not normally have told her (Taylor; Nightingale 2004). Spencer and Nightingale compare the writing to Beckett's; with an added 'warmth, and a vivid eye for detail'. 'Overwhelming in its emotional impact' (2004). Tariq Ali's political anti-Labour farce *The Illustrious Corpse* (2003) is another example.

Multiculturalism in casting is a consistent feature of most Asian plays. Anu Kumar's *The Ecstasy* (2000) and *London Fields* (2004), both produced by Kali, typically utilize an intercultural method by including black, mixed-race, white and Asian characters as does much Asian theatre.

Mythmaking and Fantasy combined beautifully in Tim Supple's dexterous rendition of Salman Rushdie's fable *Haroun and the Sea of Stories* at the National Theatre in 1997. Tanika Gupta's re-working of Rabindranath Tagore's *Skeleton* and also her plays *Sanctuary* and *Inside Out* contain elements of the supernatural and magical.[91]

The British-Asian theatre voice is often *collective*, as seen in *Tamasha* ['Spectacle'] theatre company. Run by Kristine Landon-Smith and Sudha Bhuchar, it is not necessarily a forum for feminist work, but provides encouragement to fledgling Asian women writers by staging their work. In this, they can be compared to Kali Theatre Company. Tamasha's women playwrights, however, are not politicized *qua* women. Subsumed as their gender is within the matrix of race and ethnicity by the dominant culture, they write of racialized and cultural

---

[91] For more on Tanika Gupta's work see Kathleen Starck, 'They call me an "Asian writer" as well' in this volume.

concerns such as the invention of Balti cuisine and the horror of Partition. Here, feminist concerns are suppressed under the rubric of Asian. Kali theatre company, on the other hand, concerns itself with uniquely feminist themes exploring domesticity, tradition and cultural hybridity in Britain through the eyes and experience of the Asian diasporic genderized Other. Their inaugural *Song for a Sanctuary* is in the tradition of the best British theatres-of-commitment. It explores the tensions between western liberalism and Indian tradition and the clash of cultural values within which the abused and violated Asian woman can be trapped, as western feminism proves totalizing and monolithic in its complete lack of relevance for women of different (non-western) cultures. This sophisticated engagement with practical and theoretical concerns of gender makes this tiny company (founded by Rukhsana Ahmad and Rita Wolf) a splendid forum for what broadsheet reviewers often dismiss as didactic dramatized sociology.[92] The now defunct British Asian Theatre Company had also attempted to engage with Asian-feminist issues in *Anarkali* (1986). The text negotiated with the monolithic rubric 'Asian woman' under which the gendered diasporic subject is subsumed, and rendered western feminism impotent as a solution for her problems. This failure to acknowledge or take on board the concerns of women constituted within difference is a failure of what is a central twentieth-century movement to engage with the non-western other. Such theatrical performances, then, underscore the need to restructure knowledge and power to include cultural difference.

Racism and cultural tensions are once again issues which need to be presented on the stages most affected by these practices. These issues seldom form part of British-Asian fare. This is a conservative diaspora which clings solidly to its traditions, norms and *mores* which bind it ever more closely into itself. It offers the displaced and relocated subjects a supportive network and a firm foundation on which to achieve their dreams of an ever-upward social mobility. It is often the odd radical who will engage with issues such as 'coming out', radical feminism, confronting overt racism and so forth. Hanif Kureishi's film *My Beautiful Launderette* was adapted in 1990 for the stage and is a rare instance of an inter-cultural Asian gay text, like Anu Kumar's *The Ecstasy*. The larger companies, although subversive in their variously postcolonial theatres, play it increasingly safe as they are ever mindful of their funding and media response. Tara Arts' early attempt to fuse reminders of cultural violence into the 8th-century classic *Miti Ki Gaddi* was criticized by reviewers as an unneccessary political statement (BBC Radio; Listener; City Limits 1986). In contrast to Tara's early classicism, Tamasha theatre company's inaugural performance (1990) was Mulk Raj Anand's *Untouchable*, a text which brings 'home' the roots of apartheid in ancient Indian

---

[92] For a critical study of *Kali*'s first phase see my chapter in this volume, '*Kali*: Providing a Forum for British-Asian Women Playwrights'.

cultural practice. It is a provocative text as it juxtaposes an Other's race and caste-bound exclusionary practices on the stages of modern Britain which, in turn, discriminates against the very cultures from which the practice originates. This is a contemporary re-citing of the roots of the conflictual taboos which lead to miscegenation, and carries a negative valence in both cultures.

Harwant Bains's *The Fighting Kite* reflected a savage social organization actualized in systems of cruelty never practiced in the originary Indian practice of caste untouchability or 'apartheid'. These are scattered attempts to portray 'the savage socius' which articulates 'a terror without precedent [the racist skinheads/ The National Front], in comparision with which the ancient system of cruelty, the forms of primitive regimentation and punishment, are nothing' when juxtaposed against this 'barbarian [host] socius'.[93] The racism and fascism of the National Front are similarly explored in the Royal Court debut of Karim Alrawi (1986) in *A Colder Climate*. The problem of white directors directing Asian political texts which stage racial violence is succinctly stated by Lyn Gardner, who points out that the playwright seemed not to have had been given sufficient time to refine his writing as the play seemed rushed into premature production: 'If *A Colder Climate* is merely a gentle breeze instead of the whipping icy blast it might have been I'm prepared to bet the failure lies less with the playwright than the directors' (City Limits 1986). This unconscious or subconscious refusal of a culture to acknowledge and engage with the violence immigrants are exposed to in England was brought to light in 1999 with the dramatization of the Stephen Lawrence inquiry in *The Colour of Justice*. The reconstruction of the inquiry which is based wholly on court transcripts, legitimates the voice of a marginalized social group which has been silenced by dominant groups. This was also the case within theatrical discourse in which the voice of the black subject was largely elided. The black dramatization of *The Colour of Justice* put on stage, perhaps for the first time, a chilling acknowledgement that racial prejudice exists at conscious, subconscious and unconscious levels in the collective psyche of the dominant culture/s and that this needs to be rooted out in order for justice to be meted out to victims of racist violence. The meta-discursive 'act' of the Stephen Lawrence docudrama pointed to the need for both, the dominant culture, as well as British

---

[93] (See Deleuze & Guattari, [1972] 1984:189-92). The Deleuzean 'savage barbarian socius', (see below) is a typical horizontal reference to imperial texts such as *The Heart of Darkness*, mediated chronologically backwards through *The Genealogy of Morals* achieved in a typical transverse axial-link where the savage-dark of the Conrad/Freud text ('the horror') mingles subtextually with Nietzschean paranoiac madness as it inverts and repeats itself to form the foci of the Deleuze-Guattari punning schizophrenic hyperbolic: 'the (western) despotic machine', a most barbarian socius in relation to the originary practice. (Greek 'huperbole' = excess/extravagance).

theatre itself, to take on board the fact that racial prejudice has infiltrated through the practices and institutions of British society (Godiwala 1999: 54). In 2001 I wrote that British-Asian theatre's 80s attempts seem silenced by the complete absence of this issue in the 90s and that Asian theatre needs, once again, to interrogate the still imperial hierarchies and hegemonies which determine Asian lives in Britain, and respond to the everyday experience of racism and exclusion. It was heartening, therefore, to see Tanika Gupta's 2003 production *Fragile Land* explore contemporary multicultural tensions through the lives of six inner-city teenagers from Hindu, Muslim, Afghan, mixed and white backgrounds. Apart from racial tensions this complex play depicted 'not only a struggle to grow up, but also a struggle to live in an alien culture and cope with old-fashioned, tyrannical parents' (Peter 2003).

Conclusion

Much Asian theatre in Britain is performed for the 'continuation and regeneration' of the British Asian communities. It is aware of and incorporates English morphologies and traditions. It is an example of a 'living' theatre of British-Other/s which, however, ought to remain mindful of serving or becoming an institutional state apparatus which has made so much British theatre and Indian theatre (in India) so 'deadly'. The Shakespeare of the RSC often remains a mask for the dominant ideology and is used as a tool to promote the 'authentic' version of British culture and the English language at home and abroad.[94] Likewise, the cultural imports sponsored by the Government of India are often the 'deadly' remnants of fossilized artistic practice; cultural exports which cater to and exploit the foreign capitalist market. Although subsidy and patronage is a constant need, British-Asian theatres must not be 'intellectually enslaved to the theatrical establishments [and institutional apparatuses] which support them financially' (Godiwala 1999: 55) but seek to be challenging, hybrid, oppositional if need be, and constantly subvert dominant paradigms of coloniality as it formulates new stages inscribed with a valorizing alterity within which is a celebration of the fusionary encounter of the multiple texts of east and west.

Acknowledgements: Nizwar Karanj for discussions of British theatre.
Shelley King, *Tamasha* and *Tara* for 'comps' over the years.
Jatinder Verma for photographs of Tara Arts' productions.

---

[94] Also see Colin Chambers (2004), *Inside the Royal Shakespeare Company: Creativity and the Institution* where he analyzes the institutionalized racism of the RSC.

Works cited

Ahmad, Rukhsana (1993), *Song for a Sanctuary*, in *Six Plays by Black and Asian Women Writers*, (ed.) Kadija George, London: Aurora Metro Press.
Ahmad, Rukhsana, *Kali Salwar*, unpublished. Courtesy Rukhsana Ahmad.
Ali, Tariq (2003), *The Illustrious Corpse*, London: Absolute Classics.
Alrawi, Karim (1986), *A Colder Climate*, London: Methuen.
Ashcroft, Bill, Gareth Griffiths & Helen Tiffin (eds.) (1995), *The Postcolonial Studies Reader*, London: Routledge.
Bhuchar, Sudha and Kristine Landon-Smith ([1989] 1999), *Untouchable*, London: Nick Hern.
Bhuchar, Sudha and Kristine Landon-Smith ([1991] 1999), *House of the Sun*, London: Nick Hern.
Bhuchar, Sudha and Kristine Landon-Smith ([1997] 1999), *Tainted Dawn*, London: Nick Hern.
Bourdieu, Pierre (1977), *Outline of a Theory of Practice [Esquisse d'une théorie de la pratique, précédé de trois études d'ethnologie kabyle*, 1972]*, trans. Richard Nice, Cambridge: Cambridge University Press.
Brook, Peter (1968), *The Empty Space*, Harmondsworth: Penguin.
Carter, Ruth ([1992] 1999), *Women of the Dust*, London: Nick Hern.
Carter, Ruth ([1995] 1999), *A Yearning*, London: Nick Hern.
Chambers, Colin (2004), *Inside the Royal Shakespeare Company: Creativity and the Institution*, London: Routledge.
Deleuze, Gilles and Félix Guattari (1984), *Anti-Oedipus: Capitalism and Schizophrenia* Vol. 1 [*L'Anti-Oedipe*, 1972], trans. Robert Hurley, Mark Seem, and Helen R. Lane, London: Athlone Press.
Deleuze, Gilles & Félix Guattari (1986), *Kafka: Towards a Minor Literature* [*Kafka: Pour une littérature minuere*, 1975], trans. Dana Polan, Minneapolis: University of Minnesota Press.
Eyre, Richard & Nicholas Wright (2000a), *Changing Stages: A View of British Theatre in the Twentieth Century*, London: Bloomsbury.
Gilbert, Helen & Joanne Tompkins (1996), *Post-colonial Drama: Theory, Practice, Politics*, London: Routledge.
Godiwala, Dimple (1999), 'Asian Theatre in Britain', *Hard Times*, Vols. 67/68.
Godiwala, Dimple (2001), 'Hybridity/Invention/Identity: British Asian Culture and its Postcolonial Theatres', *Journal for the Study of British Cultures*, Vol.8, No.1.
Godiwala, Dimple (2003), 'Hybridised Identity as Counterdiscursive Strategy: a Genealogy of British Asian Culture and its Postcolonial Theatres', *Journal of South Asian Popular Culture*, Vol.1, No.1.

Godiwala, Dimple (2006), 'Postcolonial Desire: Mimicry, Hegemony, Identity', in *Reconstructing Hybridity*, (eds.) Joel Kuortti and Jopi Nyman, Amsterdam and NewYork: Rodopi.

Gupta, Tanika (1997), *Skeleton*, London: Faber and Faber.

Gupta, Tanika (2002), *Sanctuary*, London: Oberon.

Gupta, Tanika (2002), *Inside Out*, London: Oberon.

Hall, Stuart (1994), 'Cultural identity and diaspora', in Williams & Chrisman (eds.), *Colonial Discourse and Postcolonial Theory*, New York: Columbia University Press.

Joshi, Abhijat ([1994] 1999), *A Shaft of Sunlight*, London: Nick Hern.

Karnad, Girish (1996), *Three Plays: Naga Mandala, Hayavadana, Tughlaq*, India: Oxford University Press.

Khan-Din, Ayub (1997), *East is East*, London: Nick Hern.

Khan-Din, Ayub (1999), *Last Dance at Dum Dum*, London: Nick Hern.

Khan-Din, Ayub (2004), *Notes on Falling Leaves*, London: Nick Hern.

Khan, Naseem (1970), *The Arts Britain Ignores: The Arts of Ethnic Minorities in Britain*, London: Arts Council of Great Britain.

Kortenaar, Neil ten (1995), 'Beyond authenticity and creolization', quoted in Ania Loomba (1998), *Colonialism/ Postcolonialism*, London: Routledge.

Kumar, Anu (2002), *London Fields* (unpublished). Courtesy Anu Kumar.

Kumar, Anu, *The Ecstasy*, (unpublished). Courtesy Anu Kumar.

Pavis, Patrice (ed.) (1996), *The Intercultural Performance Reader*, London: Routledge.

Rushdie, Salman (1990), *Haroun and the Sea of Stories*, adaptation [1998] Tim Supple and David Tushingham, London: Faber and Faber.

Rushdie, Salman (1991), *Imaginary Homelands: Essays and Criticism 1981-1991*, London: Granta/ Penguin.

Silas, Shelley (2004), *Calcutta Kosher*, London: Oberon.

Sidhwa, Bapsi, *Sock 'Em With Honey*, (unpublished). Courtesy Bapsi Sidhwa and Kali Theatre Company.

Taylor, Richard Norton (1999), *The Colour of Justice*, London: Oberon.

Newspaper reviews
Source for theatre reviews: *Theatre Record*
Adams, Sarah (6 February 2002), *Time Out*.
Anon. (23 January 1986), *City Limits*.
Anon. (31 July 1986), *City Limits*.
BBC Radio London (18 January 1986).
Coveney, Michael (3 July 2003), *Daily Mail*.
Eyre, Richard (25 March 2000), 'Why British culture needs a healthy dose of élitism',*Guardian*.

Anon. (23 January 1986), *Listener*.
Gibbs, Jonathan (9 October 2002), *Time Out*.
------------------- (10 November 2004), *Time Out*.
Nightingale, Benedict (14 February 2004), *The Times*.
Peter, John (15 February 2004), *Sunday Times*.
------------- (13 April 2003), *Sunday Times*.
Spencer, Charles (5 July 2003), *Daily Telegraph*.
-------------------- (16 February 2004), *Daily Telegraph*.
Taylor, Paul (25 February 2004), *Independent*.
Thaxter, John (6 February 2002), *What's On*.
---------------- (4 June 2003), *What's On*.

Conference papers (unpublished)
Ahmad, Syed Jamil (1999), 'Contemporaneity of tradition: the case of Pala Gan and Kamala Ranir Sagar Dighi', CAT, Dhaka: 'Natyotsav'.
Panikkar, K.N. (1999), 'Sanskrit theatre style modernity', CAT, Dhaka: 'Natyotsav'.
Rahman, Ataur (1999), 'Tradition and contemporary theatre', CAT, Dhaka: 'Natyotsav'.
Saha, Nripendra (1999), 'The Bengali theatre and the heritage of Sanskrit drama', CAT, Dhaka: 'Natyotsav'.
Vatsyayan, Kapila (1999), 'Dance or movement techniques of Sanskrit theatre', CAT, Dhaka: 'Natyotsav'.
Verma, Jatinder (1997), 'Binglishing the stage: a generation of Asian theatre in England'.

Video
Khan-Din, Ayub (1999), *East is East*.
Kureishi, Hanif (1985), *My Beautiful Launderette*.

III. HISTORIES OF THEATRE COMPANIES AND ARTS VENUES

CHAPTER FIVE

TALAWA THEATRE COMPANY: THE 'LIKKLE' MATTER OF BLACK CREATIVITY AND REPRESENTATION ON THE BRITISH STAGE

VICTOR UKAEGBU

Synopsis:
This chapter deals with the history of Talawa as a seminal, black performance-making company; its visions to promote black theatre and to become a source of inspiration and creativity for black actors, writers, directors, designers, etc and its ideological determination to present 'black' and 'blackness' on the British Stage. It will interrogate the company's performance vis-à-vis its visions for British theatre. The chapter will interrogate the company's artistic and creative legacies and stylistic approaches. The discussion of productions will cover different themes, styles and periods.

Historical Background

Talawa Theatre Company began as a project based touring company providing a single, large annual production but has since developed into a middle scale producer of two or three shows a year. The company is dedicated to establishing black performance traditions in mainstream theatre, to multicultural productions and the development of black theatre audiences. Talawa was founded in 1986 by artistic director Yvonne Brewster, actors Inigo Espejel, Carmen Munroe and Mona Hammond and is the most successful Black theatre company in the UK to date. It is a non-profit theatre organisation governed by a board of trustees. It is principally funded by the Arts Council England but receives financial assistance from the Millennium Commission and the London Development Agency. From its first outing with *The Black Jacobins* in 1986, the company has had about forty different productions[95]; many of these like the topical and highly successful *The Road* (1992), *King Lear* (1994), *Othello* (1997) and *Blues For Mr. Charlie* (2004) have earned critical acclaim for the group's artistic direction and ideological approach. Talawa began as an alternative form but, in the early years of the 21st century, can be seen to be entering a crucial phase in its transformation to mainstream British theatre. The *graduation* of Talawa actors and personnel onto mainstream theatres and their successes in other performance media[96] demonstrate its growing status, influence and contributions to contemporary British theatre.

Talawa theatre company derives its cultural edge by creating and staging performances that when not contextualising and resisting cultural and historical stereotypes, reflect the contemporary experiences of black peoples. It achieves this purpose through a creative forum that draws from black and white people's historical and cultural experiences in and about the UK society. The company's stature and artistic direction are and were a logical response to the often unedifying representation of black *peoples*, the lack of creative opportunities for actors and performances of minority ethnic backgrounds and the general marginalisation of black peoples from cultural processes that prevailed at the time of its founding. As a term the name 'Talawa' is an inauspicious but powerful, rhetorical commentary

---

[95] See list of Talawa's productions at the end of this chapter

[96] *Sample of Talawa people who have found success elsewhere:*

Danny John-Jules (*Lock, Stock and Two Smoking Barrels* and *Red Dwarf*) Shango Baku (starred with Danny in *Beef No Chicken* (1996);

Late Madge Sinclair (*The Lion*, Eddie Murphy's mother in *Coming to America*)

Collette Brown (*The Lion, Holby City*)

Joanne Campbell (*Unfinished Business* (1999), *Holby City*)

Jacqueline Kington (*Unfinished Business* (1999), *Coronation Street*)

Diane Parish (*King Lear* 1994, *The Bill, Lovejoy, The Tempest, Babyfather*)

Cathy Tyson (*King Lear* 1994, *Mona Lisa, Band of Gold, Golden Girls*)

Lolita Chakrabarti (*King Lear* 1994, *Always & Everyone*)

Norman Beaton (*King Lear* 1994, lead role in *Desmond's*)

Mona Hammond (*O Babylon!* 1988, *King Lear* 1994, *Eastenders, Us Girl, Babyfather, Blood Wedding*, co-lead in *Desmond's*)

Ellen Thomas (*Teachers, Lenny Henry In Pieces*)

Lorna Gayle (*Baby Mother, Ezme and Shaz*)

Marion Bailey (*I'll Be There, All or Nothing*)

Dona Croll (*Antony and* Cleopatra 1991, *Casualty* and *Family Affairs*)

Don Warrington (*Tis Pity She's A Whore*, 1995, *Rising Damp, Manchild*)

on the very enduring qualities that have come to characterise the group, its productions, its directorial and presentations styles and actors from inception.

[Curtain call, *The Importance of Being Earnest*. Photo courtesy Yvonne Brewster]

Aims, Mission and Vision: The Name is the *Thing*

The name *Talawa* comes from the combination of a Jamaican expression, 'Tallawah, pronounced Talawa that means 'basic sense of strong, tough, goes beyond the physical to mean dangerous' and a related proverbial phrase; "Me lickle but me talawa' (Talawa website). Conceptually 'talawa' means deceptively *little* but greatly endowed, a resilient person or outfit that is committed to and is guided by a well-defined ideological framework. At the time of Talawa's founding both expressions articulated the frustrations that black *peoples* felt about their marginalisation from mainstream performances and culture. The Jamaican expression is significant for two reasons; it contextualised the ideological position of black artists in the UK of the 1980s and their struggles to validate their own historical and cultural experiences. Secondly, "Me lickle but me talawa" sets out the company's determination to contest the misrepresentation and reduction of black cultures to tokenistic gestures and the ideological necessity for this course of action. The expression is both polemical and ideological; it draws attention to historical paradigms in the struggles of black peoples against racism and its attendant violation and erasure of black histories as well as signalling the presence of a neglected but imaginative, creative pool on which to achieve its objectives. In its origin and name, the company reflects not only its ideological position and stylistic approach, it is equally unambiguous in its deployment of productions to reaching new black theatre-goers hitherto neglected by mainstream performances as well as providing an alternative theatrical voice for black people in and beside mainstream British theatre.

Talawa's aims and Mission statement are unequivocal:

To use black culture and experience to further enrich British theatre.
To provide high quality productions that reflect the significant creative role that black theatre plays within the national and international arena.
To enlarge theatre audiences from the black community' (Talawa website)

The company's emergence on the British stage is culturally and ideologically significant. Of the hundreds of theatres scattered all over the UK, Talawa is the only theatre that provides a permanent base for black actors to train and showcase their skills. Talawa is a cultural and ideological necessity but unlike alternative forms opposed to the status quo, Talawa's opposition is more about using black performers to contest stereotypes and misrepresentations and to present authentic versions of black experiences than it is about resisting and dismantling mainstream British theatre. Talawa originated as it were from the margins of UK society and performance tradition, its *alternative* agenda is a logical counterpoint to the marginalization of black cultures and experiences while its ideological purposes are to establish black theatre and to introduce black audiences into mainstream British theatre in place of their historical marginalisation and presentation as cultural *others* (Fischer-Lichte 1990, Pavis 1992, 1996; Gilbert and Tompkins 1996). Talawa's vision is two-fold; 'to be the first Black-led and Black-managed building-based theatre producing company in the UK' and 'to become a source of inspiration, learning, talent and creativity for Black writers, actors, directors, designers, musicians, the wider community and future generations' (*Talawa: Building a Home for Black Theatre*, occasional publication). Having started at a time 'the Alternative Theatre became absorbed into the Establishment by subsidy and when the theatres of 'Trevor Griffiths, John McGrath, Joint Stock, Foco Novo' (Barker 1992: 33) became mainstream and received subsidies, Talawa's eventual transformation to mainstream theatre, given the right conditions, was only a matter of time. Talawa was, in later years, noted for the brilliance and relevance of its productions to black and white audiences.

Talawa's Artistic and Creative Legacies

Talawa is much more than a theatre company, it is a cultural institution formed from the desperation of wasting black talents frustrated by the absence of a creative outlet. One of its cherished ambitions is to provide long-term creative and artistic outlets for present and future actors and theatre artists for whom the company would be the difference between professional success and failure. This ambition depended on sustainable artistic and creative foundations from which to operate and to fill its ranks. The initial challenge for Talawa was therefore artistic and structural; its survival as a company depended as much on imaginative leadership as on its effectiveness as an education and training platform whose productions and activities capture and celebrate the rhythms of life as experienced by its mainly black audiences. In other words, although the company's recruitment and promotion of black actors was inspirational and ideological, the sustenance of its artistic vision and creative output depended on the right leadership and a permanent theatre building. These were and have since remained the cornerstone of Talawa's vision as the company worked towards transforming itself into a residency or repertory company with the history, proven excellence and *presence* on which to build a lasting artistic legacy.

The survival of a theatre organisation in a performance tradition as endowed and as diverse as the UK depends on the quality of its productions and on the availability of a secure resource base. For a company of Talawa's origins and ideology, the fulfilment of its vision depends largely on its cultural distinctiveness, its relevance and a secure base from which to challenge and to comment on issues without worrying about its funding and operational capacities. The quality of a group's performances and reception may change for good or worse but as long as it has a secure base from which to re-invent, the group is more likely to endure than disappear. For Talawa, a dedicated theatre building is not only a platform for developing new materials, for improving its repertory and generating work for its actors, writers, designers etc, a building is of tremendous symbolic significance. The planned theatre will be Talawa's home, it will accommodate other touring companies, mainstream or alternative *acts* that find themselves in such predicaments that Talawa has itself been through. Such a physical structure will symbolize the company's presence as a cultural force, a visible sign of its ideological position since 'every sign is ideology' (Easthope and McGowan 1992: 41). The theatre will be the foundation for the next important phase in Talawa's vision of promoting black performances, training actors and theatre personnel and establishing a comprehensive theatrical legacy for the present and the future.

Talawa equips its actors and young talents through education networks and skills development programmes for actors, designers, writers and community theatre / outreach workers. The company's Oral History project celebrates black histories and the pioneering work of black theatre practitioners in the UK in the 1950s and 1960s. Its productions reiterate theatre's capacity to conscientize and empower people and societies everywhere (Boal 1979, Brooker 1988, Freire 1996)). Its aims may be less revolutionary than Brecht, Boal and Freire advocated but by drawing upon contemporary British history, the purposes and results are equally thought provoking. This is to the extent that even when audiences are regaled with cultural stereotypes of black people as in *Urban Afro Saxons* (2003) they are equally challenged to reject the glaring misinterpretation of black people by dominant socio-political and historical forces. This ideological emphasis is a common feature in Talawa's utilisation of performances as site for redefining and re-locating black cultures within British history and society. The company's educational goal is equally about educating its audiences and the wider society for as Paulette Randall former Artistic director said of her production, *Urban Afro Saxons*, 'people usually perceive being English as being white ...' Urban Afro Saxons sets out to peel back the different layers in order to define who we are, how we think and how we relate to one another' (Talawa website; press release, 2003). This cultural perspective defines Talawa's stylistic approaches as well as making it a platform for presenting black culture, history and experiences on the British stage.

Talawa shares its creative processes with others, giving experiential contact with theatre making and reaching out to people through its Talawa's Young People's Theatre (TYPT) initiative. The Black Writers Group provides technical skills to participants through a series of lectures and interactive workshops with established playwrights. The writers group has been sponsored mainly by Channel 4 and in part by the BBC, the Peggy Ramsay Foundation and LWT. It provides participants with useful working sessions with leading Literary Managers and other figures from film, television and radio. A Script Development Programme assists writers to work with selected dramaturges to script ideas from concept to polished draft. Through its Script-reading service Talawa supports new and young writers to develop writing careers individually or in collaboration with the company. These programmes have produced successful writers; Grant Buchanan Marshall and Biyi Bandele-Thomas and director Michael Buffong among others.

From the inspirational leadership of first Artistic director Yvonne Brewster and Paulette Randall (appointed in 2003) to the rise through the acting ranks to the appointment of Ben Thomas as acting Artistic director in 2004, Talawa has focused on the key objectives of establishing a successful black theatre, staging culturally relevant productions and promoting black actors and talents. Each leadership contributed towards the planned transition from touring to resident company but Yvonne Brewster's leadership in particular charted the artistic vision and enduring foundation on which Ben Thomas is now leading the drive for a permanent base. There is however, no doubt that with years of effective leaderships, the company's tradition for artistic excellence and the success of its performers in other media also contributed to the funding success of £2.2 million from ACE Arts Capital Grant towards the design and erection of Britain's first black-managed, permanent theatre designed to seat 250 – 270 people. Renowned black singer, actor and playwright Kwame Kwei Armah now heads a Capital Appeals Committee charged with realising this vision.

Stylistic Approaches: To Perform is to be Ideological

In its two decades of existence, Talawa has produced over 40 plays, some on its own and some in collaboration with renowned writers and other well-established theatres throughout the United Kingdom[97]. The company's collaborations with mainstream organisations were motivated by artistic and pragmatic reasons and crucial in its development as a major force in British theatre. Collaborations enriched the artistic quotient of Talawa presentations and extended the scope of its production techniques. The collaboration with mainstream venues recognized and acknowledged the company's artistic excellence, it validated its artistic vision and stylistic approach as was the case in its production of *King Lear* (1993) directed by Yvonne Brewster with Ben Thomas as King Lear, the first black actor in Britain to achieve this status since Ira Aldridge's highly acclaimed one night performance in Hull in June 1859.

King Lear was hugely successful and acknowledged as a landmark Shakespearean production for its process and cultural emphasis. Talawa left the *text* in its original form and setting, focusing instead on migration and generational differences, two subjects with wider contemporary relevance for all sections of society. In *King Lear* the company confirmed its confidence in dealing with

---

[97] *Sample of renowned collaborating Writers, Productions/Writings and Venues:*
The Road, Wole Soyinka
An Echo in the Bone, Dennis Scott; Drill Hall Arts Centre, London
The Black Jacobins, C.L.R. James
O Babylon, Derek Walcott and Galt McDermot
Beef, No Chicken, Derek Walcott
The Importance of being Earnest, Oscar Wilde; Tyne Theatre Company
The Gods Are Not to Blame, Ola Rotimi; The Merseyside Everyman Theatre
Antony and Cleopatra, King Lear, Othello; William Shakespeare
Antony and Cleopatra (first all black cast and black Director)
The Dragon Can't Dance; Theatre Royal Stratford East

challenging subjects with a significant contribution to debates surrounding family relations and cultural identities in contemporary British society. Theatre Museum recorded every aspect of the production for the National Theatre Archive while the process workshops attracted critical acclaim for according to Melba Wilson's review in *The Times Educational Supplement* (16 April, 1993), 'Talawa Educational Workshops are an indispensable part of the process of making connections between life and art, history and culture'. The collaborations marked what may be logically described as the first stage of Talawa's development as a theatre company and a unique cultural institution.

Collaborations are useful for sharing ideas and sharpening artistic focus but in Talawa's case they served the company's vision of presenting black British theatre neither exclusively as alternative nor merely as an adjunct to contemporary mainstream British theatre but as a logical part of it. The company has collaborated with writers from all over the world and staged performances in diverse locations and spaces all over the UK, from the Cochrane Theatre in London to the NIA Centre in Manchester, The Queen's Theatre Barnstaple, the Oxford Playhouse, the Theatre Royal Stratford East (*High Heel Parrotfish!* by Christopher Rodriguez, 2005), the Young Vic, the Lyric Theatre Hammersmith and the National Theatre in London, among others. Although it started as alternative theatre, by collaborating with and locating itself side-by-side established theatres, Talawa inched closer to the mainstream without losing its ideological and cultural status. The range and diversity of its performances indicate that when not confronting and challenging stereotypical misrepresentations, Talawa productions offer authentic readings of *black* and *blackness*. Its stylistic approach encourages black and white actors and artists to work together, to take a closer look at the concept of black identity and to explore the complex, multi-layered ethno-nuances and contradictions surrounding the notions of being black and British.

Talawa's stylistic approach is eclectic, the contents and contexts of productions vary and are too diverse to be tackled in exhaustive detail in this chapter. Many incorporate other performance forms of dance and music but because the group's artistic motif is to depict black experiences, productions teem with characters that are either trapped by forces of history or are exposed to the many vicissitudes of living in a socio-political setting of which they are usually the subjects of circumstances over which they have little control. Talawa's aim is not to present these characters in tragic modes, in which case they are the hapless victims of history and contemporary socio-political forces. Its aim is two-fold; to present character types that mirror society itself and secondly, to contextualize the consequences of human actions as the products of individual choices rather than depicting them as the logical or inevitable outcome of the social forces or races around the characters. This approach produces a systematic deconstruction of ordinary people contesting against social and historical forces. Talawa confronts these forces as a condition for meaningful change, provoking thought and resisting the temptation to blame society and race for every ill suffered by black people. By highlighting the potential effects of actions or docile inactivity on the larger picture, whether these be identity crisis, nationality and immigration issues, social fragmentation, youth unemployment, crime and drug-related problems, generational conflicts and angst or communication breakdown in the family, the company contextualizes theatre's educational and entertainment functions as a laboratory for interrogating social and historical conditions that Brecht (Brooker 1988) advocated. Talawa fulfils its ideological brief without being propagandist or moralistic, its performances reject a simple analysis of problems, opting instead for a more objective interrogation of the issue(s) in question. By peeling off the layers of ignorance, secrecy and misconceptions surrounding subjects such as domestic violence as in *The Prayer*, Talawa explores Granville and his mother's cowardly silence and submission to bullying without necessarily providing answers or taking sides. Overall, Talawa contextualizes performance themes as subjects but leaves decision-making to the very individuals whose responses -- denial, indifference, proactive actions or silence -- ultimately determines their fates or transforms their circumstances.

Talawa's promotion of black actors is not to the exclusion of white and Asian performers. Being acutely aware of the potential danger in presenting races in opposition to one another, its aim is not to replace one form of stereotypical misrepresentation and cultural reductionism with another but to reveal prejudices that surround race relations and the perception of people of minority backgrounds. Whatever the source and setting of their performance texts, the company tends towards politicized if not overtly political productions. Irrespective of whether 'the form of the narrative itself is complicit with the psychocultural repression' (Sue Ellen-Case (1988) cited in Gibson 1993: 8) of black people or not, this approach allows the group to contest stereotypes of black people whilst privileging black experiences and aesthetics over the dominant canons already indicted for misrepresenting black people. Consequently, textual alterations made to *source texts* (Pavis, 1992: 137) by the group as it did in *Othello* are ultimately driven by ideology, by the needs for authentic representation and the employment of performance tropes that are familiar to black audiences. The company contests mainstream theatre's hegemony and black marginalisation by not 'making the ruling order seem a 'natural' condition or as if 'there is no alternative' (Holderness 1992: 14). For Talawa, politicising performances is important in communicating to audiences the proposition that every socio-cultural condition, whether old or new, whether fronted for or by black or white sections of society for whatever reasons, demand 'justification by political argument' (Holderness 1992: 14) of the kind it is encouraging.

Other features of Talawa presentation style are the incorporation of other performance forms; dance, music, poetry, acrobatics, ritual, carnival features and the creation of *total theatre* (Schipper, 1982) in which every art form is recognised as a significant contributor to the overall performance event. This is what the company does in *High Heel Parrotfish* and *Ska Ba Day* (2005) both based on West Indian carnival tradition. Where appropriate the company uses spectacle as an aesthetic factor and leverage for communicating with audiences. While performances include symbolic communication and gestural language as in traditional African performances, Talawa also draws from well-developed narratives and plots. Its creative process frequently involves the use of open and closed workshops to generate materials and to explore ideas. According to Ben Thomas, Talawa productions are driven by artistic quality and broad-based reception, by visionary leaderships and actors committed to establishing black theatre and presence on the British stage.

Talawa Productions: Resisting Stereotypes, Contesting Misrepresentations

Talawa productions continue to grow in numbers, in artistic range and complexity, in stylistic and textual diversity, incorporating different historical periods while parading an impressive list of actors, musicians, dancers, designers and directors whose successes reveal the individual creativity, the passion and imaginations that have sustained the company through a rich vein of challenging, thought-provoking productions. Texts come from Western and black writers, from externally commissioned and from new in-house writings, re-worked or adapted

forms. Productions may be chosen for their cultural and historical relevance, for their subjects or because of their significance to black British cultures. The *texts* range from classical European and African such as *Medea in the Mirror* and *The Road* to Shakespeare's *King Lear* and *Othello*; from traditional 'well-made plays' like *An Echo in the Bone,* to contemporary works as *Urban Afro Saxons* and *Blest be the Tie.*

I. Classics to Shakespeare

[Jeffrey Kissoon and Dona Croll in *The Importance of Being Earnest.* Photo courtesy: Yvonne Brewster]

Medea in the Mirror (Talawa 1996)

Medea in the Mirror is a re-working of Euripides' Medea by Cuban writer Jose Triana and its transposition to the cultural melting pot of pre-revolutionary Cuba in which races, religions and myths of diverse origins are transmuted into a web of social and ritual practices. Triana's text is less of an adaptation than a total re-working of ritual and the myth surrounding gender relations and power structures in a contemporary setting characterized by personal insecurities, local gossip, psychiatrists or shrinks, a social scene overflowing with musicians, gambling bars, drinking salons and ritual practices. It explores gender abuses and the consequences of society's indifference to men's infidelity in a background of women's chastity and their irrational subordination to men. In the play Talawa engages with the ubiquitous themes of gender inequality and the patriarchal marginalization of women, with the intention of deconstructing the hegemonic gender relations designed to subjugate women.

In the play, Maria Candela the central character based on Euripides' Medea, is deeply and passionately in love with Julio Gutierrez for whom she has borne two sons. Julio disappears and the whole neighbourhood is looking for him:

Maria: If he dragged me on the ground, if he made me kiss the dust,
... I'll willingly do it. I'd give my blood to see him, to know what he's thinking, to know if he still feels something, however small.... (p. 58)

Through gossip Maria finds out that he is planning to marry Esperancita, daughter of wealthy Perico Piedra Fina. Maria, furious and humiliated plots her revenge. At the wedding she poisons the bride and her father but unable to bear the separation from Julio she summons him through her secret ritual:

Maria: (staring at the knife and the doll): No, not now.
Madame: You have to do it.
Doctor: Don't lose this opportunity.
Madame: Speak the familiar words.
Doctor: So that he disappears.
....
Madame: Say it at once and once and for all. (She commences an invocation) Oh spirit from Hell...put your powers at my service.... (Maria and the wax doll fall to the ground.)
(Medea in the Mirror, Triana 1996: 65)

'Julio returns but only to collect his children. Rejected a second time, Maria's final act of revenge is devastating' (Programme Note) for Jason and tragic for the helpless sons she kills in her murderous rage;

> Maria: ... a love that calls for sacrifice and hate; a love that destroys
> everything in order to begin again.... Be still. Here are my children. Let no one wake
> them. Julio is dead and they will continue to sleep forever. (A gesture to impose silence)
> My life begins, Julio. Children, my life begins.
> Maria has found herself.... (p. 68)

    Maria's recourse to ritual for personal revenge is inexcusable just as is Julio's betrayal of her, his infidelity and insensitivity.

    The production's scrutiny of the relationship between Julio and Maria reveals the collusion between men and patriarchy in sustaining gender imbalance. It interrogated Maria's jealousy and revenge in the larger context of social and gender inequity. Transposed from homogeneous Greek society where *others* stood out for their difference to the culturally heterogeneous setting of Cuba, the production explored the universal nature of jealousy and ritual, making culture irrelevant in Maria's actions. The production therefore, contextualized Maria's murderous rage and recourse to ritual as the unfortunate actions of a woman once jilted, twice betrayed and rejected by the man for whom she sacrificed everything. Through her secret ritual, Maria generated such devastating power that Julio's lame defence and Esperancita's wealth could not withstand. Her actions destabilized gender dynamics, moving real power away from Julio and Esperancita's father to herself. In a way the performance was less concerned with ritual power than with the consequences of deploying it to such devastating self-serving purpose. This is why after trying in vain to discourage Maria the chorus 'raise her on high like a trophy' (73) in the play's final act. The chorus' action is both ironic and iconic in its re-alignment of power with women. The production however, did not diminish the tragic deaths of the innocent victims; Esperancita, her father and Julio's sons although it was less critical of Maria's ritual power. In the end, it was less censorious of Maria's ritual power for the play's tragedy than it blamed society for accommodating gender inequality and its concomitant excesses.

The Road (Talawa 1992)

    Wole Soyinka's *The Road* is an African classic. It has the format of classical Greek plays in terms of duration, plot and the relentless match of incidents towards a tragic resolution but its metaphysical scope, tragic vision and characters are different. The play explores man's fascination with causality, the experiential nature of death and the nature of the transition from life to death. It centres on the actions of shadowy, charismatic Professor, disillusioned by life's unwillingness to yield its mysteries and by his life-long failure to understand the *true* meaning of life and death. Believing that the answers lie outside the Church and scholarship,

Professor sets up his laboratory in the 'AKSIDENT STORE', a shack consisting of disused car parts collected from scenes of accidents. Here he assembles an unsuspecting rabble of social rejects and criminals oblivious of their status as guinea-pigs.

Professor wants to 'cheat fear, by foreknowledge' (*The Road*, Soyinka, 1975: 227) by seeking the secret of death from his subjects at the moment they enter the liminal threshold, when they are suspended between life and death. His tampering with road signs causes accidents in the hope of meeting his subjects/victims at the very moment of death when they are neither fully human nor entirely spirit but equally both. While performing an ancestral Egungun mask Murano was knocked down by a lorry driver. Believing they had killed him and desecrated the mask, driver and mate panic and flee the scene. Professor resuscitates Murano, now deaf and dumb, secretes him away from society and makes him the central focus of his experiment in the hope that when he eventually speaks he would reveal the secret of death. Professor deliberately assembles these odd personalities; Murano the deaf-mute, Egungun masker and his personal servant; driver and motor tout Samson and Kotonu; corrupt policeman, peddler of forged licenses and motor documents, Particulars Joe; captain of thugs Say Tokyo Kid and their more respectful accomplice Chief-in-Town, etc together for the single purpose of precipitating violence amongst them. Professor's purpose and approach are ironic and tragic in the sense that both depend on him risking lives and causing deaths as a means to understanding and cheating the very death whose true meaning lies in experiencing it. By gathering the characters together in the evenings amidst heavy drinking and fighting, Professor's hope is that in the ensuing melee one of them especially Murano would unravel the mystery in the passage between life and death.

In a session of drinking and drumming to celebrate the thugs' successful attack on their opponents the usually enervated Murano puts on his Egungun mask. He is instantly possessed and transformed in the opening sequences of a death dance. The other characters realise the implications of the dance and mask but are too late to stop him. Murano has already crossed into the spirit realm where he is less susceptible to human sentiments and emotions. Professor is eager to see the performance through; experiment, events and characters collide in a cataclysmic confrontation. Prior to being smashed to death by Murano, Say Tokyo Kid's fatal stabbing is the passage for Professor who ironically experiences death without cheating it.

In *The Road* Talawa took on a very complex play regarded by many critics as one of Soyinka's most challenging for its treatment of the contiguous interaction between people and metaphysical forces. It explores complex existential issues and metaphysical concerns that African and black people everywhere are familiar with. The production functioned on the premise that: 'The Egungun masquerader is on one level an actor playing a part... that of an ancestor, but his identification with the mask, the spirit of the dead is so complete that he becomes totally possessed by it. Murano, the mute, symbolizes the suspension of death, or the transition between life and death' ('Programme Notes'). Professor's search threatened society but viewing his death merely as a stark warning for desecrating the traditional ritual order or for using the Egungun as a mere experimental prop over-simplifies Soyinka's intention. The production was more complex in rejecting simple syllogism for a problematized interrogation of the human capacity for daring and the potential consequences for venturing beyond ritual limits. In the lead role Ben Thomas captured Professor's insane ambition and philosophical austerity in large part but communicating his attempt to straddle the metaphysical-temporal divide was more of a staging constraint. This required more of the atmosphere that was only occasionally evident but never fully captured. In an interview conducted for this chapter Ben Thomas stated that Wole Soyinka himself commended his rendition of Professor as the best he had seen till then but for Talawa, it was important for audiences to contrast between Western and African consciousnesses not by way of opposition but as a matter of differences in aesthetic and ritual sensibilities. This was important for the company for although the play has significant Aristotelian features, it conveys a different tragic vision whose lessons explain black peoples' perception of the metaphysical universe.

For Talawa, it was not only important to convey the differences between classical Western and African tragic visions it was also necessary to communicate the consequences of infringing the traditional order. Such infringements lead to *peripeteia* in Greek and African tragedies alike but while they generate philosophical and status changes for Greek characters such as Oedipus, Jason, Electra or Hecuba for their African counterparts, most especially Soyinka's tragic characters, it inevitably leads to transmutation or changes in state and form, from life to death. This is the *truth* that Samson trifles with as ordinary game or plaything, that Say Tokyo Kid warns about but which Professor ignores in his quest. Unfortunately for them all, Murano and the Egungun mask are the catalytic instruments of the metaphysical forces determined to restore the traditional ritual order threatened by Professor's experiment:

Samson (*obviously slightly drunk*): Got him? A-ah, he understands the game all right. Easy as chucking an unwilling passenger into a lorry.... (*The Road,* Soyinka 1975: 224).

Say Tokyo Kid: Stop it! Stop it!.... I say stop playing along with this sacrilege
Professor (with a terrifying roar): Play!
Say Tokyo Kid: This has gone far enough (227)

In the production Talawa highlighted the African view of human wilfulness for while Samson considered his mockery of Murano and the Egungun mask as 'play', he was also complicit in a situation of which he had little understanding. Say Tokyo Kid's belated but serious warning to Professor receives the indignant command from Professor for Murano's unauthorized misappropriation of Egungun masking from its traditional collective ritual purpose to a personal context. In this unfamiliar setting the mask remained unquestionably powerful but the attempted de-mystification of death sought by Professor amounted to a blatant challenge synonymous with denuding the mask it of its ritual power and significance. Professor's actions de-stabilized safe ritual thresholds but by releasing powers beyond his control he unwittingly obliterated the margins of his own safety. He was not only guilty of sacrilege, he was equally guilty of the deaths of many road accident victims for which he is punished.

Like Murano, Professor is already closer to death than life to heed human warnings. Talawa's intention for the production was clear; it was not necessarily contesting the tragic and social visions of Western audiences but presenting another set of traditions and values that if not applying fully to black sections of UK society, are at least implicated in the worldview of some of them. The Egungun mask was therefore, a central motif for the production and in Professor and the other characters the audience glimpsed an important but significantly different perception of the black worldview. According to Nigerian-born theatre critic and expert on Soyinka plays, Kole Omotosho; 'those who watch go away with a gift, not of the Aristotelian order but of another kind of tragic benevolence: a vision of the possibility of human dare, the vision that lies beneath all human and humane achievements. Wole Soyinka's tragedies work at his level of vision' (Programme Notes).[98]

Othello (Talawa 1997)

For this production, the company adapted Shakespeare's text drawing heavily from the similarities between Othello, the Moor of Venice in 1603 and the African American General in an English translation of Austin Clarke's essay 'Orenthal and Othello' that was first published in Italian (Programme Note) to question whether the public acknowledgement of black people's accomplishment is synonymous with race equality. The production focussed on the hypocrisy surrounding race relations and challenged the conventional gaze which regards black people as inferior. With Ben Thomas in the main role, Talawa explored the public and private faces of the racism that culminated in the wilful destruction of Othello (or the General) not for any abnormality or vice but for daring to cross race lines in a

---

[98]For more on Wole Soyinka, see Zodwa Motsa, 'A Scourge of Empire: Wole Soyinka's Notorious Theatre at the Royal Court' in this volume.

deeply racist society. The production's treatment of racism was both subtle and provoking, drawing attention to the devastating effects of racism on both individuals and on society's collective psyche. It interrogated Othello's contributions to Venetian society in contradistinction to Iago whose social and military positions depended mainly on Othello's political and military stature. In presenting Othello's delusion about his personal accomplishment and public acceptance in sharp contrast to Iago's resentment and racist rage, Ben Thomas gave black audiences at least, sufficient reasons to be disappointed by Othello's assumption about his celebrity status effectively erasing race boundaries. This is where the production located Othello's hubris and the reason for his eventual destruction.

The production explored why black people like Othello failed to realise that their acceptance in predominantly white societies is temporary and comes with the caveat; for as long as you respect race barriers and abide by our rules of play and engagement. According to the 'Programme Note',

The sentiments expressed in Los Angeles [on the O.J.Simpson trial] and those voiced in Venice are verdicts of condemnation of an entire race, or tribe. The two case histories combine time and place, and they make no distinction between the African American in 1995, and the Moor, in 1603 (1997).

By drawing on historical and contemporary references, Ben Thomas' performance explored the tragic consequences that Iago's rabid jealousy and envy had on Othello and Desdemona's fates as well as revealing the disingenuous, duplicitous pretence behind the façade of racial equality and integration on one hand and the non-discriminating effects of racism on all sections of society on the other.

Yvonne Brewster's directing was insightful and thought-provoking as Thomas presented an Othello that was not only out of touch with social realities but one whose equation of his tokenistic political stature with racial integration revealed his ignorance of the temporal nature of his position within the ruling order and its contradictory capacities to build and destroy with equal passion, anyone who ventures beyond its set boundaries. Although Othello may be forgiven for thinking he was immune from racism, Talawa's intention was not to use his destruction to discourage inter-racial marriages. The production was instead, designed to probe society's collective consciousness, to questions cultural hegemony and to shatter the many pretences surrounding racial integration. While it deliberately relegated common racial elements such as skin colour and cultural hegemony, the production placed culpability for racism on both private and public spheres.

By exposing the humanity of Othello as nothing less than his white counterparts' and by indicating that his contributions to Venetian society were by far superior to those of his white accusers put together, the production exposed why and how ugly racism manages to dilute and destroy a pure emotion like love. Yvonne Brewster's interpretation suggested that Iago's jealousy and collusion with others were merely incidental and secondary to their individual actions and that Othello and Desdemona were both the victims of the same mindless racism. The production concluded that Othello's tragedy was personal and collective; personal for the unnecessary destruction of innocent lives and collective because Othello embodied the achievements and aspirations of the black race, both destroyed by the very political forces that legislate against racism while secretly condoning it. Without resorting to stereotypes it implicated official and individual indifferences to Othello's destruction while offering both a philosophical opposition and direct confrontation of racism.

King Lear (Talawa 1994)

In *King Lear* Talawa dealt with immigration, generation differences, sibling rivalries and the angst that characterizes relations between parents and their children occasionally. King Lear's abdication and transfer of power and authority to his daughters may not necessarily figure in the frame of black people's historical experiences in the UK but the potential effects that individual actions have on other people is one they are familiar with. The play is full of timeless subjects that are of relevance to all sections of society: adultery, anger, madness and delusion, wisdom, old age and aging, family feuds, power and intrigue, betrayal, inheritance, love-hate relationships between parents and children, master slave relations, illegitimacy, the marginalization of strangers by political and cultural establishments and so on.

With a mainly black cast featuring Ben Thomas as King Lear, the production experimented with power dynamics and explored existential uncertainties and insecurities beneath the masks of family respectability and political stability. Talawa used this unusually large canvas to interrogate the consequences of choices made by people in authority and the impacts these have on people within and outside normal boundaries of state. This was a departure from the usual thematic focus on the foolishness and insanity of King Lear and the upheaval following his division of his kingdom to his three daughters, not on their abilities and wisdom but on his misguided interpretation of their flattery and jostling to demonstrate their devotion and loyalty to him. Working instead on the premise that master-servant, capital-labour, and insider-stranger oppositions are determined and sustained by both human and racial decisions, the production challenged conventional views about *other* races as outsiders and questioned the actions of especially those in authority who instead of using their positions to create racial harmony use different kinds of excuses to justify racism.

Class relation was interrogated alongside related sub-themes closer to black people's experiences. The production problematized the play by linking Cordelia's tragic death with Lear's rejection of her honesty and truthfulness in the face of Regan and Goneril's falsehood, intrigue and deception. The family setting and social fragmentation on a wider level were logical platforms for the company to interrogate racism, poverty and inter-class relationships without limiting its focus or becoming overtly propagandist. The approach and resulting performance were acknowledged as a landmark in Shakespeare productions by The Theatre Museum that went on to record the entire performance for The National Theatre Archive. The casting of a black man in the title role of King Lear challenged racial stereotypes. There was a temporal, albeit dramatic reversal of roles as the cultural positions of black and white were altered and both sections viewed each other through unfamiliar sides of the cultural prism. This was the aim of the production and Ben Thomas, the first black actor in that role since Ira Aldridge in 1859 presented a very dignified Lear whose actions, although foolish, were motivated by compassion and a generosity of heart that was ennobling as much as its outcome was devastating. According to Panayev, a critic writing in the 'Programme Note', Ben Thomas' success in the role 'was not because of "his African appearance"… not the green-whites of his eyes… but that inner flame which reveal in him a first class tragedian'.

II. Contemporary Scenes: Black Diaspora and the West Indies Context

This section focuses on Diaspora concerns that affect black people outside Africa and most especially those in the UK where people of West Indian backgrounds represent the numerous African, Asian and European influences that make up the very diverse black British population irrespective of whether the informing slavery and colonising experiences came via England, France, Spain, Portugal, the US or elsewhere. These experiences reflect contextual changes and the emergence of an altogether unique cultural expression deriving from the many cultures and peoples between Africa, Europe and the US via the West Indies. The West Indies-UK connection is unique because of a long history of immigration and settlement patterns and so differs remarkably from direct immigrations from Africa. Although Talawa promotes black British theatre, occasionally its productions mirror the specific concerns of the West Indies as a microcosm of the entire black population. Such productions derive their themes and styles from West Indies performance traditions and are characterized by a greater deployment of music, humour and comedy. In a way, while many of these productions acknowledge the historical position of the West Indies, they also reflect the common historical experiences of all black peoples in slavery and colonialism on one account and their roots and cultural links with Africa on the other.

An Echo in the Bone (Talawa 1986)

Written by Dennis Scott and directed by Yvonne Brewster, this was the play's UK premiere following its successful presentation at the Second World Black and African Festival of the Arts and Culture (FESTAC' 77) in Nigeria in 1977. Set in Jamaica of 1937, the play's narrative is based on historical fiction and ritual and although the events in the play happen within a single revolution of the sun in typical Aristotelian fashion, their antecedents lie far back in history in the marginalisation of black people and deep in their bones where these echoes reside. In the play, a white estates owner has been killed and Crew, a black peasant farmer is presumed to be his murderer. Crew is missing and believed dead. His family and friends gather for a 'Nine Night' ceremony based on the belief that the spirit of a dead person returns to its home on the ninth night. 'Nine Night' is designed to persuade the soul of the dead that all is well and to send it away amidst rejoicing. Crew's circumstances echo those of black peoples in the Caribbean and anywhere where racial discriminations exist. In the ceremony the characters (and audiences) come face-to-face with two symbolic actions that echo their own material conditions; the continuing re-enactment of their own life struggles and the need to reconnect with their life forces.

The play was written at a time of racial tension in the US and UK. Talawa used it to re-acquaint its audiences with racial relations as an ageless debate that merely reduces or increases in intensity on account of incidents on local and global settings. The setting of the play in Jamaica amidst the black-white race problems of the period had very strong resonance for the entire West Indies population in the UK where, although physically removed from the harrowing experiences that slavery left on their history and culture, they are constantly reminded of these whenever and wherever they confront subtle and blatant acts of discriminations in the UK. Its content reflected an all too frequent reality but contextualizing the text around a ritual that still exists in many names in different parts of Africa drew significant attention to the links between the West Indies and Africa. For instance, such a ritual for consigning the spirit of dead members of a community to rest is a common practice in the Igbo-speaking areas of Eastern Nigeria such as Ogwa where the 'Icho Obi' (searching for the soul) ritual is performed as in the play, only in the absence of a physical body for burial.

An Echo in the Bone is a very serious play deserving of serious treatment if the significance that Dennis Scott makes of the relationship between history and contemporary present and the self-examination he sought between the races are to be captured. The Talawa production worked on a combination of stream of consciousness, symbolic representation and realism to interrogate and expose the painful realities underneath the history of black-white relationships in a landscape in which racism and injustice are implicated in the cultural and economic exploitation of black peoples and in which meaningful freedom is almost impossible in the collusion between injustice and racism. Talawa used a series of dreamlike episodes designed 'to present a panoramic view of the history of black slavery and the continued economic enslavement of the worker' ('Programme Note'). In practice, the cast of Allister Bain, Joanne Campell, Lenny Edwardes, Malcolm Frederick, Mona Hammond, Kwabena Manso, Gary McDonald, Faith Tingle, Ellen Thomas and Leo Wringer used Sue Mayes' simple but evocative design and Richard Moffatt's brilliant lighting scheme to create an emotional canvas of painful recollections and reminiscences in which members of the audience could hear and see episodes or echoes of their own personal experiences.

A significant directorial decision by Yvonne Brewster was to frame the 'Nine Night' ritual as the setting for collective and individual soul searching, for collective healing and for re-contextualizing race relations. The quality of individual performances varied but Talawa questioned ritual retreat as a viable solution to contemporary problems and contested the relevance of any ritual that fails to challenge the kind of social order that destroys the likes of Crew. Despite finger-pointing, the production was silent on who killed the white man but was very critical of maintaining the status quo especially as Crew's guilt was neither proved nor questioned but merely assumed on the basis of his colour and material circumstances. The ritual was designed to bring closure to tragedies and disturbances of the previous eight days but its hope of restoring the personal and collective peace that social conditions denied the characters was doubtful as the production directed audiences' attention to the limitations of ritual in the play's unequal racial setting. It also drew attention to the social inequalities, personal failings and racial stereotypes that condemned Crew without trial. For Talawa, the closure that Crew's family and friends sought, although personal, was hardly political. There is nothing wrong with this as the first step towards real peace and freedom. 'Nine Night' made Crew's unjustified death and unproved guilt acceptable without contesting the injustice done him, his family and entire black race. As far as the production was concerned, such rituals should frame collective political action.

[Photo courtesy: Talawa]

Urban Afro Saxons (2003)

Urban Afro Saxons was written by Patricia Elcock and Kofi Agyemang and directed by former Artistic director Paulette Randall. It was produced in association with Theatre Royal Stratford East. The play deals with the knotty, largely unresolved problem of citizenship and identity for black people trapped between determining their identity and *Britishness* through birth and naturalisation or having the political establishment and its functionaries determine it for them on the basis of race and skin colour. In its promotion brochure director Paulette Randall asked the rhetorical question that confronts every black person in the UK: 'You have the passport, you live in the country and you even have the accent but does it take more to mean you are British?' The staging of this play during Black History Month at the time of David Blunkett's controversial citizenship tests in 2003 was significant.

With music specially composed by Delroy Murray (also of *Jack and the Beanstalk*) *Urban Afro Saxons* did not only revive the painful angst and memories that haunt many black people, it brought a new twist to the very old question of what makes anyone, black or white, British. By presenting the question to everyone, the performance exposed the duplicitous practice of different rules for different people. For instance, one of the characters Tanya, white, uses historical and cultural paradigms to link long settlement, birth and cultural diversity to the notion of *Britishness* and to de-stabilize race as the sole basis for UK nationality stating:

Tanya: There was only white people round here when my Nan was growing up. ... Everyone talked the same, everyone looked the same. It's all changed now and she can't keep up .... (To Scott) it's like he said, they just get it wrong sometimes (*Urban Afro Saxons*: 70).

The production confronted the government's simplistic position and handling of nationality but by exposing assumptions surrounding the subject, it revealed a much more complex setting in which a combination of factors; cultural reductionism, stereotyping, a history of rejection, place of birth, images and flags (skinheads and union jack), institutions such as the police or national celebrations (the Jubilee and Black History Month) have unfortunately fostered a system of hegemonic relations and white cultural dominance vis-à-vis the otherness of non-white races and their marginalisation from dominant cultural process. The brilliance and effectiveness of the production as a piece of social history and contemporary debate were obvious in its exposure of so-called natural factors as in place of birth, cultural identity and skin colour as equally weak on their own on as the basis for Britishness or UK nationality and citizenship:

[Amanda and Jay of *Urban Afro Saxons*. Photo courtesy Talawa]

Dennis: I have to admit I do have some issues with the flag. Every time I see it, I remember how the skinheads used to say there ain't no black in the union jack.
Scott: Unless it's wrapped around Linford Christie. Fuck 'em. It's our flag as much as it's theirs....
Tanya: Well I am proud of the flag and I ain't some stupid skinhead.And if you're British, then it's your flag too.
Patsy: I ain't British though.
Tanya: Yes you are. You're as English as I am.
Patsy: No I ain't
Tanya: Yes you are. You was born here.
Patsy: So? Just 'cause you born in a stable, that don't make you a horse.
[...]
Dennis: have you ever been to Jamaica?
Patsy: Yes.
Dennis: And did they class you as Jamaican
Patsy: No, they kept calling me foreigner. (72 – 73)

This dialogue highlights the true complexity of this simple and apparently innocuous question of UK nationality as well as the disingenuousness of legislations surrounding it. The presentation was helped by a hugely talented cast and by its incorporation of music as a performance trope. For the characters themselves, the difficulties they encounter convincing themselves and the authorities of their British nationality is all too real despite their actions appearing occasionally to be comic and melodramatic. *Urban Afro Saxons* was very entertaining but this did not dilute or distract from the thought-provoking message about the social instability that surrounds black people caught in the turbulent whirlpool of defining their identities on the basis of one or many factors. The production made it clear that for most black people, there are more questions than answers when it comes to dealing with their identity or with immigration and nationality laws that are deliberately designed to be problematic rather than helpful.

Blest be the tie (2004)
The play was written by Dona Daley and directed by Paulette Randall as a co-production between Talawa Theatre Company and the Royal Court at the Jerwood Theatre Upstairs. Starring Ellen Thomas, Lorna Gayle and Marion Bailey *Blest Be The Tie* is a witty tale of sisterhood, friendship and of those human failings and imperfections people see in others siblings but hardly in themselves. In the play, two estranged sisters Florence and Martha (who now calls herself Cherise) have long lived apart from each other. The two are suddenly thrown together by fate but having been raised half a world apart their coming together turns out to be anything

but a happy reunion. So much has happened; Florence and Martha (Cherise) are no more than reluctant *friends* shaped by different circumstances and as such, are as different as any set of sisters can be.

[*Blest be the Tie*. Photo courtesy: Talawa]

Florence lives in a small, cramped London council flat and enjoys going to church, watching TV and hanging out with her neighbour and best pal Eunice with whom she shares a strong friendship. Florence is satisfied with her convenient, staid life that is more remarkable for its routine than for excitement. Into this apparently organised lifestyle and setting Dona Daley introduces an outsider element, Martha, whose presence threatens to drag out a far from benign past that leads both sisters through self-examination to the truth about themselves. On her own part, Martha is a successful hairdresser with her own salon in Kingston, Jamaica, a self-assured woman who has developed the habit of speaking her mind irrespective of the situation or the people involved. Similar to Grant Buchanan Marshall's *The Prayer* in its excavation of family secrets and hurts, Daley uses the contrasting characters of the two sisters as the setting and recipe for a drama characterized by subtle, deep-rooted domestic feuds and sibling rivalry. Martha's surprise visit to London with a list of complaints and well-nourished anger does not merely threaten Florence's world, it turns it upside down as old family secrets and long buried hurts come to light. Eunice, Florence's friend is not only caught between the feuding sisters she is forced to think of an exit strategy that guarantees her friend's happiness without destroying their friendship.

The theme of the play is a familiar refrain in every household, black or white where there has been parting and reunion. The production used psychological character portraits and family history to explore the personalities of the two sisters and the effects of the past on their actions following Martha's visit. Although the text consists of eleven inter-related scenes the production itself could be viewed as consisting of three main parts, (i) Florence's world before Martha's destabilising visit (ii) Florence's anxiety-ridden world in which the sisters' personal and family secrets are deconstructed and re-packaged with understanding and (iii), a tantalisingly symbolic future that is signalled without elaboration, as rich and promising with the trophy Martha leaves for Florence on her departure. Offering no ready-made answers for family feuds other than hope arising from the sisters' newfound respect for each other and the knowledge from the sisters' years apart, the play envisions a new life that accommodates both. In place of a moralising prescription, it presented a blueprint for audiences to relate to and elaborate according to their own circumstances. Florence's two worlds are inseparable and inextricably linked to the sisters' future. By revealing the sisters' true feelings as they lurched through personal hurts, life's disappointments, broken dreams and anger against each other, the production underscored the significance of communication and openness as the basis for true understanding and meaningful relationship with other people and within family settings:

Martha: I miss my sister.

Florence: I miss my sister. Eunice seem nice... I need a friend right now.... *Martha holds a tearful Florence for a moment or two.*
Martha: .... Was there with Mama.... I decide that when I get a chance I was going to do something fe meself. Be like my big sister. Dress nice. Live in a nice place. Somewhere famous.
Florence: Clapham Junction!
Martha: Well! I was going to make it....Couldn't understand. You couldn't come home to see Mama fe the very last time.
Florence: You come and see. At the junction. Always seem to trek the wrong turning. Seemed to get further away from me destination. De children come along. Another junction, mek another plan. Archie lose him job. Another junction. Another idea. Dem tek whey we house and put we here. Another junction. Nu bodder again. Getting home wasn't going to happen again. Just rest me self and satisfy.
Martha: I used to wonder. How people deh a England so long and are send back tings ... and can't come ... ?
Florence: you getting an idea. (*Beat.*) couldn't give out the whole story. The children used to read a story about Dick Whittington and him cat and how him come to London to seek him fortune.
Martha: Yu did send something like that for my two...
Florence: I used to smile and couldn't tell them that like Mr Whittington Cat, me bury de filth and was sitting on it so that dem couldn't find it. Remember how puss dig a hole before them go a toilet and cover it when dem done? Dat's what I been doing. Smelling it an hiding it. From de kids. From you. From Mama (*Blest be the Tie*: 64 – 65)

Martha carrying the burden of *acting* Florence so their mother could die in peace was the final straw in a line of family secret that needed exorcising if closure was to be achieved. Both sisters dropped the façade of courtesy, becoming more realistic and more honest about their past and present as they buried the past for the future. Like the two sisters Eunice eventually realised their need to deal with the past and that she risked destroying her friendship with Florence altogether. Florence and Martha restore their sisterly bond from which Eunice is nearly squeezed out. For the production, securing the future was as important as dealing with the past and learning from it; the performance dealt with the necessity for digging beneath outward pretences when dealing with family problems and communication breakdowns. By rocking the psychological states and comfort zones of the three characters the presentation underscored the importance of honest self-examination if characters are to obtain the therapeutic healing that their circumstances demand desperately.[99]

---

[99] For more on *Urban Afro-Saxons* and *Blest be the Tie* see Deirdre Osborne, 'The State of the Nation' in this volume.

Conclusions: A Growing Creative Platform and the tale of Talawa's Peoples

As a creative platform Talawa's artistic and stylistic influences are undoubted and increasingly evident on the British stage and beyond. In its comparatively short history, the company has had over 40 productions including a number of award-winning plays[100]. The company's productions reflect black and white people's concerns; from angst, rejection, family and societal fragmentation to the experiences of individuals caught in the rhythm and social tides of 21st century society.

According to the company itself 'under its founding artistic director Yvonne Brewster, the company achieved a reputation for producing high quality work featuring some of Britain's finest actors and writers, many of who have gone on to successful careers in theatre, television and film' (*Talawa: building a home for Black Theatre*, n.d: 3). The list includes Danny John-Jules (*Lock, Stock and Two Smoking Barrels* and *Red Dwarf*) and the irrepressible Shango Baku who starred with Danny in *Beef No Chicken* (1996); the late Madge Sinclair (Eddie Murphy's mother in *Coming to America*) and *Holby City's* Collette Brown both of who starred in the 1993 production of Talawa theatre's *The Lion*; Joanne Campbell (*Holby City*) and Jacqueline Kington (*Coronation Street*) who both starred in *Unfinished Business* (1999); Diane Parish (*The Bill, Lovejoy, Babyfather*), Cathy Tyson (*Mona Lisa, Band of Gold*) and Lolita Chakrabarti (*Always & Everyone*) all three of who were in the 1994 production of *King Lear* with the late Norman

---

[100] *List of Awards*

'Performing Arts Company of the Decade' *by The Voice* Newspaper
OBE for Services to the Arts awarded to Yvonne Brewster, Artistic Director
Best Actress awarded to all three performers; Pauline Black, Josette Bushell-Mingo and Joy Richardson by Manchester Evening News Theatre awards in the Talawa and Contact Theatre Company production of *From the Mississippi Delta*.
Best Actress awarded to Josette Bushell-Mingo by TMA Regional Theatre Awards for her performance in *From the Mississippi Delta*.
Women in the Arts Award presented to Yvonne Brewster by the Arts Council.
1993 LWT Plays on Stage Award of £16,000 for production of new play by Nigerian playwright, Biyi Bandele-Thomas.
Regional Theatre Award for Best Supporting Actor awarded to Ben Thomas for his performance of Octavius Caeser in *Antony and Cleopatra*.
LWT Plays on Stage Award to Talawa for *Resurrections* by Biyi Bandele-Thomas.
2003 Director Paulette Randall nominated for BAFTA Award.

Beaton and Mona Hammond both of whom among other credits gained international fame and acclaim with popular Television series *Desmond's* as Mr and Mrs Desmond.

Talawa's artistic base has been very exciting and rightly diverse from the beginning. Its founding members have moved on to newer challenges, making room for the company to promote newer talents. Some of these have excelled elsewhere and successfully negotiated challenges in the transition to television and screen and back whenever they have had to do so. Mona Hammond for instance went on to successful television series in *Eastenders, Us Girl,* and *Babyfather.* Dona Croll followed her performance in Talawa's *Smile Orange* in 1992 with appearances in television in *Casualty* and *Family Affairs* while from his starring role with Amanda Symond in *'Tis Pity She's A Whore* (1995) Don Warrington went on to a very successful performance in Television classic, *Rising Damp* and a starring role in BBC's *Manchild.*

Talawa's development is built on three main factors connected with its overall cultural and artistic visions. First of all, although ideological, the company's inclusive agenda caters to multicultural and intercultural productions that are neither dogmatic nor propagandist but designed to appeal across white and black audiences. This approach has been hugely successful and is demonstrated in the diverse background and quality of actors. Secondly but more importantly, the company's ideological stance on promoting black theatre on the UK stage amidst the frustrations of the black population has made it sensitive to audiences' expectations. Thirdly, as a platform for embodying the many aspirations and visions that black artists lacked for far too long, Talawa is more than a theatre company, it is also, a cultural instrument that is committed equally to its audiences as to its actors, writers, designers and other crew. The roll call of Talawa alumni that have featured and been successful in other media demonstrate the significant contributions that the company has made to British theatre as a whole in its gradual transformation to mainstream theatre.

Talawa: List of Productions and Dates

Ska Ba Day by Patricia Cumper 2005
High Heel Parrotfish by Christopher Rodriguez 2005
Abena's Stupidest Mistake by Sandra Agard 2004
Blues for Mr. Charlie 2004
Blest Be The Tie by Dona Daley April 2004
Urban Afro Saxons by Patricia Elcock and Kofi Agyemang 2003
Itsy Bitsy Spider: Anansi Steals the Wind 2003
The Key Game by Patricia Cumper 2002
Long Time No See by Grant Buchanan Marshall April - May 2002
Itsy Bitsy Spider Dec. 2001
One Love April 2001

The Prayer July 2000
Unfinished Business Oct. 1999
Coups and Calypsos Feb. 1999
Zebra Crossing 2 by Talawa Nov. 1998
Othello Oct. - Nov. 1997
Flyin' West by Pearl Cleage June 1997
Beef, No Chicken by Derek Walcott Dec. 1996 - Feb. 1997
Medea in the Mirror by Jose Triana June - July 1996
Zebra Crossing; mixed media presentations, new writings Feb.- Mar.1996
'Tis Pity She's a Whore by John Ford Nov. 1995
Maskarade by Sylvia Wynter Dec. 1994 – Jan. 1995
Resurrections by Biyi Bandele-Thomas Sept. - Oct. 1994
Mooi Street Moves Sept. 1994
King Lear Feb. - March 1994
The Lion by Michael Abbensetts Sept. - Oct. 1993
From the Mississippi Delta by Endesha Ida Mae Holland May 1993
Arawak Gold by Carmen Tipling and Ted Dwyer Dec. '92 - Jan., 1993
Necklaces by Tariq Ali 1992
The Love Space Demands by Ntozake Shange Oct. 1992
Smile Orange by Trevor Rhone April - May 1992
The Road by Wole Soyinka Feb. - Mar. 1992
Antony and Cleopatra May – June 1991
The Dragon Can't Dance by Earl Lovelace June – August 1990
The Gods Are Not to Blame by Ola Rotimi Oct. – Nov.1989
The Importance of Being Earnest by Oscar Wilde June 1988
O Babylon! The Musical by Derek Walcott Feb. – March 1988
An Echo in the Bone by Dennis Scott June – July 1986
The Black Jacobins by C.L.R. James Feb. – March 1986

Acknowledgements: I acknowledge with thanks the invaluable help I received from Talawa Theatre Company; for the unreserved use of the company's archives, websites and video library; for access to performance texts and scores, to directors' logbooks and actors' notes and most especially to Ben Thomas, Acting Artistic director and Polly Davis, Administrator for their time and for granting interviews on short notice. This chapter is dedicated to Yvonne Brewster, founding Artistic director of Talawa and to SuAndi, Artistic director Black Arts Alliance (BAA) for the inauspicious meeting with these two visionary women whose indefatigable commitment to Black arts and performances, to nurturing and promoting black artists throughout UK and beyond drew my attention initially to the richness and diversity of black British theatre.

Works Cited

Barker, Clive (1992), 'Alternative Theatre/Political Theatre' in *The Politics of Theatre and Drama,* (ed.) G. Holderness, Basingstoke & London: The Macmillan Press.

Bratton, J.S. (ed.) (1987), William Shakespeare: *King Lear,* Bristol: Bristol Classical Press.

Boal, Augusto (1979), *Theater of the Oppressed,* trans. A. Charles & Maria-Odilia McBride, London: Pluto Press.

Brooker, Peter (1988), *Bertolt Brecht: Dialectics, Poetry, Politics,* London: Croom Helm.

Daley, Dona (2004), *Blest Be the Tie,* London: Royal Court Theatre (English Stage Company limited).

Gibson, Gay Cima (1993), *Performing Women: Female Characters, Male Playwrights, and the Modern Stage,* Ithaca & London: Cornell University Press.

Holderness, Graham (ed.) (1992), *The Politics of Theatre and Drama,* London: Macmillan.

Easthope, Anthony and Kate McGowan (eds.) (1992), *A Critical and Cultural Theory Reader,* London and Buckingham: Open University Press.

Fischer-Lichte, Erika (1990), 'Staging the Foreign as Cultural Transformation' in *The Dramatic Touch of Difference: Theatre, Own and Foreign* (eds.), Erika Fischer-Lichte, Josephine Riley and Michael Gissenwehrer, Tubingen: Gunter.

Freire, Paulo (1996), *Pedagogy of the Oppressed* (revised), trans. Myra Bergman Ramos, Hammondsworth: Penguin.

Gilbert, Helen, and Joanne Tompkins (1996), *Post-colonial Drama: Theory, Practice, Politics,* London: Routledge.

Pavis, Patrice (1992), *Theatre at the Crossroads of Culture,* trans. Loren Kruger, London: Routledge.

Pavis, Patrice (1996), 'Towards a Theory of Interculturalism in Theatre?' in *The Intercultural Performance Reader* (ed.) Patrice Pavis, London: Routledge.

Pavis, Patrice (1998), 'Do we have to know who we do theatre for?', *Performance Research: On America,* Vol. 3:1.

Salgado, Gamini (ed.) (1976), William Shakespeare: *Othello,* London: Longman New Swan Shakespeare.

Schipper, Mineke (1982), 'Oral Literature and Total Theatre', *Theatre and Society in Africa,* Johannesburg: Ravan Press.

Soyinka, Wole (1975), *The Road (Collected Plays 1),* Oxford: Oxford University Press.

Speirs, Ronald (1987), *Bertolt Brecht,* Basingstoke: Macmillan.

Archives (unpublished materials)
Elcock, Patricia and Kofi Agyemang (2003), *Urban Afro Saxons,* unpublished actors' working script, Talawa Theatre Archives, London.
Scott, Dennis (1986), *An Echo in the Bone,* actors' working script, Talawa Theatre Archives, London.
Talawa Theatre Company, *Talawa: Help Build a World-class Home for Black Theatre,* n.d., n.p., Talawa Theatre Archives, London.
Triana, Jose (1996), *Medea in the Mirror,* trans. Gwynne Edwards, unpublished actors' working script, Talawa Theatre Archives, London.

Newspaper reviews
Wilson, Melba, review in *The Times Educational Supplement,* 16 April 1993.

Websites
http://www.talawa.com/

CHAPTER SIX

'A LOCAL HABITATION AND A NAME': THE DEVELOPMENT OF BLACK AND ASIAN THEATRE IN BIRMINGHAM SINCE THE 1970S

CLAIRE COCHRANE

Synopsis:
The cancellation of Behzti in December 2004 following Sikh protests, and the troubled history of Birmingham's black arts centre, the Drum, illustrate some of the difficulties surrounding attempts to establish locally-based professional Black and Asian theatre in the city. However the ongoing record of community initiatives since the 1970s, and the work of Birmingham Rep and the MAC in nurturing Black and Asian artists and audiences, are indicative of a strengthening commitment to an inclusive theatre provision which reflects the cultural diversity of the urban environment.

On 18 December 2004 some four hundred British Sikhs and their supporters gathered outside the Birmingham Repertory Theatre to protest against the production of a play by a woman dramatist from their own faith community. The ensuing violence which marked the culmination of extended and futile attempts between theatre personnel and local Sikhs to reach agreement on the setting of Gurpreet Kaur Bhatti's *Behzti* led to smashed doors and windows, injured policemen, the evacuation of over 800 terrified adults and children and ultimately the reluctant cancellation of further performances. In the midst of pre-Christmas festivities, a theatre crisis was given the unprecedented status of top story in the national media generating widespread controversy which at the time of writing still continues.

Significantly the warring factions have not polarised neatly on ethnic lines. Robust defenders of creative freedom determined to defend the rights of artists against censorship are of multiple ethnic origin. The same can be said for the advocates of communal dignity and sacred values in the face of perceived caricature and sacrilege. As sociologist Miri Song points out 'ethnicity is not uniformly important or a fundamental part of everyone's lives'. (Song 2003: 14) However for every argument in favour of a 'postethnic perspective' (Hollinger 1995 cited by Song 2003:16) which foregrounds individual and voluntary affiliation within a cultural group, there is an equally powerful case for what has been described as 'thick' ethnic or racial ties which organise collectively on behalf of the 'symbolic elements' (Cornell & Hartmann 1998 cited by Song 2003: 14-15) which define the group's identity especially in the face of apparent discrimination.

Amidst the torrent of words one phrase stood out. In the course of a debate on BBC Radio 4's arts programme *Front Row* the Sikh theatre producer Hardial Rai scorned Birmingham Rep as 'a white space' where Asian plays were infrequently and tokenistically staged. (Lawson BBC Radio 4 2004). In fact anyone who looked at the Rep's 2004-5 Door [101]programme would have seen that the art of Black, South Asian and indeed East Asian playwrights and actors was much in evidence. Prior to the staging of the Rep-produced *Behzti*, Tara Arts had presented Birmingham-born Nirjay Mahindru's *Mandragora King of India*, Yellow Earth visited for the first time with Philippe Cherbonnier's *58* which had been partly developed with Chinese and Vietnamese communities in Birmingham. In February Rani Moorthy performed her own *Curry Tales*.

Three months after the cancellation of *Behzti*, the Door was packed with a cross-cultural and cross-generational audience for the last night of Kali Theatre's potentially even more controversial production. *Bells* is a sexually-explicit play by Yasmin Whittaker Khan about the traffic in Pakistani girls brought to Britain to be exploited in 'mujra' or courtesan clubs. *Bells* alternated with *Chaos* by Azma Dar which focused on a British Muslim family torn apart by conflicting cultural and religious loyalties post 9/11. In the Rep's main house there were large Black audiences for a co-production with the National Theatre of Kwame Kwei-Armah's *Elmina's Kitchen* and Roy Williams' *Little Sweet Thing* written specially for the Eclipse Theatre initiative. Visibly there appeared to have been a seismic shift in the demographic make-up of the audience.

Nevertheless Birmingham Rep, founded in 1913, and now the longest surviving of the regional producing theatres established at the beginning of the twentieth century, is undeniably 'a white space'. There are a few employees of non-white ethnicity, but essentially all artistic, administrative and technical policy

---

[101] The name of the Rep's studio space has varied. From 1973 to 1976 it was known as the Brum. Thereafter it was known simply as the Studio until 1998 when it became the Door.

and control lie in white hands. There is, then, an anomaly within a theatre named for the city and thus representative of a city inhabited by diverse communities of people. (Cochrane 2000: 137-47)

How can a building represent all the constantly shifting and reconfiguring communities within the city? Is it necessary—given that all citizens of whatever colour or creed are effectively stake holders in civic arts institutions through the civic taxes they pay—that communities of separate identity must willy-nilly be integrated/colonised as artists or audience into the civic enterprise? Is it more desirable to prioritise benign separate development and create institutions of 'otherness' which offer cultural autonomy and reassurance? If so on what model should these be based and where and with whom should ultimate managerial and artistic control lie? There is a further hugely contentious issue for the cultural industries as a whole. What, given the inevitable economic constraints, should be given greatest priority: the aspiring professional artist or the therapeutic and creative needs of community participants?

In attempting in this chapter to survey the way Black and Asian theatre as artistic practice, access, and participation have been developed in Birmingham in the last twenty five years or so, I intend to consider these questions and offer, not definitive answers, but a number of alternative perspectives on a complex cultural landscape. This is the outcome of research still in progress into a history of activity and initiative which, except in the most prominent examples, remains hidden and unrecorded. Much more, especially about informal networks of Black and Asian performance, and short-lived attempts at professional organisation needs to be put on record.

It is also necessary to clarify my own subject position. I am a white Birmingham-born and bred historian whose early introduction to theatre was mediated through the artistic policies of white-run theatres. My schooling was under the auspices of the educational policies of a city which, in my childhood in Handsworth in the 1950s and early 60s, was only just starting to grapple with the challenge of immigration by those who considered themselves to be British subjects, but whose appearance, voices, food, clothing and traditions of worship were so alarmingly different.

Because the provision of 'a local habitation and a name' for Black and Asian performance has been a key factor in development, the main foci of my discussion will be on particular venues, associated personalities and policies and networks of influence. This is inevitably linked to the geography of the city and the relationship between sites of performance and local communities. The broad demographic divisions of the urban landscape are very clear. The old manufacturing areas in a swathe running from Handsworth to Sparkbrook in the north east of Birmingham are littered with the relics of once-prosperous factories situated uneasily beside the unfortunate products of ill-judged 1960s regeneration schemes. To drive a few miles to the comparatively untouched leafiness of the south where Birmingham University is located near the tranquil environs of the Bournville Village Trust 'model village' feels like a major migration.

What was effectively a Birmingham City Council ghettoisation policy in the 1950s, housed the majority of post-war immigrants from Commonwealth countries in 'the middle ring' of the Handsworth, Aston, Sparkbrook and Balsall Heath districts (Upton 1993: 206-208). The preponderance of manufactory to the north offered the most employment opportunity. Inevitably when recession hit in the 1970s it was these communities which suffered the most. When, in 1992 it was proposed to build what is now flagged as the only designated Black arts centre in Britain in Newtown, South Aston bordering on Handsworth, the area was considered to have one of the highest levels of social deprivation and educational under-achievement in the country. 45% of the local population was black or Asian (Birmingham City Council 1992: 12).

As an example of 1960s urban renewal, Newtown, originally Summer Lane, renamed as one of the five post-war redevelopment areas, was a bleak, unmitigated disaster. Compounding the alienating effects of poor planning, the area is bisected by an aggressive road system where concrete flyovers dominate over the needs of the pedestrian. The success in 1992 of the Birmingham City Challenge bid provided the opportunity to spend £1.4 million on a new cultural centre as part of a major, high-profile urban renewal scheme. Social and economic need was as important as artistic vision.

What became the Drum was created out of what remained of the Aston Hippodrome, an Edwardian variety theatre which declined into strip tease and finally bingo before it was abandoned in 1980. The new centre is a large, graceful, redbrick building which inhabits a tranquil street set back from the main road and opposite the magnificent Victorian Barton Arms pub. As a venue it has a flexible theatre with the capacity for 280 seats or 700 standing places. There is a large bar/café area beside an open dance space and ample provision for exhibitions, meetings and rehearsal.

There is, however, a damaging disjunction physically, between this elegant enclave and the surrounding environment; and conceptually and psychologically, between the architects of the social and artistic vision and a community where there was no tradition of accessing western-style performance venues. The Drum has had a miserable record of financial and administrative failure which is beyond the scope of this chapter to explore in detail. But unlike the other two key venues I intend to discuss, Birmingham Rep and the MAC (Midlands Arts Centre) the Drum is figuratively speaking built on the relics of other shifting locations. That instability is emblematic of the tangled history of attempts to create black-led artistic autonomy.

Birmingham Rep also has had to contend with the ghost of another building and location, but largely because in its day the 'Old Rep' was one of the most famous regional theatres in the Britain. The much-enlarged 'new' Birmingham Rep was built in 1971 as a monument to civic pride in what for decades had been envisaged as an ambitious civic centre on Broad Street. With the opening literally next door of the multi-million pound International Convention Centre in 1991, the location on Centenary Square became the most dominant in the City (Cochrane 2003: 135).

High-profile buildings (and the Drum also comes into this category) and community outreach do not usually sit comfortably together and the Rep has had a long, difficult-enough battle to attract audiences from the old indigenous Birmingham population let alone the new plural population. The challenge for so-called 'white spaces' is to make non-white audiences feel comfortable. A Black-Caribbean man interviewed for a 2000 ACE research report on ethnic minorities and the arts described the problem in graphic terms 'It's like a dalmation with five black spots in the audience'. (Jermyn & Desai 2000: 60) An Asian interviewed in 1993 as part of the research into Black and Asian attitudes to the arts in Birmingham described the considerable discomfiture felt as the only Asian in the audience for a Rep production of *The Merchant of Venice*. (Harris Research Centre 1993: 30)

The third venue, the MAC (Midlands Arts Centre) is sited in a park a mile or so south of the city centre. One side of Cannon Hill Park opposite Edgbaston cricket ground is firmly located in the area associated since the nineteenth century with the homes of the civic and academic elite. The other side of the park, however, borders Balsall Heath, notorious for decades for its slum housing and red light district. As Chris Upton points out in his history of Birmingham, in the 90s Asian culture has transformed the shopping streets of both Balsall Heath and Sparkbrook with distinctive garment and jewellery shops, Halal butchers and Bangladeshi and Pakistani restaurants. (Upton 1993: 209) On fine days throughout the year the park is thronged with young people and families from the different communities, many of whom wander into the MAC. Also of course the cricket ground is a natural point of diverse convergence.

The Midlands Arts Centre for Young People was established in 1963 with the aim of making 'culture and cultural activities' an integral part of young people's educational experience. Virtually monochrome white, undeniably middle class and with more than a hint of cultural patronage in its early years, the priority given to the enjoyment of, and participation in, the creative and expressive arts made it a pioneering project. Now facilitating access to the creative arts for all generations, it is one of the largest organisations of its kind in the UK with more than 500,000 visits in 2003. It has also evolved into the most effortlessly multi-cultural of all the venues under discussion. In 1990 SAMPAD, which is a development agency regionally and nationally for South Asian arts, began to use the MAC as its administrative base. Founded by Indian-born dance specialist Piali Ray, SAMPAD promotes a range of artforms originating in India, Pakistan, Bangladesh and Sri Lanka.

Birmingham is the second largest city in the UK and at the 2001 Census had a total population of 977,099. Big, yes, for Britain, but much smaller than London. Inner London alone has a 2 million- plus hugely diverse population. However by 2011 demographic trends suggest that Birmingham will become Britain's first multi-cultural city.[102] In 2001 70% of Birmingham's population was categorised as white although this included Irish and 'other' ethnicity. The national and regional average was about 90%. Almost 20% of Birmingham's population was from one of the Asian groups with those of Pakistani ethnic origin in the majority. About 6% were designated Black or Black British with the Black Caribbeans in the majority. 2.9% were of 'mixed' (or more sensitively 'dual heritage') background so it was possible to see population growth based on inter-ethnic alliances. (http://www.birmingham.gov.uk/GenerateContent?CONTENT_ITEM_ID=729&C ON)

For the purposes of this discussion it is worth noting that the statistical dominance of the Asian community does not date back very far into the twentieth century. The first wave of post-war non-white immigration into Birmingham was largely from the Caribbean. In the 1970s and 80s it was within this community that most of the grass-roots arts activity was to be found. It is important also to differentiate much more carefully amongst national/ethnic origins. There are of course major language differences which include not only the range of distinctive South Asian languages, but even the versions of English spoken in the Caribbean islands. There are significant economic and social differences which are again beyond the obvious class divisions of affluent Indian doctor and Bangladeshi waiter. As Malcolm Dick has pointed out the Caribbean islands have different traditions, cultures and outlooks. Inevitably this impacts on the capacity to access theatre as audience or artist and the resultant attitudes and expectations. (Dick in Grosvenor, McLean & Roberts 2000: 38)

The life stories of three people who were born outside Britain and have in some way influenced the record of theatre in Birmingham will serve to illustrate the distinct differences in background as well as some common concerns. Tyrone Huggins, the actor, writer and director who ultimately became a Board member at Birmingham Rep and, at the time of writing, sits on the West Midlands Regional Council of Arts Council England, was born in St Kitts and arrived in Birmingham

---

[102] This is controversial because there are other contenders for the prospective title like Leicester and Bradford. However sociologist Tahir Abbas, amongst others, has calculated that by 2011 non-white communities in Birmingham may reach 50%

in the early 1960s. His father worked as a welder while initially the family shared accommodation with other black families in one of the big old houses in the rapidly changing Handsworth. His encounter at school with a dynamic drama teacher who turned him on to a completely eclectic diet of theatre is a familiar factor in many actors' lives. He also went on to acquire a degree in metallurgy. But, as he told the 2001 Eclipse Conference on combating racism in theatre, the other familiar minority ethnic experience of inadequate support structures to develop Black theatre companies and effective institutional racism on a more personal level, came later. (Huggins recorded in Arts Council England 2002: 45-50) He has just decided to dissolve his company Theatre of Darkness.

Bob Ramdhanie, however, one of the pivotal figures in the development of grass roots arts in Birmingham, arrived in Handsworth via a completely different life trajectory. He described his childhood in Trinidad: 'you were encouraged to respect each other, value time and education and always believe in yourself' (Ramdhanie 1994: 50). Despatched to Britain to obtain the necessary qualifications to fulfil the family expectations of an elite career he graduated from Sheffield University with a degree in engineering. In 1977, however, he arrived in Handsworth to a life-changing job as a senior officer and first black appointment in the West Midlands Probation Service. He went on to found Kokuma Dance Theatre Company and Black Voices.

Theatre director, filmmaker and multi-media artist, Pervaiz Khan whose father had served in the British and Pakistani army came to England, initially to London, as an infant from the Mirpur District of Kashmir. At primary school in Birmingham's Sparkbrook district, he was the only Asian in a thoroughly multicultural class of children. At secondary school, in the context of Enoch Powell's anti-immigration rhetoric, he suffered the worst kind of peer-group racist abuse This was exacerbated by the failure of teachers to understand ambitious young Asians who wanted to be more than factory workers like their parents (*Birmingham Post*: 2000). Wholly committed to Birmingham as his home, in 1992 Khan served as part of the consultancy team on the creation of an Asian, Caribbean and African Arts Strategy for West Midlands Arts. Together with Afro-Caribbean actor Michael Aduwali, he currently directs Duende theatre company predicated on a belief in the widest possible definition of 'black'.

Arguably it was through the social needs of the growing numbers of young people from migrant families that the first initiatives towards establishing performance opportunity together with spaces for performance, began to emerge in the early 1970s. In 1973, the year the first black actor, Nigerian Olu Jacobs, performed on the main stage of Birmingham Rep, the Rep's studio space, the 'Brum', began to play host to performances by the newly-formed Birmingham Youth Theatre, a relationship which continued until the mid-1980s.

Founded by two locally-based white school teachers, Derek Nicholls and Ray Speakman, the group rapidly began to diversify with black teenagers joining to work on a series of plays written by the two leaders on issues relevant to their lives. In 1977 the dilemmas of young Anglo-Muslim children of *East is East*-style 'mixed' marriages encountered by Speakman in the classroom stimulated the jointly-authored *The Seed*, the first adult play performed in the Studio by a professional company which included the Indian actor Darien Angadi, and Renu Setna, the Pakistani actor well-known in the television soap opera *Crossroads* (Cochrane 2003: 90).

That same year over in Handsworth, Bob Ramdhanie provoked consternation amongst his managers by the insistence, just nine months into his post, that purchasing a building for a cultural centre to enable alienated and truculent young blacks access to the creative and therapeutic power of the arts might be an effective strategy to turn them away from criminality. As he later put it 'what galvanised me into community development, neighbourhood programmes and the use of arts in our daily lives, was the witnessing of a process which marginalised many and which orchestrated a system of self doubt and self denial' (Ramdhanie 1994: 50).

The Handsworth Cultural Centre, funded by the Probationary Service, and one of the first ventures of its kind in the UK, was launched in 1978 as an experiment in working with the local community as well as offenders and potential offenders. The Centre was housed in a large, rather elegant building not far from Handsworth Park which would become in 1984, the location for the Handsworth Carnival. The Cultural Centre offered workshops and training in a variety of art forms and promoted performances in collaboration with other venues. Importantly there was no stigma attached to being a Probation Service client. Everyone using the Centre as participant or audience was issued with a pass so that both participants and audience were 'normalised'. The aim was to offer 'creative channels so that its members could experience for themselves new opportunities and visions' (Ramdhanie 1994: 49).

The Centre persisted in its work even after the Handsworth riot of 1981. Ramdhanie's next move was to find a larger space for exhibitions, theatre, dance and music performance. A disused 1930s' cinema on the Moseley Road in Basall Heath which was later used to show Asian films, was converted in 1983 to the CAVE (Community And Village Entertainment). Again financed by the Probation Service, this second location was to benefit from the relaxed bohemianism to be found at the interface between Balsall Heath and the traditional arts-oriented Moseley. The 120 seat venue rapidly became a great success regularly selling out for professional shows, community performance and popular evenings of local home-made entertainment. To the suggestion that both the Cave and the Cultural Centre had the potentially negative effect of linking black people and art to crime, Ramdhanie's response was that this was a white perception of black creative work within the criminal justice system. The deeper-rooted problem also lies in the unacknowledged influence of crude stereotypes about Black people and criminality (Song 2003: 35).

What was of particular significance, however, was a much more fluid approach to art-form boundaries as well as the boundaries between amateur and professional, and education and recreation. A theatrical event at the CAVE might well be a formal text-based play about the Black South African experience by Athol Fugard performed by visiting professional actors. But dance and music were also part of a programme which presented itself unashamedly as entertainment as well as exciting art.

At the Midlands Arts Centre—by 1979 identifying minority ethnic arts as a developmental goal—music and dance which reflected popular or culturally specific forms became increasingly powerful instruments of integration. Derek Nicholls became Centre Director in 1980, thus extending and building on the philosophy behind the intercultural success of the Birmingham Youth Theatre which by then had two homes: the Rep and the Centre which had become its operational base. A steel band, the Maestros led initially by Trinidadian Roy Jacob for Black Caribbean youngsters was a phenomenal success which eventually attracted white players and audiences. By 1984 the Centre had even set up its own steel pan manufactory to keep up with the demand for playable pans. Break dance was introduced in 1983 with several local break dance crews encouraged to rehearse, share skills, perform and effectively compete with each other. Specialised Indo/Pakistani dance classes including Kathak and Bharatnatyam became a regular feature of the formal education programme. Piali Ray led an Indian folk dance troupe, *Natyam*, using students from her weekly classes. Kathak dancer Nahid Siddiqui was not only a resident tutor, but also performed in her own right as did Bharatanatyam dancer Chitralekar Bolar.

At the Rep, when a black actor appeared only rarely on a 'need to cast' basis, the annual/biannual Studio performances by the Birmingham Youth Theatre signalled other possibilities. As the Arts Centre's 1984 Annual Report stated, BYT's actors were 'from inner city districts as much as from the suburbs; they are black as well as white, unemployed and in full-time education. They appeal to audiences as diverse in composition as their own' (Canon Hill Trust 1984: 1-18). At a time when there were few training opportunities for black and Asian actors nationwide, the BYT produced actors of the calibre of Adrian Lester, Joe Dixon and Lorna Laidlaw, and writers Roy Mitchell and Nirjay Mahindru.

The Arts Centre had always presented visiting professional theatre companies since its inception, but by the 1980s there was a more proactive policy of hosting the work of the emerging black and Asian companies which were beginning to tour nationally. During the 1982-3 season Tara Arts presented Jatinder Verma's *The Lion's Raj* while Black Theatre Co-operative came with Edgar White's *Trinity*.

The South African artist Soyikwa performed in *Egoli*. The Centre also went into partnership with the Handsworth Cultural Centre to promote the visiting Little Carib Theatre of Trinidad. The following season Black Theatre Co-operative confirmed the Arts Centre as its major regional base coming with two shows: Edgar White's *The Nine Night* and Sam Shepherd's *Tooth of Crime*. The Company returned with Frank McField's *No Place to be Nice* while Tara Arts presented Shudraka's *Miti Ki Gadi*.

However occasional visiting theatre companies and several hundred happy young people break-dancing, steel-banding and learning complex Indo/Pakistani dance forms did not, of course, amount to a thriving locally-based professional arts culture for Black and Asian artists. Neither, pace Ramdhanie, was it possible to ameliorate sufficiently the simmering tensions which erupted in the Handsworth riots on 9 September 1985. The two-day confrontation between black youths and the police at Aston Cross led to extensive rioting and looting in the Lozells area. Ironically Asian shopkeepers suffered the most destruction.

'A Different Reality,' the report commissioned by the West Midlands County Council damned Birmingham as 'the capital of racial discrimination in Britain'. Abuses included an 'apartheid' system where officials in the Department of Health and Social Security exchanged files with the police to check on blacks who signed on the dole. Discrimination was rife amongst teachers and employers. Firms working on inner-city housing projects did not employ local black people and black business men were not given a share in contracts. The Report stated firmly 'In 1986 black people in Birmingham are saying that they are not alien, they are not part of an undesirable chunk of surplus labour to be eradicated. They are not a problem as depicted by the Government and the media, and they will not accept anything less than equal treatment, justice and control of their own destiny' (*Guardian* 1986).

Zygmunt Bauman has written powerfully about the way all societies 'make strangers if the strangers are the people who do not fit the cognitive, moral or aesthetic map of the world'. Each society produces strangers in 'its own inimitable way'.

If they, therefore, by their sheer presence, make obscure what ought to be transparent , confuse what ought to be a straightforward recipe for action, and /or prevent the satisfaction of from being fully satisfying, pollute the joy with anxiety...if...they befog and eclipse the boundary lines which ought to be clearly seen; if, having done all this they gestate uncertainty, which in its turn breeds the discomfort of feeling lost—then each society produces such strangers (Bauman in Werbner & Modood 1997: 46).

What had happened in Birmingham on a micro level reflected the macro situation nationwide. People had come to Birmingham, at least initially, assuming familiar rights but had been made strangers for all the reasons Bauman posits above. A lot was to change after 1985, but even as the *Behzhti* riots demonstrate, the 'strangers' still have the capacity, 'to confuse what ought to be a straightforward recipe for action'.

It seems obvious, given that riots also took place in Brixton, Toxteth and Peckham a few weeks after Handsworth, that the Arts and Ethnic Minorities Action Plan launched by the Arts Council in February 1986, was in direct response to 'grave social and cultural problems' (Arts Council 1986) manifested in these urban disturbances. Naseem Khan's seminal 1976 report 'The Arts Britain Ignores' warning that valuable arts activity amongst minority ethnic communities was doomed to wither due to lack of resources and adequate support structures, had provoked some response in the form of the national Minority Arts Advisory Service (MAAS) set up in the immediate aftermath of publication. But substantive action had been desultory to say the least.

The 1992 'Asian Caribbean and African Arts Strategy' consultation document commissioned by West Midlands Arts Regional Arts Board (WMA) at a time of major structural change, acknowledged the extent of WMA's contribution to developments in the region (Qnun Ltd. 1992). A decade earlier the West Midlands Ethnic Minority Arts Service (WMEMAS) set up an office at Holyhead School/Community Centre in Handsworth. Ethnic Arts Co-ordinator Laxmi Jamdagni worked with a designated WMA Community Arts Assistant Jane Wilson to advance the work of what was an umbrella organisation offering support and advice. At that point the extent of the direct financial support amounted to about £25,000.[103]

In truth these were chilly times under Margaret Thatcher's government when there was a real fear that she might seek to get rid of public funding for the arts altogether. The 1984 National Arts Strategy *The Glory of the Garden* was very much an iron fist in a flower-scented glove, insisting on adherence to market values as well as more community and educational outreach. But it took two years (and the riots) for the requirement in the strategy to consider the work of ethnic minority artists and arts organisations to be made an urgent priority. Just three months before Secretary General Luke Rittner sent out the letter of instruction to the Regional Arts Associations, he and other key figures in the Arts Council were criticised for not attending personally the Black Artists, White Institutions Conference held in London in November 1985.

As Diane Abbott, soon to become Britain's first black woman MP, told the conference it was important that Black British artists should understand the workings of White institutions. It was necessary to be wary of the 'gate keeper'

---

[103] Details of these initiatives and consultations including the action plan cited above are recorded in various WMA correspondence to be found in Birmingham City Archives in a file marked 'Black Theatre Development 1979-1988' MS 1620

syndrome where predominantly white arts officers acted as buffers between artists and the funders and decision makers. Then a writer and academic, Colin Prescod argued the necessity of 'awakening' out of the cultural, ideological and economic ghetto which had placed black artists in a subordinate position. Succumbing to an internal definition of themselves as 'other' meant that in negotiations with white gate keepers of white institutions (however well-intentioned) meant a social transaction where all the power lay in white hands (Smith 1985).

The flurry of activity in Birmingham in late 1985 and through 1986 resulted in a strengthened WMA support base through the appointment of principal drama officer Alan Rivett with a particular interest in developing black theatre. He in turn mentored a new black trainee officer, Nigerian Yomi Babayemi, Hugh Edwards (aka Black Caribbean stand-up comedian John Simmit) was appointed as a trainee officer in marketing. The only two local black theatre companies which were identified: *Dark Movers* and *Black Ebony* (which was white-led) were consulted along with WMEMAS, but neither were considered professional or indeed strong enough to sustain a major new venture (CAVE 1986). The only black 'institution' in Birmingham which could conceivably offer a base for a focused theatre initiative was the CAVE and that of course existed within the much more encumbered structure of the Probation Service.

The problem of growing black and Asian companies locally, was and remains compounded by the fact that most artists who wish to organise and develop independently, function most successfully in London. Not only, as we have seen, does the huge population of London include the largest proportion by far of ethnically-diverse communities, but the capital has long had a tradition of small-scale 'other' theatres and venues. The companies coming to the Birmingham venues in the 1980s were, on the whole, London-based. The theatre experience and skills of Don Kinch were imported to Birmingham where initially he was funded by WMA to work with the *Dark Movers* group.

Kinch, a Barbadian-born teacher and writer who had founded the London-based Afro-Caribbean company Staunch Poets and Players some seven years previously, was installed as animateur at the CAVE in June 1986 jointly funded by WMA and the Probation Service. Third Dimension, the company which Kinch assembled at the CAVE in the hope of creating a focal point for black theatre in Birmingham and the West Midlands, came into existence with great optimism that locally-based practitioners could become fully professional.

When Two Shifts Meet, the first play by the fledgling company, went right to the heart of the dreams and disappointments experienced by those who left the Caribbean to come to England in the 1940s. The title refers to the different shifts of black workers who shared housing, rooms and beds literally on the basis of alternating patterns of work. Through the story of the central character, Benjy, a soldier in the British army who comes to England with his wife and child, the play moves from the 1940s to the 1960s to explore the emotional and psychological consequences of uprooting and replanting. The twelve-strong cast included poets and singers coming together to create a ritual drama fused with song and dance, poetic prose and poetry.

What Kinch wanted was to inculcate a range of performance skills in music, poetry, dance and physical theatre associated with the black cultural tradition. Part of the programme at the CAVE was a series of training workshops and performances. For many radical black artists that meant not just drawing on the Caribbean experience but identifying very directly with African and Afro-American performance traditions. The Barbadian Theatre Company, Stage One performed for an unprecedented three nights at the CAVE in August 1986, while their director Earl Warner conducted training workshops. Part of the overall vision was to invite other Caribbean, African and American practitioners to boost the Birmingham enterprise.

When Two Shifts Meet was a great success playing to enthusiastic audiences at the CAVE and the Rep Studio. But as Kinch himself conceded, in a report written in December 1987, the second production, *Carnival Fire,* was less successful even though there was now more funding from other sources and the company was attracting new writing, directorial, administrative and technical skills. As Kinch prepared to detach himself from the company to extend the project elsewhere, it had become clear that a major problem was the lack of a permanently available rehearsal and development space (Kinch report in Black Theatre Development File 1979-1988: 1987).

The fault line running through the whole enterprise was the role and function of the CAVE and its work in the community in relation to the Probation Service. Priorities clashed in the explosive personalities of Don Kinch himself, and Hermin McIntosh, community arts worker, administrator and dance officer, who became manager of the CAVE in October 1986 (McIntosh 1990). In early 1987, Kinch moved the administrative base of Third Dimension to another Probation Service property, while still using the CAVE for rehearsals and performance. A key bone of contention was the lack of clarity over whether the CAVE's primary aim was to nurture community arts or serve as a showcase for established artists imported from outside the region.

What was also obvious, however, as Kinch pointed out, was that the other mainstream Birmingham venues were increasingly offering dynamic performance opportunities to Black companies. In the autumn of 1989 when Kinch orchestrated Kajoyo '89, a celebration of black arts hosted in venues across the city, the Rep was vigorously promoting work focused on the Afro-Caribbean and Asian experience in both its main house and Studio spaces. *Heartlanders*, performed on the main stage by some 300 local people drawn from all the communities, was written by three locally-based playwrights David Edgar, Stephen Bill and Anne

Devlin. Three narrative strands of encounter and convergence were woven together in a journey through Birmingham which emphasised cultural diversity. This was followed by a brilliantly-coloured, sun-soaked Caribbean-set production of *Twelfth Night* where the entire cast of characters apart from Viola and Sir Andrew Auguecheek were black. In a parallel programme in the Studio, there was a plethora of black companies and black themes including as part of Kajoyo, the Soweto-based company Bahumutsi presenting *Bring Back the Drum*, while Staunch Poets and Players staged a 'folklore parable' *Changing the Silence*.

While small local initiatives were attempting to launch a separate black-led initiative, professional black artists were being vigorously dragged out of the ghetto and into the Birmingham mainstream in a hitherto wholly unprecedented way. The artistic leadership of Birmingham Rep had changed significantly. In the 1985-6 the year Derek Nicholls was invited to become Associate Director at the Rep, the first black company Temba came to the Studio with Nigel Moffat's *Mamma Decembra* followed by Foco Novo playing an adaptation of Gorky's *The Lower Depths* by Tunde Ikoli. The arrival of John Adams as the new Artistic Director in 1987, meant a deliberate policy of bringing in small locally-based companies to the Studio, and extending the regular appearances of visiting black companies which included Tara Arts and Staunch Poets and Players (Cochrane 2003: 127).

For the first time programming also offered more substantive opportunities to black actors on the main stage. Admittedly some plays chosen were of white authorial origin like stage adaptations of Harper Lee's *To Kill a Mocking Bird* and Steinbeck's *Of Mice and Men* which presented black characters as subordinate or victims in some way. But actors like Tyrone Huggins, who was praised for his performance as the crippled farm hand Crooks in *Of Mice and Men*, could get noticed. In his last season in 1992, however, Adams presented the world première of *Biko*, a chamber opera composed by Pritti Paintal about the black South African activist, which attracted an audience drawn from the elite of all Birmingham's communities. Adams' final production as Artistic Director on the main stage was the European première of Derek Walcott's Trinidad-set *The Last Carnival* which placed white characters and black characters, and thus actors, in narrative equilibrium (Cochrane 2003: 148-9).

Adams and his associate directors, Gwenda Hughes and Anthony Clark, subscribed enthusiastically to a controversial policy which made the Rep one of the leading regional proponents of integrated or so-called 'colour blind' casting. Access suddenly opened up to the entire English classical canon as well as modern plays. On the level of simple transposition, it was manifested in *Twelfth Night*. In 1988, Joe Dixon played the Theseus/Oberon double in *A Midsummer Night's Dream*. Much more disruptive of critical and aesthetic assumptions were black actors playing major roles in Restoration or eighteenth century comedy. There was also a critical kerfuffle when Gwenda Hughes cast black actors in such classic white northern sagas as *Hobson's Choice* and *When We Are Married* (Cochrane 2003: 141-2). This was not uncontroversial in the black artistic community. The director of Talawa, Yvonne Brewster, who had staged an all-black *The Importance of Being Earnest* disliked casting that 'makes nonsense of life' and singled out the casting of black and white actors, Jude Akuwudike and Michael Bertenshaw as brothers in Adams' 1990 production of Vanbrugh's *The Relapse* (Brewster-Billington interview, 'The Colour of Saying', *Guardian* 1990). Discussing integrated casting in 1993 in the light of his own transposition and reinvention of European classical drama for an Asian setting, Jatinder Verma was clear that he did not want to 'mask Blackness'. This he claimed was to deny 'the particularities of ourselves... I cannot ignore my colour in modern Britain, no more than my audiences can. And, in any case to do so would be to deny what makes me human' (Verma in Shank 1993: 58).

The counter argument from John Adams was to insist on a policy in Birmingham which reflected the multi-racial pluralism of the region he served and which he hoped—naively as it turned out—would attract more representative audiences. The policy also meant that a regional theatre programme, typically based in a certain kind of English repertoire, could go on staging the same texts by mediating the cultural heritage of the 'old' English *through* and *to* the 'new' English. Black and Asian actors educated in the English literary tradition could enjoy playing roles which they had been encouraged to admire, but previously only at a distance.

An artistic policy based on challenging 'the figment of pigment' (Horowitz 1971 cited in Stone and Dennis 2003: 33) i.e. that racial categorisation is no more than 'an arbitrary grouping of dissimilar people based on phenotypical differences such as skin colour and hair type' (Song 2003: 10) is clearly one way of essaying a therapeutic hybridity in theatre. The policy of integrated casting continued beyond Adams and is now widely practised albeit more cautiously. The problem, however, lies in the perception that it is yet another way of assimilating and appropriating and denying other kinds of cultural heritage.

Third Dimension and ultimately WMEMAS disappeared. Even, in a move now condemned by artists, the CAVE was closed long before the Drum was remotely a viable alternative. Ironically the Rep under John Adams and his successor Bill Alexander went through major financial crises which threatened their survival. (Cochrane 2003: 139-40, 176-201). To a lesser extent so did the MAC. But both organisations were rescued by the City Council and the Arts Council. The 1992 WMA Strategy document commented sharply on the disparity between black and Asian enterprises and their peer White organisations in this respect. Black organisations 'have been able to go so far and then get stuck...they have been unable to access resources to grow... It leads to the harsh but essentially accurate perception voiced to us: 'Asian, Caribbean and the African arts organisations have inferior status because few if any are untouchable—you can lose WMEMAS but not the MAC, African People's Theatre[104] but not the Belgrade'(Qnun 1992: 24-5).

As other 1990s' consultation documents demonstrate, attention began to shift to the issue of audiences without whom, of course, no venue can survive. At the Rep artistic relationships continued to strengthen. Key black actors like Jeffery Kissoon and Rakie Ayola became very familiar especially in classical drama. Kissoon, designated an RSC-style Associate Artist, played Othello, Prospero and Macbeth. He and Ayola were paired as Mirabel and Millimant in Congreve's *The Way of the World*. Ayola played Ariel and Viola. Cathy Tyson was cast as Portia. Audiences in general, however, were poor.

No amount of artistic success could attract sufficient audiences of any colour. In 1994 Gwenda Hughes' production of *Once On This Island*, an exuberant musical set in the French Antilles starring black American rock star P.P.Arnold and Black British Clive Rowe played to thin audiences in Birmingham. It transferred to the Royalty Theatre in London where it won an Olivier Award as Best New Musical. In 2000, Indhu Rubasingham directed Peter Oswald's adaptation of *The Ramayana* with a multi-cultural cast choreographed by Piali Ray. Attempts to attract a large South Asian audience failed in Birmingham. At the National Theatre it played to packed houses.

The Studio/Door, however saw a fruitful artist-audience relationship forged with Tamasha Theatre Company which began in 1994 with Abhijat Joshi's *A Shaft of Sunlight*. Ayub Khan Din's *East is East* was premièred in 1996. The Bollywood spoof *Fourteen Songs, Two Weddings and a Funeral* not only packed the Door with Asian audience over the 1998 Christmas period, it ultimately returned to the Rep's main stage after London success. In 1999 for *Balti Kings* based on life in Birmingham's famous Balti houses, the entire Studio was converted into a balti kitchen (Cochrane 2003).

In 2002, however, Tara Arts brought to the Rep main stage their epic trilogy *Journey to the West* which charts the twentieth century migratory experience of three generations of characters from India to East Africa to Britain.[105] Director Jatinder Verma wove his own personal history of what he described in 1993 as 'transformation' in which 'I have been changed by Britain as much as, I hope I am contributing to changing Britain's idea of itself'(Verma in Shank 1993: 57). On the last night in Birmingham, the main auditorium which seats 824 was packed with a large South Asian audience. Community workshops had been included at every

---

[104] Don Kinch set up African People's Theatre in 1988 as a performance facilitating organisation again resourced by the CAVE. It closed down in 1994 through lack of funding.
[105] An early version was also staged at the MAC.

stage of the company's tour and before the performance entirely mixed groups of local young people were given an opportunity to present their own devised work on the *Journey* theme.

What an event such as this recognises is that Asian, Caribbean and African communities are moving from being immigrant to indigenous members of the population. Thus the indigenous culture itself is now irrevocably diverse and new generations of British people have a hybrid identity both modern and here and now, and rooted in other memories and places. Performance is a way of exploring that hybridity, and educational and community outreach is pursued vigorously in all the Birmingham venues.

The MAC has since the late 90s developed a strong record of participatory community productions with mixed casts which have used music and dance to tell stories derived from black Caribbean, Afro-American and South Asian traditions and concerns. These have included *Gangsta Rapture*, an original youth musical based on *Macbeth* and set in the Birmingham's club underworld in 1997, and in 2002 a revival of *King,* a musical based on the life and death of Martin Luther King. The choreography of the 1996 production of the Philip Glass opera *Satyagraha* based on Gandhi's activism in South Africa benefited from the relationship with SAMPAD. There have been open air co-productions of two Indian-Pakistani versions of the Romeo and Juliet story: *Heer Ranja* in 1997 and *Layla Majnun* in 2003 which Piali Ray choreographed.

As a major regional development agency which promotes nationally, SAMPAD works right across the city and has access into South Asian communities which permits a much greater understanding of attitudinal and economic constraints and opportunities. Effectively hidden from white, mainstream perspectives, there is a well-established culture of informal promotion of professional performance, much of it organised very quickly, often at great expense, and focused around visiting artists from India or Pakistan. Amateur drama groups work on home language plays. These can range from the Bengali Association of Theatre which consists of doctors who work towards single performances of Bengali plays to a Bangladeshi group mostly made up of young men, and a Punjabi-Hindi speaking group.

ArtSites, Birmingham, born at the MAC as a concept, and now an independent company based at the MAC, works to promote access to, and participation in, a whole range of artforms in a network of ArtSites established in combined schools and leisure centres across the city. Areas with high levels of economic deprivation and social exclusion have been targeted and the demographic varies considerably from mostly white working class communities in Castle Vale to densely black and Asian in Perry Barr and Sheldon Heath. An educational project showcased in early 2005 at the MAC included a devised piece around GCSE work on R.C Sherriff's classic 1920s war play *Journey's End*. Performed by a wholly monochrome brown group of mixed South Asian origin from Golden Hillock Secondary School where the young Pervaiz Khan once suffered so much racist abuse, it was an exercise in cultural hybridity which generated unexpected enthusiasm and excitement.

The MAC is a battered assemblage of spaces badly in need of capital resources for rebuilding. The Drum, by contrast, is still eerily pristine. Since the opening date in 1995 was delayed in order to raise more funds from the National Lottery and the European Regional Development fund, the venue has opened and closed three times. Structural problems in the building especially in the auditorium have had to be addressed. There has been a high turnover of staff especially at managerial level. The company is currently trying to achieve financial targets monitored by the Arts Council through their 'Recovery' plan.

And yet the potential to create a uniquely exciting resource for multi-cultural Birmingham is enormous. Local artists like Don Kinch and Tyrone Huggins insist there must be more artistic leadership and consultation. SAMPAD, together with local companies like Duende and Don Kinch's Nu Century Arts, which Kinch now directs from the Community Roots Enterprise Centre in Handsworth, have contributed to programming. As I write, former community arts programmer Mukhtar Dar has been appointed Director of Arts tasked with creating a winning mix of highly-skilled Black British and British Asian dancers with visiting artists from the Caribbean, Africa and South Asia. To woo the community into a family venue there will be events like the Mirpuri Musical Extravaganza which brought local and national poets and folk musicians and dhol players to create an evening of 'at home' entertainment.

What has certainly enhanced Black and Asian audience engagement in other venues has been a greater understanding of social networks and cultural boundaries. SAMPAD is now functioning effectively as a city-wide performance promotion agency and indeed assisted in the promotion of *Behzti*. While not entirely uncontroversial, the Arts Council's New Audiences Programme promoted by Birmingham Arts Marketing, has prompted the establishment of groups of 'ambassadors' associated with venues which has focused on 'word of mouth' marketing (Khan 2002: 13).

Where a theatre like Birmingham Rep enters a potential minefield is when it offers an ambitious artist like Gurpreet Kaur Bhatti the opportunity to challenge what Miri Song calls 'collectively prescribed scripts of behavior' (Appiah & Gutmann 1996 cited in Song 2003: 48-51) in order to express anger at culturally-condoned practices which blight lives, especially of women. *Behzti (Dishonour)* was developed through the Rep's Writers' Attachment Scheme, as was her first critically-acclaimed play *Behsharam (Shameless)* in 2001. For the first time the Rep entered into a consultation which gave designated leaders of that Sikh community the misleading impression that they could change a work of art. It is worth saying that there has been some 'creative tension' between different departments of the theatre.

Birmingham's Caribbean and Asian communities have come a long way since the ghettoisation of the 1950s. Community leaders are in the forefront of a mature civic democracy where inevitably there are different cultural agendas and political factions. The next stage for Birmingham's performance spaces and indeed for organisations across the UK is to address the need for high-level British Black and Asian leadership of arts organisations. As the 2001 Eclipse Conference declared there is still considerable 'institutional racism in British theatre' blocking access to creative authority and control.

Acknowledgements: I would like to thank the following people for conversations which have helped me in my research: Steve Ball, Jonathan Cochrane, Jacqueline Contré, Tyrone Huggins, Iqbal Husain, Abid Hussain, Don Kinch, Sue Longfils, Derek Nicholls, Ben Payne, Bob Ramdhanie, Alan Rivett, Piali Ray, Geoff Sims, Fiona Tait, Dorothy Wilson.

Works Cited

Arts Council (1993), Harris Research Centre, *Black and Asian attitudes to the arts in Birmingham*, London: Arts Council, Great Britain.

Arts Council (2002), *Eclipse: Developing strategies to combat racism in theatre: Report from a conference looking at how the theatre industry can develop strategies to combat institutional racism in theatre*, London: Arts Council England.

Bauman, Zygmunt (1997), 'The Making and Unmaking of Strangers', in Pnina Werbner & Tariq Modood (eds.), *Debating Cultural Hybridity: Multi-Cultural Identities and the Politics of Anti-Racism*, London: Zed Books.

City Challenge Implementation (1992), *City Challenge 1992, Newtown South Aston*, Birmingham: Birmingham City Team, Council.

Cochrane, Claire (2000), 'Theatre and Urban Space: The Case of Birmingham Rep', *New Theatre Quarterly* 62.

Cochrane, Claire (2003), *Birmingham Rep: A City's Theatre 1962-2002*, Birmingham: Sir Barry Jackson Trust.

Dick, Malcolm (2002), 'Travelling through time: migration and the black experience' in Ian Grosvenor, Rita Mclean & Sian Roberts (eds.), *Making Connections: Birmingham Black International History*, Birmingham: Birmingham Futures Group.

Jermyn, Helen and Philly Desai (2000), *Arts—what's in a word? Ethnic Minorities and the arts,* London: Arts Council of England.

Khan, Naseem (1976), *The Arts Britain Ignores: The arts of the ethnic minorities in Britain*, London: The Commission for Racial Equality.

Khan, Naseem (2002), *Towards a greater diversity: Results and legacy of the Arts Council of England's cultural diversity action plan*, London: Arts Council of England.

Qnun Ltd. (1992), *Asian Caribbean and African Arts Strategy for West Midlands Arts Board*, Birmingham: West Midlands Arts.

Ramdhanie, Bob, (ed. & researcher) (1994), ACAAN, *African Caribbean Asian Arts Networks in Birmingham and the West Midlands*, Birmingham: ACAAN.

Song, Miri (2003), *Choosing Ethnic Identity*, Cambridge: Polity.

Stone, John (2003), 'Max Weber on Race, Ethnicity, and Nationalism' in John Stone and Dennis Rutledge (eds.), *Race and Ethnicity: Comparative and Theoretical Approaches*, Malden, MA: Blackwell.

Upton, Chris (1993), *A History of Birmingham*, Chichester: Phillimore.

Verma, Jatinder (1993), 'Cultural Transformations' in Theodore Shank (ed.), *Contemporary British Theatre,* Basingstoke: Macmillan Press.

Unpublished Documents

'Black Theatre Development File 1979-1988', West Midlands Arts Correspondence held in Birmingham City Archives, MS 1620. This includes:

Smith, Pippa, Notes on the Black Artists White Institutions Conference held at the Riverside Studios on 4 November 1985; Arts Council: Internal Memo, 13 November 1985;

Arts Council of Great Britain, 'The Arts and Ethnic Minorities—Action Plan—February 1986';

Notes from a meeting held at the CAVE, March 1986;

Don Kinch, Report dated December 1987.

Reports

Canon Hill Trust Limited, 'Report and Financial Statements, 1 April 1984.

West Midlands County Council (1986), 'A different reality: an account of black people's experiences and their grievances before and after the Handsworth rebellion of September 1985', Report of the Review Panel, West Midlands County Council.

Newspapers and Radio

Anon. (21 February 1986), *Guardian,* Commentary on 'A different reality: an account of black people's experiences and their grievances before and after the Handsworth rebellion of September 1985', 1986 Report of the Review Panel, West Midlands County Council.

Anon. (27 December 2000), 'Birmingham and the Wider World', *Birmingham Post.*

Billington, Michael (1 November 1990), 'The Colour of Saying', *Guardian.*
Lawson, Mark (20 December 2004), BBC Radio 4, 'Front Row', interview with Hardial Rai.

Websites
McIntosh, Hermin, 'Community and Village Entertainment: The CAVE, an examination of the relationship between social intervention and black culture', Selected papers from the 1st Symposium on Therapeutic Recreation, Curators, University of Missouri, 1990. http://www.lin.ca/lin/resource/ html/yg001%5B16%5d.pdf

CHAPTER SEVEN

TARA ARTS AND *TAMASHA*: PRODUCING ASIAN PERFORMANCE – TWO APPROACHES

DOMINIC HINGORANI

Synopsis:
This chapter provides a historical overview of the work of Tara Arts since the company began in 1977 to the present time. It also contains a historical account of the work of Tamasha Theatre Company from their first production in 1989 until their production of Strictly Dandia. The theoretical context of the work will examine the way in which the theatrical work of these two British Asian theatre companies operates to destabilise the conceptual binary of British and Asian and put them literally into 'play'.

I. A History of *Tara* Arts: From English to 'Binglish'

Jatinder Verma has described himself in interview as a 'translated man' (Verma 1991) by applying Salman Rushdie's concept of translation (Rushdie 1991) to post-colonial migrants like himself who, 'bear upon them the traces of the particular cultures, traditions, languages and histories by which they were shaped' (Hall 1992: 310) while simultaneously inhabiting a new cultural location. Jatinder Verma was born in Dar-Es-Salaam, Tanzania on 17 July 1954 of Indian parents, grew up in Nairobi and came to live in Britain at the age of 14. This diasporic biography is worth citing as it intersects powerfully with Tara Arts' theatrical practice which aims to 'confront ethnicity through drama'(Verma 1990c). Indeed, Jatinder Verma's negotiation between British and Asian cultural spaces, as Artistic Director of Tara Arts for more than a quarter of a century, has 'translated' to the stage over one hundred productions and created the innovative theatre form of 'Binglish'.

Since the inception of Tara Arts in 1977 there have been three major theatrical movements in the company's history. Firstly, their early work from 1977 to 1984 which concerned itself with a range of subjects including the postcolonial reworking of historical events on the Indian subcontinent in *Inkalaab 1919* (1980)[106], the presence of Asians in Britain long before post-war immigration in *Vilayat or England Your England* (1981) to young Asians growing up in contemporary Britain in *Chilli In Your Eyes* (1984) but all primarily underpinned by a theatrical methodology of text-based realism. Secondly, the period dating from the first production of *Miti Ki Gadi* (*The Little Clay Cart*) in 1984 that heralded the creation of Jatinder Verma's unique hybrid performance methodology 'Binglish' and led the company to the 'centre' of the British theatre establishment at The National Theatre in the early 1990's with adaptations such as Molière's *Tartuffe* (1990) and Rostand's *Cyrano* (1995), transposed to an Asian setting. Thirdly, the creation and performance of the epic *Journey To The West Trilogy* (2002) which married the 'Binglish' performance methodology to a postcolonial mission to document and dramatise the stories of the Asian diaspora from India to Kenya and then to Britain over the course of the last century.

'A brave company could develop a theatre that examines the place of tradition in a new society' (Khan 1976: 71)
The catalyst that led to the formation of Tara Arts was the tragic murder of an Asian youth, Gurdip Singh Chaggar, killed in a racially motivated attack by whites in Southall, West London in 1976. Jatinder Verma, in his final year of University at that time, has described how the 'sense of anger and of trying to understand what's happened and of trying to say something, led us to make our theatre' (Verma 1996b). This political imperative has consistently manifested itself in the work of Tara Arts with its insistence on looking at the world from a marginal position in order to speak for the 'migrant' and the 'outsider' (Verma 2004 & 1996b: 84, 285).

Naseem Khan's ground breaking report 'The Arts Britain Ignores' in 1976 officially recognised that 'ethnic arts' should not be regarded as an 'exotic' extra operating outside of British theatre but should be understood, funded and fostered as though they were a *part* of British theatre. The arrival of Tara Arts made concrete the hope expressed in that document that an Asian theatre company would come and 'find local writers and sometimes look at the British setting' (Khan 1976: 71).

Initially, Tara Arts held meetings on a Wednesday evening at The Milan Centre in Tooting Bec, London hosted by the founding members Sunil Saggar, Praveen

---

[106] *Inkalaab 1919* concerned the incident in which the colonial British army opened fire on Indian civilians gathered at Jallianwala Bagh.

Bahl, Vijay Shaunak and Jatinder Verma and would encompass poetry recitals, lectures and discussion as well as drama. The members of Tara Arts were aware that 'Asians here do not, as a matter of course, have an appreciation of *established* theatre [in Britain] so our tours have been ...in community centres, in homes wherever Asians gather in large numbers'(Verma 1984d: 9) and so were very much in the traditions of 'Community Theatre' which began in the early 1970's and was defined by 'a desire to perform to different, non-theatre going audiences, and to engage them in a different relationship' (Khan 1980: 61).

The first play performed by Tara Arts in 1977 was *Sacrifice*, adapted by Jatinder Verma from a play by Rabindranath Tagore, *Balidaan*. Tagore had translated the play into English in 1917 which he had written in support of World War I pacifists.

[The Programme Cover featuring the goddess Kali for Tara Arts' first production *Sacrifice*, 1977]

The play is set in 16th Century Bengal and focuses on Jaising, the daughter of the priest Raghupati. The King has banned blood sacrifices in the temple and in response to the perceived threat to his power, Raghupati tells Jaising she must kill the King. Jaising, who agrees with the King, is morally unable to do this and torn between the duty to her father, who represents cultural tradition, and to her own beliefs, commits suicide. Indeed, Jaising's rhetorical cry before her death, 'can you not rejoice in two truths – must you grant victory to one' (Verma 1977: 25) acts as a 'call to arms' for Tara's mission of 'reflecting or remarking upon various aspects of Asian historical or contemporary experience...in an effort to provide a perspective on our lives here today' (Programme notes, *Sacrifice*, 1977).[107]

From this very first production, Tara used an 'all Asian' cast and this casting policy was to become established as one of the signs of a 'Binglish' performance. However, in contrast to the multi-lingual 'Binglish' text, the decision taken for those early productions such as *Sacrifice* was 'to work in English... since they reject what they regard as the backward looking nature of much Asian theatre'(Khan 1980: 75) or 'Language Theatre'. While this policy was driven by

---

[107] **[It also draws attention to and is a metaphor for the twin histories of culture and theatre that Asian theatre performs. Ed.]**

Tara's desire to recognise the contemporary British site, they found that it became increasingly restrictive in the expression of a heterogeneous Asian identity and cultural difference.

From *Sacrifice* (1977) to the *Journey to the West Trilogy* (2002), Tara's work has had a postcolonial provenance implicit in 'that very act of finding a text which was unknown or part of the hidden history of England' (Verma 1996b: 282). However, the critical gaze of the company has not been limited to the non-Asian community as can be seen in *Sacrifice* which 'linked Race to Communalism, as being part of the same spectrum of Oppression...an uncompromisingly twin pronged stance' (Verma 1989c: 772). This 'twin pronged stance' exemplifies the approach that Tara Arts have adapted since that time of critiquing the Asian community from within as well as the wider community from without.

Chilli in Your Eyes (1984), directed by Yogesh Bhatt and written by Jatinder Verma was based on three weeks of research on the experiences of young Asians growing up in the London borough of Newham. The play followed the lives of five young Asian characters Jag, Nalini, Sonny, Rit and Gaz from a range of different Asian backgrounds, Sikh, Muslim and Hindu as they battle against the 'traditional' cultural values of their own families and the unwelcoming and racist outside world. We can see Tara's 'twin pronged stance' in operation in *Chilli in Your Eyes* with

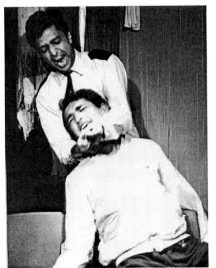

reference to two scenes. The first shows Sonny as the victim of racist police brutality as he is beaten up by a policeman and another which shows the attempted rape of an Asian girl by a gang of Asian boys; a scene although 'based on actual testimony of people living in Newham' (Verma 1989c: 772) was not designed or destined to court popularity within the Asian community.

['Interrogation' scene with Harmage S Kalirai & Sheetal Verma from *Chilli in Your Eyes* © Chris Ha, 1984]

While the content of *Chilli in Your Eyes* fitted Tara's brief, there was growing disenchantment from Jatinder Verma with the form. Although, in those early years the company had no formal theatrical training in Western conceptions of realism Tara 'found [themselves] slipping into a kind of convention which was the usual thing, drama and right speaking and tables and chairs and so forth'(Verma 2004: 84). So began a journey into finding a form 'not restricted by the dead hand of naturalism' (Verma 2002b) through which they could explore the hybrid British Asian cultural site which would lead to the creation of 'Binglish'.

'[T]he heaping together of fragments of diverse cultures is what I characterise as a Binglish process' (Verma 1998: 126-134)
Jatinder Verma recognised there was a need to develop a distinct theatre approach in order to culturally locate the British Asian subject because 'we are not talking about the subcontinent...nor are we talking about Britain as it is...it is a peculiar mix of the two' (Verma 1984d: 9). This 'peculiar mix of the two' led Tara Arts to create 'Binglish' in response to the hybrid cultural location of their work. Jatinder Verma uses the term 'Binglish' 'to denote a distinct contemporary theatre praxis: featuring Asian or Black casts, produced by independent Asian or black theatre companies...to challenge or provoke the dominant conventions of the English stage'(Verma 1996a: 194). While Tara Arts were in straightforward accordance with the first of these two tenants, in order to 'challenge and provoke' they drew on Eastern as opposed to Western forms such as the *Natyashastra* , the

Indian treatise on acting dating from circa 200BC, Indian folk forms such as Bhavai and the Bollywood film genre which led them to a hybrid 'Binglish' performance methodology in which 'movement and music ...are not ancillary to the spoken word but form an integral part of the 'text' of performance' (Verma 1996a: 200).

[*The Little Clay Cart* at the National Theatre in 1991 – 'The Torture Scene' with Stanley Townsend & Shehnaz Khan © Simon Annand]

The 'Binglish' text was also to address the linguistic flaw, which meant 'in rehearsal we negotiated across several languages, and yet none of these languages are on stage' (Verma 2004: 91). Indeed, the performance of Asian languages alongside English as they 'form part of the linguistic map of modern Britain.... and cannot be expected to be absent from modern British theatre' (Verma 1996a: 198) is a powerful force for inscribing cultural difference on the British stage.

Furthermore, the employment of a range of Asian languages, as exemplified in the 'Binglish', such as Hindi, Punjabi, Gujarati and English, also demonstrates the plurality of the signifier 'Asian'. In this way, the creation of a 'Binglish' aesthetic may 'be viewed as cultural and political, an attempt to demolish the white Eurocentric way of looking at the world and replace it with another' (Peacock 1999: 175), in this case, a culturally hybrid understanding of the British stage, Britain and indeed, 'Britishness'.

The non-European text that became the focus for the development of Tara's 'Binglish' theatrical methodology was *Miti Ki Gadi (Little Clay Cart,* 1984) ascribed to Shudraka who is said to have written the Sanskrit drama *Mricchakatika* between the 7th and 8th Century A.D. and was first performed by Tara in 1984. Tara Arts went on an extraordinary journey with *The Little Clay Cart* from the 'margin' to the 'centre' of British theatre when it was performed in1986 at the Arts Theatre to open the third 'Black Theatre Season' and then revived and revised for a production in the Cottesloe Theatre at The National in 1991.[108]

The play, unlike other Sanskrit works of this time, is peopled with low characters as well as the more exalted classes. The story unfolds against a backdrop of a revolution that results in Aryaka, a peasant, being made king. This representation of normally marginalized groups, whose political agency results in the subaltern being placed literally centre stage very much reflects the decentring aspirations of a 'Binglish' production.

In *The Little Clay Cart* the non-naturalistic 'Binglish' performance is exemplified in each actor having a 'characteristic gait' (Hall 1986), which created a stylised movement vocabulary. A great deal of the exercises employed in the rehearsal process focused on the body, exploring posture and rhythm, and the rehearsal records show the importance attached to the physical manifestation of character (Verma 1984c & 1986). This resulted in the actor playing the hero, Charudatta, walking with a very upright posture with his heels kicked up high behind him at each step while his friend Maitraya, the Brahmin, walked with a wide waddling gait constantly bent at the knee as if sitting. These stylised movements also facilitated the actors moving freely and recognisably through a range of characters throughout the performance. The play was also interspersed with songs and dances and music, provided by live musicians on Asian instruments, and was integrated throughout. The theatrical challenge being mounted by Tara Arts in their 'Binglish' methodology 'blending conventions of Indian classical acting...with western realism' (Rea 1984) was being recognised by critics who warned that 'a few more shows like this and western linear theatre will start looking primitive' (Wardle 1991).

---

[108] For more on Black Theatre Seasons, see Alda Terracciano, 'Mainstreaming African, Asian and Caribbean Theatre: The Experiments of the Black Theatre Forum' in this volume.

Around the late 1980s, Tara began to produce the texts of 'classical' European playwrights, employing 'Binglish' methodology so that in their productions of *The Government Inspector* (1989), *Danton's Death* (1989), *Tartuffe* (1990) *Le Bourgeoise Gentilhomme* (1994), *Troilus and Cressida* (1993), *Marriage Of Convenience* (1990) – and a double bill of Brecht's *The Emperor and The Dog* and Chekhov's *The Proposal*, they were 'viewing Gogol, Buchner, Moliere, Shakespeare, Sophocles, Chekhov, Brecht through Asian eyes and ears'(Verma 1998: 126-134).

[The programme for *Tartuffe* with the Indian deity Ganesha taking centre stage © RaRa designs]

The methodological implications in Tara's approach to these texts are exemplified in this extract of Jatinder Verma's production notebook for *Tartuffe*:

I am setting out to translate a seventeenth century French farce through an all-Asian company of performers. This entails a double translation: once from the French original to English; and secondly to an English spoken by Asian actors, who have their own history of the acquisition of English speech. In other words, who are themselves 'translated' men and women – in that they (or their not-too distant forebears) have been 'borne across' from one language and culture to another. In order then to lay bare the full dimension of 'translation', I must take account of the specificity of my performers (their history): by conveying Molière's original playtext into a form that allows the performers to make creative connections between their ancestral traditions and their English present.... (Verma 1998: 126-134).

These 'creative connections' were realised as a result of Jatinder Verma's historical research, which led to him framing Molière's *Tartuffe* as a play-within-a-play being performed at the court of the Moghul Emperor Aurangzeb to a French traveller, Francois Bernier. Jatinder Verma also describes how he drew on Bhavai, the Indian folk form, as a performance resource equivalent to the Commedia Del'Arte which he felt had influenced Moliere's theatre.

The 'provocation' of this 'Binglish' 'translation' of Tartuffe should not be underestimated for the audience at the National Theatre as, 'the first sight that greeted them was this bunch of darkies, beautifully costumed, terribly lush, coming out to the strains of some Eastern flute and speaking in Urdu' (Verma 1996b: 282). However, this production remains a critique of religious hypocrisy but Tartuffe becomes 'Binglished' to Tartuffe-ji, an Indian fakir in saffron robes.

['The Seduction Scene' featuring Nizwar Karanj as Tartuffe-ji and Yasmin Sidhwa as Almirah in *Tartuffe* (1990) at The National Theatre © Simon Annand 1990]

The aim of this theatrical form is also experiential in that a 'modern white audience in Britain experiencing a 'Binglish' production could be said to be oscillating continuously between the sense of the native, the familiar and the foreign' (Verma 1996a: 200) as it insists on placing cultural hybridity at the 'centre' of the stage.

∇

Journey to the West Part I -- Dhows, Deserts and Dirty Tricks 1896 – 1901

[The workers' journey from India to Africa on the dhow.
© Stephen Vaughan 2002]

Fateh, a Sikh from the Punjab, leaves his famine struck home and goes to work as indentured labour for the British to build the East Africa railway. *Dhows, Deserts and Dirty Tricks* celebrates the pioneering spirit of the Asian workers and also makes visible the colonial exploitation of the Asian workers by the British who refused to honour their promise of land after the work was completed. The play ends as Fateh finds an abandoned baby on the railway tracks who he adopts and names Kala Singha (Black Lion). This baby 'born on the waters between India and Africa' symbolises the racial ambivalence and irreducible hybridity of the Asian identity as a result of diaspora.

Journey to the West Part II -- Rifts, Refugees and Rivers Of Blood 1968

[The chorus of Asian women washing saris in Kenya. © Stephen Vaughan 2002]

Part II opens in post independence Kenya and follows the friendship of three teenagers Ranjit, Sita and Liaquat who are descendents of the workers in *Part I*. The religious plurality and almost idyllic cohesion of the Asian community symbolised in the close friendship of the three friends, a Sikh, a Hindu and a Muslim is counter pointed with the rising animosity of the African people to the insularity of the Asian community. The scene then shifts to Britain as the three arrive as part of the Asian 'Exodus' in order to beat the impending legislative deadline restricting Kenyan Asian immigration. The play charts the increasing politicisation of the Asian community in the face of racism whilst also foregrounding a friendship between Ranjit and a white girl, Lesley. However, *Part II* ends on a pessimistic note with Ranjit being stabbed to death in a racist attack which echoes the actual killing of Gurdeep Singh Chaggar in Southall by white youths; this murder was the catalyst that led to the formation of Tara Arts.

Journey to the West Part III – Bhangra, Bollywood and British Bulldog 2002

[Kamaal listens to stories of the Asian diaspora on his grandfather's lap.
From a production of *Revelations* that became *JTW Part III*
© Nick White 2001]

The genealogical narrative link continues in *Part III* as the protagonist, Kamaal,
is the son of a Hindu mother, Sita, and Muslim father, Liaquat, whom we met in
Part II. We follow Kamaal on his journey, by road this time, to scatter his
grandfather's ashes at Hadrian's Wall on the border of Scotland and England. This
is a metaphorical as well as literal journey on which Kamaal attempts to reconcile
his desire to 'belong…in a team, a group, a gang, a tribe' with his hybrid Asian
identity that makes him 'part Hindu part Muslim, part Indian, part Pakistani, part
African, part English.' On his journey Kamaal passes through two allegorical sites,
the first espousing cultural assimilation and second cultural separatism, both of
which he rejects. His arrival at Hadrians Wall,a tangible reminder of England as a
once colonised nation as well as coloniser, heralds Kamaal's acceptance and
celebration of his hybrid identity as he determines to 'make this England, our
England, full of all your long journey's West'.

The Journey to the West Trilogy

Tara's *Journey to the West Trilogy* (*JTW Trilogy*) maps an Indian diaspora to Kenya and Britain over the course of the last century. *Part I* follows the thirty two thousand Indian workers who were transported to Kenya at the turn of the last century to work as indentured labour for the British to build the East Africa Railway. *Part II* is focused around the experience, shared by Jatinder Verma, of the Kenyan Asian 'exodus' to Britain in 1968, whilst *Part III* interrogates a hybrid British Asian identity in contemporary Britain in the light of this diaspora. While the postcolonial provenance of the *JTW Trilogy* is in part a straightforward attempt to recover and make visible an Asian history overwritten by and inextricably linked with colonial power, it also attempts to give agency to a 'subaltern' Asian voice through the methodology that underpins the theatrical realisation of the work.

In this way Tara Arts' *JTW Trilogy* aims to provide a theatrical counter-narrative located in the 'performative moment' of the nation that in Homi K. Bhabha's work 'disrupts the signification of the people as homogenous' and results in the construction of the nation being 'marked by discourses of minorities, the heterogeneous histories of contending peoples, antagonistic authorities and tense locations of cultural difference.' (Bhabha 1994: 148).

The *JTW Trilogy* had an overt autobiographical provenance as the initial strand, *Exodus*, concerned with the forced emigration of Kenyan Asians to Britain, drew on Jatinder Verma's personal experience of coming to Britain on Valentine's Day in 1968. He was part of a rising level of Kenyan Asian immigration to Britain triggered by the increasingly restrictive 'Africanisation' policies that came into force against those Asians unwilling to take up Kenyan citizenship after Kenya gained independence from British rule on 12 December 1963. In Britain, Enoch Powell's dire warnings of 'a nation busily engaged in heaping up its own funeral pyre' (Powell 1968: 1-2) symbolised the apocalyptic tone of the 'non-white' immigration debate. Indeed, the Labour Government's 'Commonwealth Immigrants Act' of 1968 which was passed in just three days 'had the effect of treating Kenyan Asians with valid British passports as 'aliens' (Jones & Gnanapala 2000: 15).

The *JTW Trilogy* signalled a change of emphasis for Tara Arts as they focused on re-connecting with the Asian community from which they had sprung in 1977. Perhaps a tacit admission that whilst Tara Arts had found critical acclaim and a mainstream profile at the National Theatre in the early 1990s with *Tartuffe* and *The Little Clay Cart*, they had lost touch with their constituent Asian audience. For Jatinder Verma 'the project was about artistically rebuilding a bridge with the Asian community' (Hussein 1998: 1) and this was to be achieved methodologically by going out and interviewing members of the community and documenting the stories of their experience of living in and then leaving Kenya in the 1960s as source material for the performance.

In order for that initial contact to be made, invitations were circulated in Urdu, Hindi and Gujarati to a range of societies and meeting places in London, Leicester, Birmingham and beyond. Those who came forward for interview were recorded on

 digital video and transcripts were made with the emphasis on getting as much detail of life in Kenya as possible: schooling, housing, entertainment, marriage as well as the relations with Whites and Africans.

[The cast of the Exodus production with some of the interviewees at Battersea Arts Centre. © Tara Arts, 1998]

The actors' duties included conducting the interviews; this also facilitated their process, as they were able to build characters 'based on real evidence, real research, first hand experience' (Ganatra 2001: 3). As the research developed between the interviewees and actors it became more practically interactive as they learnt skills such as making Gujarati & Punjabi rotis as well as learning nursery rhymes, card games and Swahili songs of that time. Indeed the naïve misconceptions of the Kenyan Asian immigrants to Britain dramatised in *Part II* who believe 'an underground train from Heathrow... will take you straight to Manchester' (Verma 2002a) was based on the real reminiscences of the interviewees.

Building on the front of house success of the performance of *Exodus* at Battersea Arts Centre in 1998, at which there was 'the distinct aroma of beedees and dhoop sticks.... as you are greeted with statues of Greek Gods dressed in saris and salwars' (anon. review 1998) the performance of all three parts of the *JTW Trilogy* on a Saturday would turn the front of house into a chaandi (silver) bazaar. To create the bazaar, Tara Arts invited stallholders to sell Asian fashions and crafts and had live demonstrations by rangoli and henna artists in the foyer of the theatre. Asian caterers also provided food especially tailored to provide for an audience watching the compete *JTW Trilogy* which would entail spending over seven hours in the theatre.

This 'Binglish' epic utilised the theatrical conventions of mask, a sutradhar (narrator), a chorus and allowed the actors to directly address the audience and play multiple characters. The 'Binglish' text of the *JTW Trilogy* is made up of an array of languages including Punjabi, Hindi, Gujarati, Swahili and English, introducing the audience 'to a greater auditory experience and, by implication, challenging them (Verma 1996 a: 198). The provocative nature of the linguistic 'Binglish' methodology is evident from this reflection of a work-in-progress performance during which the Asian-speaking members of the audience 'understood the 'in jokes' – for whom 'gora khuta' (white dog) meant something' (Hussein 1998: 24). The corollary to this was 'observing the non-Asian children at times I felt that they were left out, but then I thought how regularly Asians are left out of the 'mainstream' (Hussein 1998: 24) which demonstrates how the 'Binglish' performance can give the non-Asian language speaking audience members a powerful experiential understanding of marginalisation.

Jatinder Verma also insisted the actors study Valmiki's epic *The Ramayana* and *The Odyssey* 'to provide the company with another vision which contrasted with the realism of the Exodus story.' (Hussein 1998: 24). The application of this rehearsal methodology realising intertextual connections to Asian myth can be seen in *Part II* when Ranjit's mother, Daljeet, has to take a job in England and is told that for reasons of 'health and safety. No saris in the work place.' (Verma 2002a: 27). As the official slowly gathers in the seemingly never-ending sari the resonance of the episode in the Mahabharata in which Dussashan, younger brother of Duryodhana, attempted to disrobe Draupadi is clear. In the legend, Draupadi appealed to Krishna for protection and he made sure her sari did not unravel before Dussashan fell exhausted at her feet. However, with no Krishna to intervene this time, Daljeet is stripped of her sari and left standing centre stage metaphorically 'naked' in slacks and a blouse.

The lyrical final image in the *JTW Trilogy* of Kamaal, sitting high above the stage picking stars from the firmament as he finally acknowledges and, indeed, celebrates his hybrid Asian identity by promising to, 'make this England our England, full of all your long journey's West' (Verma 2002a: 31) could be read as the mission statement for Tara Arts over the past quarter of a century. It is Tara's insistence on the recognition of the Asian presence in the construction of British identity that has led to the creation of their innovative theatrical form of the hybrid 'not quite English' (Verma 1996a: 200) 'Binglish', whose performance has not only irrevocably destabilised the borders of British theatre but also provided a site of resistance from which Tara Arts can and does 'disturb those ideological manoeuvres through which 'imagined communities' are given essentialist identities' (Bhabha 1994: 149).

II. *Tamasha* Theatre Company: Practising 'Authenticity'

Tamasha Theatre Company has produced thirteen new writing shows of great diversity since the company was founded by Kristine Landon-Smith and Sudha Bhuchar in 1989. Their theatre work ranges from adaptations of Indian novels such as *Untouchable* (1989) and *House of the Sun* (1991), through evocations of a 'second generation' childhood in 70's Britain in *East is East* (1996), to the innovative staging of a Bollywood film, *Fourteen Songs Two Weddings and a Funeral*(1998 & 2001). Whilst this diversity epitomises Tamasha's adherence to their culturally explicit yet artistically expansive mission statement to 'reflect through theatre the Asian experience from British Asian life to authentic accounts of aspects of life in the Indian subcontinent' (Bhuchar & Landon-Smith 1998), their stated aim of 'authenticity' promotes a single minded methodological approach.

Whilst the name of the company derives from the Hindi word *tamasha*, meaning a show, spectacle or commotion, it does not draw on the traditions of *tamasha* as a 16th century Indian folk theatre form. Indeed, Tamasha Theatre Company was keen to adopt 'a British Western style of acting, naturalistic and realistic' (Bhuchar 1999e) and it is this methodological approach to acting that consistently underpins their work and differentiates it from that of Tara Arts. Although both Sudha Bhuchar and Kristine Landon-Smith worked with Tara Arts as actors, their performance style does not attempt to 'challenge the dominant conventions of the English stage' (Verma 1996a: 194). However, it must be recognised that while Tamasha's acting methodology may be 'western', the Asian provenance of its theatrical subjects, the methodological use of linguistically hybrid texts, its use of largely Asian casts, as well as the training it provides to new Asian writers, actors, directors and designers, demonstrates the company's insistence on placing the performance of cultural difference at the centre of the British stage.

The genesis of Tamasha Theatre Company in 1989 was the result of an intercultural exchange in 1988 when Kristine Landon-Smith was invited to teach and direct the second year students of the New Delhi National School of Drama under the auspices of the British Council. Ironically, sponsored by the British Council as a *British* practitioner of theatre, she initially planned to mount a production of *The Seagull* by Anton Chekhov. Perhaps recognising that this choice of production was an implicit acceptance of an exclusively Eurocentric construction of British theatre, Kristine Landon-Smith decided mid journey to India to devise a performance piece based on the novel *Untouchable* by Mulk Raj Anand. Written and set in 1932, *Untouchable* highlighted the plight of the 'untouchable' caste in India. Kristine Landon-Smith and Sudha Bhuchar subsequently formed Tamasha Theatre Company in 1989 in order to reprise the play in Britain and *Untouchable* was first performed at The Riverside Studios, London on 4 December 1989.

[Sudha Bhuchar playing Gulabo, a washerwoman, in *Untouchable* © Jenny Potter 1989]

Tamasha's desire for 'authenticity' was apparent from their first production, *Untouchable,* which follows a day in the life of seventeen-year-old Bakha, a 'Chamar' (sweeper) or lavatory cleaner, and portrays the injustices that he and his family as members of that caste must endure. As the audience entered, the aim was to make them feel as if 'they are transported to an Indian village' (Anon. review 1989: 9) so the actors were already in place and improvising in character. The realism and cultural specificity of Tamasha's acting approach could be crystallised in this production in the image of Bakha as he sat on his haunches smoking a 'bidi', a crude form of Indian cigarette rolled within a leaf. Such detailed accuracy in the performance, even down to the cigarette that is being smoked, led critics to remark on the 'authenticity clinging to both action and actors

throughout the play' (Chaudhari 1989) and that 'the impression of people going about their daily affairs is remarkable.' (Kingston 1989).

[The publicity flyer for *Fourteen Songs, Two Weddings and a Funeral* which mirrored the style of the Bollywood film publicity posters]

The staging of the Bollywood film *Hum Aapke Hain Koun (Who Am I To You),* which was adapted by Kristine Landon-Smith and Sudha Bhuchar and re-titled *Fourteen Songs Two Weddings and A Funeral,* was a very different methodological challenge. The plot is simple, yet full of melodramatic twists until a romantic resolution is finally achieved. Rajesh and Pooja are to marry, and their respective brother and sister, Prem and Nisha also fall in love and want to marry. However, disaster strikes as Pooja is killed in an accident and Nisha must forsake her love for Prem and step in to marry his brother, Rajesh, as is the 'duty' of the younger sister. All turns out well as Rajesh realises Prem is in love with Nisha and heroically steps aside so they can be together for a happy ending.

Kristine Landon-Smith wanted to find an acting style that would not lead to a parody or 'send up' of the Bollywood genre. However, the British Asian actors in the production although familiar with the Bollywood genre were mainly trained in a naturalistic style of acting. In order to explore this unfamiliar style the director would set the actors exercises such as finding their character's most Bollywood 'moment' in the play. They would then present this and attempt to analyze it in acting terms, deconstructing it vocally, physically and emotionally in order to build a vocabulary the company could share and work with.

Whilst the genre has stock characters who may appear unashamedly melodramatic to a Western audience, it was important to the director that the actors should 'never lose the fun to be had with a stock character but …don't push them too far so as not to believe or empathise with them.' (Landon-Smith 1998 [programme notes]) From this we can see the creation of a hybrid Tamasha acting methodology which determinedly reaches towards an embodiment of the signs of the Bollywood genre yet remains anchored within a Stanislavski based psychological realism. This balance achieved praise for the production for 'the way it combines the gentle poking of fun at that genre's unusual conventions with sensitivity and conviction when it matters most.' (Logan 1998). *Fourteen Songs* …went on to win the Barclay's New Musical Award in 1998 and the BBC Asia Award for Achievement in the Arts in 1999.

This realistic methodology also had to create a stage language that would represent Asian speech to a largely non-Asian language speaking audience. *Untouchable* was played on alternate evenings in Hindi and English versions and Sudha Bhuchar and Kristine Landon-Smith had to develop a script for the 'English' version that aimed to represent the Indian locale as authentically as possible in the performance. The 'English' script was not a direct translation of the Hindi script but was linguistically hybrid as, 'in English we have tried to do the new language, streetwise without being Cockney, contemporary but with the regular Hindi phrases and rhythms' (Bhuchar 1990). The following example of Lakha, the father, calling to his son Bakha, the main protagonist of *Untouchable* demonstrates how this hybrid text operates by mixing Hindi and English in order to achieve a believably colloquial style that attempts to replicates the social context.

LAKHA: Bakha –are uth (get up) –come on, get up ma da chodh suer ke bache. Come on – you getting up or not? Get up you bastard or I'll give you a kick up the arse. (7)

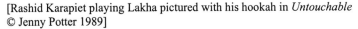
[Rashid Karapiet playing Lakha pictured with his hookah in *Untouchable*
© Jenny Potter 1989]

The methodological difficulties of achieving these 'authentically' hybrid scripts were exemplified in Tamasha's third show, *Women of the Dust,* because of its intercultural provenance. The play was commissioned and funded by Oxfam to mark their fiftieth anniversary and for the first time a new writer, Ruth Carter, was employed by the company. *Women of the Dust* dramatised the lives of Rajasthani women who have to leave their villages for half the year to work as migrant labour on building sites in various cities in India. The subsequent tour to India in 1993 marked the first international tour for Tamasha and also a remarkable intercultural event in which a British Asian theatre company from Britain were to perform a piece of theatre based on Asian women's experience in India for an Indian audience. This allied to the not insubstantial methodological problems of performing a play about Asian women in India to a British/British Asian audience.

Women of the Dust, along with *Balti Kings* and *Strictly Dandia* exemplified the company's theatrical aim to produce 'new writing based on factual research of a particular subject or community.' (Bhuchar & Landon-Smith 1992: programme notes). However, Kristine Landon-Smith recognised there was a methodological question to answer in how 'you transpose the rhythms and cadences of an indigenous dialect into English without sacrificing a crucial degree of credibility'(Subramanium 1999). To address this, Sudha Bhuchar, Kristine Landon-Smith and Ruth Carter travelled to the village of Tilonia, in the Ajmar district of India in order to meet and research the lives of their dramatic subjects. Sudha Bhuchar interviewed the women in a mixture of Hindi and the local dialect and then she translated these conversations for the writer Ruth Carter.

We recorded the women speaking a dialect of [Rajasthani], and we tried to do that not just in the writing but in the way we delivered it. It was nasal it was higher …for instance they would all be talking over noise...it was kind of shouted...we tried to capture the speech and it's not always putting in odd Indian words ….the women talked very different from urban speech …if you ask them are you hungry ..they would say something like 'is the sky blue', 'does the camel carry water', it was littered with metaphors. (Sudha Bhuchar, 1999e).

After the interviews the writing/directing team would go through the tapes listening not only to *what* the women said in terms of content and syntax but also crucially *how* they said it in terms of pitch, pace, intonation and musicality. The British critical reaction took as read the 'authenticity' of the hybrid language remarking on the 'sing song cadences of the women's speech' (Curtis 1992) while praising the production for its documentary realism that created a 'credible slice of life'(Armistead 1992).

[The set for *House of the Sun* adapted by Sudha Bhuchar and Kristine Landon-Smith at Theatre Royal Stratford East 1991 © Alistair Muir]

The designs by Sue Mayes for Tamasha have played a significant role in achieving Tamasha's realist vision of performance and this was evident in their second show, *House of the Sun*. Adapted from the novel by Meira Chand and premiered at Theatre Royal Stratford East, this production demonstrated the integral part that design has played in Tamasha performance. *House of the Sun* focuses on the Sindhi residents of the fictional Sadhbela apartment block in Mumbai who, as Hindus, were forced to flee their homeland around the Indus after partition and were, in effect, made stateless and homeless. The very episodic structure of *House of the Sun* with thirty short scenes, constantly cutting between households in order to structurally interweave the stories of the inhabitants, which accentuated the interconnectedness of their lives and gave the audience a sense of the Sindhi community at large was aided by the set.

The remarkably realistic set contained a working lift as well as stairs and screens that could slide up or down in order to cover or reveal the action. This allowed the audience to see into the apartment block like an open dolls house and feel that they were eavesdropping on the lives of the inhabitants whose 'fourth wall' had literally, in this production, been removed. This, allied with a writing process which was a mixture of devising, research and re-writing, seemed to have realised Tamasha's aims as critics recognised 'the improvisation afforded by

Tamasha's semi-devised script lends each scene a sense of slice of life realism.'
(Feay 1991).

[The set for *Women of the Dust* with Shobu Kapoor mixing cement. Note the 'working' cement mixer © Jenny Potter]

Sue Mayes also provided a working set for *Women of the Dust*, with the women using an operating cement mixer on the building site. Kristine Landon-Smith astutely exploited the set, 'that leaves little to the imagination ....cement mixer, trays of bricks' (Lawson 1992: 12-19) by having the actors realistically perform tasks such as climbing ladders, carrying bricks and mixing cement as would happen on a real building site in Delhi.

The design was also central to *Balti Kings*, which was based on research carried out by the production team in Birmingham and was set behind the scenes in the fictional Shakeel's Restaurant. In the play, the restaurant is engaged in, and losing, a 'curry war' with its rival, Karachi Karahi. The play unfolds over a day as the staff prepare thirty-five dishes for the buffet that evening for the 'Curry-oke' competition that will hopefully save the ailing fortunes of the restaurant. The actors were aided by a very realistic kitchen set in giving the illusion of actually cooking the 'Grand Bollywood Buffet' as the performance of *Balti Kings* progresses. During the play, which is performed in the round, the actors actually chop and peel vegetables, make samosas and cook on the stoves which had working gas hobs. Kristine Landon-Smith's production, performed in the round, tried to get the audience as close as possible, literally, to the 'world' of a Balti kitchen as, 'spices fill the air... [and]... the tomatoes are slopped into vats on a stove almost splattering the audience on that side.'(Walsh 2000).[109]

Tamasha were always keen that their work set in India should be of political relevance to their British Asian audience by drawing parallels between characters in the Asian setting and the position of the Asian migrant in Britain. In this way, an analogy was drawn with the treatment of Bakha , the sweeper in *Untouchable*

---

[109] [Ironically, *balti* cuisine is a British invention and not available in India. *Balti* simply means bucket, and the invention of balti food can be traced to Birmingham's Asian restaurants of the late 80s and early 90s. Ed.]

because 'Asians will recognise Bakha's situation as being similar to their own experiences as victims of racism.' (Bhuchar 1989). The examination of the Sindhi community in *House of the Sun* espouses an approach to culture based on hybridity and fluidity rather than one of assimilation or insular diversity for the diasporic migrant.

[The 'working' kitchen for *Balti Kings* © Jenny Potter]

Fourteen Songs was categorised as an 'irresistibly charming and shamelessly enjoyable family play' (Peter 1998), perhaps not unsurprisingly as the success of the original film was based on its 'return to romance and song' (Mishra 2002: 146) against the trend of more violent and sexually adventurous films. The return to 'traditional values' epitomised by *Hum Aapke Kaun Hain Koun* was problematic in respect of the gender politics of the film, particularly when played in the British location. The extended family 'order' was 'within a dominant patriarchal Hindu order where a woman's sexuality/sensuality is circumscribed by respectable social norms and where the model is ....as the devotee of her husband-lord.' (Mishra 2002: 218). While Prem's compliment to Nisha that 'I am already a fan of your singing and dancing. Now I am a fan of your cooking' (Bhuchar & Landon-Smith 2001: 40) underlines the traditional tone of the text, there were more problematic instances. When Bhagwanti, the stock character of the interfering social climbing auntie goes 'too far' in suggesting that recently widowed Rajesh should remarry and have his son brought up by an 'ayah' (nanny), her husband slaps her across the face.

(ARUN slaps her)
ARUN: It is this sour nature of yours that has kept us childless all these years. (52)

However, traditional or not, the non-western form of the musical was indeed provocative to one critic who was non-plussed by the evident enjoyment of the British Asian audience 'laughing both at and with the actors'(Myerson 2001). His admonishment that Tamasha needs to 'befriend those of us with Western theatrical expectations' (Myerson 2001) was to miss the point that this was now a *British* product.

As has been pointed out, the British critics accepted the verisimilitude of the portrayals in *Women of the Dust,* whereas on the Indian site, claims of 'authenticity' were of course more problematic. Indeed, the critics pointed out that because of the ungrammatical English syntax used by the women workers in the hybrid text, there was a risk of creating 'an orientalist stereotype of native incompetence ...the Indian who uses English wrongly...the Rajasthani who doesn't use even his own language properly' (Aurora 1994). However, the synthesis of English language with Rajasthani inflexion and cadence was 'so deceptive ...that at first one is left a little confused...it sounds like Rajasthani Hindi but one can't get the words' (Vaish 1994), suggests that this hybrid 'text' transcends stereotype and operates on the creative intercultural terrain between British and Asian to destabilise discrete constructions of both terms.

It was with *East is East,* written by Ayub Khan-Din, and developed in a writers' workshop held by Tamasha in collaboration with the Royal Court Theatre and The Birmingham Repertory Theatre Company that Tamasha found mainstream success and critical acclaim. The play moved from 'fringe' to film, from its first performance at the Royal Court Theatre Upstairs at The Ambassadors Theatre on 19 November 1996, before playing Theatre Royal Stratford East and then transferring to the Royal Court Downstairs in the Duke of York's Theatre in the West End from the 26 March 1997 before being made into a feature film directed by Damien O'Donnell and produced by Film Four.

East is East was set in a working class family in Salford in 1970 and is a largely autobiographical portrayal of the mixed 'race' children of a Pakistani father and an English mother. The play was very much in the vein of Tamasha's 'slice of life' realism, or indeed Royal Court 'kitchen sink' drama and brought Tamasha critical and popular success with both Asian and non-Asian audiences becoming the first British Asian play to go to the West End. The play was well received by the critics with John Peter in *The Sunday Times* setting the tone with his view that 'first plays don't come much better than this' (Peter 1996). The play includes some tremendous farcical set pieces, one of which culminates in Tariq's art work, a realistic 'sculpture' of a women's vagina, ending up thrown onto the po-faced prospective mother-in-law's lap after the 'hair' has come off in his mother's hand. Whilst *East is East* exploited the comic potential of well-observed, but previously unrepresented, British Asian characters, it also focused on questions of cultural identity for British Asian children growing up in a northern working class family.

East is East was critically praised for its 'withering comic satire at the expense of fathers who exude swanky materialism and parade their religious correctness.' (De Jongh 1996: 48). Indeed, the rather unsympathetic portrayal of the Asian father, George, or Genghis as the children referred to him, was exacerbated by him being the central and *only* Asian character in the play. This drew accusations of veering too close to stereotype so that critics noted that 'what stays in the mind is his readiness to knock his wife down' (Kingston 1997). Ayub Khan-Din did little to defend himself from accusations that he was, 'betraying the Asian community'(Hattenstone 1997) in his portrayal of George Khan and he was unrepentant about his depiction of the father on the grounds that 'my Dad was like that .....[I] am not interested in what people want me to say' (Hattenstone 1997).

[*East is East:* Imran Ali playing Sanjit, a character based on the author Ayub Khan-Din, wearing his trademark Parka © Robert Day]

However, the portrayal of the father is not solely negative. Indeed, one of the most lyrical moments in the play occurs in the second act as we see George, alone, practicing his Muslim prayers. His movements are described as 'poetic and gentle' in the stage directions and this 'gentleness' carries over into the comforting embrace he gives to his son immediately after his prayers are finished. Abdul, the eldest son recognises this as something he wants for himself when he says 'when I got home my dad was here praying ....and it was right to be here ...to belong to something' (Khan-Din 1996: 49). Indeed, *East is East* as a 'problem' play dramatises some robust arguments between the children over cultural identity which brooked no preciousness as the nickname of Gandhi for the most devout Muslim among the children, Maneer, suggests.

The portrayal of the children in *East is East*, who are neither 'English nor Pakistani' (Spencer 1996) can be read as a model espousing a hybrid and fluid understanding of cultural identity. Although one of the children in particular, Tariq, rebels against his Asian heritage in his desire to assimilate claiming, 'we speak English not Urdu' (Khan-Din 1996: 40), it is his brother, Abdul, who recognises that 'no one round here thinks we're English, we're the Paki family who run the chippy' (Khan-Din 1996: 39). Indeed, the play points out that the cost of assimilation for Abdul is having to laugh at racist jokes, a price he finds too high as he realises, 'I don't want that out there...it's as alien to me as me dad's world is to you' (Khan-Din 1996: 49).

In this way, *East is East* refuses to accept the narrow and exclusive definition of 'Britishness' that cannot encompass British Asian cultural difference. However, these signs of cultural identity are shown to be fluid rather than fixed as the children in *East Is East* speak with northern accents and greet in Urdu, mime along to Bollywood film songs, dress in both traditional Asian clothes and western ones, and attend mosque as well as helping out when the catholic parade is short handed. Indeed, Ayub Khan-Din's assertion that *East is East*, both the play and subsequent film, are 'as much Northern pieces as they are Asian pieces' (Khan-Din 1999: 6) clearly locates its hybrid British Asian provenance.

Indeed, the success of plays such as *East is East*, as well as *Balti Kings*, and *Fourteen Songs*... and their latest production, *Strictly Dandia*, set in the London Gujarati community during the festival of Navratri, suggests Tamasha's commitment to 'pioneering the attendance of large culturally diverse audiences to culturally specific work' (Landon-Smith 2002). Furthermore, Tamasha's performance methodology of research based realism underlines their commitment to the 'authenticity' of this 'culturally specific work' and gives credence to their aim of producing theatre which 'makes cultural connections that are a celebration of complexity rather than a dilution of the diverse' (Landon-Smith 2004).[110]

Acknowledgements: Dominic Hingorani would like to thank Jatinder Verma, Kristine Landon-Smith and Sudha Bhuchar for their time and understanding.

Works cited

Bhabha, Homi, K. (1994), *The Location of Culture*, London: Routledge.
Bhuchar, Sudha and Kristine Landon-Smith (2003), *Strictly Dandia*, London: Methuen.
Bhuchar, Sudha and Kristine Landon-Smith (2001) *Fourteen Songs, Two Weddings and a Funeral*, London: Methuen.
Bhuchar, Sudha and Kristine Landon-Smith (1999a), *Untouchable*, London: Nick Hern Books.
Bhuchar, Sudha and Kristine Landon-Smith (1999b), *House of the Sun*, London: Nick Hern Books.
Bhuchar, Sudha and Kristine Landon-Smith (1999c), *A Tainted Dawn*, London: Nick Hern Books.
Carter, Ruth (1999), *Women of the Dust*, London: Nick Hern Books.
Carter, Ruth (1999), *A Yearning*, London: Nick Hern Books.

---

[110] For more on Tara and Tamasha in this book, see Dimple Godiwala, 'Genealogies, Archaeologies, Histories: The Revolutionary "Interculturalism" of Asian Theatre in Britain'; Alda Terracciano, 'Mainstreaming African, Asian and Caribbean Theatre: The Experiments of the Black Theatre Forum' and also Jatinder Verma, 'The Shape of a Heart'.

Craig, Sandy (ed.) (1980), *Dreams and Deconstructions – Alternative Theatre in Britain*, Derbyshire: Amber Lane Press.

Hall, Stuart (1992), *Modernity and Its Futures,* (eds.) Stuart Hall, David Held & Tony Mulgrew, Cambridge: Polity Press.

Hingorani, Dominic (2004), 'Binglishing Britain: Tara Arts: Journey to the West Trilogy', *Contemporary Theatre Review*, (eds.) David Bradby and Maria Delgado, Volume 14 (4).

Joshi, Abhijat, *A Shaft Of Sunlight*, London: Nick Hern Books.

Khan, Naseem (1976), *The Arts Britain Ignores – The Arts of Ethnic Minorities in Britain,* London: The Commission For Racial Equality.

Khan-Din, Ayub (1996), *East Is East*, London: Nick Hern Books.

Landon-Smith, Kristine (1998) Programme notes, *Fourteen Songs Two Weddings and A Funeral* 'Why adapt a Bollywood film for stage'.

Mishra, Vijay (2002), *Bollywood Cinema – Temples of Desire*, London: Routledge.

Peacock, Keith (1999), *Thatcher's Theatre*, New York: Greenwood Press.

Rushdie, Salman (1991), *Imaginary Homelands*, London: Granta Books.

Verma, Deepak (2001), *Ghostdancing*, London: Methuen.

Verma, Jatinder (1998), 'Binglishing the Stage: A Generation of Asian Theatre in England' in *Theatre Matters*, (eds.) Richard Boon and Jane Plastow, Cambridge: Cambridge University Press.

Verma, Jatinder (1996a), 'The Challenge of Binglish: analyzing multi-cultural productions', in *Analyzing Performance: A Critical Reader,* (ed.) Patrick Campbell, Manchester: Manchester University Press.

Verma, Jatinder (1996b), *In Contact With the Gods,* (eds.) Maria Delgado & Paul Heritage, Manchester: Manchester University Press.

Verma, Jatinder (1989c), 'Transformations in Culture: The Asian in Britain', The Sir George Birdwood Memorial Lecture, Wednesday 22 March 1989, *RSA Journal.*

Archives

Aurora, Keval (3 February1994), *The Pioneer (Delhi)*, 'In search of a voice' [Tamasha Archive].

Bhuchar, Sudha, Kristine Landon-Smith, Chris Ryman, Rehan Sheikh and Richard Vranch (2002), *Ryman and The Sheikh*, [Tamasha Archive].

Bhuchar, Sudha and Shaheen Khan (1999), *Balti Kings*, [Tamasha Archive].

Bhuchar, Sudha and Kristine Landon-Smith (1998), 'Tamasha Theatre Company - Into the Millennium', A Mission Statement [Tamasha Archive].

Bhuchar, Sudha and Kristine Landon-Smith (1992) Programme Foreword for Indian Production of *Women of the Dust* [Tamasha Archive].

Hussein, Iqbal (1998), *I Will Be a Text* [Dramaturgical Notes] [Tara Arts Archive] Trilogy Background Files, no.TB28, p.1

Landon-Smith, Kristine (2004), *Tamasha Theatre Company Gala Programme*, 15th Anniversary Fundraising Gala, 12 February at the Lyric Theatre, Hammersmith [Tamasha Archive].

Sawalha, Nadim (2003), *All I Want Is a British Passport*, [Tamasha Archive].

Verma, Jatinder (2002a), *The Journey to the West Trilogy*, Parts I, II & III [Tara Arts Archive]

Verma, Jatinder (1995), *Cyrano* [Tara Arts Archive].

Verma, Jatinder (1994), *Le Bourgeoise Gentilhomme*, [Tara Arts Archive].

Verma, Jatinder (1993), *Troilus and Cressida*, [Tara Arts Archive].

Verma, Jatinder (1990a), *Tartuffe*, [Tara Arts Archive].

Verma, Jatinder (1990b), *A Marriage Of Convenience*, [Tara Arts Archive].

Verma, Jatinder (1989a), *Ala Afsur (The Government Inspector)* [Tara Arts Archive].

Verma, Jatinder (1989b), *Danton's Death*, [Tara Arts Archive].

Verma, Jatinder (1984a), *Chilli in Your Eyes* [Tara Arts Archive].

Verma, Jatinder (1984b), *Miti Ki Gadi (The Little Clay Cart)* adapted from Shudraka [Tara Arts Archive].

Verma Jatinder (1984c &1986) Production Rehearsal Notebook *Miti Ki Gadi (The Little Clay Cart)* [Tara Arts Archive].

Verma, Jatinder (1981), *Vilayat or England Your England* [Tara Arts Archive].

Verma, Jatinder (1980), *Inkalaab, 1919* [Tara Arts Archive].

Verma, Jatinder (1977), *Sacrifice*, adapted from Rabindranath Tagore, [Tara Arts Archive].

Newspaper reviews

Anon. (30 October 1998), review of *Exodus, Eastern Eye.*

Anon. (17 November 1989), review of *Untouchable, Asian Herald.*

Bhuchar, Sudha (11 December 1989), 'Untouchable Misery 50 Years after Gandhi', *Independent.*

Curtis, Nick (11-18 November 1992), A Review of 'Women of the Dust, *Time Out*

Chaudhuri (November 1989), review of 'Untouchable', *Bazaar.*

Feay, Suzi (24 April 1991), A Review of 'House of the Sun', *Time Out.*

Hall, Fernau (11 January 1986), review of Miti Ki Gadi (The Little Clay Cart), *The Daily Telegraph.*

Hattenstone, Simon (29 January 1997), 'What country friend, is this?', *The Guardian.*

de Jongh, Nicholas (26 November 1996), 'This father's authority rules, not OK', *The Evening Standard.*

Khan-Din, Ayub (31 October 1999), 'I speak English not Urdu...', *Observer Review.*

Kingston, Jeremy (11 February 1997),'Zipped-Up culture clash', *Times.*

Kingston, Jeremy (December 1989), review of 'Untouchable', *Times*.

Landon-Smith, Kristine (6 July 2002), 'Who's who in new British theatre', *Guardian*.

Lawson, Peter (12-19 November 1992), A Review of 'Women of the Dust', *City Limits*.

Logan, Brian (17 November 1998), Review of 'Fourteen Songs...', *Time Out*.

Myerson, Jonathan (20 February 2001), 'A Load Of Old Bollywood', *Independent*.

Peter, John (1 December 1996), 'Crossed Countries', *Sunday Times*.

Peter, John (15 November 1989), A Review of 'Fourteen Songs...', *Sunday Times*.

Rea, Kenneth (13 December 1984), Review of Miti Ki Gadi (The Little Clay Cart), *Guardian*. [Tara Arts Archive].

Spencer, Charles (25 November 1996), 'Rich mix of culture and comedy', *Daily Telegraph*.

Subramanium, Arundhathi (29 January 1999), 'A Nation Polluted with Saviours', *Statesman*. [Tamasha Archive].

Vaish, Arti (5 February 1994), 'Labouring hard to construct reality', *Economic Times* (Delhi). [Tamasha Archive].

Powell, Enoch (21 April 1968), 'Explosive race speech by Powell', *Sunday Times*.

Walsh, Maeve (16 January 2000), 'A bit too much on their plate', *Independent on Sunday*.

Wardle, Irving (8 December 1991), Review of Little Clay Cart at The National Theatre, *Independent On Sunday*. [Tara Arts Archive].

Television and radio

Verma, Jatinder (February 1991), *The Late Show*, Interview by Jim Hiley, BBC 2 [Tara Arts Archive].

Verma, Jatinder (2002b), *The Bone In The Kebab*, BBC Radio 4, Producer Mukti Jane Campion, 11.30 a.m. Thursday 21 February.

Interviews

Bhuchar, Sudha (5 January 1990), 'Double Helping of Indian classic tale is a "first"', interview with Liz Gilby, *Leicester Mercury*.

Bhuchar, Sudha (22 January 1999), interview with Dominic Hingorani, London: the Tamasha offices.

Ganatra, Ravin (2001), interview with Dominic Hingorani [Tara Arts Archive].

Verma, Jatinder (12 April 1990), 'Bound by Traditions' interview with Nick Smurthwaite, *Stage and Television Today*.

Verma, Jatinder (20 January 1984), 'Staging the Asian Experience', interview with Rick Bhanot, *ilea contact*.

Verma, Jatinder (2004), 'Encounters with the epic-an interview', interview with Jane Plastow, *Contemporary Theatre Review*, Vol.14 (2).

IV: CONTROVERSIES

CHAPTER EIGHT

DRAMA IN THE AGE OF *KALYUG*[111]: *BEHZTI* AND SIKH SELF-CENSORSHIP

ANTHONY FROST

Synopsis:
Events surrounding the closure of Bhatti's play after protests by offended Sikhs are described and compared to similar occurrences in India. A tragedy of rights in collision is discussed and the historical and political circumstances - in India and the Sikh diaspora - which have produced the current over-determination to defend a beleaguered Sikh identity are sketched. Rather than being the work of an apostate, it is suggested that the play encodes a fundamental, though critical, belief in Sikhism; and that theatre might provide a 'creative space' in which such clashes could be resolved.

Religion and art have collided for centuries, and will carry on doing battle long after my play and I are forgotten. The tension between who I am, a British-born Sikh woman, and what I do, which is write drama, is at the heart of the matter. These questions of how differences in perspective and belief are negotiated in Britain today will, I hope, continue to bring about a lively and vital debate (Gurpreet Kaur Bhatti, Guardian, 13 January 2005).

The '*Behzti* Affair' presents a nexus of apparently irreconcilable forces in collision. There is a deeply tragic collision of multiple viewpoints, all of which have some claim to be in the right. The purpose of this chapter is to examine these conflicting claims, and to locate the play in a context of apparently increasing British (and Subcontinental) Sikh militancy and censoriousness, seen principally as

---

[111] According to Sikh and Hindu theology, mankind lives in the *Kalyug*, or Evil Age - the fourth and last cosmic age - the age of strife and falsehood.

a struggle between two crucially opposed articulations of social identity - one of which seeks to defend a beleaguered traditional view, the other attempting to define a new, more complex (but less palatable) vision. This polarisation has actively prevented the play from being heard as a cautionary voice from within the Anglo-Punjabi community, and rather posited it as fundamental apostasy.

In December 2004, the presentation of a new play at the Birmingham Repertory Theatre, *Behzti* (or 'Dishonour') by the young Watford-born playwright Gurpreet Kaur Bhatti was disrupted by angry protests from members of the West Midland Sikh community. In summary, protesters argued that the play was blasphemous, particularly in the writer's choice of setting. The action of her play (which, it must be admitted, is fairly lurid, involving rape and murder) takes place inside a *gurdwara*, or Sikh temple. The gurdwara is the 'gateway to the Guru'; here the Sikh holy book, the *Sri Guru Granth Sahib,* is kept and venerated, and for that reason, all of a gurdwara's precincts may be regarded as sacred territory. Bhatti's play depicts corruption at the heart of the community, and her symbol for this is the violent action which unfolds at the centre of the community's most precious space, culminating in a retributive blow struck with a sacred *kirpan,* or Sikh sword.

For the Birmingham Council of Gurdwaras, a generally humane and moderate body, (consulted in advance of the production), the symbolic location and action firmly situated the play as an attack on the religion itself, rather than on its misuse or abuse, and they called for changes. The creation of the gurdwara setting was not achieved through realistic scenery, but made use of key props and visual references - which some saw as denigrating the symbols of their faith. Alarmed by the play's content, they were nonetheless willing to see the play performed, but with what seemed to them great tolerance asked for the setting to be changed to a community centre or non-religious venue, where the issue of blasphemy would not arise. At this point, they discovered that a right to be *consulted,* as so often in British politics, actually translates as a right to be *informed.* Consultation did not, apparently, mean that they had the right to ask for changes. When they did, Bhatti, and the Birmingham Repertory Theatre, refused.

The Council of Gurdwaras acknowledged that any institution, religious or otherwise,

is open to corruption, abuse and political ambition. Like the child-molesting priests of the Catholic faith, or the bigotry of some Imams of the Moslem faith and the Pundits of Hindus, the Sikh institute is no different.... To stage a play about the corruption of its institute is always welcomed by the Sikh faith, as it welcomes debate, reform and criticism, so that it improves its practice along the lines as stated by our Gurus. We do not have a problem with this ('Statement by Sikh Groups on Behzti', 17th December 2004; later re-published on Asians in Media Website, 13 May 2005).

The community leaders did not condemn the representation of the rapist Mr Sandhu, the corrupt Chairperson of the play's gurdwara. They pointed out that in reality British legal measures exist to prevent such a person from gaining pre-eminence in any gurdwara's organisation (and – somewhat chillingly – suggest that Sikhs know how to deal with such people anyway). Instead, they deplored both the use of the gurdwara setting and the depiction of Sandhu's 'bedraggled' brother Jaswant, the comic *Giani* figure, whom they regarded as holding the faith up to ridicule. ('Giani' is loosely translated as 'priest' in the play text, though 'religious scholar' would be more accurate, since Sikhism has no ordained priesthood).

> Whilst the Chairperson justifiably meets his demise and we applaud it, (in real life, if the background of such a person was known, the community would simply never bring him into the committee. In fact people have been known to be killed when such a person tries to get into a committee) it is the caricature element of the Giani that we have major issues with…. He is portrayed as being irresponsible and out of depth of the principles he is supposedly preaching ('Statement by Sikh Groups on Behzti', 17 December 2004).

They conclude that there is something decidedly sinister about Bhatti's depiction of both the temporal and spiritual figureheads at the gurdwara and the production's only intention, therefore, is 'to demonise the Sikh institute.' They reason that the play

> says more about the arts establishment which continues to use public funds to promote offensive productions on minorities in the name of art. Writers from minority communities who have little knowledge of their own communities but are willing to write highly offensive material continue to be sought by the white arts establishment. Is this not racism? ('Statement by Sikh Groups on Behzti', 17 December 2004).

Bhatti, naturally, disputed this reading of her play, and insisted on the validity of her choice of metaphorical setting, her understanding of Sikhism, and her characterisations. Hence her refusal to accept the requested changes.

As the first protests against the play emerged, the Rep (under the Executive Directorship of Stuart Rogers) were adamant in their support of the playwright. The theatre would 'never yield' to threats of intimidation; 'the writer's right to write' was sacrosanct. As the protests grew in size and ferocity, however, the West Midlands police warned that they could not guarantee the safety of audiences attending the play. And when the crush of increasingly hot-headed protesters pushed back a police cordon, one of the theatre's distinctive large exterior glass panels was broken. At this point, mindful of the theatre's glasshouse structure, and the vulnerability of those attending the building, the theatre cancelled the play on Health and Safety grounds.

When the play was withdrawn, Kim Kirpjalit Kaur Brom, a local councillor and protestor, congratulated the Rep and claimed that 'commonsense' had prevailed

(Branigan & Dodd, *Guardian*, 21 December 2004), while Dr Kanwaljit Kaur-Singh, Chair of the British Sikh Education Council, welcomed the ban, commenting 'it is insulting the religion by portraying murder and sexual abuse in a Gurdwara. If it was in a community centre... I would have been offended but I would not have called for its banning' (*Guardian*, 22 December 2004).

Following news reports of the situation, and the publication on a liberal newspaper's front page of part of the play's text (*Independent*, 21 December 2004), there was considerable support from Britain's theatre community – seven hundred prominent signatories to a letter of support – and a surprisingly mealy-mouthed response from Fiona Mactaggart, the Home Office Minister for Race Equality on the Radio 4 *Today* programme. Despite this generally vociferous support from the arts community, and offers to stage the play from other theatres in Birmingham and elsewhere (Neil Foster of the Birmingham Stage Company offered to do the play, as did the Royal Court in London), permission has not been granted, and the play remains in limbo.

As does Bhatti herself. A friend, film-maker Shakila Taranum Mann, is quoted as saying 'She has been threatened with murder and told to go into hiding by the police... She feels this is an attempt to censor her. It is mob rule' (Branigan & Dodd, *Guardian* 21 December 2004). Bhatti herself contacted Neil Foster after he made his offer to re-stage her play, and asked him to withdraw it, largely because the threats against her had increased (Jury & Pettifor, *Independent*, 22 December 2004: although Bhatti denies having vetoed the play and suggests that, when the time is right, she will sanction future productions; Bhatti, *Guardian*, 13 January 2005). Essentially, she remains in hiding as I write this, six months later.

In the interim, however, Gurpreet Kaur Bhatti has been awarded the Susan Smith Blackburn Prize (an American prize worth $10,000, awarded annually to the best English language play by a woman). In awarding the prize, one of the judges, theatre critic Matt Wolf, said: 'Ms Bhatti writes with courage, intelligence and skill about family dynamics within a larger, ceaselessly fascinating social and cultural context.' (*BBC News Website*, 9 March 2005). This judgement is indicative of how sympathetic 'neutrals' view Bhatti's situation, but almost certainly overestimates the play (is it really the 'best' drama by a woman writing in English this year?), and does little to explain or palliate the extraordinary violence generated by its first performances.

I will relate the *Behzti* affair to the current Indian outcry against the film *Jo Bole So Nihaal*, and attempt to argue that, with Sikh identity hypersensitive to any misrepresentation in India, the issue for diasporic Sikh communities is equally acute. Surrounded by alien cultures, and partly assimilated into them, the choice for many appears to be a return to orthodoxy and a violent (if necessary) defence of traditional values. For others, the multicultural world of the West is something to be embraced, offering a chance to go beyond the patriarchal limits set by some manipulators of tradition, and, in Bhatti's own words, to challenge the imprisoning 'mythology of the Sikh diaspora' (Foreword to *Behzti*, p.17; see Hall 2002: 209 n.14).

Finally, as the Birmingham Rep stages Yasmin Whittaker Khan's Anglo-Pakistani play *Bells* (about the prevalence of *mujra* brothels in British Muslim communities), the wider Asian community may look to *Behzti* as a model - positive or negative - for staging a questioned cultural identity. Asian theatre companies such as Tara and Tamasha, and established writers like Tanika Gupta, Rukhsana Ahmad, Meera Syal, Nandita Ghose, Harwant Bains, Hanif Kureishi, Ayub Khan Din, Shahid Nadeem (many of whom are discussed elsewhere in this volume) have all staged works articulating the conflicts between and within Asian communities, generations, families or sexes. In a context in which violent protest can visibly lead to the silencing of uncongenial opinions, the furore surrounding *Behzti* may make it harder for such important issues to be aired in future. And that makes discussion of the issues of self-censorship here relevant and crucially important.

∇

To create a context for that discussion: Sikhism in India saw itself explicitly threatened in the period following 'Operation Bluestar' (the 1984 military attack on Sant Jarnail Singh Bhindranwale in the Darbar Sahib at Amritsar and the destruction of the Akal Takht). The response to this was the later assassination of Indira Gandhi by two Sikh members of her security detail, followed within hours by the brutal massacre of several thousand Sikhs in New Delhi and beyond. These actions (and the way in which they appeared to be Government-sponsored and police-supported) politicised many Sikhs on the Subcontinent and in the diaspora.

Gurharpal Singh, Professor of Inter-religious Relations at Birmingham University, argues, however, that by the 1990s, the explicit calls for the creation of a Khalistani homeland had largely subsided (although the political situation in Punjab remains distressed), leaving a partial political vacuum 'in which the politics of agitation has given rise to professional lobbying' (G. Singh, *Guardian*, 24 December 2004).

Professor Singh argues that the 1990s saw a rise in 'a more aggressive assertion of Sikh identity' (G. Singh, *Guardian*, 24 December 2004) in contrast to the more defensive – and successful – campaigns and agitation for changes to legislation affecting Sikhs prior to that period. It is also true that, in the reprehensible tide of anti-Islamic prejudice following '9/11', bearded Sikhs in Britain (and in the USA and Canada) were frequently attacked – either because mistaken for Muslims, or because latent hostility to all brown-skinned people could seemingly be justified as righteous in that aftermath. Certainly, such attacks have sharpened a sense of defensiveness and, as with many Muslims, polarised young Sikhs in their beliefs. Feeling rejected by their British peers, many have been tempted to abandon a compromised and complex 'British' identity for a reassuringly simple 'Indian' one - even though, as Kathleen Hall convincingly argues, its apparent simplicity effectively conceals the constructive processes – encoded in the scriptural *rahit-namas* and *gur-bilas* – which have produced it.

> The imagined spiritual community of 'the Sikhs' represented in the entextualized tradition of Sikh religion, martyrdom, and martial strength incorporates a construction of culture as monolithic, timeless, and traditional. The martial image, in particular, is a powerful potential source of identification for young Sikhs – particularly for boys, due to its masculine construction (Hall 2002: 132).

That monolithic, combative image, however constructed, may appeal strongly to the disaffected and offer a justification for immersing oneself in the Sikh *khalsa* (brotherhood) which goes beyond the purely religious. At one extreme it may lead to membership of the British radical Khalsa Dal activist group. Overt religiosity - beyond question genuine - can also become a way of producing a social identity which works by excluding the complex simultaneous temptations and rejections of the non-Sikh, or 'Western' world.

Meanwhile, back in India (where many Sikhs are acutely aware of the Birmingham issue due to widespread newspaper reports and on-line coverage) a parallel situation and a similar mobilisation of aggressive protest has arisen in respect of the film *Jo Bole So Nihaal*. The title derives from the Sikh *Fateh* slogan and battle cry, *Jo Bole So Nihaal: Sat Sri Akal*, [roughly 'He who hears this shall be blessed: Truth is the Eternal Lord'] and its misappropriation is one of the reasons for Sikh outrage at the film.

In this Bollywood farrago, the Punjabi actor Sunny Deol plays an apparently Sikh policeman (with a clipped beard in some scenes and no beard at all in others [112]). The film also contains 'scantily clad' female performers and, elsewhere, mixes in shots of the Sikh scriptures. A widespread outcry was spearheaded by Bibi Jagir Kaur, President of the powerful Shiromani Gurdwara Parbandhak Committee (SGPC). She called on the Indian Central Board of Film Certification to ban the work, claiming that it not only offended Sikh sensibilities, but that the film itself 'is polluted and has shown religion as well as Sikh character in a bad light'. Not only does the title offend, but scenes in the film 'which are enacted in the presence of the *Guru Granth Sahib* should be removed and also those scenes where the

---

[112] One of the *panj kakke* (or 'Five Ks' which are the external symbols of Sikhism) is *kesh*, or uncut hair. A seriously-taken Jat Sikh village copper would be luxuriantly *kesh-dhari* (James 1974: 48). Deol's character subordinates religious and cultural correctness to Bollywood film star glamour.

Gurbani [Sikh scripture] is quoted with distortions' (*OutlookIndia* website: 23 May 2005). To make matters worse, the film appears to glorify an unpopular Punjabi police force.

The issue has divided the Sikh community. Jagir Kaur herself is viewed by many with suspicion, following the apparent murder of her daughter. Then, some weeks before the release of the movie, activists of various radical Sikh groups (the Amritsar-based Shiromani Akali Dal, Dal Khalsa, Shiromani Khalsa Panchayat, Khalra Mission Committee and Sikh Students Federation) blamed the Akal Takht *jathedar*, Giani Joginder Singh Vedanti, 'for allegedly conniving with the distributors of the film. Ludhiana traders had released cell-phone recordings of the jathedar in which he is heard giving his assent to the film screenings. The jathedar denies the reports' (*OutlookIndia* website: 23rd May 2005).

There is also evidence that Punjabi Sikhs may have taken a more extreme view than their metropolitan cousins, for political reasons. The same report quotes Delhi Gurdwara Management Committee chief Paramjit Singh Sarna as saying:

Our members had also seen the movie and they did not find anything controversial in it except the name, which was a religious slogan being used. We also did not receive a single complaint from any Sikh in the Capital relating to the movie (OutlookIndia website: 23 May 2005).

The film was released on 13 May 2005, but has now been banned in many Indian states (including the Punjab, Haryana and West Bengal). In New Delhi, however, the situation escalated. On 22 May 2005, bombs were planted at two cinemas showing the movie, claiming one life and injuring as many as seventy others. The bombings were instantly blamed by the Indian authorities on 'Sikh militants' (because of their publicly stated objection to the film), although later forensic analysis has begun to suggest other, even possibly Islamist, groups may have been involved. For Bibi Jagir Kaur, the bombs were 'a conspiracy to defame Sikhs' and an attempt 'to show the peace-loving Sikh community in a bad light' (*OutlookIndia* website: 23 May 2005). She blamed the Government for not taking steps to prevent the outrage after being warned (although the only step they could have taken was to ban the film outright, which they were reluctant to do).

The two issues – the English play and the Indian film – cross refer. In the film (and in an earlier movie, *Bewafa*), Sikh identity is subject to apparently deliberate misrepresentation, and the various Sikh agencies have been activated in defence of that identity. Producer 'Ponty' Chadha and director Rahul Rawail, himself a Sikh, of course disagree, claiming that their film doesn't offend against Sikhs or Sikhism, and that the Board of Film Certification understands film better than religious activists.

There is of course a long context of misrepresentation to which Sikhs (as an often beleaguered minority) are acutely sensitive. Sunny Deol's 'simple Punjabi cop' character is seen by many as a poor '*Sardar*' stereotype (much as the Irish, Scots and Welsh have often felt insulted by simple-minded stereotyping in books, films and plays in Britain), even before the issue of religious offence is considered. Proposed solutions to the problem of such misrepresentation take the form of a reasonable demand from SGPC President Bibi Jagir Kaur for Sikh representation on the censoring authority; and a perhaps less reasonable demand that the SGPC be given the right to approve, before screening, 'all television serials and films depicting Sikhs and their way of life' (*BBC News World website*, 23 May 2005). One sees in this manoeuvring something which goes beyond the outraged defence of the community from what is, in reality, merely an exploitative, insensitive and fairly banal film. One can sense the jockeying for advantage between political rather than purely religious groups and between communities - liberating the enormously dangerous energy of the insulted and opening the way for inter-communal violence.

But Bhatti's play is not intended as casual exploitation or insult. Whether or not one agrees with her articulation of the many issues of the play (e.g. the self-oppression of women, commercialism, loss of faith, generational clashes, bi-culturalism, the 'shame culture' of *izzat* [113] and *behzti*), it is clear that none of this is done to make money; (and in any case, playwrights in Britain earn pathetically little from their plays, compared with screenwriters). Rather, these issues are raised, and the near certainty of communal censure is faced, because she believes that, it is vital

... for any community to keep evaluating its progress, to connect with its pain and its past. And thus to cultivate a sense of humility and empathy; something much needed in our dog-eat-dog times (Foreword to Behzti: 17).

She believes, and the liberal theatre establishment supports her belief, 'that drama should be provocative and relevant'. As to such drama's liability to offend, the veteran playwright Arnold Wesker argues that there is:

an unavoidable risk that ... what we say and write may cause offence to others. It is an inescapable hazard of living and must be considered a sign of intellectual and emotional maturity when accepted (Wesker, Independent, 22 December 2004).

Accepted, that is, on both sides. Wesker divides offence into three categories; 'gratuitous, calculated, and unavoidable'. He denies that Bhatti's work gives

---

[113] '... the ideology of family honor, supports status rankings ... within Sikh caste communities, influencing, most significantly, the arranging of marriages....' [Izzat] 'is a quality possessed collectively; it is reinforced or ruined in social transactions, most significantly by the actions of unmarried daughters' (Hall 2002: 15 and 167).

ignorant or mindlessly gratuitous offence; nor does it set out with calculation to attack or hurt. Rather, he finds it lamentable that:

> A young colleague who has chosen the art of theatre to explore the truth of her experience, must [now] think twice about her belief that art is where one can courageously pose dangerous questions. The question the Sikhs should be asking is not does the play Behzti insult us, but are the claims of this play true? (Wesker, *Independent*, 22 December 2004).

Gurpreet Bhatti herself clearly understood the risk that her work would be misunderstood by the community it addresses. In November 2004, while the play was in rehearsal, she pre-emptively defended her work thus:

> I wrote Behzti because I passionately oppose injustice and hypocrisy. And because writing drama allows me to create characters, stories, a world in which I, as an artist, can play and entertain and generate debate (Foreword to Behzti: 17).

And, far from giving unthinking offence to decent members of the Sikh *Panth*, she voluntarily enters into the fray because she feels the conflict is, in Wesker's terms, 'unavoidable', and because she believes that such debate is essential.

> The writers I admire are courageous. They present their truths and dare to take risks while living with their fears. They tell us life is ferocious and terrifying, that we are imperfect and only when we embrace our imperfections honestly, can we have hope. Such writers sometimes cause offence. But perhaps those who are affronted by the menace of dialogue and discussion need to be offended (Foreword to Behzti: 17).

While militants gathered to defend their religious and cultural identity, and Sikh activists resisted the symbolic depiction of human frailty at the centre of the gurdwara, theatre workers in Britain and beyond – as well as many Sikh artists like the poet Roshan Doug (*Daily Telegraph*, 22 December 2004) – recognized her stance as important and brave (and were no doubt glad they weren't having to make it).

The director of the Oxford Stage Company, Dominic Dromgoole, compared Bhatti's situation (if not yet the quality of her writing) to that of O'Casey and Shakespeare. Having praised all sides for their admirable restraint and spirit of compromise in the build-up to the protest, he writes:

> Though the scale of the violence is a surprise, this is nothing new in the theatre. Sean O'Casey, a Protestant socialist, fell foul of the fresh-minted purity of the new Irish state. His Plough And The Stars was yelled from the stage by a mob when he besmirched the birthpains of Irish nationalism and the shibboleths of Irish Catholicism. The greatest problem for Shakespeare was the zealotry of the sour-faced Puritan element ... who contested that all drama was immoral. Euripides was thought a little out of control by the

controlling Greek religious authorities. Gurpreet Kaur Bhatti ... is in an honourable tradition. (Dromgoole, Guardian, 20 December 2004).

The point is not that theatre is controversialist for its own sake. Rather, it exists to facilitate inter- and *intra*-communal dialogue about difficult and intractable issues.

Theatre asks for this trouble. It has to. Nonconformity is as natural to theatre as conformity is to religion.... Now, more than ever, it is theatre's role not to be bullied by religious or ideological sensibilities. Now that various forms of fundamentalism are queuing up to close the shutters on the windows of enlightenment - and Sikhism ranks a great deal beneath Christianity for potent offence at this moment - it is more important than ever that theatre finds various ways of saying no to the various blind yeses that are so ardently promoted. It's what it does (Dromgoole, Guardian, 20 December 2004).

In the British Sikh context, Gurharpal Singh writes of the promotion of religion in public life which has led to the legitimation (under New Labour) of what he labels 'rotten' multiculturalism – 'where culture has long given way to religion, particularly if it is capable of delivering ethnic minority votes' and can be used to deliver peaceful outcomes by defusing dissent. This analysis goes some way towards explaining Fiona Mactaggart's highly equivocal response to the *Behzti* problem (which she defends in an interview with Nick Britten, *Daily Telegraph*, 22nd December 2004). Professor Singh argues that, although the frequently expressed sentiments of inter-religious dialogues are noble,

the result is often to stifle dissent within religions and essentialise particular traditions as representing the Sikh, Muslim, Christian or Hindu way. In a highly plural and secular society, nothing could be further from the truth (G. Singh, Guardian, 24 December 2004).

He describes a constituency of third and fourth generation British Sikhs

seriously disaffected from a tradition that remains obstinately rooted to the politics of the homeland while being ambivalent or unresponsive to the challenges of British society. Community leadership appears incapable of addressing their concerns. The choice before it is stark: relapse into a narrow agitational Sikhism or recognize the need to accommodate young British Sikhs' voices (G. Singh, Guardian, 24 December 2004).

Gurharpal Singh has very little time for Bhatti's play as such (seeing her as 'an unsophisticated playwright' with 'grasping backers'), but he argues that banning her play has dire consequences for British Sikhism:

Behzti is not an aberration.... [It is] symptomatic not only of a fatal attraction between third-rate talent and British libertarianism with a penchant for titillating tales of minority voyeurism; it is above all, the playing out of community traumas in public. The tragedy is that multiculturalism has shied away from creating spaces for the peaceful resolution of these dilemmas (G. Singh, Guardian, 24 December 2004).

What I want to argue here is that *theatre* (stripped of its associations with cheap and fleshly entertainment and centred rather in the very notion of imaginative exploration and dialogue), might offer precisely that kind of space.

V

Every playwright, every actor and, ultimately, every spectator knows that theatrical events are not to be confused with reality. (As Doctor Johnson famously put it, 'The spectators are always in their senses, and know, from the first act to the last, that the stage is only a stage': Johnson [1765] 1983: 431). A play like *Behzti* is not a documentary and audiences are normally quite able to distinguish symbolic representations from actuality. It is not claiming that these events literally happened in such and such a temple in Birmingham, Wolverhampton, Huddersfield, or Southall. Nor does it purport to be actually taking place *in* a gurdwara, but rather (on an open and simple set, and by the use of certain indicative props and musical sound effects) it is bringing a gurdwara to mind for the purposes of the narrative.

Despite that, we know of innumerable cases where it has suited politicians to confuse such issues (for example, the case of Edward Bond's 1968 play, *Early Morning*, which was banned *in toto* by the Lord Chamberlain for addressing the legacy of 'Victorianism' via the person of a comically unhistorical lesbian 'Queen Victoria'). It may be that, here, the refusal to accept this indicated 'gurdwara' as a dramatic, and metonymic, representation of Sikhism corrupted and in need of cleansing, and the insistence that instead it is a blasphemous representation of a real gurdwara is a similar attempt to resist the argument of the play, rather than engage with it.

Although *Behzti* is a symbolic rather than a documentary play, its images and metaphors appear torn from an appreciation of Sikhism, rather than a rejection of it, and from a reading of Sikh history and scripture which does not seem superficial to those involved in its rehearsal and performance, nor to many of its Sikh recipients (though I must of course defer to Sikh scholars on this point).

It is also, as Gurharpal Singh might have to acknowledge, an emotionally engaged dramatic projection and articulation of observed social and cultural issues. The lived experience of female self-oppression (in both *Behzti* and the earlier play *Behsharam*) is clearly observed and powerfully expressed through contemporary language and stage images. The issue exists precisely in the space between Gurmukhi scripture and British vulgarity - there is no other space for it to occupy other than the culturally-confused territory in which these displaced and excommunicated women (Balbir and Min) are driven to reside.

Is it not possible that there exists a metaphorical level in *Behzti* that the raised passions about the play prevent us from seeing? As Sunny Hundal points out, there is a visual pun even in the play's poster – reproduced on the cover of the printed play text – which represents a woman in *shalwar kameez* (presumably Min) holding up a comically enormous pair of pants (presumably belonging to Balbir). The visual reference to airing one's dirty linen in public is obvious. But so, too, is the substitution of these absurd knickers for proper Sikh *kachh*. The image immediately identifies the cultural dichotomy of the play's central figures, and the irreconcilable worlds they are doomed to inhabit. On one hand the traditional outer garment represents modesty and social as well as religious conformity; on the other, the prominently displayed undergarment becomes an admittedly comic, but strangely disturbing icon of Westernisation, the aging body, and the outward sign of the *patit*, or apostate life.

As the narrative of *Behzti* unfolds, we become aware of a dreadful loss of status, a fall from power occasioned by the loss and betrayal of Balbir's husband, Tej. Balbir and her daughter have been, for twenty years, outcast and excommunicated, ever since the disgrace and suicide of the homosexual, drug-using Tej. Their house, which Balbir, Teetee and Polly recall with such nostalgia, has been sold 'Before his ashes were flung over Brighton Pier' (*Behzti*: 78). They now live in a high-rise council flat, attended only by a West Indian care assistant. Balbir's former status is obliterated by this past dishonour, just as her present capacities have been eroded by a recent stroke.

Maninder (her name simplified and Westernised as 'Min') has been brought up in ignorance of her Sikh faith as a result of Balbir's ostracism, and subsequent apostasy. The opening scene is full of subtle inversions of Sikh practice: the old woman, naked, turns what should be a ritual bath and prayerful preparation for her return to the gurdwara for the *gurpurb* celebrating Guru Nanak's birthday, into wallowing in self-pity and self-indulgence. She is returning to the gurdwara because she seeks Mr Sandhu's list of eligible marriage partners for her lumpen 'buffalo' daughter rather than because she has rediscovered her faith (although her rapid translation of the prayer for Min confirms she has never forgotten her own baptism – symbolised by the 'Kaur' in her name). I suggest that these inversions are not clumsy or insulting; they are deliberate signs of a desperately misconceived and empty existence.

We glimpse Min's estrangement from her faith in the first scene, too, where she appears dressed in mismatched Western clothes with uncombed hair, trying to learn the words of a *shalok* [114] before visiting the gurdwara for the first time since childhood. Min is unable to develop her own identity until, arguably, the end of the play. For much of the time she is stranded between worlds and identities. To be a dutiful daughter, she has to act like a mother, while being denied the opportunity to become one. Sacrificed to Balbir's need to reclaim *izzat* by getting her daughter married; Min loses her innocence, and her honour, in the most violent way possible. Min is an innocent; she has as little knowledge of the wider world as she does of the world within Sikhism. Not even a *sahaj-dhari*, Min is simply ignorant of most of the tenets and practices of Sikhism, as much as she is unsure of Punjabi. At first sight, it may appear that she has simply fallen into the spiritual void of Westernisation and lost her Sikh and Indian identity. It transpires that she has been raised in ignorance by Balbir, and is naturally drawn to her religion.

Language is critical here. As well as creating cultural gaps between immigrants and their forebears, and between second generation offspring and their parents, 'neglect of language cuts Sikhs off from their spiritual heritage' (Cole 2003: 182). A stage direction informs us that 'her Punjabi is broken and her accent imperfect' (*Behzti*: 25). Min is linguistically severed from Sikhism, literally excommunicated by her inability to read or understand the *Gurmukhi* script of the *Guru Granth Sahib*; cut off from the language of prayer and the words of salvation. One wonders how fluent Gurpreet Kaur Bhatti is.

When Balbir reluctantly translates the prayer for her, Min literally dances (albeit to the music of Michael Jackson!) When she finds love, it is embodied in the multi-cultural person of the sympathetically-portrayed black care assistant, Elvis, drawn (like the non-Sikh audience) into the strange dream world of this gurdwara where he is tempted and symbolically made (briefly) into 'Elvis Singh' by the mocking women.

But why should audiences see these actions as signs; or see the play as metaphorical rather than literal? The character names may alert us. 'Balbir Kaur' and 'Tej Singh' are significant names in Sikh history. Balbir shares her name with a member of a famous *shahidi jatta* (martyr group) of the 1920s, who laid her dead child on the roadway and continued advancing towards the British until herself cut down (Dogra & Dogra 2003: 51). Tej was the name of a universally despised traitor who was given the title of 'Raja' by the British for bringing about the destruction of the army under his command in the Anglo-Sikh war (Dogra & Dogra 2003: 440: and cf. Gopal Singh 1988: 543 ff.). Balbir will similarly appear to abandon her daughter before redeeming them both; and Tej's betrayal is endless and irreversible.

---

[114] A verse staff or couplet, part of Sikh hymnology; the term *Ślok* (Sanskrit *sloka*) is transliterated as *salokh* by Bhatti, in *Behzti*: 25. See McLeod 1984: 163.

In other words, Bhatti's play in no way seeks to mock or to denigrate Sikhism. Her friends, like Janet Steel, *Behzti's* director, regard her as a religious woman, and she herself refers to the importance of Truth in her religion.

> Truth is everything in Sikhism, the truth of action, the truth of an individual, God's truth (Foreword to Behzti: 17).

Her play attacks with great passion what she perceives as certain levels of social and institutionalised hypocrisy, and the valorisation of the strong at the expense of the community's weaker or less successful members.

Valerie Lucas will elsewhere discuss the way in which the play encodes a portrayal of female oppression. I will simply note here that, in both her plays, as well as strong but lost and damaged women, Bhatti depicts weak - and thereby dangerous - men.

The very recognisable Indian demand for a son by the poet Father in *Behsharam* causes the mutilation of all the women in his household: literally in the case of his first wife and youngest daughter, spiritually and morally in his mother, second wife and eldest daughter. Even his much longed for boy is eventually taken from him; Westernized and feminized.[115] He fails his family, and his poetry significantly deserts him: his poem, ultimately expresses only a longing for death (*Behsharam*: 42). The strong women of the play, are irreparably damaged and scarred by his abdication of responsibility for them.

In *Behzti*, similarly, Sikh male authority figures have abdicated or failed, and are also in search of death. These guilty and evasive men masquerade to themselves and others as upright, *kesh-dhari* Sikhs. In Sikh terms, all the characters are depicted as *man-mukh* (worldly-minded) rather than *gur-mukh* (God-conscious and God-filled). They are ensnared in *maya* (not the cosmic illusion of classical Vedanta, but the Sikh vision of the material world, God-created and therefore reality, but capable of distracting man from God-centredness:) and *haumai* (self-reliance). Spiritually adrift, they are prey to all the Sikh 'deadly sins' of *kam* (lust), *lobh* (covetousnous), *moh* (wordly attachment), *krodh* (wrath), and *ahankar* (pride). (See Cole & Sambhi 1978: 68, 77, 82-85: See also the *Guru Granth Sahib* p.466: 'In haumai there is worldly attachment (maya) and its shadow, doubt').

Tej and Sandhu have been lovers; Tej and Jaswant have abused drink and drugs. Sandhu's sexually omnivorous nature is metaphorical of his spiritual emptiness and terror, rather than rooted in naturalistic psychology. His predations on the community's women (which they condone because they seek the worldly

---

[115] The spoiled, pampered Raju is showered with piano, tennis and tap-dancing lessons: later, we learn that his mother enters him in ballroom dancing competitions: the Father 'can't face looking at him' (*Behsharam*: 38, 91-92).

advantages his patronage might bring) is similarly metaphorical; and the women repeat the violence done to them through continued oppression, trading *izzat* (family honour) for *behzti* (dishonour) in an endless cycle. Teetee's mother watches her rape, then beats her and calls her 'shameless' (*behsharam*); and Teetee repeats the behaviour. Balbir is expected to fall into the same self-deluding pattern of acquiescence. Not a literal, but a metaphorical pattern.

The disputed figure of Jaswant tries to remain invisible: like the central character 'O' in Samuel Beckett's *Film*, he fears that 'to be is to be perceived', and prefers to be neither. He scuttles away whenever anyone approaches in case they ask him something, or in case he has to deal with reality. His food addiction reduces him to the most basic level of physical humanity. He has been thrust into the role of giani by his brother. Roused from a drug-fuelled stupor at the death of Tej and sent back to India to be symbolically fed and clothed anew, he should be *gur-mukh*. But, far from being a genuine scholar, he is filled with the shadow, doubt. Without mind, he appears to only eat and defecate (simultaneously in one scene), and the stress of being asked for advice means he soon needs to go and change his undergarments. He is inadequate, bemused and remote; another of Bhatti's weak men, in awe of his brother and hiding behind the veil of scripture. Utterly enmeshed in *maya*, he means well, and sometimes appears curiously perceptive. But ultimately he embodies the ineffectualness of the religious adviser to cope with the complexities of contemporary urban life, hiding behind all-purpose platitudes which at first Min finds 'flipping well brilliant!' (*Behzti*: 72), but later discovers to be empty. In the end, cowering in the corner, he cannot even respond to the most basic greeting, '*Vaheguruji kha khalsa*', with the required formula '*Sri Vaheguruji khi fateh*'. (*Behzti*: 136, and 139 [116]). At the play's conclusion, Min completes it in response to Balbir's touch, even as she reaches out to clasp the hand of Elvis.

The final act of vengeance, the taking up of the sacred *kirpan*, is again not blasphemous: it is another symbolic act. Min plays with the sword earlier, not understanding its significance. But Teetee and Balbir both know exactly what its meaning is. Betrayed and abused, they literally follow the seventeenth-century Guru Gobind Singh's famous *Zafar-nama* to the Mughal Emperor Aureng Zeb: 'When an affair is past every other remedy, it is righteous, indeed, to unsheathe the sword.' Teetee's contempt for Sandhu and herself mingles frustration at the collapse of her own selfish plans, and grief at the diminution of former *communitas* to such corruption. It is the *patit* (apostate) Balbir, rather than the *amrit-dhari* ('baptised' Sikh) Teetee, who wields the cleansing blow, and restores a chance of progress to Min and Elvis.

---

[116] Roughly 'The brotherhood belongs to God: The victory is God's'. Frequently used as a greeting and the culmination of *Ardas*, the Sikh prayer which ends religious worship.

Given the decision to build her passionate play out of religious metaphors, the extreme stage language (verbal and physical) is essential to the plays themes. And those shocking expressions *must* clash with a cultural view that says 'There is nothing wrong. Be silent'. They *must* cause offence to those who would maintain, in the face of both reason and history, that there can be no difference of outlook between Sikhs born and raised in Britain and their parents and grandparents in the Punjab. They are bound to offend those who claim, on the one side, that gurdwaras are protected by rules and regulations to prevent corruption, and on the other that such corruption has led to vigilante killing in some extreme cases. It is going to anger those who argue that apparently religious Sikhs cannot be homosexuals or users of prostitutes (see James 1974: 13) or predatory rapists. It is that very dissonance which is the play's subject. That is the dirty linen that needs to be aired.

But, if that were the only point, then Gurpreet Kaur Bhatti should just have circulated a pamphlet on issues of Sikh hypocrisy. No need to write a play at all. No need to air those ridiculous pants in public.

It is rather the *enactment* - the vicarious and emotional living through - of that series of clashes which may highlight 'the tension between assertions of cultural authenticity and essentialized identities and the celebration of new forms of cultural hybridity' (Hall 2002: 9). The anthropological ethnographer Kathleen D. Hall, examining the social production of identity among young British Sikhs thirty years after Alan James's pioneering study, here employs Judith Butler's invocation of identity as 'a strategic provisionality' constantly under political scrutiny to determine its usefulness; and notions of mobile, 'hybrid' identities flexibly produced in response to social contingencies. Hall 2002: 209 n.9). The tension she identifies can remain static, either side of a widening gulf; or some mechanism can be found to bring the two poles into apposition, into dialogue.

It is that shocking dialogic encounter in the safe space of a theatre auditorium which is intended to produce a sharpened experience of what W.E.B. Du Bois called 'double-consciousness' - of seeing one's culture 'from the outside' (Hall 2002: 9, again, cites Du Bois' 1903 essay 'Of Our Spiritual Strivings' in which he writes about the sense of always 'looking at one's self through the eyes of others' which marginalised or immigrant populations naturally acquire: Hall 2002: 194). Victor Shklovsky might have termed that theatrically-heightened experience *ostraneniye*; Bertolt Brecht might have called it *verfremdung*: but these words connote coolness and reasonableness, and that is not the aesthetic mode of Bhatti's writing.

Whether or not she would accept the attribution, Bhatti's play assimilates formally to Aleks Sierz's model of 'in-yer-face' theatre (and for liberal sophisticates is no doubt tarnished by that association, too). Having scripted a number of naturalistic episodes for *Eastenders, Crossroads* and the World Service soap *Westway*, and written screenplays, Bhatti came to live drama just at the point when 'in-yer-face theatre had become a new orthodoxy' (Sierz 2001: 248) and was actually ceasing to shock audiences with its insistent use of obscene language and florid action – most of which, of course, is never actually seen onstage any more than the rape and murder are directly represented in *Behzti*.

It may well be the case that, as for other writers, the style proves to be 'an arena, an imaginary place that can be visited or passed through, a spot where a writer can grow up, or where they can return to after other adventures' (Sierz 2001: 249). Its value, Sierz maintains, lies in 'restoring the writer to the centre of the theatrical process, and reminding society at large that living writers are not only symbols of theatre's vitality but also a crucial resource for the whole culture' (Sierz 2001: 249 – And it's not in the slightest facetious, in the light of the threats Bhatti received, to stress the importance to the 'whole culture' - meaning explicitly Punjabi Sikhs and British Sikhs and non-Sikhs - of keeping the writer *living*).

Some of the most disturbing images of the *Behzti* episode appeared in Mark Dowd's Channel 4 *Dispatches* documentary, 'Holy Offensive'. The programme noted the obvious parallels between Sikh outrage in Birmingham and the Christian Voice attempts to force the BBC to ban the screening of *Jerry Springer: The Opera*. Recalling the violence of Islamic protests against Salman Rushdie's *Satanic Verses* in Bradford and elsewhere, and the later murder in Holland of Theo van Gogh, the documentary suggested that the Sikh success in closing down *Behzti* encouraged the Christian objectors in their orchestrated, but unsuccessful, e-mail campaign to suppress the broadcast, and was evidence of a resurgent religious militancy not confined to Sikhism.

Mohan Singh, of the Guru Nanak Gurdwara in South Birmingham, emerged as a very articulate spokesperson for the religious point-of-view, again putting the case that the play should have been relocated to 'a community centre', rather than a religious building, and allowing the cameras to enter his gurdwara to see the *Guru Granth Sahib* being read and tenderly cared for. By contrast to the now-familiar dark newsreel footage of the jostling crowds outside the Rep, the brightly lit main hall of the gurdwara appeared to be a tranquil refuge.

The small screen appeared to amplify the number of demonstrators outside the theatre, and the blurred camerawork emphasised the restless energy threatening to spill over into violence. Mohan Singh rejected the Rep's claims to be a bastion of free speech, and calmly suggested that rather than these few hundred milling protestors, at least thirty thousand (of Britain's 336,00 Sikhs) lived within a forty minute drive of the theatre and could easily be called into action if the play were not immediately cancelled.

Asian performers Yasmin Wilde, Shelley King and Madhav Sharma (who portrayed Min, Balbir and Mr Sandhu respectively), together with the director Janet Steel, were all incensed, frustrated, intimidated and saddened by the ultimate decision to discontinue the performances under this kind of pressure. As Yasmin

Wilde put it; 'A lot of testosterone was thrown at this little female play' (*Dispatches:* 21 February 2005).

Floodlit newsreel footage of the overwhelmingly masculine protestors surging against police lines outside the theatre fuels the suspicion that the suppression of *Behzti* is misogyny masquerading as religious outrage (an issue which Valerie Lucas discusses elsewhere in this book). Certainly, the protestors pushing against the police were predominantly male. But, within the gurdwara, there were many female voices raised against the play. These elderly women (Punjabi-speaking, though possibly English-competent) were first generation Jats from, say, the Jullunder Doab - the very people with whom Gurpreet Bhatti's dialogue should be taking place.[117] We might say, she should be talking symbolically to her own mother or grandmother, *bucharee* ('poor girl').

These women raised the most chillingly resistant oppositional voices to emerge from the affair; their opinions were delivered very succinctly, and with some brutality. It is worth quoting their comments verbatim.

WOMAN 1:We're worried about what effect this will have on our children. She shouldn't have said it.

WOMAN 2: Everyone's faith is the same. We shouldn't say anything bad about anyone's faith. She has insulted her own faith.

WOMAN 3:This is her own fault. She is the daughter of Sikhs. Remember when the *Satanic Verses* came out. People came out and protested and burnt the book. It's good that that happened. That soon put a stop to it, didn't it?

WOMAN 1:That's what should happen to Bhatti. Making money out of bad-mouthing Sikhs in this way. She might upset other religions too, one day. Far better to put a stop to her now, before she does any more harm (*Dispatches*, 21 February 2005).

And this is the real problem of the protests. The very ladies whose metaphorical condition is being dramatised won't go to see the play. Bhatti's critique of the way such Sikh women may invest so much in their cultural identity that they end by supporting its atrocities and becoming complicit in their own oppression goes unheard. They have determined, perhaps even before their spiritual leaders, that the play has no value.

Perhaps the act of theatre itself is resisted - equated with the debased eroticism of some Punjabi *nautanki* (see Jaywant *et al*, 1998: 131; but also Yarrow 2001: 84), or associated with the Guru's disapproval of public dance-drama forms such as the *Krishna-Lila* ('For money all such mime-makers tune their instruments....

---

[117] Such Jat characters populate her plays - as indicated by their typical *got* (Hindi *gotra*) names; Grewel, Sandhu, Dhodhar... and, of course, Bhatti (Dogra & Dogra 2003: 308; James 1974: 6-7: McLeod 1976: 89).

Such dancing and capering is only the expression of the mind's passion', while the true dance is inward - the ticking of the mind to the harmony of the holy word: see *Guru Granth Sahib*: 465 and 368: and Dogra & Dogra 2003: 107). The *Sukhmani* of Guru Arjan, the Hymn of Peace from which Min and Balbir quote (*Behzti*: 25- 6), elsewhere refers to God as playwright and actor in the ultimate drama of His own creation - with whom no mortal dramatist could compete: 'God Himself sets His play in motion.... He Himself has staged His own dramas; O Nanak, there is no other Creator.... He Himself is the Performer in His own plays .... He causes whomever He pleases to play in His plays.' (*Guru Granth Sahib*: 287-292).

And, of course, the very act of theatregoing requires an excursion into the secular public sphere: to see, but also to be seen. In one sense, this is no different from visiting the gurdwara, but the cultural intention makes it seem very different and alien, and conservatism precludes it.

$$\nabla$$

My chief concern in writing this chapter is to avert a situation, if it can be managed, where it becomes impossible for the various sides to hear each other over the racket of their entrenching tools. The situation surrounding *Behzti* is complicated, and admits of multiple readings, all of which have some claim to truth. Clearly, the play has offended some Sikhs. Put another way round, some Sikhs have allowed themselves to be offended by the play, while others have understood the play in the way its author seems to have intended. Clearly, there are important issues of bi-culturalism and assimilation versus the protection of Sikh religious and cultural identity. Put another way, there are those who are protecting an unreflective perception of Sikhism at odds with the way their own children and many Sikh scholars currently perceive it.

If it is at all possible to reconcile some of these conflicts, it should be attempted. Censorship is a dangerous practice of absolute last resort - for this community and for all communities. The advocacy of free speech is not merely a rhetorical, or even an ideological, stance on the part of British humanist liberals out of touch, and out of sympathy with the views of their religious Sikh neighbours. Rather, dialogue with alternative views is the only means of genuine spiritual, as well as political, growth. As philosopher A.C. Grayling put it:

> Freedom of speech is not a decorative amenity in a liberal democracy. It's fundamental to its structure. Without it, other rights and freedoms are effectively empty, because they cannot be asserted, and still less defended, when free speech is forbidden (Independent on Sunday, 26 December 2004).

Free speech is a fundamental belief which Sikhs and non-Sikhs share, a common ground arrived at from different starting points. The historian Patwant Singh, writing of frustrated attempts to open discussion on matters of Sikh theology within the Indian context, reminds us that:

> Integral to the principle of equality is the right to free speech - also ingrained in the spirit of the Sikh faith. Any diminution of this principle distorts the very concept of Sikhism, since all its traditional practices … are based on the republican ideal of encouraging people to invoke their right of free expression, a right Sikhs have enjoyed from the beginning, unfettered by the dictates of a self-centred few (P. Singh 1999: 259).

He goes on to warn that 'attempts to censor freedom of expression within Sikhism lead in the direction which proponents of *hindutva* [the movement of Hindu self-assertion] is taking Hindus…' (P. Singh 1999: 261), and he quotes I.F. Stone's famous dictum derived from the fate of Socrates, 'We must not be angry with honest men' (Stone 1989: 222). Or women.

Gurharpal Singh has identified a serious flaw in the multicultural project; the lack of creative spaces in which to address potentially divisive major community issues such as religious orthodoxy, sexual role and identity, language and the endlessly developing relationship to the host culture. That address must imply theatre, in whatever form, since it implies the *processes* of theatre; dialogue, imaginative projection, empathetic exploration of otherness, listening and responding to the issues dramatised without confusing metonymy for actuality.

> The closing of the play has triggered a series of timely and valuable discussions. However, there can never be any excuse for the demonisation of a religion or its followers. The Sikh heritage is one of valour and victory over adversity. Our ancestors were warriors with the finest minds who championed principles of equality and selflessness. I am proud to come from this remarkable people and do not fear the disdain of some, because I know my work is rooted in honesty and passion. I hope bridges can be built, but whether this prodigal daughter can ever return home remains to be seen. (Bhatti, Guardian 13 January 2005).

I want to suggest (with deliberate naivety) that rather than boycotting the play and becoming further entrenched in their irreconcilable positions, the warring participants in the intercultural tragedy of *Behzti* should agree to share the creative space that theatre affords, and respectfully – perhaps in the manner of Augusto Boal's 'Forum Theatre' – perform and re-perform and re-make the play for each other.[118]

---

[118] For more on *Behzti* in this volume, see Valerie Kaneko Lucas, '"Shameless" – Women, sexuality and violence in British Asian Drama' and Claire Cochrane, '"A Local Habitation and a Name": The Development of Black and Asian Theatre in Birmingham since the 70s'.

Works cited:

Bhatti, Gurpreet Kaur (2001), *Behsharam (Shameless)*, London: Oberon.
Bhatti, Gurpreet Kaur (2004), *Behzti (Dishonour)*, London: Oberon.
Cole, W. Owen, & Piara Singh Sambhi (1978), *The Sikhs: Their Religious Beliefs and Practices*, London: Routledge & Kegan Paul.
Cole, W. Owen (2003), *Sikhism*, London: Hodder & Stoughton.
Dogra, Ramesh Chander and Urmila Dogra (2003), *The Sikh World: An Encyclopaedic Survey of Sikh Religion and Culture*, New Delhi: UBS Publishers Distributors.
Hall, Kathleen D. (2002), *Lives in Translation: Sikh Youth as British Citizens*, Philadelphia: University of Pennsylvania Press.
James, Alan G. (1974), *Sikh Children in Britain*, (for Institute of Race Relations), Oxford: Oxford University Press.
Jaywant, Jasmine, Ranbir Singh and Ravi Chaturvedi (1998), 'Indian Theatre' in Don Rubin (ed.), *The World Encyclopedia of Contemporary Theatre*, Vol. 5., Asia/Pacific, London & New York: Routledge.
Johnson, Samuel (1765), 'Preface' to 'The Plays of William Shakespeare', in Donald Greene (ed.) (1983), *The Oxford Authors: Samuel Johnson*, Oxford: Oxford University Press.
McLeod, W.H. (1976), *The Evolution of the Sikh Community: Five Essays*, Oxford: Clarendon Press.
McLeod, W.H. (1984), (trans. & ed.), *Textual Sources for the Study of Sikhism*, Manchester: Manchester University Press.
McLeod, W.H. (1995), *Historical Dictionary of Sikhism*, London: Scarecrow Press.
Sierz, Aleks (2001), *In-Yer-Face Theatre: British Drama Today*, London: Faber and Faber.
Singh, Gopal (1988), *A History of the Sikh People, (1469-1988)*, New Delhi: Allied Publishers.
Singh, Patwant (1999), *The Sikhs*, London: John Murray.
Stone, I.F. (1989), *The Trial of Socrates*, New York: Anchor Books.
Yarrow, Ralph (2001), *Indian Theatre: Theatre of Origin, Theatre of Freedom*, Richmond: Curzon.

Quotations from the *Sri Guru Granth Sahib*, or *Adi Granth* and *Dasam Granth*, are from various translations, including the on-line *Khalsa Consensus Translation* by Singh Sahib Dr. Sant Singh Khalsa (at *www.sikhs.org/english/frame.html*) against which page references have been checked.

Newspaper articles

Bhatti, Gurpreet Kaur (13 January 2005), 'This Warrior is Fighting On', *Guardian*, (repr. *SikhSpectrum.com Quarterly*, Issue No. 19, February 2005).

Bhatti, Gurpreet Kaur (21 December 2004), 'An offensive act?' *Independent*. (First publication of part of the *Behzti* text).

Branigan, Tania & Vikram Dodd (21 December 2004), 'Writer in hiding as violence closes play', *Guardian*. Also see Editorial, 'Playing with fire'.

Britten, Nick (22 December 2004), 'Violent protests will benefit axed Sikh play, says minister', *Daily Telegraph*. Also see News: 'Minister defends rights of protesters as Sikh play closes'; and Editorial: 'Running scared'.

Burleigh, James (22 December 2004), 'Royal Court considers staging drama', *Daily Telegraph*.

Dodd, Vikram, Tania Branigan and Charlotte Higgins (22 December 2004), 'Arts and community leaders to discuss freedom of expression', *Guardian*.

Doug, Roshan (22 December 2004), 'There's more to art than Bollywood', *Daily Telegraph*.

Dromgoole, Dominic (20 December 2004), 'Theatre's role is to challenge religion', *Guardian*. Repr. online, *Guardian Unlimited*, n.d.

Grayling, A.C. (26 December 2004), 'You too can be tolerant', *Independent on Sunday*.

Jury, Louise and Tom Pettifor (22 December 2004), 'Playwright goes into hiding and blocks plan to perform work that offended Sikh community', *Independent*.

Singh, Gurharpal (24 December 2004), 'Sikhs are the real losers from *Behzti*', *Guardian*.

Wesker, Arnold (22 December 2004), 'Can offence be avoided in this life?' *Independent*. Also see Editorial and Opinion.

Televison and Radio

Dowd, Mark (writer & narrator) (21 February 2005), 'Holy Offensive', *Dispatches* TV documentary, directed and produced by Bruno Sorrentino for Angeleye, Scotland: broadcast by Channel 4.

Mactaggart, Fiona (20 December 2004), Home Office Minister, contribution to *Today* programme, BBC Radio 4.

Websites

BBC News World, South Asia; 'Why Sikh row dogs Bollywood film', 23 May 2005. (http://news.bbc.co.uk/1/hi/world/south_asia/4573619.htm)

BBC News Website; Matt Wolf quoted on Bhatti's award of the Susan Smith Blackburn Prize, 9 March 2005. (http://news.bbc.co.uk/1/hi/england/west_midlands/4332317.htm)

Hundal, Sunny, 'The violent reaction to Behzti is despicable and hypocritical', 20 December 2004, *Asians in Media* Website (repr. 5th June 2005). (http://www.asiansinmedia.org/news/article.php/theatre/746)
OutlookIndia.com, 'A conspiracy to defame Sikhs', *OutlookIndia.com* website, 23 May 2005. (http://outlookindia.com/outlookarchive.asp?war=ignore&s=4)
Sikh Groups, 'Statement by Sikh Groups on *Behzti*', 17 December 2004, *Asians in Media* Website (repr. 13th May 2005). (http://www.asiansinmedia.org/news/article.php/theatre/743

V: THE DRAMATISTS

CHAPTER NINE

'BLACK AND FEMALE IS SOME OF WHO I AM AND I WANT TO EXPLORE IT':[1] BLACK WOMEN'S PLAYS OF THE 1980S AND 1990S

KATHLEEN STARCK

Synopsis:

This chapter looks at the increasing number of plays by Black female authors and tries to give explanations for such a development. Against this background, individual plays are examined which deal with such diverse topics as migration, unplanned pregnancy, drug trafficking, Black Lesbianism, the Black community, 'Black' health and the Christian nativity story. In the light of the ubiquity of many of these themes, a move of Black Women's Theatre from fringe to mainstream seems possible.

The emergence of plays by Black[2] women writers in Britain is a later phenomenon in the context of 20th century dramaturgy. Although there were male Black playwrights such as Errol John, Wole Soyinka, and Derek Walcott whose plays had been produced by the end of the 1960s and later those such as Caryl

---

[1] Mcleod in Stephenson and Langridge 1997: 99.
[2] I use the term 'black' as referring to women of Caribbean or African descent only.

Phillips and Mustapha Matura, women remained largely invisible until the late 1970s/early 1980s.[3]

This is a tendency which, although somewhat earlier, can likewise be observed for white women playwrights who have found it much more difficult to have their plays produced than their male colleagues. Yet white women profited largely from the Women's Liberation Movement and the emergence of feminist literary criticism from the 1960s onwards (and saw the first wave of women playwrights from the 1970s onwards). In spite of the early notion of a 'universal sisterhood' among all women, Black women often did not feel represented by their white sisters' writings. In addition to white women's oppression based on gender and class, Black women's experience not only included but often placed at the centre the category of race. Thus, coinciding with the theorizing of issues of national, cultural, sexual and ethnic identities in cultural, literary, lesbian and feminist studies, Black women in Britain started finding 'stage voices' of their own only from the 1980s.

Opportunities to do so were provided for example at the Royal Court Young People's theatre through workshops as well as through the Second Wave Young Women Playwrights' Festival at the Albany, established in 1982 by the Second Wave Young Women's Project under Ann Considine. The project

> [...] provided a support system for young women who want to write and produce films and plays. [...] they have offered workshops in improvisation, comedy, songwriting, storytelling, rap and dub all geared to creating for new writers that moment when the creation of something that will live on a stage no longer seems an impossibility. Workshop participants have the opportunity to have their early efforts scrutinised not [...] with a view to rejection, but in order to suggest developments. Even more valuable are the open rehearsals and rehearsed readings [...] These writers [...] challenge existing theatre conventions or choose to create their own. (Gray 1990: 10-11)

Another initiative was 'The Write Stuff' at Theatre Centre, where Associate Director Sita Ramamurthy set up 'a forum for experienced black writers to explore the craft of playwriting' (Ramamurthy 1993: 12). During a series of workshops different aspects of playwriting, such as structure, plot, character, and treatments and the requirements of young people's theatre were examined so that in the end the writers were able to make proposals to Theatre Centre. Likewise, the 'Talking Black' workshops led by Jude Alderson, have encouraged Black women playwrights such as Bernadine Evaristo, Patricia Hilaire, Paulette Randall and Carol Williams (Croft 1993: 85).

---

[3] For a more detailed analysis of male playwrights see, in this volume, Deirdre Osborne, 'Writing Black Back: An Overview of Black Theatre and Performance in Britain' and for Soyinka, see Zodwa Motsa, 'A Scourge of the Empire: Wole Soyinka's Notorious Theatre at the Royal Court'.

Some white women's theatre groups such as the Women's Theatre Group and Women and Theatre started employing multi-racial politics in the 1980s. These were to ensure the presence of Black women in the companies and led to, for example, the first all-Black production by the Women's Theatre Group of Sandra Yaw's *Zerri's Choice* in 1989. In addition, the Women's Theatre Group (now Sphinx) have worked with Paullette Randall, Jackie Kay and Winsome Pinnock. Likewise, other groups such as Theatre Centre Women's Company, the Women's Playhouse Trust, Red Ladder and Monstrous Regiment have performed plays by Black women (Croft 1993: 86), while Clean Break has commissioned, among others, *Mules* (1996) by Winsome Pinnock and *Hyacyth Blue* (1999) by Kara Miller.

Black women's theatre groups that emerged are, for example, The BiBi Crew (women comedians), The Women's Troop (formed by the Black Mime Theatre and emphasising the explicitly Black *British* experience in their work), Imani-Faith (founded by Jaqueline Rudet), Sistren (originating in Jamaica and, according to Lizbeth Goodman, in their practical social action comparable to Clean Break Theatre Company (Goodman 1993: 163)), Talawa (directed by Yvonne Brewster and drawing on West Indian and African traditions), and Theatre of Black Women. However, it was 'well into the 1980s [that] the Theatre of Black Women was one of very few groups to provide opportunities for aspiring women playwrights' (Ponnuswami 2000: 219). Founded in 1982 by Bernadine Evaristo, Patricia Hilaire and Paulette Randall, the company's declared aim was to encourage a 'bonding between Black women [...] in their fight against oppression which helps them to define 'feminism' on their own terms' (Aston 1995: 89). In addition to developments within the UK, many Black women playwrights found themselves inspired by African-American Ntozake Shange's *for coloured girls who have considered suicide, when the rainbow is enuf* which received a West End production in 1980.

Mirroring the slow emergence of opportunities for Black women playwrights is also the fact that it was only in 1987 and 1989 that the first two volumes of Black British plays, edited by Yvonne Brewster, who in 1982 became the first black woman drama officer at the Arts Council, were published by Methuen. Further 'early' anthologies to include plays by Black and Asian women playwrights are Nick Hern's *First Run* series and Aurora Metro Press's *Six Plays by Black and Asian Women Writers* (1993) which was edited by Kadija George. Similarly, a scholarly interest in plays by Black women playwrights has only developed over the last fifteen years or so. Books that have explicitly dealt with the subject are Trevor R. Griffiths and Margaret Llewellyn-Jones' *British and Irish Women Dramatists Since 1958*, Lizbeth Goodman's *Contemporary Feminist Theatre: To Each Her Own*, Elaine Aston's *An Introduction to Feminism and Theatre*, Elaine Aston and Janelle Reinelt's *Cambridge Companion to Contemporary British*

Women Dramatists, to some extent J. Ellen Gainor's *Imperialism and Theatre*, Dimple Godiwala's *Breaking the Bounds: British Feminist Dramatists Writing in the Mainstream since c. 1980*, and, at the time of writing, Gabriele Griffin's *Contemporary Black and Asian Women Playwrights in Britain*.

As the interest in Black playwriting is growing, there has also been a shift in the self-perception of the authors. According to Griffin many of today's Black women playwrights

> do not necessarily view themselves as 'other' within Britain and [...] are now claiming their place at the table of British high culture. Their points of reference – in theatrical terms – are thus not the rituals, performances, or theatre works that are prevalent in [for example] the West Indies [or] parts of Africa [...], but those of contemporary British theatre. (Griffin 2003: 5)

In line with this, Mary Karen Dahl, when writing about Black British theatre, includes an analysis of Kay's *Chiaroscuro* and Oshodi's *Blood Sweat and Fears*, under the title of 'Black Voices at the *Centre*' (Dahl 1995: 46-52, my emphasis).

However, regardless of the authors' later shift in self-perception, many early plays by Black women were produced on the fringe (which once more proves that it is not merely self-perception which defines one's identity). A large number focus on Black women's history, particularly looking at the generation which came to Britain during the 1950s and 1960s. Something that many Black playwrights share is an obvious concern with the quest for an identity by ethnic minority women. This holds true not only for characters of the older generation, but also for their children, members of Black communities of the second and third generations. Griffin explains this phenomenon as follows:

> Indeed, many of their plays [...] focus on issues of race, colour and ethnicity as key determinants of their characters' experiences. This is almost inevitable given the political climate in Britain in which questions of difference, migration, ethnicity, and regulation are perennially high on the agenda. (Griffin 2003: 8)

Plays that particularly address issues of identity and belonging are *Leave Taking*, *A Hero's Welcome* and *Talking in Tongues* by Winsome Pinnock, *Chiaroscuro* by Jackie Kay, *England is De Place for Me* by Killian M. Gideon, *When Last Did I See You* by Lisselle Kayla, *No Place Like Home* by Roselia John Baptiste, *Running Dream* by Trish Cooke, *Basin, God's Second in Command* and *Take Back What's Yours* by Jacqueline Rudet, *Zerrie's Choice* by Sandra Yaw, *Leonora's Dance* by Zindika, *Cricket at Camp David* by Jenny McLeod, Valerie Mason-John's *Brown Girl in the Ring,* and to an extent also Rudet's *Money to Live.*

Other topics addressed in Black British women's plays are awakening sexuality and unplanned pregnancy which signify a break with the black community's values (Grace Dayley's *Rose's Story* and Roselia John Baptiste's *Back Street Mammy*), making a living as a family or singly (Liselle Kayla's *When Last Did I See You* and Jacqueline Rudet's *Money To Live*), the (ab)use of black women as drug trafficking 'mules' (Winsome Pinnock's *Mules*), Black Lesbian identity (Jackie Kay's *Chiaroscuro* and *Twice Over* and Valerie Mason-John's *Sin Dykes*), exploring through biography the history of one of the first Black British papers, the *West Indian Gazette* (Winsome Pinnock's *A Rock in Water*), prison life (Kara Miller's *Hyacinth Blue*), the outsider position of a Black woman in a white society (Jenny McLeod's *Raising Fires*), ('Black') health and disability (Liselle Kayla's *Don't Pay Dem No Mind* and Maria Oshodi's *Blood Sweat and Fears*), the heterogeneity of 'the Black community' and problems this entails (Maria Oshodi's *The S Bend* and Jackie Kay's *Chiaroscuro*), and later, contemporary notions of a Black artist's life in Britain and what it means to be 'authentically Black' (Winsome Pinnock's response, *Water*, to Alice Childress's *Wine in the Wilderness*) and the Christian nativity story adapted to a Creole West Indian setting (Geraldine Connor's *Carnival Messiah*).

Due to the theme's prominence, I will begin my analyses with some of the plays addressing issues of migration and belonging: Killion M. Gideon's *England is De Place for Me*, Liselle Kayla's *When Last Did I See You*, Roselia John Baptiste's *No Place Like Home* (all three plays were developed during the Second Wave Young Women Playwrights' Festival at the Albany Empire between 1986-1988), Trish Cooke's *Running Dream*, and Zindika's *Leonora's Dance*.

Directed by Paulette Randall, *England is De Place for Me* was one of the Second Wave works which received a mainstage production. It was first performed at the Albany Empire in 1988. The play focuses on the character of Rose who decides to stay on in England after divorcing her unfaithful husband Winston and seeing her friends Dickie and Wilma return to Jamaica for their retirement. Apart from the question of migration, *England is De Place for Me* addresses issues of racism, gender, class, spiritualism, and first and second generation immigrants' adaptation to their host/home country.

All the characters show signs of nostalgia thinking about Jamaica. Thus, Rose is convinced that she and Winston would have been able to afford a house 'back home' (I.ii), Winston mourns the fact that he would have been promoted to the rank of detective had they stayed on (II.ii), and Dickie persuades his wife to go back by claiming, 'You know you can stay aweh from de country you born fe ah while but dere's no place like home' (II.i). However, at the same time they are having second thoughts about returning. Winston warns that 'Enuff man guh back home and can't settle dere no more ... dem stey aweh too long' (II.iv). Wilma, on the other hand, worries about the financial situation: 'Wha dere to guh back to? How we guh mek a living? Don't feget dat is what we left Jamaica for. We older now. Dere's not even wuk for de young, how we guh survive?' (II.i).

Gideon presents two 'solutions'. Wilma and Dickie start saving and finally, after having seen their children through school, emigrate back to Jamaica. Although in the epilogue Wilma claims that it takes time to adjust, she also admits, 'Dat Dickie is like him neva leave de place' (Epilogue). This is confirmed when Dickie once more claims, 'home is home' (Epilogue). Rose, on the other hand, does not have much of a choice. Divorcing her husband and having to support her children she must stay on in England. Thus, she woefully writes to her friends, 'Maybe if tings had wuk out wid me and Winston all of we could be where you is now' (Epilogue). Yet, at the end of the play she tells Wilma that she has passed her driving test which clearly is symbolic of her liberation from a bad marriage. It also might mark a new beginning by providing Rose with a new freedom of movement. Gideon does not state a preference for one or the other decision.

She does, though, make a statement concerning ethnic identity by making extensive use of Jamaican English throughout the play. Interestingly, it is also language which marks one of the differences between first and second generation and signifies an estrangement between 'Jamaican' parents and 'English' children. Thus, Wilma complains about her son Leo, 'Sometime Leo ah talk some breed ah Cockney me naw understand. I haffe tell him to slow down ... ah no Cockney in dis house' (II.ii).

Liselle Kayla, in *When Last Did I See You*, is explicit about her choice of language:

> for too long the Afro-European based languages of the Caribbean have been regarded as almost without value. [...] For more of these languages to be elevated to a position of pride, we must begin to play a part in the process by recognising that they have worth within themselves. In this play I have celebrated the language of Jamaica, showing it without compromise, as it has been fashioned by passing generations of people from the island. (Notes on the Language of the Play from the Author)

Kayla concentrates on the differences between first and second generation by contrasting the fifty-year-old Miss Mary with her friend Blossom's teenage offspring. Both families emigrated to Britain during the 1950s due to their desperate economic situation in Jamaica and UK government schemes luring cheap Jamaican labour to England. However, whereas Miss Mary is a Jehovah's Witness who clearly adheres to the 'old ways', Claudia, Shirley and Lloyd were born and brought up in England. Thus Mary scorns Lloyd for not finding a job, 'If you did stop talking wid de bad English and start comb you head and fling 'way de old frowsy hat, you would find job' (p. 110). Moreover, Miss Mary and the 'children' have a debate about spirituality and the Day of Judgement. Whereas Miss Mary lives in constant anticipation of it and keeps her suitcase all packed under her bed, the teenagers make fun of her and advise her to spend some more time living before she starts planning her death. In addition, Miss Mary complains about her friend Blossom's way of life of going out to clubs and enjoying an ever changing string of boyfriends. Thus, Mary's last sentence is symbolic of the absence of the 'old ways' from her friend's family's life, 'Is a long time now me don't see her' (111). It is very likely that Mary will not see the 'old' and 'pure' Jamaican Blossom ever again since immigration has changed her and the way she brings up her children.

As the title suggests, Roselia John Baptiste's play *No Place Like Home* explores the implications of the term 'home'. In a foreword to the play the meaning is described as follows: '[…] the country where one was born, the members of your family, the place where one likes to be, the place of origin'. Furthermore, the 'point' of the play is stated explicitly: 'For Black [Britons], those who were born or who have lived in Britain for a number of years, the word is difficult to define' (p. 141). In accordance, the play offers different notions of what represents 'home' for the different characters. Thus, Maggie, the mother, clearly mourns her 'lost' Dominican life and loses herself in whisky. In contrast, her husband Thomas is more realistic and tries to embrace the here and now and although he admits to his children that he is thinking about going back constantly, he is convinced that

[…] a man has to go forward, no sense looking back … Your modder now, she is living in de past, mess up your mind to keep on looking back on things. […] in a sense I'm more English than Dominican. I've been here more years than I was over there. (152-3)

Likewise, when challenged with his own wish to go 'home', he explains to his daughter Anne who has never been to Dominica, 'Home? You don't understand Annie. My Dominica is in my head, yours is in your heart ... and your mammy's… (*looks at the bottle of whisky*) […]' (153). Thomas is aware that the Dominica 'in his head' does not exist any more in reality. He differentiates his own memory of the country and his daughter's imagining it from her mother's tales of the past. Interestingly, Maggie's passing on her memories to her daughter is undercut by the girl's English surroundings. Thus, when she tells her father how she pictures the country of her ancestors he replies, 'You see through white man's eyes' (154). This is certainly not supported by Maggie's insistence that she wants her daughters to 'have more' than she had. She informs their older daughter, Marcie, 'I send you to school to do better than me. When Etta send me to school, I never go. But you, you can read and write – you should know better. You have an education in England' (144). Marcie, on the other hand, accuses Maggie of trying to turn her into someone English and claims that she is neither English nor Dominican. So whereas the other characters are quite certain about their identities, Marcie, unlike her younger sister Anne, is the one character 'in between' and she has not quite arrived yet in this 'third space'.

What is striking about Gideon's, Kayla's and Baptiste's plays is that all three address the tension or even estrangement between first and second generations which are brought about by the anglicizing of the latter. Although it would be too simplistic to assume an auto-biographical basis to the plays, the impression that these are pressing issues for young black women in Britain during the 1980s is undeniable.

Generations are also at the centre of Zindika's *Leonora's Dance*. Yet here it is not the difference between the age groups, but more the continuance of traditions, the passing on of knowledge and spirituality from mothers to daughters, the linkage between the generations which are emphasised. Leonora, who is described as 'a young middle-aged woman', had come from the Caribbean to England as a young girl in order to pursue a ballet career. As the daughter of a black Caribbean fieldhand and a white English colonel, what she had not anticipated were the racism and discrimination she was faced with in England. As a consequence, a spirit, called Medusa, has taken possession of her and her house. Leonora has spells of confusion, panic attacks and shows acute signs of agoraphobia (reminiscent of Sue Townsend's play on agoraphobia, *Bazaar & Rummage*). None the less, she is unwilling to face the fact that she never 'made it' in England. When finally her mother Frieda comes to England to fetch her back home to take her position as the eldest daughter of 'Aunt Frieda', the obeah woman, Leonora refuses. Instead, Frieda finds a follower in the young black lodger Daphine who is a distant relative, whose mother sees spirits, and who has a daughter to whom she could pass on the calling.

The focus on generations includes Frieda's calling on all her ancestors to help 'save' Leonora:

> I shall have to call them all – no matter how far away they are; Ivory Coast, New Guinea, Benin, Bermuda,, and Burundi. I shall go way back, past the middle passage, to the old world, to Africa. (II.iv)

However, what is made very clear by Frieda is the fact that it is the matrilineal link which counts.

Whereas this plot values and supports the notion of a cultural identity and one's purpose in life 'predestined' by an original shared culture/ethnicity before colonialism (a contradiction of Stuart Hall's argument in *New Ethnicities*), the second plot undercuts this idea. Chinese-British Melisa is hiding in order to escape an arranged marriage. She seeks help from the spirit of one of her heroines whom she tries to procure by witchcraft. In the end, she realises that she has to take action herself instead of waiting for help from some spiritual being. When she finally leaves her bedsit in order to run away from the threatening marriage, she addresses her parents and ancestors as follows:

[…] slave and chattel I shall be not. To endure marriage is to endure hell. Mama you should know that. I am too infatuated with freedom to sacrifice that. […] I think tradition is a dead man's revenge on the future.' (II.iv)

Interestingly, Melisa is mainly in fear of her father, whereas in Leonora's case it is her mother who has come to use her power over her daughter. In the first case, the play suggests a refusal of tradition, in the latter an embracing of it. Thus it seems the preserving of female traditions is ascribed a higher value than those of patriarchy.

With respect to dramatic means, Zindika describes her own writing as 'magic realism' (Author's Notes). She fuses very realistic scenes with the appearance of the spirit Medusa who addresses the audience as well as the characters. When Frieda tries to rescue Leonora, a battle between Medusa and the obeah spirit, between European/Western versus Caribbean traditions ensues:

Frieda:Come mediators, convenors of life and rituals. Come overseers of the past. Come voice of the people. Come myals, speakers of parables, come sisters of the spirit.
Medusa:This is the house. […] A house built on unstable ground…distorted dreams, stagnant lives…a house where souls compete.
Frieda:Come bring us wisdom and love in all its potency. Come like the rhythm of the drum. Come if you are able (*makes drum noises – whilst moving forward as if to stop Medusa. She appears to freeze.*)
Medusa:(*Looks at Frieda. Walks around her*) This is my house. My name is Medusa – the name that launched a thousand spells. […] Come on move me if you dare. You'll wish you'd never heard my name. […]. (II.iv)

However, in line with Zindika's emphasis on lineage and heritage, it is the obeah spirit who wins since at the end of the play Medusa is run over by a lorry. The different generations of her own family is what inspired Trish Cooke to write *Running Dream* when she was asked to write a play for Second Wave Youth group in Deptford (Author's Note). First produced in 1993, the play deals with three generations of Dominican women, the three sisters Clementine, Grace and Bianca, their mother Florentine, and their grandmother, Ma Effeline. Once more, the main theme is that of belonging. As a young woman Florentine follows her husband to England, leaving Grace and Clementine in Dominica to be brought up by their grandmother. After some years and giving birth to Bianca, she sends for Grace to join them in England. As a consequence, Clementine feels left out and develops a bitter resentment. What she does not realise, however, is that Grace feels completely uprooted and out of place when she comes to England. In addition, she cannot connect to her new sister in the same way she did to Clementine. Bianca and Grace do not share the same culture and although Bianca understands patois she hardly speaks it. Bianca is the character with the most explicit identity crisis. Whereas her mother and her two sisters clearly define themselves as Dominican, Bianca does not know the country of her mother and sisters. When, as an adult, she visits Grace and Clementine in Dominica she tries to explain this feeling to a family friend:

Bianca:Everything must be straight-forward for you though.
Dennis:[...] Why you say that?
Bianca:Because this [the beach, the sea] is yours.
Dennis:What? You're joking. The only thing that is mine is what you see in front of you. I make no claims on this island.
Bianca:You were born here.
[...]
Dennis:[...] So because you were born in England you would say England is yours?
Bianca:That's my point, it's not. (Part 2: 223)

Florentine, too, regrets her decision to follow her husband William. When, just before she dies, he returns to her and says that he has been thinking about going 'home' she replies, 'You know how long I been waiting for you to say that to me?' (Part 2: 224). During the same conversation the symbolism of the play's title is revealed with William contemplating his life:

When you run so far forward you forget what you running from you start to think maybe you should stop and look...especially when you think you getting somewhere and you turn and see you still in the same place... [...] I always thought there was something there, for me, on the other side, so I ran to take it. I never stopped to see that what I was running to reach I already had. (Part 2: 225)

Cooke also highlights the bonds which exist between mothers and daughters. Thus Florentine knows when Effeline dies before she receives Grace's phone-call from Dominica. Likewise, just before her own death, Florentine can feel her mother calling her. And finally, while their mother dies in England, the three sisters are united on the Dominican beach, embracing each other with the creaking noise of the dead Grandmother's rocking chair in the background.

Cooke's play is non-realist. She employs a chorus, sound effects are created by actors (e.g. the creaking rocking chair, the sound of waves) and drums are used throughout the play to imitate running, the ticking of a clock, and to punctuate comments of the chorus. Further, Cooke makes extensive use of Dominican patois. As well as this, *Running Dream* comes close to a circular form as it begins and ends with the grandmother's creaking rocking chair, repeating the same words addressing her daughter and granddaughters, 'Ah dou dou / Ah dou dou [my dearest]' (Part 2: 227). This creates the impression of the grandmother's presiding over the actions of the play and underlines the role she plays in the life of her (female) descendants.

What is remarkable is that these five plays addressing the subject of belonging share the focus on tension and bonding between different generations created by migration, the trauma of leaving relatives behind, and the disruption caused by the plays' black men's unfaithfulness to their wives.

Rose Dayley in *Rose's Story* also concentrates on the clash of generations. Yet, in this case the conflict grows out of two extremes: Rose's pregnancy at the age of fifteen on the one hand and her father's religiousness which borders on fanaticism on the other. The play, first performed in 1984, developed from personal experiences of the author and its production also reflects some aspects of the cast's lives:

> [...] the women in the cast surpassed themselves. Men were difficult to come by and proved even more difficult to keep, especially when the going got rough. This could have been linked to the actual content of the play, as nearly 50% of the women in the cast were unmarried mothers and could probably make analogies with their lives [...] (Author's Note).

The play starts with a scene at a GP's in which he not only confronts her with the consequence of having a baby, but treats her in a rather patronizing way, assuming that she is not able to make any decisions. This scene foreshadows many others. Again and again Rose faces adults like her parents, a social worker and a policewoman trying to tell her what to do. By most of them it is seen as a given that Rose will not keep the child – Rose's opinion is of not much interest. Thus, when she tells the doctor that she wants the baby he replies: 'How can you be so sure? You've hardly given this vital piece of information time to lodge in your mind. Do you realise a baby will change your life completely?' (I.i). The social worker is less subtle in her implications: 'Have you thought about the difficulties ahead if you decide to have the baby and keep it? I think you should seriously consider having an abortion' (II.i). Rose, on the other hand, is determined to have the baby and not to let anyone take things out of her own hands. Yet her boyfriend, Leroy, is of no help. Although thrilled by the idea of becoming a father, he is not mature enough to understand the consequences. The character of Leroy once more gives rise to the question of how Black men define themselves, their masculinity and their relationship to their families. Becoming a father marks a rite of passage for Leroy. It proves his ability to produce offspring and thus his masculinity – it makes him 'a man'. Obsessed with 'being a man' he does not realise, however, his own childish behaviour and is not able to take any advice. Thus, in the end, Rose understands that she cannot rely on Leroy and goes into a Mother-and-Baby-home.

The vast rift between the generations becomes particularly visible in Rose's father, a minister. Running away from home and falling pregnant deviates so much from this Black community's values that Rose's father cannot forgive her and refuses to take her in again. On the other hand, he forbids her to have an abortion because this is prohibited by the scripture. So Rose is exiled and alienated from her family and community in several ways. She has to acknowledge Leroy's inability to support her, her father's rejection, as well as her mother's complicity with the social worker and policewoman. Yet there is a trace of hope at the end of the play when Rose says, 'And this is where the story *really* begins' (II.iv).

Dayley's extensive use of Jamaican English and her characters' code-switching add to the play's realism which is only undercut by Rose's soliloquies which are addressed to the audience and provide a frame to the plot. What should be emphasised, though, is that Dayley does not necessarily want to show a particularly 'Black' situation, but instead insists that 'it could happen to anyone irrespective of race, colour or creed' (Author's Note).

An issue hinted at as one of the problems to be expected by Rose is at the centre of Jaqueline Rudet's *Money to Live*: how to make ends meet. The play was first performed in 1984 at the Royal Court Theatre Upstairs. The main character is Charlene, a West Indian woman in her twenties who lives in London. She has moved out of her parents' house and finds it hard to survive on the money she makes. An old friend introduces her to the scene of clubs, go-go dancing and stripping. She decides to increase her income by stripping. *Money to Live* raises issues of sexism, sexploitation, dignity and abuse.

Although Charlene's parents do not particularly approve of her part-time job as a Go-go dancer, both agree that she is a grown-up woman and cannot be told what to do. In addition, Charlene's mother, Olive, reveals to her daughter that she has stooped much lower than her. 'Your mother was a prostitute' (Scene vii). 'Your father never knew […]. There was no way I could have kept house on his money' (Scene vii). This is reminiscent of Kay Adshead's play *Thatcher's Women* in which Northern English housewives go to London for a fortnight and prostitute themselves in order to support their unemployed families. Yet, although Rudet seems sympathetic with Charlene's part-time job and her need for more money throughout the play, she undercuts this with the character of Charlene's sister Jennifer. She brings into play quite a different perspective:

Jennifer: When the show's over, where do they go?
Charlene: Home.
Jennifer: But if they're excited, and they don't live with a woman, how are they going to relieve themselves?
Charlene: By their own efforts.
Jennifer: What if they don't want to do that?
Charlene: Go out and find a girl.

Jennifer:What happens if they can't find a girl who wants to sleep with them?
Charlene:Go to a prostitute.
Jennifer:What happens if they can't afford a prostitute?
Charlene:They'll have to go without, won't they?
Jennifer:But if the guy is really excited, he won't want to go without.
Charlene:Are you saying that guy's going to rape someone?
Jennifer:More than likely, or try to rape someone, and it will have been your fault. You excited him. [...] all of you dancers, all of those nude models, all of those blue movie actresses; you make women seem like all they've got on their mind is sex. (Scene iii)

The discussion prefigures the last scene of the play in which Jennifer visits her sister late at night and gets molested by a man on her way. In addition, she refuses Charlene's offer of a holiday on the grounds that the money was earned stripping. She relates this, of course, to what has just happened to her:

I looked into his eyes and saw nothing but inherent, deep, deep disrespect. He wanted merely one thing from me. It wasn't my heart. And it wasn't my consent. Why do all men think that all women are just waiting to be approached? What, have I got an entrance sign over my head? (Scene xiii)

This is very much in line with feminist anti-pornography writing such as Andrea Dworkin's (1981) and plays such as Sarah Daniels's *Masterpieces* which proposes a connection between pornography, sexist jokes and the rape of women (see Godiwala 2003). Likewise, in her own words, Rudet is

not overly concerned with relations between black and white people. Of course, since the first 'black' plays were written, life has remained as appallingly racist as ever, but I think it's time for black people to be shown as more than just 'black' (Author's Note).

In contrast, Winsome Pinnock's *A Rock in Water* is very much concerned with the condition of being black. Premiered in 1989 at the Royal Court Theatre Upstairs, it follows the journey of Claudia Jones from a young Jamaican-American girl who accompanies her mother on her search for work and ends just after Jones's death in London. Pinnock traces Jones's development from an angry child who hates her mother for having to clean white women's homes to a communist activist throwing leaflets from the Statue of Liberty, to a prisoner trying to bond with her guards on the basis of women's oppression and class, to an exile in London, to the 'inventor' of the Notting Hill Carnival and successful editor of the *West Indian Gazette*, one of the first Black British papers. However, according to Pinnock, Jones died alone and by the 1980s had virtually been forgotten. The author makes it very clear that she wants to redress this development:

[...] a heroine who never forgot her roots, a fearless campaigner who gave up an ambition for 'political stardom' in order to work at grass roots level – comforting, encouraging and fighting on behalf of a people who could so easily have given up the struggle in those turbulent days of the mid-50s. But they didn't give up. And the play is as much about them as about Claudia. They're still fighting and so, in a way, is she (Preface).

This note of hope for Claudia Jones's cause is particularly visible at the end of the play. Dina, one of Claudia's closest friends and colleagues at the press, learns about Claudia's death and feels unable to continue her work. However, co-editor Donald tells her that Claudia would have wanted them to continue and he 'picks up a notebook and pen and starts to write' (I.xx).

A later play by Pinnock, *Mules*, although requiring a mixed ethnic cast, is according to Pinnock not concerned with issues of ethnicity: 'I don't see why one can't just see them as characters and that there are other areas being explored apart from race' (Stephenson and Langridge 1997: 52). However, I would like to challenge this statement and claim that in addition to class and gender, ethnicity is one of the themes of *Mules*.

Based on true-life stories, Pinnock wrote about women who make a living by smuggling drugs. The play is set in contemporary London and Jamaica and changes back and forth between these two locations. The two Jamaican sisters Lyla and Lou cannot find sufficiently paid employment. So, as a last resort, they agree to work for Bridie, an American who is in the drug business. Bridie has 'cast off' her Jamaican background and adopted an American accent since this makes her appear superior to the Jamaican women she hires who speak Jamaican English. In addition, both the title of the play and the ethnicity of four of the characters conjure up notions of slavery. The drug-smuggling women are called mules, they are merely 'containers' carrying the commodities, i.e. drugs. Like slaves, they are valued for their labour only. Being Jamaican and Nigerian they symbolise the origin of the large-scale slave trade that was conducted by various European countries. In addition, their plane trips echo the experience of the middle passage in that the women have to avoid drawing attention to themselves and thus cannot move freely. Moreover, some women die of an overdose when the drug-filled condom inserted into their vagina bursts. This and the danger of being caught by the customs police make it necessary to have several 'mules' on the same plane. Thus, a high enough profit is ensured even when some 'cargo' is lost – a practice paralleled by that of slave traders who threw overboard ill slaves because the insurance money would be higher than the price that an infirm slave would attract. Although Pinnock employs humour to provide some comic relief, she does not show a way out – Lou and Lyla's situation is very much the same at the beginning and the end of the play.

Black Lesbian identity is what Jackie Kay investigates in *Chiaroscuro*. The play was written for Theatre of Black Women and first presented in 1986. The title translates as 'light and dark' and thus hints at the play's concern with 'different kinds of Black'. *Chiaroscuro* is highly symbolic and set in a non-realist mode. It makes use of oral traditions such as story telling and poetry. Kay's symbolism employs dance, music, masks, pantomime and props.

The four black women of the play try to come to terms with their own or their friends' homosexual, black/mixed-racial identity. Most important, they are also in search of a name for black lesbian women, a name that is different from the derogatory ones given to them by the (white) lesbian and the black (homophobic) community. This lack of a name and thus a lack of Black lesbian history is best illustrated in one of the characters' songs:

> [...] They had no one to name me after
> in so many different ways
> so tell me what do you call her
> a woman who loves another like her [...]
> where are people
> who are her ancestors
> tell me what is her name [...]
> so many women have been lost at sea
> so many of our stories have been swept away [...]. (II.79)

All four characters have undergone changes by the end of the play. This once more serves Hall's concept of the New Ethnicities and is in line with Mirza: 'Identity is a living process; though it is temporal, spatial and shifting, it can be transformative through risk, desire, decision and struggle' (Mirza 1998: 17). Kay frames the play using identical tableaux (except for redistributed props standing for parts of the characters' identity) in the first and the last scene. Thus, the search for names/identities is not over, and similar struggles will have to be lived through many more times.[4]

Another approach to Black lesbian identity, bolder due to its emergence twelve years after *Chiaroscuro*, is offered by Valerie Mason-John in her play *Sin Dykes*. Her realist characters are white and black, lesbian and out, and some of them engage in sado-masochism. Thus, lesbian sexuality as such is not the issue anymore. However, notions of what black women ought and out not to do play a major role. So although the lesbian community seems to have accepted black women, there are still 'rules' of the black community to abide by. Mason-John

---

[4] For more on *Chiaroscuro* see Dimple Godiwala, 'The Search for Identity and the Claim for an Ethnicity of Englishness in Jackie Kay's *Chiaroscuro* and Valerie Mason-John's *Brown Girl in the Ring*' elsewhere in this book.

challenges the validity of ideas such as: 'You got no excuse to check white gal, now you know where the black women's scene is. [...] I can't understand how you can have relationships with the enemy' (Scene iii). In addition to rules about inter-racial relationships, there also are strong ideas of what defines a black lesbian identity. Among these, 'Black women don't do SM' (Scene iv) is a prominent one in *Sin Dykes*.

Although Mason-John supports the attitude 'I love women, and I refuse to be trapped by my colour' (Scene iii), she leaves room for an awareness that ethnicity does matter in power relationships. *Sin Dykes* makes this clear with the character of Trudy, an African-Caribbean 'Brixton babe' who would like to try out SM practices. Formerly she refused to do so with her white lover Gill. After they have separated she nonetheless asks Gill's advice since she is planning to have SM sex with another black woman. She explains to Gill:

> So many of black-white relationships in this society are based on the fact that black people have very little power. How do I know that when I give up my power to you in the bed, that you're not thinking 'nigger, slave, mugger'? And if you are, how do I know you won't play those thoughts out on my body? (Scene iv)

This, however, is undermined when Trudy finally acts out her SM fantasies with Clio, another black woman, and gets carried away with her power over Clio: 'Clio remains sexual in her whipping style, while Trudy becomes excited, dangerous, out of control, unsafe, going beyond boundaries' (Scene v). Clio's final shout of 'Stop!' (Scene v) proves Trudy's explanations of her fear of inter-racial SM sex questionable. Power and its abuse can be dangerous regardless of ethnicity and skin colour.

In contrast to this last statement, skin colour makes all the difference in Jenny McLeod's *Raising Fires*, which was first performed at the Bush Theatre in 1994. The play is set in the Essex of 1603 and tells the story of Tilda, a West Indian girl who was brought to England by a minister who had found her starving, next to her mother's body. As a young woman Tilda has an affair with the Marshall of the town and falls pregnant. Simultaneously, a number of fires has been troubling Tilda's home town Gravestown. The Marshall's wife, Ruth, seizes this opportunity to take revenge and accuses Grace of witchcraft. As so often in real witch hunts, more and more people join in the accusations, making ever bolder and more absurd claims: 'I saw her too, and she had a broom stick that took her to the top of the church [...]' (I.ix). 'She's brought fire, death and starvation, brought misery and curses on all of us' (I.ix). In the end, Tilda is left to the mob.

So far the plot resembles a rather 'conventional' witch hunt. However, McLeod makes a point of Tilda's ethnic otherness. When people start making accusations, they quickly introduce Tilda's skin colour as the reason for and proof of her witchcraft. Thus her adopted brother laments: 'This is what becomes of bringing *her kind* into our house and making her call us kin' (I.viii: my emphasis). The othering of Tilda by people around her is already introduced in scene four when Tilda says, 'The first thing I noticed about me was other people' (I.iv). She also hints at at least one, if not several, rapes she has experienced. So Tilda was not only labelled 'the other', but treated accordingly. Her probable death at the end of the play is therefore merely the consequence of her isolation in the white community. McLeod explains her motivation for writing *Raising Fires* as follows:

> When I talk to my white friends about what it feels like for me walking around the streets of London, it's a complete shock to them. They just don't understand how things work when you're black. Raising Fires looks at that. Tilda's father had no idea of the effect that bringing her to 1603 Essex would have on her. [...] Witches were scapegoated in much the same way as black people in this society. (Stephenson and Langridge 1997: 101)

On the other hand, McLeod states that 'When people get scared about their position in society, they look for difference around them. It's not white nature. It's human nature' (Stephenson and Langridge 1997: 101).

A condition limited solely to people of Afro-Caribbean descent is at the centre of Maria Oshodi's *Blood, Sweat and Fears*. It was first performed in 1989 and deals with sickle-cell anaemia. Oshodi explains that she wanted to 'accurately present the trauma of the disease, but also show some of the social implications' (Author's Preface). The play stresses white society's neglect and ignorance of an illness they know cannot affect them. Thus Ben is wrongly diagnosed for a long time before his condition is correctly identified: 'You might be allergic to something', 'Just a juvenile case of eczema', 'Mild case of gout' (I.ii).

Despite its bleak topic, *Blood, Sweat and Fears* is praised by Yvonne Brewster:

> Its wit, humour and lack of overkill strike a telling blow at much larger prejudices. In this zany, fast-moving play the punch and accuracy of the dialogue is particularly commendable, and the situations keep the action on the boil, focusing on the central theme, throughout (Brewster 1989: Introduction).

Oshodi has continued to take an interest in issues of health and the arts. In 2000 she and Damien O'Connor registered Extant, 'the first arts production company in the UK, managed by blind arts professionals who seek to promote the arts and culture of blind artists' (http://www.damianoconnor.zetnet.co.uk/2about/2html, 2002).

In contrast to the plays introduced so far, I would like to finish with the brief mention of something that is rather a musical or a festival than a play – Geraldine Connor's 2000 *Carnival Messiah*. The piece values the Trinidad Carnival as a serious form of theatre. It tells the

Christian nativity story using eight pieces of music from Handel's Messiah, along with a virtual sampling of world music: dub, reggae, calypso, Orisha chanting, gospel, tassa drumming and steelband music, all unified in the idiom of Trinidad Carnival (Ramcharitar 2004).

It was very successful and highly praised. The *Guardian's* Alfred Hickling writes: 'until you've heard the heavy dub version of For Unto Us a Child Is Born, you haven't lived' (Hickling 2002). So when in 1993 Susan Croft wrote that 'Black women playwrights clearly intend to make themselves heard' (Croft 1993: 98), *Carnival Messiah* can be seen as a fulfilment of this prophecy. Likewise, it is proof that Black women's writing in the new millennium might finally move away from the fringe and have a lot to say to and about the mainstream. Although Black women playwrights often do write about specific Black experiences, thus talking to and possibly about the mainstream, they likewise address topics, such as making a living, drug trafficking, prison life, health and disability, teenage pregnancy and the Christian nativity story, which concern a much wider audience. Even the many quests for an identity in Black women's plays are by no means restricted to one particular ethnicity.

Works cited

Adshead, Kay (1988), *Thatcher's Women*, in Mary Remnant (ed.), *Plays by Women Seven*, London: Methuen.
Aston, Elaine (1995), *An Introduction to Feminism and Theatre*, London: Routledge.
Baptiste, Roselia John (1987), *No Place Like Home*, in Ann Considine and Robyn Slovo (eds.), *Dead Proud: from Second Wave Young Women Playwrights*, London: The Women's Press.
Brewster, Yvonne (ed.) (1989), *Black Plays II,* London: Methuen.
Cooke, Trish (1993), *Running Dream* in Kadija George, (ed.) *Six Plays by Black and Asian Women Writers*, London: Aurora Metro Press.
--------------- (1990), *Back Street Mammy*, in *First Run 2* (ed.), Kate Harwood, London: Nick Hern Books.
Croft, Susan (1993), 'Black Women Playwrights in Britain,' in Trevor R. Griffiths and Margaret Llewellyn-Jones (eds.), *British and Irish Women Dramatists since 1958*, Buckingham: Open University Press.
Dahl, Mary Karen (1995), 'Postcolonial British theatre: black voices at the centre,' in J. Ellen Gainor (ed.), *Imperialism and Theatre,* London: Routledge.
Daley, Grace (1988), *Roses's Story*, in Michelene Wandor (ed.), *Plays by Women Four*, London: Methuen.

Daniels, Sarah (1997), *Masterpieces*, in Sarah Daniels, *Plays 1*, London: Methuen.

Dworkin, Andrea (1981), *Pornography – Men Possessing Women*, London: The Women's Press.

Gainor, Ellen J. (ed.) (1995), *Imperialism and Theatre*, London: Routledge.

George, Kadija (ed.) (1993), *Six Plays by Black and Asian Women Writers*, London: Aurora Metro Press.

Gideon, K.M. (1990), *England is De Place for Me*, in Frances Gray (ed.), *Second Wave Plays: Women at the Albany Empire*, Sheffield: Academic Press.

Godiwala, Dimple (2003), *Breaking the Bounds. British Feminist Dramatists Writing in the Mainstream since c. 1980*, New York & Oxford: Peter Lang.

Goodman, Lizbeth (1993), *Contemporary Feminist Theatre: To Each Her Own*, London: Routledge.

Gray, Frances (ed.) (1990), *Second Wave Plays. Women at the Albany Empire*, Sheffield: Academic Press.

Griffin, Gabriele (2003), *Contemporary Black and Asian Women Playwrights in Britain*, Cambridge: Cambridge University Press.

Harewood, Kate (ed.) (1989), *First Run: New Plays by New Writers*, London: Nick Hern Books.

Kay, Jackie (1988), *Chiaroscuro*, in Jill Davis (ed.), *Lesbian Plays*, London: Methuen.

Kayla, Liselle (1987), *When Last Did I See You?*, in Ann Considine & Robyn Slovo (eds.), *Dead Proud: from Second Wave Young Women Playwrights*, London: The Women's Press.

Mason-John, Valerie (1999), *Sin Dykes*, in Valerie Mason-John, *Brown Girl in the Ring*, London: Get a Grip.

McLeod, Jenny (1994), *Raising Fires*, London: Bush Theatre.

Mirza, Heidi Safia (ed.) (1998), *Black British Feminism: A Reader*, London: Routledge.

Oshodi, Maria (1989), *Blood Sweat and Fears*, in Yvonne Brewster (ed.), *Black Plays II*, London: Methuen.

Pinnock, Winsome (1989), *A Rock in Water*, in Yvonne Brewster (ed.), *Black Plays II*, London: Methuen.

-------- (1996), *Mules*. London: Faber and Faber.

-------- (1989), *Leave Taking*, in *First Run: New Plays by New Writers* (ed.), Kate Harwood, London: Nick Hern Books.

Ponnuswami, Meenakshi (2000), 'Small island people: black British women playwrights,' in Elaine Aston and Janelle Reinelt (eds.), *The Cambridge Companion to Modern British Women Playwrights*, Cambridge: Cambridge University Press.

Ramamurthy, Sita (1993), 'The write stuff,' in Kadija George (ed.), *Six Plays by Black and Asian Women Writers*.

Rudet, Jaqueline (1986), *Money to Live*, in Mary Remnant (ed.), *Plays by Women Five*, London: Methuen.

Stephenson, Heidi and Natasha Langridge (eds.) (1997), *Rage and Reason: Women Playwrights and Playwriting*, London: Methuen.

Townsend, Sue (1995), *Bazaar & Rummage*, London: Nick Hern Books.

Zindika (1993), *Leonora's Dance* in Kadija George (ed.), *Six Plays by Black and Asian Women Writers*, London: Aurora Metro Press.

Reviews

Hickling, Alfred (2002), 'Carnival Messiah', *Guardian*, 1 July.

Websites

http://www.damianoconnor.zetnet.co.uk/2about/2html, 2 June 2002.

Ramcharitar, Raymond, 'Geraldine Connor, Carnival Messiah' *Nou*, http://www.nou-caribbean.com, 15 May 2004.

CHAPTER TEN

THE SEARCH FOR IDENTITY AND THE CLAIM FOR AN ETHNICITY OF ENGLISHNESS IN JACKIE KAY'S *CHIAROSCURO* AND VALERIE MASON-JOHN'S *BROWN GIRL IN THE RING*

DIMPLE GODIWALA

Synopsis:
The trope of identity-formation is central to the experience of blacks who grow up in – and are thereby formulated within – white society. The need to construct a sense of self which is independent of the self-hatred forged in the black psyche by the discrimination of the dominant society is what these plays enact in a debunking of Fanonian racial and sexual stereotypes as they stage a creative response to Albert Memmi's 'two answers of the colonized'.

The search for identity in a society which denies blacks a voice and constructs itself in an exclusion of blackness is perhaps the most important issue to be staged by black women dramatists. Albert Memmi theorizes: 'The body and face of the colonized are not a pretty sight. It is not without damage that one carries the weight of such historical misfortune' (Memmi [1957] 1965: 119). Maya Chowdhry speaks of Britain's 'African/Asian-descent lesbians [who] exist in a racist and homophobic society, and their concerns are viewed as marginal by the mainstream' (in Mason-John 1995: 131). Kay and Mason-John's plays demonstrate that the oppression Memmi and the later Chowdhry speak of is an on-going one, as blacks born in white society experience the condition of racism which is leveled at young children and adults to formulate them in a psychology of self-hatred. The plays go beyond this however, to enact the 'two answers' Memmi formulates: 'He [the colonized] attempts either to *become different* or to *reconquer all the dimensions which colonization tore away from him*' (Memmi [1957] 1965: 120 emphasis mine). In both plays the characters 'become different' as they experience or progress toward self-love and self-acceptance, which they have been robbed of as they were growing up in white society; in Mason-John's play the character boldly appropriates all that colonialism has denied her as a black subject in Britain.

Chiaroscuro[5]

The text of *Chiaroscuro* (1986) negotiates the oppositions and contradictions of History/ Silence, Normal/ Other, Heterosexual/ Lesbian where heterosexuality and whiteness are deemed 'normal' within and without the marginal racialized space. Typical of lesbian coming-out plays with an intrinsic difference in the ethnicity of the constitutive subjects, the text explores coming-out in the face of prejudices within the community and also the formation of black identity within the larger white society. This is done using the resonance of poetry, songs and music in a text which balances naturalistic dialogue as it flirts boldly with an experimental form resulting in a portrait of what it feels like to be black and lesbian within a society which is overwhelmingly inscribed with prejudice, or as Kay herself put it, 'a racist and homophobic society' (Kay 1987: 82-83).

> [C]ommissioned by the Theatre of Black Women [Chiaroscuro] is a delicate but potentially powerful piece written in a mixture of forms [...] in which cultural histories, friendship, 'coming out' as a lesbian and the difficulties of communication in a largely white-dominated and heterosexual world are confronted and overcome (Griffiths and Woddis 1988: 194).

'I am committed to change, personal and political, and everything I write comes out of this commitment. Writing *Chiaroscuro* was a challenging and terrifying experience', says Jackie Kay, the Glaswegian poet who turned successfully to drama before writing her acclaimed first novel *Trumpet* (1998). Influenced profoundly, as have been other black poets and dramatists, by Ntozake Shange's internationally performed play, *for colored girls who have considered*

---

[5] I am grateful to Peter Lang for permission to reproduce some of the material on *Chiaroscuro* which was first published in my monograph *Breaking the Bounds: British Feminist Dramatists Writing in the Mainstream since c. 1980*, New York & Oxford: Peter Lang, 2003.
For more on *Chiaroscuro* see, in this volume, Kathleen Starck, 'Black and Female is Some of Who I Am and I Want to Explore it: Black Women's Plays of the 1980s and 1990s'.

suicide/ when the rainbow is enuf, Kay blends theatre with poetry and transgresses conventional form. Perhaps comparing the result with Shange's, Kay felt that 'some of the dialogue was so naturalistic that the poetry jarred with it rather than complemented it' (Kay 1986: 83). Shange's text uses the poetic speech rhythms of Black America which are influenced by jazz and rap and the blues, whilst Kay attempts to draw on similar traditions which seem surpassed by her own poetic talent which informs the songs. Her imagination is a poetical one, and the experimental format allows for the interplay of naturalistic dialogue with the music and the poetry.

The four actors remain in character/s throughout as the themes of blackness and lesbian-ness are developed with some dexterity. The consciously symbolic[6] use of minimal props against the nearly bare dominantly grey set gives the play a certain depth of imagination against the surface play of the spot-lighting which throws each speaking character into relief. Dressed in all-in-one suits, the actors function as a double-sign enabling them to enact the community whilst remaining in character. There are five objects which dominate the stage. These are the photograph album, symbol of black women's personal and political history; the mirror, symbol of the identity and image-of-difference of black women in a white society; the black doll which serves as a representation of the black woman, responses to which reflect the levels of prejudice toward blackness in the larger community. Thus the doll is both (Black) Self and (Black) Other. The cushion, used to signify the newly born child symbolizes the lack experienced by the four women: there is nothing that cushions them in white society. Kay intended the chest to be 'an important symbol; it functions as the past and also as the chest in the human body. In order to breathe, these four women have to get things 'off their chest'. Everything that is important to them is contained in the chest' (Kay 1986: 83). In the production the chest also takes on the added function of being a symbol of secrets and intimacy as each reveals the negative identity she has formed – thus it is the symbol of revelations as each retrieves the symbol of her fragmented identity from it.

The opening is formal and stylized as the women sit, backs to each other, rotating in turn to tell of their naming against the grey of a dreary landscape. Kay speaks of her obsession with naming: 'What do we call ourselves as lesbians and black women? How did we get our names? How do we assert our names? What are

---

[6] I mean for there to be a difference between a *sign* and a *symbol*. Whilst almost everything from prop to actor is a signifier signifying a signified or signifying a signifier as the case might be, a symbol is something (in this case five props) explicitly and consciously used to signify a signified which has a strata of meanings, making the symbol function on the level of the conscious, the sub-conscious and, as the case may be, the unconscious, all of which may be collective.

our past names? Each of the characters tells the story of her name. She is also searching for another name. She is in flux, reassessing her identity, travelling back into memory and forward into possibility' (Kay 1986: 83). Thus we find the need for history in a racial, cultural as well as individual way.

In an attempt to erase the traces of the double-inscription of colonization and patriarchy on their patronyms, they attempt a matrilineal tracing of origins through autobiographical narration. Necessarily beginning at a time when their ancestors were located in their lands of origin, Aisha, the Indian, traces back to: 'my grandmother was born in the Himalayas at dawn'; while 'My daddy told me he called me Beth because my grandmother's African name was whipped out of her'; and the homeless orphan, always in flux, was named Opal, after 'a stone that was both jewel and rock... a rainbow, changing with the light'. And they chant in unison, 'For we have to remember it all'. The opening is the necessary baptism-through-fire: the ritual of naming the nameless ones, a ceremony which bestows upon them a past and a history which is individual and political. This is the start of their politicization which will move them into the necessary space of (re)discovery as they enter a positive threshold of self-definition and identity. This is of essence as their previous constructions-of-self are markedly negative. The Nigerian Yomi's doll serves as a displacement for Yomi's self-hate. In *Black Skin, White Masks* Frantz Fanon recounts his experience of being black in a white society. Hailed as:

'Dirty nigger!' Or simply, 'Look, a Negro!'
I came into the world imbued with the will to find a meaning in things, my spirit filled with the desire to attain to the source of the world, and then I found that *I was an object* in the midst of other objects.
[...]
The black man among his own in the twentieth century does not know at what moment his inferiority comes into being through the other.
[...] In the white world the man of colour encounters difficulties in the development of his bodily schema. Consciousness of the body is solely a negating activity. It is a third-person consciousness (Fanon [1952] 1967:109-110).

Viewing themselves through the eyes of white society, a 'third-person consciousness' constructs a self-hatred as the blacks learn to see themselves as 'dirty' aliens, the negative remanences of white identity. Opal's mirror reflects her negative self: 'her face was a shock to itself'; and Beth's photo album reveals the negative history of her blackness. Negotiating through a constructed self-negation, they establish a history of self but display a simultaneous lack of identity because it is formed in a space posted as a negativized site by the cultural condescension of western cultures which support, consciously and unconsciously, the 'truth' regimes of white cultural superiority over races of colour.[7] As Jean-Paul Sartre put it, 'It is the anti-Semite who *makes* the Jew.' In Frantz Fanon's later formulation, 'The feeling of inferiority of the colonized is the correlative to the European's feeling of superiority [...] *It is the racist who creates his inferior'* (Fanon [1952] 1967:93).

Thrust into, and formed within, the discursive space of cultural and patriarchal domination each reveals her displacement. Dark of skin and alien of culture Aisha's Asian parents 'were the invited guests who soon found out they'd be treated like gatecrashers'. Yomi holds up the quilt, symbolic of the multicultural patchwork of society that constitutes modern Britain: 'in what language are these threads?' Like the quilt the play is also a patchwork of scenes where themes interweave to work towards a whole or wholeness of being of the four women to enable the formation of an integrated identity for the doubly ostracized black lesbian women.

The songs take the women back to 'the country of origin' as they long to be accepted in society, to 'be welcomed, not a stranger/ for who I am and feel at home'. The longing for 'back home' is a longing for countries they have never known or seen, an attempt to claim a lost Self in longago-lands-of-origin which are fictionalized and idealized as a result of the rejection of their present Self by the predominantly white cultures which posit themselves as culturally superior.

Complicating their variously black lineage which excludes them from the mainstream white society, Beth and Opal become lesbian partners. In their nascent relationship they demonstrate fairly 'typical' romantic behaviour, their feelings typifying those of heterosexual couples in early courtship:

Beth: maybe I should just give her a ring now. (She picks up an imaginary receiver and replaces it.) This is ridiculous! it's too soon. I could always ring her tomorrow. Oh, I just don't know what to do.

and

Opal: I can't believe I'm feeling like this. It's crazy. I've only seen her three times and seen three very good films into the bargain! Not the sort I'd usually go and see but when I'm with her it doesn't seem to matter what we do. [...] Sometimes, you just meet someone like that. (She snaps her fingers) and you feel like you've known them all your

---

[7] It took the Stephen Lawrence inquiry to get a culture to acknowledge that racism operated at the level of the unconscious: '*The Colour of Justice* [which was the 1999 dramatization of the inquiry] puts on stage [...] a chilling acknowledgement that racial prejudice exists at conscious, subconscious and unconscious levels in the psyche of the dominant culture/s [...] [I]t points to the need for the dominant grouping/s to acknowledge and come to terms with the fact that racial prejudice has infiltrated through the practice and institutions of British society.' Dimple Godiwala, 'Asian Theatre in Britain', *Hard Times*, 1999. p.59.

life. I feel that way with Beth. Somewhere I believe I was meant to meet her that day in that café before the sun went down and the summer slipped away (Act I).

Kay establishes that desire is universal, that the feelings of a lesbian couple do not differ in a marked way from heterosexual romantic love.[8]

Whilst Beth and Opal engage in lesbian courtship, the other actors enact the differing attitudes of friends and community. While some put on conscious blinkers (Aisha), others are blind to the existence of lesbians amongst friends or are denunciatory of lesbianism (Yomi).

The theatricality of the play derives from the freezing technique used in *for colored girls*. The effect is cinematic and stylized as is, for example, the scene from Act I where the four women mime playing pool. Naturalistic dialogue gives way to 'freezing' three actors whilst the fourth is in a spotlight, directly addressing the audience in character:

Beth pots the black. They freeze.
Spot on Opal.

Opal: My face was a shock to itself. The brain in my head thought my skin white and my nose straight. It imagined my hair was this curly from twiddling it. Every so often, I saw me: milky coffee skin, dark searching eyes, flat nose. Some voice from that mirror would whisper: *Nobody wants you, no wonder. You think you're white till you look in me. I surprised you didn't I?* I'd stop and will the glass to change me. Where did you get that nose? (Act I)

As Fanon explains it:

Out of the blackest part of my soul, across the zebra striping of my mind, surges this desire to be suddenly *white*.
I wish to be acknowledged not as *black* but as *white*.
Now – and this is a form of recognition that Hegel had not envisaged – who but a white woman can do this for me? By loving me she proves that I am worthy of white love. I am loved like a white man (Fanon [1952] 1967: 63).

In a reversal of Fanon's theorizing which is riven with feelings of the constructed self-hate of the colonized and the overwhelming *need* of the black man to be *white* which he voices over and over again in his text, the play, though

---

[8] This is by no means to be read as the definitive form of lesbian desire. See, *e.g.,* Jill Dolan, *Presence and Desire*, University of Michigan Press, 1993 or, for an overview, see Tamsin Spargo's introductory essay 'Foucault and Queer Theory', Icon books, 1999. See Valerie Mason-John's *Sin Dykes*.

acknowledging painfully that black and black lesbian identity is indeed mis-shapen as the blacks grow up in white society, formulates the black lesbian characters in a journey toward self-love and self-acceptance in an act where black skin meets and loves black skin. The previous scene continues:

> Aisha, Yomi and Beth unfreeze.
> Beth goes up to Opal. Aisha stands near them.
> Yomi sits on the chest, watching.
>
> Beth: Do you still feel alone when you look in there?
> Opal: No.
> Beth: I don't feel alone anymore, either. When I first met you, you were so familiar, a dream I never expected to come true. Like seeing my own reflection. I used to feel that I was the only black lesbian in the world, you know. Serious. Just me on my tod (Act I).

The dialogue intertwines negative/ positive as mis-shapen black identity greets lesbian comfort. Negative-construction-of-identity (like) meets positive-feeling (like). The hetero-normativity of the world outside the space the characters occupy impinges upon the play by inference of the implied heterosexual reader. Bound up in this interpretation is also the threat present within the play: the threat felt by the characters as the society they live in formulates their black and lesbian subject positions within/ outside its Anglo-heterosexual systems of normalization.

The effect achieved by combining naturalism of dialogue with an innovatively deployed experimental, semi-Brechtian theatre technique of a multiplicity of char-actor re/presentation/s results in a character analysis of some depth whilst the cultural conditions are conterminously offered up for examination. The economy of the minimal set, the quick scene changes (effected efficiently by the use of spotlighting), and the optimal use of four actors are thrown into relief by the skilful use of deeply symbolic props. The quick changes of mood allow the multitudinous strands of the play to develop in short spaces of time, whilst Kay's resonant poems and songs add depths of nostalgia, and develop the real need for a past and a history by the lesbians and displaced black peoples.

Emotion is evoked sparingly, and always with the need to establish a vital thread such as the societal rejection felt by the partner: 'she is suddenly dead/ I am at her funeral/ and no one there knows what we meant/ to each other/ and all her remaining relatives wonder -/ who is the sobbing woman in the dark/ coat/ at the back with a pew to herself?' Whilst exploring difference, the dramatist posits the tenuousness of lesbian relationships and the vulnerability of human beings (Opal) within hetero-normal feelings of emotion and attachment.

Aisha, the carpenter who builds things, is essential to the build up of the themes of difference (herself different, an Asian brown-ness in African and

Caribbean blackness) and the dramatic structure as she serves as both, interlocutor and character.

The scene changes to the people of the community: they are robots, infiltrated by the dominant heterosexual ideology, they adhere to their fixed agendas representing unquestioning hetero-normativity as they are riven with negativity and prejudice. The actors wear blank masks as they mechanize their walk and gestures and become the faceless unthinking masses: 'What do they do what do they do these les-bi-ans? It is easy to imagine what men do - but women, women. The thought turns the national stomach, stomach.' Society is thus enacted as an unthinking machine constructed of repressive structures.

Lesbian desire is expressed through poetry - as are their hopes and fears:

Then I see another picture
we lie close talking tongues
she is under my skin
we are each other's dream
she and her opalescent eyes
me and my fire flies
we are dawn and dusk together (I)

The dinner-party vignette focuses on prejudice against lesbians amongst 'friends' and the need for black women to share in a sisterhood so their minorities don't feel isolated:

Alone in it all - the black solo
searching for it in the rain
we were looking for
that meeting place
and we needed it bad
show us we are not the only ones (I)

Act II opens onto Opal's monologue to her self in the mirror - only now the audience serves as a mirror as Opal speaks directly to them. Her inability to come to terms with her black skin and her different facial features take away from her sense of self. While a mirror reflects an unchangingly same reflection, the monologue (ideally delivered to the audience with a breaking of the fourth wall) serves as an appeal to society to see her (a black person) differently, an eloquent expression of a need to encounter different attitudes when she next meets the Others whose responses, conscious and unconscious, serve to locate the marginalized subject within negativized sites of construction and meaning.

Opal's reverie is interrupted by Beth, who has come to terms with her blackness through an engagement with black culture/s, but, sadly, only by effecting a rejection of her host culture.

> Sometimes I feel such a sham. When I was eighteen I rushed out and bought the black records that had never sat on my shelves, the blues, funk, jazz and soul I'd been missing. It was a whole new world. James Baldwin. Toni Morrison. C.L.R. James. I was excited. I dumped Dostoevsky, Dire Straits and Simon and Garfunkel. I pretended I'd never sang Joni Mitchell's 'Blue-oo-oo-oo-oo-oo-oo' to myself in the mirror (Act II).

It is as if subjects constructed in radical difference can never participate equally of culture/s they inhabit, but nevertheless this speech signifies a journey to an acceptance of the rejected self by finding valorized objects/ subjects of same-ness (James Baldwin. Toni Morrison). Ironically, the valorization (of these writers) comes from the same dominant cultures which construct the negativity of the black subject, but the character is unaware of this as the re-construction is necessary, and identifying with a valorized same-ness enables self-validation and helps erase the feelings of self-hate.

The black characters have to journey to a place of integrity. A need for acceptance of one's Otherness in terms of a valorized culture and the appreciation of a different racial aesthetic is established, as each is now depicted at different stages of awareness and formation of identity.

Again, the prejudice of the larger normalizing community is enacted, this time to depict attitudes to persons of differing sexual orientation. A patient in a hospital falsely accuses a black lesbian nurse of touching her. As the nurse stands in a position signifying crucifixion her judges 'fire questions like bullets' thereby effecting a metaphoric execution. The vignette signifies the precarious position of the gay and the lesbian in society especially in caring jobs, such as a doctor or a nurse's. It is easy for them to become society's scapegoats as a result of ignorance, prejudice and outright hatred. Yomi, Aisha and Beth each represent the community as Opal is crucified. They simultaneously remain in character, thereby making the partner's 'bullet' a betrayal of their personal relationship as also of their black sisterhood: As she 'fires' she says, 'Is it because you are too ugly to get a man?' as she simultaneously represents the prejudice of the ignorant masses.

While the blacks have a history the lesbians do not and the songs wonder at (the lack of) black lesbian roots:

> They had no one to name
> me after
> in so many different ways
> so tell me what do you call her
> a woman who loves her another like her

what do you call her
where are her people
who are her ancestors
tell me what is her name
tell me what is her name

I want to find it all now
know our names know the others in
history
so many women have been lost at sea
so many of our stories have been swept
away
I want to find the woman
who in Dahomey 1900
loved another woman
tell me what did they call her
did they know her name
in Ashanti, do they know it in
Yoruba, do they know it in patois
do they know it in Punjabi...

The play ends in a remembering of names, the names of their selves with which
the play opened, thus giving their journey a sense of present closure, leaving the
women with an identity with which to go forward. 'oppression/ makes us love one
another badly/ makes our breathing mangled'.[9] The women learn to accept and
love one another as prejudice is curbed and attitudes re-learned, and they sing of
the self and their history and hope:

If we should die in the
wilderness
let the child that finds us
Know our name and story...
let us never forget to remember
all our heres and theres
let a hot sun shine on our wishes
let the rain fall without our tears

With *Chiaroscuro*, Jackie Kay broke the silence on black lesbian issues and
'there is little doubt that time will prove the play to have been a turning point in
black women's theatre in Britain' (Griffiths and Woddis 1988: 194).

---

[9] Kay is quoting Ntozake Shange's *Three Pieces*.

Brown Girl in the Ring

Journalist, writer and performer Valerie Mason-John aka Queenie's collection *Brown Girl in the Ring* (1999) contains the plays *Sin Dykes* and the self-confessedly autobiographical *Brown Girl in the Ring*. The poetry and prose in the book are both agonistic and celebratory of black lesbian identity and include an historical look at the black presence in Britain.

The assertive and confident monologue *Brown Girl in the Ring* contains grim echoes of childhood racial abuse and a mis-shapen identity which Jackie Kay explored so brutally and frankly in *Chiaroscuro* (1986). Although Mason-John writes that her race cannot be separated from her sexuality (Mason-John 1999: 15), the solo piece is more about a wilful self-assertion in the face of being marginalized as black in Britain than it is about lesbian identity.

[Photo credit: Simon Richardson]

Brown Girl in the Ring is dedicated to Mason-John's lover and reflects the identification of the author-performer 'with the royal, the rich, the famous' with whom, 'as a Barnardo child [she] socialised regularly'[10] (Mason-John 1999: 99).

Queenie, a quintessentially English aristo-brat — with a dark shade of cocoa, is by no means an assault on royalty, but more an extension of our vision of royalty. After all, nobility comes in many colours (Kevin le Gendre, http://www.valeriemason-john.co.uk/profile.html).

Her research revealed that French and English aristocracy had some African antecedents [see Valerie Mason-John's essay in this anthology].

Brown Girl reveals the character Regina's identity as formulated within a fiction of English aristocracy and western styles and forms of theatre, gesture and diction. Seizing upon an ethnicity of aristocratic Englishness, Regina enters the auditorium to the strains of Beethoven, dancing ballet-like movements, 'speaking

---

[10] At the age of four, and until the age of thirteen, Valerie Mason-John was placed in a Barnardo's foster home in Essex.

in an exaggerated upper class English aristobratish voice,' dressed in several layered petticoats and pearls. A throne dominates the set (Mason-John 1999: 101).

The character is one of the most startling subversions of racial imagery you're ever likely to see on any side of the social divide. Queenie's strength lies in both the sheer shock value of the persona's appearance and the well-bred ambiguity of her manners (Kevin le Gendre, http://www.valeriemason-john.co.uk/profile.html).

As Frantz Fanon put it in *Black Skin, White Masks*,

Every colonized people – in other words, every people in whose soul an inferiority complex has been created by the death and burial of its local cultural originality – finds itself face to face with the language of the civilizing nation; that is, with the culture of the mother country (Fanon [1952] 1967: 18).

This culture is to Queenie, aka Regina of the solo piece, an intense identification with the upper classes of Britain, a status denied her all her life until she decides to make it 'real' in performance. Royal status conflated with her role as lesbian queen, Queenie performs a piece which is bound up with her identity as a black lesbian in Britain. 'Born to be a Queen, I wasn't prepared for society's stigma towards my colour, gender, race, sexuality, culture and attitudes […] Due to colonial racism, many of us are constrained to live in a class lower than our real one and denied our true social status amidst the many struggles we are faced with to survive in Britain' (Mason-John 1999: 91). As she hitch-hiked the world with her best friend, pretending to be someone else came naturally to Mason-John. They found they attracted attention when they passed as famous black women such as Whoopi Goldberg and Tracy Chapman (Mason-John 1999: 102).

Brown Girl in the Ring attempts to regain for the first generation British-African performer an identity which the structures of English society deny its black subjects: Englishness. Englishness as an ethnicity is constructed in a fierce denial and exclusion of the black other. Englishness through the centuries has been constructed as a whiteness, a racial rather than nationalistic characterization which excludes blackness in a forced difference (see Young 1995).

Valerie Mason-John writes and performs what could be seen as an ethnic Englishness clothed in the blackness of her skin as Regina, Queenie, author, performer, royalty, royal subject, woman and dyke. The monologue begins with an upper class condescension directed at the invisible waiter who seems to question her unusual hybrid-ethnic order of 'Caviar… and rice and peas', with 'hashish for starters'. He seems to mistake her for an 'aborigine' and a wog to which she asserts good naturedly but with tongue firmly in cheek:

No no, you don't quite understand. *I am as English as Her Majesty.*

My title is Regina
Not vagina, Regina
W!O!G! My poor poppet you do seem to be losing it.
I am most definitely not a Western Oriental Gentleman. (102, emphasis mine)

Now Regina/ Queenie regresses to an 8 year old who chants sadly, over and over, the refrain of 'sticks and stones will break your bones/ but names will never hurt me' as she enacts the response to the hostility of the mother culture the young girl so identifies with. She grows adult again to recount the naming of her history and lineage. From Kunte Kinte and Martin Luther King to Muhammed Ali and Bob Marley the blacks do have a history, despite the assertions of Hegel and Marx. The character Regina has descended 'from a royal lineage of Africans'. The fiction of the royal African family 'who were captured and brought to France in the 16th century' and descended through the alcoholic strains of 'Dom Perignon', 'Pink Lady', 'Lanson' and 'Moët et Chandon' to produce 'by some idiosyncratic malfunction [...] a fine specimen of a daughter, red curly hair and green eyes' (pp. 104-5) serves to emphasize the chromatism practiced by the blacks in Britain towards each other: 'The blacker you were the uglier you were.' Mason-John recounts in her prose that the names she has been called 'ranged from "tar baby" to "ace of spades" and "Teflon"' (p. 113). In *Brown Girl in the Ring* the character of Regina is 'a throwback' as her twin brother has 'blonde hair and blue eyes'. The citation of the incongruous family history by Regina demonstrates the colour prejudices rife even within black communities as they regard light skin as aesthetically and culturally superior.

Regina/ Queenie goes through the stereotyped responses which construct blacks within the inferiority complex which is their legacy from within and without their communities as she tries to 'erase' the colour of her skin by rubbing her cheeks in vain; 'learns' that she has descended 'from the apes' at school as her teacher 'says if I go to the zoo I'll see lots of animals who look like me' (p. 107).

Wilfully created and spread by the colonizer, [the] mythical and degrading portrait [of the colonized] ends up by being accepted and lived with to a certain extent by the colonized. It thus acquires a certain amount of reality and contributes to the true portrait of the colonized. [...] In order for the colonizer to be the complete master, it is not enough for him to be so in actual fact, but he must also believe in its legitimacy. In order for that legitimacy to be complete, it is not enough for the colonized to be a slave, he must also accept his role (Memmi [1957] 1965: 87-89).

This excerpt from Albert Memmi's influential text which analyzes the roles of the colonizer and the colonized emphasizes the internalization of negative traits that the colonizer ascribes to the colonized in a Hegelian tendency which creates and re-creates the self of the colonizer in a hierarchical and superior role. It is when the black subject accepts and internalizes the negativities the white man has formulated him in, that he acquires an inferiority complex as he now sees him/herself as lazy, greedy, ape-like or whatever he has been told describes his/ her personality.

Which is precisely what makes Mason-John's solo piece so compelling, as the posh-acting Regina seeks to identify with and internalize the traits of the one who possesses the most power in the land: the Queen. And she insists that she is as English as the Queen may be.

Underlying the posh deportment of Regina's exterior self which reconstructs Englishness through the subjectivity of an adult black woman lies a reservoir of childhood abuse which turns into self-hatred. The adult Regina's frequent lapses

into regressive childhood have no memory of self-validation but a litany of meanings of what blackness connotes to the young girl raised in white society:

> I look like the golly
> On the jam jar jar jar
>
> I look like the mould
> In the cheese, cheese, cheese (108-9)

Valerie Mason-John says: 'I've transcended a lot in my childhood and adolescence to get where I've got to; I've had to struggle for everything I've got' (Hensman in Rapi & Chowdhry 1998: 218).

[Valerie Mason-John as Regina.
Photo credit: Vanda Playford]

The repetition of 'sweep it under the carpet', literal at first as she instructs the waiter to sweep the remnants of her broken champagne glass, becomes more and more figurative as the shards of the negative self imaging of her childhood cut through in the frequent regressions played in an 8 year old voice. The regression into a nervous breakdown leads to more racial and female stereotyping from her shrink and the piece ends on the slurred speech of someone on sedatives.

My shrink says I need an electric shock
I took stock
My shrink says all negroes are manic

I didn't panic (111).

Valerie Mason-John says: 'At times I do find performing painful. Certain material is cathartic. [...] there's a lot of painful stuff in [*Brown Girl in the Ring...*] As a performer, your work does take you on particular journeys, sometimes painful.' (Hensman in Rapi & Chowdhry 1998: 215). The play bravely confronts the trials that blacks experience by virtue of the colour of their skin in white society. The triumph of the writer-actor is that she is able to reformulate and shift the boundaries of what it means to be English. Surely being born and brought up in England ought to confer upon black subjects a 'natural' English heritage which they share with their white others? The writer's adamant insistence on partaking of western culture from classical music and dance to inheriting a royal heritage makes her piece a bold and innovative celebration of her personal formulation of Englishness which is inclusive. Yet she remains balanced, indicting society for its ills practised on blacks since slavery began. *Brown Girl in the Ring* is courageous as it indicts the evils still practised toward blacks in western societies whilst still accepting of the aspects of western culture which the character finds interesting, useful, aesthetic, educational, indeed part of the make-up of her individuality as British or indeed English.

The two plays are positive images of how black women can attempt to re-discover and re-envision their selves. These are plays which confront prejudices, 'sweep them under the carpet', and begin again, in an attempt to empower the black British woman.

Works cited

Fanon, Frantz (1967), *Black Skin, White Masks*, [*Peau Noire, Masques Blancs* 1952], trans. Charles Lam Markmann, NY: Grove Press.

Godiwala, Dimple (1999), 'Asian Theatre in Britain', *Hard Times,* Vol. 67/68.

Godiwala, Dimple (2003), *Breaking the Bounds: British Feminist Dramatists Writing in the Mainstream since c. 1980,* New York & Oxford: Peter Lang.

Griffiths, Trevor R., and Carole Woddis (eds.) (1988), *The Bloomsbury Theatre Guide,* London: Bloomsbury.

Hensman, Savitri (1998), 'Presentation of Self as Performance: The Birth of Queenie aka Valerie Mason-John' in *Acts of Passion: Sexuality, Gender and Performance*, Nina Rapi and Maya Chowdhry (eds.), New York & London: The Haworth Press.

Kay, Jackie (1986), *Chiaroscuro* in Jill Davis (ed.) (1987), *Lesbian Plays*, London: Methuen.

Mason-John, Valerie, (ed.) (1995), *Talking Black: Lesbians of African and Asian Descent Speak Out,* London: Cassell.

Mason-John, Valerie (1999), *Brown Girl in the Ring,* London: Get a Grip.

Memmi, Albert (1965), *The Colonizer and the Colonized,* [*Portrait du Colonisé precede du Portrait du Colonisateur* 1957], trans. Howard Greenfield, Georgia: The Orion Press.

Young, Robert (1995), *Colonial Desire: Hybridity in Theory, Culture and Race,* London: Routledge.

Websites

Le Gendre, Kevin, http://www.valeriemason-john.co.uk/profile.html

CHAPTER ELEVEN

A SCOURGE OF THE EMPIRE: WOLE SOYINKA'S NOTORIOUS THEATRE AT THE ROYAL COURT.

ZODWA MOTSA

Synopsis:
This chapter explores the activities of emerging playwrights at the Royal Court, focusing primarily on Wole Soyinka, a writer hitherto scantily researched as one of the Angry Young Men. The discourse addresses three writers who presented their plays at the Royal Court in the late 1950s. These plays were the dramatists' first attempt in George Devine's theatre. The discussion also examines newspaper reviews of the plays' performances, a critical factor in their reception as new playwrights. It is hoped that the relationship dynamics between the Court and its protégés, like Wole Soyinka, may be better understood.

The so-called Angry Young Men of 1950s England are usually perceived as white and British. Research in modern drama does not faithfully capture the full array of nationalities that participated in the theatre renascence of post-World War II England. For instance, Wole Soyinka, the 1986 Nobel Literature laureate, was one of these 'angry young men.' In the late 1950s to mid 1960s, Soyinka staged some of his very first plays with Britain's leading contemporary playwrights, popularly known as the 'Angry Young Men.' Although he worked and performed at The Royal Court Theatre with Edward Bond, Arnold Wesker, and John Arden,

Soyinka's presence at this momentous period in English theatre is often underplayed by research. The principal question is, why? This chapter explores the interactions of Wole Soyinka and the Angry Young Men in the late 1950s to mid-1960s, seeking to establish the nature of the society in which Wole Soyinka first presented his early works.

From 1958 to 1959 Wole Soyinka was attached to The Royal Court Theatre as a play-reader. This occupation allowed him the opportunity to test his skills as playwright, director and actor in his own works. As a play-reader, Soyinka had to invite, screen and evaluate manuscripts for the emerging British theatre, Gibbs explains (Motsa 2000[11]). Soyinka was also a co-teacher of English at local London high schools (Lindfors 1982:111-112). Additionally, he worked for the BBC as both journalist and anchor person for the programme known as 'Calling West Africa.' It is at The Court that he met many literary artists of renown and enhanced his experience in professional theatre. Soyinka spent about eighteen months in self-styled apprenticeship to George Devine at The Court. Britain at the time was beleaguered with myriad storms of change. Amongst these was the theatre revolution in London, a transformation that was to eventually become a consequential event in the history of British theatre. The Royal Court directors, George Devine and Tony Richardson set out to establish an experimental theatre that was poised to offer a very different type of dramaturgy to the hitherto conventional styles in the mode of Shakespeare and other older established playwrights, like the proponents of the well-made play. The orthodox theatre ignored the working-class and younger population's interests and favoured the bourgeoisie in taste and affordability. In contrast, George Devine's avant garde theatre catered for the interests of the young and the poor. Hitherto unknown playwrights began to find their way to popular theatre. This occurred in the wake of John Osborne's groundbreaking *Look Back in Anger* (8 May 1956). Amongst these young writers were John Arden, Arnold Wesker and Wole Soyinka – the three dramatists on whom this chapter focuses.

Osborne's cutting edge play emerged in the middle of major theatrical events. The year before, London had received Samuel Beckett's début, *Waiting for Godot* (1955), in the West End and three months after *Look Back in Anger*, witnessed the first visit of Brecht's Berliner Ensemble theatre troupe around August 1956 (Findlater 1981:29). Brecht, who had died on 14th August 1956, a few weeks before his company visited England for the first time, presented the British theatre with stage techniques that were strange. Similarly, Devine's theatre was renowned for its freedom of expression and socialist inclinations, a stance that probably did not rest

---

[11] This subject has been fully discussed in my doctoral research, '*A Tiger in the Court: The Nature and Implications of Wole Soyinka's Interactions at The Royal Court Theatre: 1956 – 1966.*'

well with conservative Britain. This was a very defining moment in post World War II British theatre history. The socio-political milieu in which Soyinka and his British contemporaries first presented their serious stage works was to become the watershed of English theatre between the older illusionist and the new wave non-illusionist theatre.

Such an effervescent climate afforded nascent playwrights an opportunity to stage their works at the Court's 'Sunday Night without decor' sessions,[12] an arrangement that enabled the company to save costs by producing a play at £100 as opposed to £5, 000 for a full production (Findlater 1981:42). Conditions were ideal for neophyte playwrights to respond to the socio-political challenges of the time as they experimented with a variety of styles emulating Beckett, Brecht or Shaw and drawing from their own pre-knowledge of theatre.

Soyinka's activities at The Court can be better explored in a comparative study of these three dramatists' premier plays, and their reception by the reviewing media, a very critical standards control agent. The three playwrights came to the Royal Court around the same time. Their plays addressed the common theme of the importance of human and personal freedom in a society ravaged by strife and war. Colonial atrocities in Kenya, Egypt and South Africa particularly preoccupied Soyinka's works at this time. Despite these obvious similarities in theme among Devine's protégés, there is disparity in their début plays' reception by both the London theatre reviewers and Devine himself.

All three playwrights had written plays and prose works before coming to the Royal Court. They had each won at least one national prize in England. While at Leeds University, Soyinka had made noticeable inroads in writing and winning prizes in literary contests.[13] Soyinka's premier Royal Court performances comprised two poems and a play entitled *The Invention* (1959). The poems were 'Telephone Conversation' and an untitled piece protesting against the use of the Sahara to test nuclear armament. Owing to the absence of an adequate (black) cast in London at this time, *The Lion and the Jewel* (1963) was only staged in 1966, despite its enthusiastic reception by the Court in the 1950s (Moore 1978). In these

---

[12] These sessions accorded producers time to preview a play to a select audience to gauge its impact before showing it to a larger audience for more commercial gain and critical input.
[13] At Leeds, Soyinka won a second prize in 'The Margaret Wrong Memorial Fund' for his fiction, 'Oji River'. He also produced short prose like, 'Madame Etienne's Establishment' (*Gryphon*: University of Leeds, March 1957:11-22), 'A Tale of Two Cities' (*Gryphon*: University of Leeds, Autumn 1957:16-22), and 'Another Tale of Two Cities' (*New Nigerian Forum London* 1:2 1958:26-30). Similarly in 1956, John Arden obtained a prize for his radio play, *Life of Man*.

early works, the voice of anger and protest against the domination of Africa by Europe is patent. Interestingly, Soyinka's theatre was received with hostility and patronising incomprehension in London, both in 1959 and 1966.

The selection of newspaper reviews from the British Theatre Museum, London, captures part of the playwrights' evaluation. In the main, the reviewers appear to have been more intolerant of Soyinka than was the audience. *The Times* (2 November 1959) reports that the audience warmly responded to Soyinka's poetry and drama – 'Telephone Conversation' and *The Invention*. While it extols Soyinka's outstanding skill as a wordsmith, the review also depicts him as an artist who is very shy, if not suspicious, of the English accolades. The reviewer states:

> We must hope that the reception given at the Royal Court last night to verses and song by Mr Wole Soyinka and to his one-act play, The Invention, will make this Nigerian writer less suspicious of the London theatre than he gives the impression of being. Whenever he allowed a reader or a character to speak directly to the audience the audience responded ... even when Mr Soyinka plainly was not addressing it. If he thinks this was prompted by the thing he hates most, a patronising attitude on the part of the audience, it will be a pity. It was prompted by respect for his gift for words.

This review discloses Soyinka's aversion for the patronisation of 'the minorities.' It further points out that although Soyinka's words were at times very clear, he had the weakness of tending to repeat himself. The deep-set culture of realistic drama in the reviewer's criticism of the structure of Soyinka's play is manifest here. Commenting on the ending of the play, this reviewer expresses the misgiving that Soyinka's final message on the relationship between the black and the white races is not clearly conveyed because:

> ... instead of making [a clear comment] at the end of The Invention, he made a joke, or else, figuratively speaking, he mumbled. So the comment was lost. For us, a pity' (The Times 2 November 1959).

Judging by the nature of such comments, it is clear that even in 1959, theatre critics still upheld the dictum of a solid moralistic conclusion to a play, a rule ascribable to realistic drama. When an artist deviated from this 'norm', leaving the 'unravelling/discussion' in the hands of the viewer, he incited dissatisfaction and judgements of artistic failure to communicate clearly. Contrary to convention, Soyinka's play was presenting the *idea* of apartheid and racism's absurdity, not preaching a moral.

Alan Brein's most racist review is sarcastically entitled, 'Where Spades Are Trumps' (*Spectator* 6 November). Satirically attacking the Court for blindly promoting obviously weak artists, Brein condemns the decision to produce

Soyinka's play, as a patronising gesture, a ploy to score points of political correctness on the part of the Royal Court. His opinion is:

[The] presence of a Negro in a play is becoming very near to being a guarantee of a masterpiece. Two blacks do not make a white – but two blacks trying to make a white is still good box-office theme. In the Thirties, Left-wing intellectuals consistently over praised anything written by a worker. In the Fifties they over praised anything written by a Negro. In both cases their amazed delight that someone from the lower depths can actually put words into sentences is not only irrelevant but also betrays an unconscious contempt for the very group they are supposed to be championing.

'Spade' is a pejorative term for Black people. Brein eloquently uses racist discourse and manipulates the words 'spade' and 'trump', as used in a game of cards, to attack the patronage of the British left wing liberals, as represented by the Court. Is Brein justifiably exposing the phoney attitude of the Court that wants to overrate even an inferior product simply to accommodate 'the minorities', or he is actually feeding into the racist attitude that does not see anything good in a black writer attempting to write in English? The review concludes with the advice that The Royal Court must 'be persuaded to support the really new and genuine achievements produced there – such as John Arden's *Serjeant Musgrave's Dance*' (1959). Brein overlooks the fact that *Serjeant Musgrave's Dance* was Arden's third production at the Court, while *The Invention* was Soyinka's very first. Arden was a major disaster with the box office and set back the Court by ten thousand pounds in costs but Devine repeatedly put him back on stage[14]. Devine's leniency with Arden's third play is more glaring when set against the treatment of Soyinka's first and only attempt in the 1950s. Incidentally, Arden's and Soyinka's drama were similar in that they were the most 'deviant' by their use of Brecht's and Beckett's style as opposed to the 'conventional' dramaturgy of Osborne and Wesker. Could it be that both Devine and the theatre reviewers were reacting to something more than 'unorthodox theatre' in Soyinka's works?

Six years later, the reviews of Soyinka's second play at The Court (*The Lion and the Jewel*) remain unchanged. Jeremy Kingston (*Punch* 21 December 1966) still makes similar assumptions as were made half a decade earlier. Kingston continues to look for European influences on the African art. Questioning the playwright's ingenuity to create, he cites possible European sources of influence on

---

[14]Arden exposes Devine's partiality, stating: '... as an illustration of this doctrine [the playwright's right to fail] ... [Devine] would frequently quote the case of *Serjeant Musgrave's Dance* - a play which lost the theatre ... Ten Thousand pounds, but which he had ... insisted upon presenting in the teeth of hostile critics and different audiences until acceptance of its qualities was finally secured (Arden 1977:5; Motsa 2000:79).

Soyinka's *The Lion and the Jewel,* but sorely overlooks the most probable progenitor, African folklore. This attitude is reflected in such statements as:

> The wily man who pretends to be impotent in order to win a pretty maid is a character almost as old as the art of storytelling. He crops up in Greek comedy, the Decameron, the Arabian Nights.

The opening remarks of Felix Barker (*Evening News* 13 December) are also noteworthy for their racist slant and attack on the play's badness of taste. Barker explains:

> We were in for a Nigerian play with an all-coloured cast, The Lion and the Jewel, by Wole Soyinka, and if the director of the English Stage Company thinks it is a masterpiece, that is just too bad.

Even though such racial references are excusable in their historical context, one would never find statements like, 'Arden's *The Waters of Babylon* (1957), with an all-white cast.' Hereafter, Barker continues to state his conviction that this play is an imitation of some European work, declaring:

> To find a playwright today beating an African drum about female emancipation is rather like encountering a modern Ibsen black-face, and while Mr Soyinka's play has some occasional felicities it does not go very deep. It lacks dramatic excitement and is unconvincingly acted by an obviously inexperienced cast.

This parochial outlook erroneously propagates the view that the subject matter of women's emancipation, as championed by Lakunle, is the sole monopoly of Europe and can only be addressed by dramatists like Ibsen. The anonymous critic from the *Illustrated London News* (24 December) is even more acerbic. He registers his disappointment with an unidentified newspaper for daring to rank *The Lion and the Jewel* not far too short of a masterpiece. In disbelief he proclaims:

> Could it have looked like that from the front rows? Glumly, I doubt it. What I saw and heard from the middle of the house was a mild and artless Nigerian comedy, with an occasional good line, a few dances, and a cast – endearing, I agree – that offered charm instead of technique ... These enterprising visitors and their dramatist, Wole Soyinka, have still much to learn ... Maybe we shall watch their progress on later visits to the Court.

Evidently, Soyinka's strange dramatic idiom presented itself as fair game to the London reviewers, a fraternity generally inhospitable in its reception of premiere plays. The reviewers' hostility often masked ignorance or unwillingness to acknowledge and welcome innovative experimental work.

The exploration of the playwrights' début productions at the Court remains paramount in establishing the nature of their interactions. Hence in addition to performance reviews, a critical textual examination of the plays is still essential as a tool by which we evaluate the issues raised by the dramatist. In the ensuing analysis the discussion favours the hitherto lesser known *The Invention,* Soyinka's first Court production, while it under-represents the more familiar *The Lion and the Jewel,* Soyinka's second production there. Privileged by early publication, the artistic qualities of *The Lion and the Jewel* have become widely known. So, to provide fuller exposure to Soyinka's embryonic works, it becomes necessary to give more prominence to the newly published *The Invention*[15].

A close study of *The Invention* shows that what Bernth Lindfors (1982:127) terms an extravagant political satire, is a complex drama that exposes the plight of black South Africans in the hands of a racist white government. It is a forthright and blunt attack on social ills. Set seventeen years into the future – the winter of 1976 in South Africa – this one-act play is a futuristic, aptly prophetic comic satire that depicts the devastating effects and pettiness of racial discrimination. It features three white super-powers and proponents of racism of the 1950s: the British, South Africans, and the Americans of the Deep South. July 1976 is ironically important for being the celebration of the 200th anniversary of the 'Declaration of Independence, and ... the Declaration of Human Rights' in America (Soyinka 1959:1), and for a different reason, the winter of 1976 is of greater significance to Black South Africans—the time apartheid began to crumble. On this day in the play, America sends an isotonuclear bomb to explode in Jupiter, hopefully without endangering human life. Unfortunately, the rocket strays and shoots from Massachusetts to Madagascar to the icebergs of the Antarctic sea, it goes twice beneath the North Pole distorting every dial on earth. It disappears for two days from sight and radar, only to resurface three days later, hovering over the Cape of Good Hope and lands in a disused Johannesburg mine. It soon explodes, killing humans and distorts their racial composition, which makes it impossible to distinguish blacks from whites because of the black's loss of pigment. Consequently, everyone must submit to racial testing in a laboratory where handpicked scientists work on the testing. One of these scientists invents a testing machine – 'the invention' of the play's title – that shows within seconds what race each 'specimen' is.

While exposing humankind's diabolic folly, *The Invention* addresses the themes of nepotism and academic dishonesty, as depicted in the inventor who

---

[15] This analysis is based on the original manuscript acquired from James Gibbs in 1996. However, in July 2005 University of South Africa Press published *The Invention* for the first time in the collection titled, *Wole Soyinka: The Invention and The Detainee* (Motsa 2005).

cruelly steps over fellow researchers and steals their ideas to attract all the glory. Soyinka's characters deftly advance the theme of the far-reaching extent of dehumanization. Before the opening line is uttered, the stage directions bluntly advise that the actors' '... faces could be hideously deformed or simply pasty with sickly grayishness [*sic*]' (Soyinka 1959: i). All the researchers must wear white overalls, symbolising an external reflection of the depleted humanness in the whites. Clearly, Soyinka is drawing from the Brechtian technique of using representational characters to create distance between the actor and the role. This technique is also common in Yoruba oral performances, where the suggested mask-like deportment of a character emphasises his representational role (Götrick 1984:108-110). A group of people simply called 'the guinea- pigs' also forms part of the cast. These guinea-pigs are projected as voices, they never appear on stage, except for the desperate off-stage cries of protestations of the 1st Voice, 'I don't want to be a guinea-pig; I am only a simple farmer ...' (Soyinka 1959:9) – a technique echoed decades later in *King Baabu*'s mass killing scene (Soyinka 2002). Soyinka cynically exposes the cruelties of elevating an ideal over human life in the cupidity of the scientists. After the explosion of the first invention killing the Inventor, his fellow scientists heartlessly remark:

DESTUS: What do you say now, oh Bytron? We're on the run again.
CRUGER: (*Suddenly beginning to run*) Bodies! Bodies! Fresh specimens for research! ...
(*Destus and Cruger are fighting for the possession of one head.*)
CRUGER:Finder's keepers!
DESTUS:Don't make a fuss, old boy. It's mine! (Soyinka 1959:12).

They scramble for this new supply of human bodies as for a treasure trove. This use of typological characters advances the satirical theme that derides the treatment of non-white races as inferior. The biting humour is not confined to the Americans only. The British also receive the brunt of the dramatist's satire seen in the stereotypical landlady, Mrs Higgins and when Soyinka jibes at 'the[ir] law of bathing once a week.'

The play builds on a number of satirical incidents. For instance, the failure of the South African scientific experiment is an echo of the failed American spacecraft experiment. These failures are the writer's satirical jeer at the childlike preoccupations and wasted efforts of racist antics. Witty dialogue between characters further accents the satire, for example, the interaction between Kalinga and Prosecutor as well as the sentiments expressed by the latter in the prologue that, '... amidst this carnage, the only fact that distresses my countrymen is that they can no longer tell who is black and who is white' (Soyinka: ii). The climax presents the punch line of the humour and end of the story where, after much secrecy, the South African team is to display the invention to their visiting and eagerly waiting counterparts from overseas. Concealing that the original machine blew up, the scientists try and deceive their visitors by presenting a newly constructed imitation. Sadly, this replacement is received as the most horrid thing by the British envoy, and as disgusting with an unprepossessing appearance by Briklemaine the Ku Klux Klan adventist. At this bathos, the idiot giggles, 'The emperor is naked!' He takes off his coat to lend to the 'emperor'. This appears as a parody for Britain's 1851 'Great Exhibition', the iron glass which was displayed at Hyde Park solely to demonstrate the British supremacy of design and technique, but failed dismally as it was later perceived to be the most atrocious monstrosity of creation (Altick 1973:11).

The Invention is teeming with features of a 1950s period piece. The subject matter and setting clearly attest to this. The play is set in the science laboratory, counterpoising the kitchen-sink set of its European contemporaries. Additionally, it daringly stages nations as characters and pointedly exposes social maladies, like the idiocy of racism, as the Director of the laboratory proudly explains to Mrs Higgins that:

DIRECTOR: ...one of our methods of telling a black native from someone who was merely coloured was to pass a pencil through his hair. If it went through, he was coloured. If the hair stopped it, he was pure native. It is quite a time-tested method. ...it was used as far back as 1959... (Soyinka 1959: 23).

Political drama was the mainstay of popular plays at the Royal Court. Similarly, the plays of Edward Bond, Arnold Wesker, and John Arden all dealt with topical political issues like the war or the disadvantaged Jewish families. The Invention projects a theme of anger but, unlike in Osborne's Look Back in Anger, the voice of the angry primary hero/victim is not heard at all. Instead the folly of the perpetrator is exposed through the satirisation of the British; white South Africans and white Americans. In the light of this similarity in theme, it remains unclear why the play was taken lightly. Given the political era and the place where The Invention was staged, the subject matter of apartheid and racism was perhaps inconsequential to England, despite the play's topical tone of disdain and anger which the audiences had welcomed in plays like Look Back in Anger and Chicken Soup With Barley.

Like all greenhorn works, The Invention has its demerits, but its infantile death robbed African literature's early exposure to the seedbed of Soyinka's great works. Although many Soyinka scholars agree that it is not one of Soyinka's best creations, The Invention's strength lies in its boldness of theme that testifies to the seriousness of mind and bravery in the young Soyinka. It is unequivocally 1950s period drama, a seedbed for committed art. Describing canonical works of 1950s'

London revolutionary theatre, Peter Brook reminds us that these plays were aimed at:

> ... crackling the spectator on the jaw, ... douse him with ice-cold water, then force him to address intelligently what has happened to him, then kick him in the balls to bring him back to his senses again (Sanders 2000:620).

Could this have been the effect of Soyinka's theatre at The Court?

The Invention's debacle may suggest that the playwright was still finding his feet in theatre. However, noteworthy is the fact that Soyinka's Royal Court experience was in fact not his first and only experience in the performance arts. Two of his three serious plays, *The Swamp Dwellers* and *The Lion and the Jewel* had been performed elsewhere in the preceding two years, the University of London Drama Competition (1958) and the Arts Theatre in Ibadan (1959) respectively.

∇

John Arden's history compares well with Wole Soyinka's. As early as 1955, Arden had also started to present plays for production. He had already produced his first play in Edinburgh and had aired the radio play that had won the 1956 prize. The Royal Court's staging of *The Waters of Babylon* (20 October 1957) was his first milestone in the meaningful breakthrough sought by aspiring playwrights. Like Soyinka, Arden did not confine himself to the Royal Court in these early years but continued to produce plays with other companies, like the Central School of Speech and Drama in London.

The third playwright, Arnold Wesker, also has an interesting pre-Court history. In 1956 Wesker had shown Lindsay Anderson his short story, *Pools*. Anderson, who had read *The Kitchen* and *Chicken Soup With Barley*, brought these plays to Devine's attention for staging possibilities, but Devine did not stage these plays immediately. It is unclear why Devine was not so enthusiastic about the plays. He passed *Chicken Soup With Barley* on to the Belgrade Theatre where it was produced on 24 May, and later at The Court on 7 July. *The Kitchen* was only produced at The Court on 11 September, 1959. The Belgrade Theatre gave Wesker a first taste of the productions of *The Kitchen* (1958) and *I'm Talking About Jerusalem* and *Roots* (1959). At Sloane Square, all three dramatists started in the 'Sunday night without décor' slot. This account serves to illustrate the three playwright's parity in stage history.

The Invention (Soyinka), *Waters of Babylon* (Arden), and *Chicken Soup With Barley* (Wesker) were all first Royal Court attempts for each dramatist. Of the three, Wesker was the most successful at the box office. Arden, however, started off very poorly with box office ratings. His *Live Like Pigs* filled 25% of box office capacity, *Serjeant Musgrave's Dance*, 21% and *The Happy Haven*, a shameful 12% (Findlater 1981:44). Despite this glaring disaster, Devine's support for Arden never flagged. Devine even wrote to Neville Blond urging, 'We must support the people we believe in, *especially* if they don't have critical appeal' (Findlater 1981:44). As seen in the newspaper reviews, Soyinka was received with strong derision by the London theatre reviewers. His work was ascribed to European influences and he was accused of lacking originality and skill but perceived to be staged merely for political correctness. What could have been the source of such negativism?

The themes presented by the three dramatists were comparable and familiar to the post-World War II audience in their forthright address of the subject of injustice and disillusionment, protest and anger against the powers that ruled. However, their theatrical styles differed. Arden and Soyinka used a very 'deviant' form of dramaturgy, while Wesker brought back the familiar mode of the well-made-play that critics and theatre-goers were used to. Wesker's use of the familiar realist theatre mode earned him more favour than was accorded either Soyinka or Arden. Explaining the dramatists' predicament, Jeffrey Roberts explains that:

> The works of playwrights such as Harold Pinter [who was emulating Beckett and Ionesco] and those of John Arden [influenced by Brecht] ... seemed both foreign and puzzling to the British audiences, compared to those of Osborne and Wesker which were received with warmth and enthusiasm (Wike 1995:4).

Wesker's kind of drama was what the viewers were familiar with. Heavily influenced by Brecht, Beckett and Yoruba lore, Soyinka's drama was very foreign and unacceptable to reviewers, like Pinter's and Arden's.

In *The Waters of Babylon*, Arden addresses topics like prostitution, the ethics of local government, British foreign policy on immigrants and local citizens, sponsored gambling, and the motley of foreign ethnic groups residing in the heart of London. Arden's title is an allusion to the verse 'By the Waters of Babylon, there we sat down and wept, when we remembered Zion' (*Holy Bible* Psalms 137:1). This text bemoans the despair of the Jews in captivity. Another significant biblical reference could be the Babylon of corruption referred to in Revelations 17:5 that states, 'Babylon the great, mother of harlots and of earth's abominations.' These allusions jointly point to the premise on which the characters and theme are based. London is a 'Babylon', an island of people in exile, and the activities of Krank echo the moral decay of the symbolic Babylon of the end of times.

The audience may have been frustrated by the seemingly unclear standpoint of the writer on issues raised. Arden merely depicts issues without conveying any personal view or attitude. Conventional criticism would single out a hero that embodies the central idea – and a supportive group of foreground characters. These characters' attributes of good or bad usually work as a guide to the revelation and understanding of the moral bent of the playwright and the statement being made. Such compartmentalisation of character into the conventional types is not found in *The Waters of Babylon*. The audience's psychological expectations of finding a former Nazi soldier to be an outright villain are thwarted when Krank is presented as a benevolent pimp citizen of England. Joseph Caligula, the upright 'Negro' who attacks racism with Sunday spiritual rhetoric, falls prey to the flirtatious Bathsheba's enticing schemes; he capitulates and sleeps with her. Characters like the parliamentarian Mr Loap and Henry Ginger are all too complex to easily pigeon-hole into a category as, '... there is no clear separation of the people ... into good and bad, heroic and villainous ...' (Wike 1995:11). Arden's characters stand as individuals with both virtues and flaws; they do not represent any specific type in society. The technique of not focusing on a single heroic protagonist, as we would like Krank to be, but to have the action cover the whole range of the post-war theme with a myriad of personalities, is a typical Brechtian device of the epic theatre (Innes 1992:25).

Arden's non-committal handling of theme and depiction of character makes critics conclude that he doggedly refuses to take sides with any of his characters and to wind up the issues of debate raised through characters' action. Perhaps, like Artaud (Bermel 1977), Arden avoids the use of character to preach an argument, but prefers to engage character to expose the audience to certain situations. Unfortunately, this evokes the ire of some critics, who assert that he never puts across any concrete statement, but touches on issues and leaves them hanging. This may be true about some of Arden's plays, but the same cannot be said of *The Waters of Babylon*. In this play can still be detected the underlying idea of vanity and illusion interwoven in the action. This subject matter challenges the intellect of the viewing audience.

The critics' dissatisfaction with Arden's style may be attributed to the expectations of having a single hero who embodies a palpable idea – this clearly comes from a society that desires heroes while the playwright may be wanting to demystify that very concept of heroism. Arden's *The Waters of Babylon* presents an idea which is sustained from the beginning of the play to its conclusion. If for instance, we could take entire cast as a 'collective hero' (Gassner 1965:36-37), and the society – represented by the audience – as the 'antagonistic force', we could establish Arden's theme. Hence, if the individual characters were not isolated as carriers of specific statements but viewed as a group-hero, it would emerge that each character embodies a segment of the whole – the concept of the sullied persona (the anti-hero). Similarly, Soyinka's defect-fraught cast (*The Invention*) depicts a physically and psychologically marred society. Consequently, there is no single hero to talk of in *The Waters of Babylon* and *The Invention*.

Like Soyinka, Arden metaphorically uses negative character-traits to point out a larger societal flaw. The minor difference is that Arden's characters display personality flaws not physical defects like Soyinka's. For example, Krank, the should-be hero, runs a brothel by night and has a shady past connecting him to the Nazis; Councillor Caligula the 'Negro' and self-appointed liberator of black people ends up in bed with the prostitute, Bathsheba; Butterthwaite sees no wrong in rigging the lottery and defrauding the state and several politicians of local government, like right-wing extremist Henry Ginger, are not exemplary in behaviour. They readily engage in espionage activity, selling out and backstabbing colleagues without remorse. Blackmail, lying, and clandestine deals are the order of the day in this 'Babylon'. All are tainted. The society is the antagonistic force whose financial policies, social affairs and political ideals have had a major role to play in the shaping of these flawed personae. The characters therefore do not reflect society, but reveal what society does to humankind. The negative influence of the wider European socio-political structure is seen in the travails of Krank, whose life seems to succumb to the strong force of the whirlpool of circumstance: first the Polish war offices, the Russian camp, the Nazi camp, and now the shadow of the past that engulfs and kills him as he tries to escape it. As the curtain falls, Krank dies an emotional death, marked by a lengthy speech of self-exposition. The question posed is, whose hands are clean?

The idea of identity is cast in developmental phases throughout the play. It centres on the life of Krank. This theme is developed by use of three major technical devices; clothing, name, and verbal utterances. Arden starts gradually with the elementary device of costume change, moving on to name change he ultimately ends with the utterance of highly philosophical statements. In typical Brechtian style, Krank addresses the audience, thus distancing it even more from the illusion of the play.

The most sophisticated presentation of the theme of identity-crisis is in the characters' philosophical statements. These utterances, made mainly by Krank, are tied to the concept of one's dwelling place as a clue-bearer to identity. Conventionally, people are identified by their places of abode and the countries of citizenship, so that one's base becomes a component of one's identity. Contrary to this, Arden's characters continually avoid a personal concrete base; they are forced to assume a 'floating identity'. Krank, the proponent and defender of this philosophy, disclaims citizenship of any place, whether of Poland or England. When Paul, the committed Polish nationalist, urges him to help in the assassination of the coming Russians to show Polish patriotism and the acknowledgement of his roots, Krank's outburst is, 'I am no longer a citizen of anywhere' (Arden 1974:37).

The binary of illusion and reality complements the theme of identity discussed above. Unlike the tautly structured layout of the theme of identity, the idea of illusion comes out elliptically until it is fully explored toward the end of the play through statements and song. Like Brecht, Arden disturbs the audience's comfort zone by using a battery of background information that is loosely connected to the central story, yet very important. Furthermore, Arden creates a play within-a play wherein some of the characters assume the role of director. Although clearly a technique that can be traced back to the Shakespearean tradition, this device enhanced the Brechtian distancing effect by distorting all meaningful distance between reality and illusion. As the sense of reality is teased, the audience keeps asking, 'What is life, what is play?' – typically, a Brechtian principle.

The audience has been long conditioned to figure out the theme of the story, but this time, it cannot. Evidently, it becomes difficult to pin Arden down to the specific moral position propagated by Krank in this play. Naturally, this can disturb an audience that wants to grasp the theme of the play, but find it opaque. Jeffrey Roberts remarks that in *The Waters of Babylon,* Arden, a maverick of the 'New Wave', '... has a perplexing tendency to withhold judgement of [whatever] order or ... behaviour of [an] individual who struggles within it ... [perhaps] because he is much more aware of the irrationality of human experience' (Wike 1995:5). *The Times* (21 October 1957 dismisses the play as '... a noisy and shapeless work ... [which] even at the end [is still] full of fanfare, [while] the theme, [the supposed] purpose in writing the play remain[s] obscure'. It is the same newspaper that vilifies Soyinka two years later for not communicating clearly at the end of *The Invention.* The desire to end a drama with a solid statement is still paramount. *The Waters of Babylon* illustrates that there are no simple answers to problems. The audience is subjected to a battery of facts and postulations and must ferret out their significance. This makes compelling, Jeffrey Roberts's opinion that Arden's is the theatre of illusion and as such it is also '... a theatre of persuasion. Like Shakespeare's – like Brecht's – [it] is a theatre of scepticism and questioning' (Wike 1995:7). Arden's intricate model of a questioning theatre is not understood by the audience that is conditioned to orthodox dramaturgy.

In addition to the absence of a theme-bearing hero, Soyinka and Arden further compare in their use of techniques like the breaking of the fourth wall, and stock characterisation, all of which point to the hesitant beginnings of non-realist theatre which the reviewers failed to note.

In contrast, Wesker's dramaturgy is very orthodox. *Chicken Soup With Barley* traces the course of gradual deflation of political commitment in a West End Jewish community. It displays a panoramic time setting that spans two decades, (4 October 1936 to December 1956). The dramatic style is teeming with the conventional features that the audience of the time was accustomed to. The central theme is enunciated toward the end. The sense of despair in the young is brought about by capitalist Great Britain's indifference toward people of socialist inclinations, like the European Jews living there. In the mode of realist theatre, most of Wesker's stage directions depict true-to-life scenes, for example:

A fire is burning. One door, at the back and left of the room, leads to the bedroom. A window, left, looks up to the street. To the right is another door which leads to the kitchen, which is seen...
[SARA KAHN is in the kitchen washing up...] (Wesker 1959:13).

This 'kitchen-sink' hallmark also shows in the place setting which introduces the audience to the play. Wesker's use of song is very different from the Brechtian style in Arden's *The Waters of Babylon*. Wesker's play is characterised by the scarcity of poetry and song, features which are common in Arden's play. Wesker only refers to song to emphasise setting and theme. None of his characters advance the plot by singing lyrics that reveal new aspects of the story as do Arden's in the mode of Brecht. Wesker does not specify the exact songs instead, he mentions them as part of the stage directions, explaining setting and casting the mood thus: '[SARA KAHN IS...] *humming to herself*, and '*From outside we hear a band playing a revolutionary song*' (Wesker 1959:13).

Another striking difference between Wesker and Arden is the 'absence of the audience' in Wesker. Like a true box-set, Wesker's play unfolds in front of the audience without once acknowledging its presence in speech or action, the kind of theatre the reviewers were accustomed to.

Jeffrey Roberts' comment assists in establishing an answer to the lingering question why Wesker triumphs where Soyinka and Arden do not, that:

The majority of these new playwrights, including Wesker and ... Osborne, chose more often the conventional styles traditionally associated with social realism, dating back to Shaw and Ibsen. ... [This kind of drama] had cultivated and satisfied the urge of the audience to identify itself vicariously with the stage characters and their circumstances; as a result most of the anti-realist forms – expressionism, epic theatre [and] absurdism – were still met by qualified reception (Wike 1995: 3, 4).

This is the kind of theatre the British reviewers expected as the slant of their commentary attests.

Interestingly, even though Arden failed at the box office, he did not fail at the Royal Court, a proponent of experimental theatre. He was accorded more leniency than normal. Soyinka was not. Why? Many postulations can be made in response to this question. Could it have been a case of inadvertent segregation against the minorities or it was all due to the British's unfamiliarity with Soyinka's foreign subject matter, presented in an equally foreign mode of dramaturgy? Alain Ricárd does not perceive this as a racist act. He believes Devine might have been torn between the task of building a national theatre and accommodating a foreign dramaturgy whose idiom could be better understood in its place of origin, Nigeria. Seeing that Nigeria was soon to be independent, Ricárd opines that Soyinka had a better chance of making an impact there than in Britain. Ricárd further explains that perhaps Devine, '... saw that [Soyinka] had invented a dramatic language that was really rooted in Africa. Maybe [Britain] couldn't make use of [Soyinka's] kind of drama (Motsa 2000:82).' Hence it was more sensible to urge the playwright toward establishing himself in Nigeria.

Ricárd's argument raises the concern that perhaps England was not the right platform for Soyinka to test his excellence of skill; implicitly, he may have been 'singing the Lord's song in a strange land' in 1950s England. This marginalisation of Anglophone African art by England reflects a love-hate relationship between 1950s England and her colonies whose artists England could not readily assimilate into the English literary mainstream. It is evident that the British social structures in which Soyinka emerged as a playwright were very complex. Consequently, his seeming marginalisation may be better understood by making a more detailed analysis of British society and its structures at the time. Nonetheless, when one considers Devine's partiality, the overtly racist reviews, Soyinka's own 'paranoia' with the patronising gestures of the British toward the so-called minorities, one perceives indubitable evidence of racial discrimination against black artists who dared to compete with the colonial master in his own turf. It is all the more comprehensible why Soyinka later lamented, '... it was here in England, in the 1950s, that I faced the most raw brunt of racism with bus passengers, landlords and landladies, and shop stewards' (Soyinka 1986). The validity of the argument that Soyinka was still a novice in theatre notwithstanding, the view still holds that his race and the foreignness of his theatrical idiom contributed considerably to his inhospitable reception. It becomes obvious that, this New Wave experience was very apathetic to anything foreign. Lacey points out that in fact, this was more an English than a British occurrence as it even marginalised a thriving post-war non-realist Scottish theatre which had emerged before Osborne (Lacey 1995:3). Accordingly, it is hardly surprising why a non-British black dramatist was met with an antagonistic reception despite his presentation of a topical play in an angry, blunt and deviant voice, as was the style of his English contemporaries: his was an anger directed at the entire White system of oppression which included Britain.

A progenitor of protest and 'deviant' non-illusionist styled drama; *The Invention* appeared at a seminal moment in English literature. As the vanguard for Wole Soyinka's drama, this play pioneered a drama that was to become the voice of the politically disenfranchised in an oppressive society. Through satire, Soyinka's strange drama sought to expose the social disease rampant not only in Nigeria but in Africa and the world over. Soyinka's dramatic idiom which experiments with an amalgam of forms from home and abroad started with *The Invention* and 'Telephone Conversation' at the Court. However, it continued as the voice of the voiceless, satirically staging the ruling powers in various socio-political contexts.

Unsurprisingly, Soyinka found the right seedbed in The Royal Court which, in its pursuit of relevance in a fast changing Britain, implemented action programmes primarily aimed at grooming new voices for the theatre. The Court had sought to conscientise the writer and the society about contemporary issues which theatre had to explore in the wake of post-World War II. Undoubtedly, Devine was very keen on taking theatre beyond the confines of Britain, hence the distinct and continuous inclusion of plays by foreign playwrights such as Arthur Miller, Beckett, and Ionesco in the repertoire of the early production list at The Court (Browne 1975:103-104). The kind of foreign theatre that Devine desired to blend into his project included a wide variety of traditions, such as was seen in the array of foreign playwrights, whose works were shown in London and seemingly instituted as canons to emulate. Devine openly embraced these non-English theatre-ideals like those of the German Bertolt Brecht and Samuel Beckett, who, though of Irish origin, wrote in French and English. Devine's sense of blending local British with 'foreign' techniques was ostensibly confined to Europe and the United States. Backed by experience, Brecht and Arthur Miller were welcomed as worthy contributors to the new British theatre. Correspondingly, Soyinka and other youths answered Devine's call and offered 'the different voice' to the familiar. Regrettably, Soyinka did not form part of the canon. His African oral-lore imbued theatre could not find room alongside Brecht's and Beckett's – ironically also his sources of inspiration. Despite this pernicious reception by 1950s England, Soyinka treasured the Court experience; he later testified that, '...the days at the Royal Court were marvellous. It was good to experience this change in theatre – a move toward social realism for rising playwrights like Osborne, Wesker, Bond, and so forth ...' (Motsa 2000: 299).[16]

A history of productions

Wesker, Arnold, *Chicken Soup With Barley*. 7 July 1958, Belgrade Theatre, Coventry. Dir. by John Dexter. Design\music by Michael Richardson. Royal Court Theatre, London, 14 July 1958; 7 June 1960.

Soyinka, Wole, *The Invention* (unp.). Dir. by Wole Soyinka, Royal Court Theatre, London, 1 November 1959; 1965.

Soyinka, Wole, *King Baabu*. Dir. by Wole Soyinka et al. Spoornet State Theatre, Pretoria, October 2002.

Soyinka, Wole, *The Lion and the Jewel*. Dir. by Desmond O'Donovan. Design\music by Jocelyn Herbert, Marc Wilkinson & Sanya Dousanmu

---

[16] For more on Soyinka in this book, see Victor Ukaegbu, 'Talawa Theatre Company: The 'Likkle' Matter of Black Creativity and Representation on the British Stage'.

(music). Nigeria December 1959; The Royal Court London, 12 December 1966.

Osborne, John, *Look Back in Anger*. Dir. by Tony Richardson. Design\music by Alan Tagg, Thomas Eastwood (music). Royal Court Theatre, London, 8 May 1956.

Arden, John, *Serjeant Musgrave's Dance: An Historical Parable*. Dir. by Lindsay Anderson. Design/Music by Jocelyn Herbert, Dudley Moore (music). Royal Court Theatre, London, 22 October 1959; 9 December 1965.

Arden, John, *The Waters of Babylon*. Dir. by Graham Evans. Royal Court Theatre, London 20 October 1957.

Works cited

Altick, Richard D. (1973), *Victorian People and Ideas*, New York: W.W. Norton & Company.

Beckett, Samuel (1982), *Waiting for Godot*, New York: West Houston Street.

Bermel, Albert (1977), *Artaud's Theatre of Cruelty*, New York: Taplinger Publishing.

Browne, Terry W. (1975), *Playwrights' Theatre: The English Stage Company at the Royal Court Theatre*, London: Macmillan.

Findlater, Richard (ed.) (1981), *At the Royal Court: 25 Years of the English Stage Company*, New York: Groove Press.

Gassner, John (1965), *Directions in Modern Theatre and Drama: an Expanded Edition of Form and Idea in Modern Theatre*, New York: Holt Rinehart and Winston.

Götrick, Kacke (1984), *Apidan Theatre and Modern Drama: A Study in Traditional Yoruba Theatre and Its Influences on Modern Drama by Yoruba Playwrights*, Stockholm: Almqvist & Wiskell International.

Holy Bible (RSV) (1972), Nashville: Thomas Nelson.

Innes, Christopher (1992), *Modern British Drama 1890 – 1990*, Cambridge & New York: Cambridge University Press.

Lacey, Stephen (1995), *British Realist Theatre: The New Wave in its Context 1956 – 1965*, London & New York: Routledge.

Lindfors, Bernth (1982), *Early Nigerian Literature*, New York: African Publishing.

Moore, Gerald (1978), *Wole Soyinka* (2nd ed), London: Evans Bros.

Motsa, Zodwa (2000), *A Tiger in The Court: The Nature and Implications of Wole Soyinka's Interactions at The Royal Court Theatre: 1956 – 1966*, (Unpublished Doctoral thesis), University of the Witwatersrand. Johannesburg.

Motsa, Zodwa (ed.) (2005) *Wole Soyinka: The Invention & The Detainee*, Tshwane: University of South Africa Press.

Sanders, Andrew (2000), *The Short Oxford History of English Literature* (2nd ed), Oxford: Oxford University Press.

Wike, Jonathan (ed.) (1995), *John Arden and Margaretta D'Arcy: A Case Book*, New York: Garland Publishing.

Television

Soyinka, Wole (27 February 1987), interview with Maja-Pearce. 'A Combative Soul', *The Nobel Prize in Literature '86*. Channel 4.

CHAPTER TWELVE

THEATRE AS EDUTAINMENT: SOL. B. RIVER'S DRAMATIC BURDEN

ASHLEY TELLIS

Synopsis:

This chapter uses Godiwala's theory of textual performativity[17] to analyze the plays of Sol. B. River, a young and innovative Yorkshire-born British-Caribbean playwright. A central contradiction is located in his dramatic project and this is examined from within the dynamics of the plays. Successful plays are pitted against unsuccessful ones to make an argument for when and how a theatrical practice which seeks to combine social messages with entertainment fails and when and how it does not.

Sol. B. River's plays come with a set of resources that are nothing short of dazzling. Mixing elements of film, music (a very eclectic range, symbolic of the 'new' Britain), performance poetry, the internet, mobile phone messages into traditional drama, he seems at the cutting edge of theatrical invention. Thematically, too, his resources are no less wide-ranging. Incorporating elements from African postcolonial history, African-American civil rights struggles, the

---

[17] In this chapter, I will be analyzing River's plays only on the page, following what Dimple Godiwala has called 'the performativity of the dramatic text', implying that a critical reading of a play can contain a 'performative possibility, and is a performance theory located in the dramatic text.' See Dimple Godiwala, '"The performativity of the dramatic text": domestic colonialism and Caryl Churchill's *Cloud Nine*', *Studies in Theatre and Performance* Vol. 24 No. 1 5-21.

West Indian history of slavery, British West Indian cultural and intellectual figures, his plays are palimpsests that open out in interesting ways for the individual viewer/reader.

The central danger that lurks beneath this dizzying dramatic array, however, is that all of it has been assembled as a series of effects, pyrotechnics, and, as such, is reducible to little more than its various parts. Is there a theatrical framework, an intellectual matrix that orders this diverse and rich material or is it the reader/viewer's task to create one for herself?

One place not to go for an answer to this is the slim body of River's own Prefaces to the various dramatic pieces that he has published, or his autobiographical prose, like the piece 'Serious Business' in this volume. This is not because of some naïve reading of Barthes' death-of-the-author thesis, but merely because River is not the most articulate of writers. His prose is meandering, his theses often contradictory and his aims and claims somewhat diverse and ill-formed.

However, if we are to discern two central premises to which he returns over and over in his prose writing, and they are that a) his plays are 'infotainment' or 'edutainment' (River 2003:15) – entertainment with a social conscience, a message, a form of education and b) that he aims to remain true to the rhythms of the world and the characters he sees around him, then we locate a central contradiction in these two claims.

Theatre as education or as a form of accounting to one's conscience does involve the moulding of reality; it is not merely reality recorded. Further, this idea of merely recording the conversations and rhythms of the world runs the risk of characterizing dramatic art as mere mimetic observation, which it is not. Yet the naiveté of this contradiction is the source of River's dramatic creativity as a dramatist, even as it also frequently is the source of his foundering.

In this chapter, I will concentrate, initially, on two of his plays, one each from the two broad kinds of plays River writes, which fall on either side of the contradiction noted above: i) the artfully created lineages of intellectual and political history he creates in many plays, of which I will be concentrating on *Moor Masterpieces* and ii) the plays he writes with his ear to the ground, merely capturing characters and their lives, of which I will be concentrating on *Two Tracks and Text Me* (2003).

My division of the two plays into River's schema must not give the impression that I think the plays can or should be contained within such a schema. Indeed, part of my point will be that River might improve his dramaturgy as a whole if he lets the two mingle more and that the flaws of his plays often lie in his too-schematic distinction between education and entertainment, between artifice and the ordinary, conversational rhythms of lived lives. Through an analysis of two more of his plays *48-98* (1998) and *To Rahtid* (1996), I will then show the success he manages to achieve when he lets the two work together, something he needs to build on for his future dramatic work.

Moor Masterpieces

Moor Masterpieces is a re-working of *Othello* as if Othello were a historical character. It mixes his own narrative as a fictional-turned-historical character with the narratives of several others (Solomon, Iago, the Prince of Morocco, West Indian migrants) and, through that, River creates a certain kind of history of the Black present. The play opens with a voice-over detailing various dates and events of the history of Black slavery.

This is followed by a Solomon as Ur-Black man, entering to songs by Terence Trent D'Arby and Des'ree. Solomon's narrative establishes a certain vision of history, a certain lineage and it becomes clear that this is a history of men, a male genealogy. He says:

I, being me, was allowed to see, like Othello before me. Although he is me and I he,...
the great leaders of my kind, all black and comely, and each time I ask these men what
will deliver the Moor of the 21st century? (Moor Masterpieces, Act I)

All the Black leaders through various historical moments have one message to offer and this is the central message of the play, repeated over and over:

They all answered the same. An exodus, a return, in mind and body, physically or
mentally to that place all Moors should go (*Moor Masterpieces*, Act I).

This message can be read both literally and symbolically to mean, one imagines, a return alternately to oneself with a sense of integrity and dignity or to the homeland of Africa. In either case, the message seems dated (Black Pride) and reactionary (Africa as origin, Africa romanticised). Solomon ends his narrative with an exhortation to Black men to wake up from their slumber and follow the instruction that these great Black men have left behind.

The central narrative by Othello that follows in Act II, Scene i, continues with this male-centred history and does not really dwell upon the question of gender at all, even though it is central to the Shakespearean play. Not a word is spoken about Othello's sexism, his investment in patriarchal notions of honour, purity and the play's distrust of women. Instead, the focus is on his own betrayal by white history, his being short-changed because of his race. Indeed, he accuses the audience of siding with Desdemona and sees that as racially predetermined. He says he gave his heart to Desdemona over the Nubian princess and the words 'Nubian princess' haunt him to this day, implying that his was a racially wrong choice that doomed him. He accuses Desdemona of not being an adequate partner:

But as for my mind that makes decisions for me in peace and my peace I thought was
Desdemona, but not even she knew the pain that chased me around my own mind. (II, i)

Othello then goes on to repeat that refrain that is the onus of the Black man, but
not before insulting the Prince of Morocco (the Arab) as inferior and not worthy of
his attention, as subject of an inferior pain and history. This is a shockingly
insensitive slur on River's part, even though he later recuperates him into a joint
position of being duped by the White Man. He then frames Shakespeare as the
white imperialist and ends his discourse with an implicit exoneration of himself
and an explicit blaming of Desdemona:

> And so, infatuated a Moor should not be. Instead his own life and destiny he should take
> care of and uphold. It is imperative that he understands the basics of the economy and
> having said that his own mind must be structured and composed to the extent that he
> understands the beginning of wisdom, which is to get insight. I whisper now into the ears
> of my brothers, choose your love wisely, choose, but choose wisely, let your manner be
> close to God. (II, i)

In Act II, ii Solomon returns to build a genealogy of Black leaders and
historical figures from Benjamin Bannecker to Martin Luther King, with only two
women (Edmonia Lewis -- seen only relationally, as lovingly sculpting Jean de
Sable -- and Elaine Locke) in a roster of fourteen men, not counting Othello and
Solomon himself.[18] The scene ends with Solomon collapsing under the pain and
martyrdom of these Black figures, mainly men (with a token reference to Black
sisters), seen in his taking off his clothes and raising his arms, becoming a sort of
Black Christ figure, orgasming after the circle-jerk of Black male history.

Act III is a palimpsest of slave male voices (with only two small references to
women being enslaved and raped) through letters, testimonies and autobiographical
accounts. It ends with the freed slave, who gets rid of his chains, finding himself on
a slave ship to the United States, once again repeating the central refrain, marked
with a solidarity with fellow men:

> I prayed to the ancestors that I would die soon if they didn't give me the strength to rise
> above it. And I knew that from now on, seeing all my fellow men in a strange land that

---

[18] As will be noticed by now, River sees the United States as an important part of his legacy.
Indeed, he has an entire play about Civil Rights figures James Meredith (*Walk Against
Fear*). While this can be a productive move, it also has its dangers as it flattens out historical
trajectories. In River's case, it ignores the richness of West Indian British histories, only
because its figures are not as popular. See *West Indian Intellectuals in Britain* ed. Bill
Schwarz (Manchester: Manchester University Press, 2004) for a full history of these figures
and movements. One area of further exploration needed is River's romanticisation and use
of the United States with which he works in close relation.

only an exodus [...] to that place we should go before it is too late. (Moor Masterpieces, Act III)

An Old West Indian man and a Young Man share Act IV, offering an inter-generational perspective on Black Britain from the first, big West Indian migration in the late 40s and 50s. The Old Man's wife, a presence only in his narrative and never appearing on stage in person, returns to the West Indies because she is a proud woman and cannot stand the humiliation of being in Britain, especially as she is a trained teacher. She too repeats the refrain, arguing that 'black people here were going to be lost' and this is where the return motif takes on literal significance, going back to the homeland (not that Jamaica is the original homeland anyway, but this is not problematized)[19].

The Young Man, toward the end, offers another list of Black figures and that too contains just one woman Harriet Tubman (referred to only as Tubman) in a list of five men. The narrative of the young West Indian man does not give us a complex picture of the new, multicontextual Britain at all. He merely rages against the racism and then is told by the Old West Indian man to look to his ancestors for inspiration, and he promises to do that.

The play ends on yet another invocation of that central refrain, this time put in the mouth of the protagonist's mother, which, as we have noted, at best can be interpreted as Black pride and, at worst, as a romantic return to Africa, but what's worse is that it stands in for a more nuanced picture of race-based politics. If racial problems in Britain could be fixed with an invocation of a racial genealogy or a return to some fictional point of 'origin,' that would be simple enough. While a looking inward is much-needed in Black communities in Britain and elsewhere in the West, it is a more reflexive and critical looking that is needed, not a nostalgia-based evocation of some racially pure history or pure racial politics.

The point here, furthermore, is not just the numerical scarcity of women mentioned in this vision. The world-view of the play is not just gendered conservatively - the only two women who have parts are not presences, but merely referred to by the men: the wife of the old man who leaves him and returns to the West Indies and the mother of the young man who taught him that all people were equal, pitted against white mothers who teach their children to stay away from Black kids; the women form the tail-end of a list of male greats, an afterthought. It is that the didacticism and demagoguery of the vision creaks embarrassingly. Blacks are faultless in this vision of history; Black Pride means just reconnecting with great male leaders of the past who have all the answers.

---

[19] Indeed, River uses Jamaica and Africa interchangeably as homelands or points of origin without any interrogation. His problematic construction of Jamaica is most evident in his play *The Witch of Annie Hall* which was produced in Jamaica, subject for another play

In both the narratives of historical-fictional figures like Solomon, Othello and the Prince of Morocco, on the one hand, and the lived figures like the slave and the Old and Young West Indian men, on the other, gender roles remain unquestioned and history is configured in fairly straightforward black-and-white terms. The Black guys are the good guys and the white guys (and Arabs) the bad guys/exploiters/fools. This is a somewhat hagiographic and simplistic narrative and what the theatrical contribution of such a historical staging is remains not quite clear, apart from, as has been noted, a resuscitation of a naïve notion of Black Pride that had its moment in the seventies but has surely passed its sell-by date.

There is no reconstruction of the experience of slavery or account of what it was to be among the Blacks arriving in Britain on Windrush (apart from one powerful image of the cold hands of the labourer) that changes standard available accounts of these phenomena. *Moor Masterpieces* is an exercise in feel-good maleness that simplifies and irons out all the complexities of Black existence in Britain or through history.

Two Tracks and Text Me

Two Tracks and Text Me is a play set in contemporary Britain among several young Black protagonists, a group of young men on the one hand, and two girls - both dub poets - and a minor girl on the other. Once again, the gender politics of the play leave much to be desired. The men talk a certain crude, commodifying language, they want to 'grind that gal like a dog' (*Two Tracks and Text Me*, Act I) and liberally spew misogynist and homophobic abuse:

SHUN: Bitch, ass, hoe
HOE: Bitch arse, mother fucking, fuck, fucking hoe.
SHUN: Batty hole, fucking, fingerfucking hoe ass, frigging, bitch, mother fucker. Punni lipped dirty semen spreading shit (*Two Tracks and Text Me*, Act I).

but turn out to be angels in the end. The women talk of love (Kat) and if they don't believe in it are made to be in denial of their true feminine selves (Yazza). While Beeves and his girlfriend Yazza are both cheating on each other, only Yazza gets blamed for it. The problem figure is Yazza who needs to be reprimanded, told to shut up, tamed and who is sleeping around because she is not in touch with her true femininity, while her friend Kat is, which is why she is monogamous and finds true love with a man.

[Shun, Beeves and Hoe in *Two Tracks and Text Me*
Photo courtesy Sol B. River]

[Yazza and Kat.
Photo courtesy Sol B. River]

Yazza and Kat have a long
discussion about what love is and
what they want from men. Kat is
trying to save Yazza from
destroying herself. Yazza is
cheating on Beeves, sees through
the whole charade of love, knows
that Beeves is also cheating on her
and is not mystified by the sexual act, but sees it for what it is. This, according to
Kat (and the moral order of the play), is her problem:

KAT: Wait Yazza
YAZZA: Wait for what? Wait for you to follow me?

KAT: Yazza
YAZZA: Yazza, Yazza, Yazza…You said you wanted to be me.
KAT: Like you…And I don't anymore.
YAZZA: Then pick some other sorry ass to follow because I've got my own shit to deal with. I've got stuff you know, stuff inside. You think I'm confident, don't you, you think I know.
KAT: Talk about it.
YAZZA: I don't want to talk about it… I'll deal with it in my own time, I don't need you Kat, because I'm strong. I can fight any bastard and I can fight on my own terms.
KAT: You're a beautiful girl, whatever is in there needs to come out (*Two Tracks and Text Me*, Act I).

While Yazza is given a history and an interiority, it is only to pathologise, not understand her. She has strayed from the path of good femininity, while Kat has not, and, therefore, will find her true love:

KAT: But I can't stand confusion. Everyone has their shit to deal with. Every other person you pass on the street has a story. I'd say tell it. Every boyfriend…all three of them Yazza. Since nineteen years old I've had three boyfriends and they all wanted to use me as a punch bag just like my father did who unlike yours was there , I wish he

hadn't been. I got help. I got some help. I talked, I thought, I faced it. Yazza, look yourself in the eye and decide what you need. Not what you want but what you need. So, if you need a hug. It is waiting for you.

(*YAZZA is stopped in her tracks.*)
It has taken me so long to find a man, to trust a man Yazza. It takes time to get over and time to discover. (*Two Tracks and Text Me*, Act I).

[Louise.
Photo courtesy Sol B. River]

While Kat also has a pathological history, she is healed and restored by her acceptance of conventional femininity and redemption through men. Louise, too, finds such redemption. She is a young girl in the play whose father is pimping her out as a prostitute till she is 'saved' by the benevolent young men, Hoe and Beeves, 'rescued' by the heroes from the abomination of her fate, 'her dilemma.' (*Two Tracks and Text Me*, Act I). Her own desire as a twelve year-old is deemed irrelevant, never mind that all her messages (read as pleas for help) are sexual; infantile female sexuality can have no place in this patriarchal universe.

Louise is merely an object to be saved to show the greatness of the male figures, never mind that they constantly objectify women themselves and were ready to do it to Louise too till they discover she is 'Shit, twelve.' (*Two Tracks and Text Me*, Act I) Hoe assuages Louise's sexual abuse with some gobbledygook about there being a reason for everything and about entering music and about simple misuses of love. He reduces her to tears and bad poetry from her earlier sexual SMS missives. All that remains is for her to be rescued by him but not before some misunderstanding that facilitates the male reunion. As both thematic and dramatic technique, paedophilia is the most pathetic trick in the book. It allows for no interrogation of the messy business of sexuality and eases the process of the iron hand of male control's coming down with great moral heft.

[Louise and Hoe.
Photo courtesy Sol B. River]

Adult female sexuality has no place either, for that matter. Yazza, by far the most interesting character in the play, is first reduced to a caricature – she makes a sexual pass at Hoe, her boyfriend's best friend (who refuses her only because she is, as he tells her, 'my spar's girl'), then as vindictive as she tries to implicate him as the one who made the pass, tries to put the best friends against each other by accusing Hoe of paedophilia and finally as the shrew who won't stop talking and needs to be tamed and domesticated by Beeves (who, while no angel himself, is restored as patriarchal godhead) in a narrative of male ordering of female disorder:

BEEVES: Just keep it shut for a damn second. Listen, one of the greatest skills is for somebody to have the ability to listen. You don't know the facts you don't know, and you don't even wait for a sentence to finish before you have your say. I'm fed up of your... Oh if you could listen to yourself. See yourself for a just a minute. Your mother didn't bring you up to behave like this... (*Two Tracks and Text Me*, Act Two).

while Kat goes off into the sunset with Shun in monogamous, heterosexual bliss.

The men are the heroes of the day. Indeed, Hoe turns out to be a policeman (!), that arch figure of violence against Blacks in Britain, and the men touch fists and end in homosocial bliss, with Beeves leaving young Louise in the paternal policeman's care of Hoe. Male bonding is the crux of the play and the homosocial bond between Beeves and Ho is restored in the play, despite its temporary disruption at the hands of the devious woman, Yazza. This conservative and frequently misogynist sexual narrative in the play undercuts all the radical mixing of genres (video, internet, film, TV, mobile phones) and the inventive use of music (from Jill Scott to Diana Ross and Outkast to Aquemini) reinstating Caribbean patriarchy and big boy bonding above all else.

48-98

By contrast, *48-98* combines British West Indian history with the particularities of lived lives in a way that is dramatically satisfying. Smartly juxtaposing different forms – filmic narrative, stand-up comedy, family drama and inventive music collages – the play offers the blend of historical consciousness and rich entertainment without the didacticism and moral heavy-handedness of the earlier two plays.

The play opens with footage from Roy Boulting's classic 1948 film *The Guinea Pig*, foreshadowing issues of assimilation, a museum attendant speaking of West Indians both as artifacts and offering a racist narrative of their sojourn in Britain in the 50 (and then 100) years since Windrush and the voice of a West Indian man. The play swiftly moves into a family scene – father (Merwin), mother (Dorothy) and son (Tony) and various scenes are played out, usually the same scenes with various possible outcomes. Characters leap out of the domestic scene and become other characters; the son Tony for example becomes a stand-up comic. Indeed, this is one of the best scenes in the play, for its breath-stopping mixture of humour and the sheer violence of the West Indian boy's initiation into masculinity at the hands of the violent father. The multiple levels at which this narrative works – social commentary, pathos, gendering – are remarkable:

Do you remember…do you remember getting beat…fun wasn't it. All dads did it differently, my dad had what he called the strap that hug behind the cellar door. All you heard my Dad say is, 'go and get de strap'. I'd have just come in from school and as soon as he'd see me he'd think of something to beat me for and it was probably something that happened three days earlier… (Mimes father.) 'Oh yes an go an fetch de strap'…and he's get his words out in-between chewing out the marrow bone from the biggest bowl of soup you'd ever seen. (Mimics father.) 'Go (Chews bone.) an (Chew.) get (Chew.) di strap'. So you walk off knowing where the strap is but you're afraid to find it, then you'd shout back 'I can't find it' while stuffing magazines down you're pants and you're hopeful that he's rethinking.

And there are other times when it's just pure action. It's like going to the gym wasn't the fashion the like now so dads had nowhere to go and work off their frustration…so back then beating your kids was as good as doing a circuit, some weights and a spot on the running machine. And then you'd get emergency beatings, the ones that you weren't expecting and your dad grabs anything at hand like his shoes or my brother used to have this plastic car track. And you know one last thing…my dad when he finished beating you and you were like trying to be brave and hold back the tears, but you couldn't and one would slip out and start rolling down you face or your bottom lip would start to quiver. He'd look at you and he'd say, what you crying for?

You've been a lovely audience, thank you very much, next week it's afro picks, waist bands and flares. Good night God bless.

(TONY comes back to the sitting room where the previous family scene continues, mum is cleaning the television, MERWIN is off) (48-98, p. 37)

Both Dorothy and Merwin are given monologues in which we enter their minds and get a keen sense of their interiorities. Their alienation even in their togetherness, and the gendered nature of their alienation is well-portrayed, their link to Jamaica as homeland which alienates their British-born child are real and we see both the particularities of their lives and the broader canvas of twentieth-century British history without being preached to or without an arch construction of the self as located in history. In vignettes, the husband and wife hug each other and speak their thought out loud from within the hug, thoughts they can't in their joint suffering, share with each other, even as they console each other:

MERWIN: First I have to make myself happy... I don't know...a big man like me in dis country feeling lonely...first time I feel my eye red with water because a de pressure. An I have to keep my suit clean to look presentable at de most basic tings. Stubborn me, stubborn, but I'll get through.

DOROTHY: First I had to make myself satisfy...I don't know... a little girl like me in dis country feeling lonely. I feel my eye red with water cause I survive de pressure. An we have to keep our hearts and minds clear to stay presentable in a thick atmosphere. Stubborn me, stubborn us. But I'll get through (*48-98*, p. 46).

Just these few lines embody gendered universes that open their resonances to the readers.

The play is circular in structure and ends not with the parents return to Jamaica but with the moment of the West Indian first landing on British soil off the ship. This undercuts the romanticising of the homeland. Jamaica, through the play, is invoked as tropical paradise (not the eviscerated landscape of Stephanie Black's *Life and Debt),*[20] a trope that plagues much early British Caribbean writing. In ending the play at the point of entry into Britain, River points to the reasons why the paradise was left in the first place and disallows a false nostalgia, even as the play recognises the importance of that idea for earlier generations of immigrants.

---

[20] Black's film which shows how the IMF and World Bank destroyed Jamaica borrows heavily from Jamaica Kincaid's literary work *A Small Place.*

To Rahtid

Finally, *To Rahtid*, a shorter, more experimental piece, also manages to capture that mixture well. Spoken by a character called MOUT, it involves just a mouth speaking in a dense Caribbean patois, recalling Beckett. However, unlike a Beckett character, this character is marked very obviously with history. Though the geography and history of this character's monologue is ambitious in the extreme - the history of slavery, historical and contemporary Jamaica, historical and contemporary Britain and Africa – River never loses hold of the fragile texture of human subjectivity. The images are tactile, the human is never lost against this vast historical landscape, nor does it end on any hagiographic recuperation.

Indeed, the historical references open out to several resonances for the reader/viewer, like the repeated invocation of the John Crow mountains, which make one wonder if this narrative is not also the voice of the eighteenth-century African queen Nanny who hid her people in times of conflict in the John Crow mountains and who made a vow to fight the British to death. Jamaica still has Nanny Town and in 1997 she was awarded the honour of National Heroine (See http://www.moec.gov.jm/ heroes/nannycont.html). River's narrative deftly moves from past to present but in each case, his sense of a closely intertwined suffering and resistance retrieves the narrative from abstraction and a pious invocation of Black history which marks *Moor Masterpieces*.

Consider this narrative of wanting a yam in the barren, colourless markets of England:

> people jus a watch me...me race...it always cole...dem watch me freezing nu understanding...freezing bret...slow bret...we did never...we can't speak...all dis time...how me survive!...urban life...in de town...busy concrete jungle...market...list wat me want...yam, ackee, plantain...big ol bag.. den me wait...big length of time...dem don't have what me want...turn dupy...eyes turn big...bottom lip drop...big ol bag full o potato...den me gawn... me nu say ta ta...how me can stan!... and now freezing bret...see me bret...slower bret... tink...what is dis...deal wid dis!...blaggage... me nu feel so gud...mad is crazy...not potato...where de yam/...me lip say...no yam...vital food gone...lickle most...strive I strive...I feel... me feel... I feel too... deal wid dis... mout quivering (To Rahtid, p. 55).

Despite the hamfistedness of too many 'deal wid dis' in the play, we can 'mek something of it' (*To Rahtid*) by ignoring that injunction and just listening to the pain and the perseverance of the human spirit. That in the end is the triumph of dramatic art and that in the end is what changes us, the change that Sol. B. River aims to engender through his plays.

Works cited:

Godiwala, Dimple (2004), '"The performativity of the dramatic text": domestic colonialism and Caryl Churchill's *Cloud Nine*', *Studies in Theatre and Performance* Vol. 24 No.1.

River, Sol. B (1997), *Plays*, London: Oberon.

River, Sol. B (2003), *Plays Two*, London: Oberon.

Schwarz, Bill (ed.) (2004), *West Indian Intellectuals in Britain*, Manchester: Manchester University Press.

Websites:
http://www.moec.gov.jm/heroes/nannycont.htm

CHAPTER THIRTEEN

BEYOND VICTIMHOOD: AGENCY AND IDENTITY IN THE THEATRE OF ROY WILLIAMS

ELIZABETH BARRY AND WILLIAM BOLES

Synopsis:

Roy Williams's is a naturalist theatre that aims to challenge racial stereotyping and to make a probing analysis of issues that black Britons face. His early work looked at the experience of emigration from Jamaica to Britain, and the relationships that individuals were able to build between the two cultures. His later work, on which this chapter concentrates, has explored what he has called the 'painful' experiences of a young, urban, black population, dealing with violence, racism within the law, gang conflict and sexual politics. The linguistic idiom of Williams' work makes an important contribution to contemporary theatre, both using the energies and distinctive rhythms of contemporary black British speech and exploring how this language is coming to dominate youth culture in general. He has also made some important collaborations, including those with the director Indhu Rubasingham, and the designer Ultz, to create a distinctive visual idiom: stark urban settings and a striking physicality in performance that serve to bring out the relationships between sport, sexuality and violence, and to represent their overlapping territories.

*I am giving the audience a slice of something they have not
seen before — Roy Williams*

Michael Billington, reviewing London theatre in 2003, commented that British
theatre had 'suddenly woken up to the big issues' (Billington 2003). Prominent
among those who were responsible for this awakening for Billington was the
playwright Roy Williams, whose critically acclaimed play *Fallout* the critic had in
the same year described as 'dazzlingly' overturning expectation in its depiction of
the fraught relations between the British police force and the black urban
population. Williams writes about British society as a whole, but he also aims in
his work to think about the particular issues facing second or third-generation
immigrants whose own community is divided and troubled. In the playwright's
own words: 'Is multiculturalism a mask? Where do we fit in? Are we fighting the
same fight as our mums and dads, to be accepted? Where do we stand?' (Crompton
2003).

Indhu Rubasingham, the director of Williams' first four plays, notes that the
playwright 'creates contemporary characters familiar to so many people in a way
that has never been done before in theatre. His plays capture a world that is
immediately recognisable but very rarely seen on stage' (Williams 2002: xxi-xxii).
The first such world is that of the Jamaican immigrant to Britain and the
subsequent generations of Afro-Caribbean Britons. Williams' early plays, *The No
Boys Cricket Club* (1996), *Starstruck* (1998), and *The Gift* (2000), draw on his own
family history to examine the situation of blacks in Jamaica, and subsequently in
Britain, and their struggle in choosing between their island heritage and the
potential financial opportunities in England. In 1999, however, Williams found a
second and much more localized focus as he turned his attention to contemporary
London and the stories to be found with its black inhabitants in plays such as *Lift
Off* (1999), *Clubland* (2001), *Sing Yer Heart Out for the Lads* (2002), *Fallout*
(2003), and *Little Sweet Thing* (2004).

With these works Williams provides the multicultural perspective absent from
mainstream British theatre, and in particular from the work of the new playwrights
writing at the Royal Court, the 'New Brutalists' or 'In-Yer-Face' generation such
as Butterworth, Kane, and McDonagh who were felt to characterize the 1990s
revival in British theatre. Williams' work shared with theirs an honest reflection of
the violence, prominent but de-eroticized sexuality and political disaffection
perceived to characterize their troubled generation. It also embraced a wider set of
issues, however, in following a postcolonial theatrical tradition, established by
playwrights like Mustapha Matura, Hanif Kureishi, Caryl Phillips, and Winsome
Pinnock, which addressed 'the erosion of cultural traditions, the conflicts between
first- and second-generation immigrants, the pull of assimilation, violence, racism,
discrimination, and poverty' (Dahl 1995: 39).

While Williams offers two sets of plays that feature new theatrical voices, this chapter will focus on his later urban plays, and their representation of the true condition of contemporary multicultural Britain. The emergence of a voice such as that of Williams is, as many commentators have pointed out, a timely one. Mary Karen Dahl, writing in 1995, observed that reviewers of the existing naturalist strand of black and Asian British theatre still tended to concentrate on its treatment of racism, and ascribe the primary agency in the play to this racism. The white 'us' of British society was still made the subject of such discussions. Taking the example of Hanif Kureishi's 1981 play *Borderline*, Dahl argues that twentieth century black and Asian theatre has deliberately tried to locate agency elsewhere, in the individual decisions and community actions of the black subjects themselves (Dahl 1995: 44). Roy Williams, in particular, has made this principle central to his work.

In fact, as Williams shows, the question of agency is now complicated by the fact that the dominant cultural expression among urban young people is becoming one identified with black youth. As Winsome Pinnock puts it, 'black rhythms of speech, a kind of street argot, have become the benchmark for all youth culture' (Pinnock 1999: 29). The post-colonial model whereby the colonised subversively mimics the language and behaviour of the coloniser has been turned on its head. White boys, in particular, are starting to emulate their black peers, responding to a cultural formation wherein machismo, strength, and sexual potency are all being aligned to the signifier 'black'. The white family in Williams' *Sing Yer Heart Out for the Lads* bring to light some of the more negative elements of this cultural phenomenon:

Jimmy [of Glen's music]: Just tell me what you get from it.
Glen: Loads.
Gina. Yeah, like learning to call a woman a bitch. (Williams 2004a: 135)

While the prominence of black culture in general is a cause for celebration, a 'moment of triumph' as Pinnock puts it (Pinnock 1999: 29), a particular strand of urban black youth culture also endorses a less welcome set of practices, something that Williams feels a particular responsibility to explore.

Paul Gilroy has written of how the role of the black character in British literature, even when written by black writers, has historically been that of either problem or victim. Central to the work of Roy Williams is its endeavour to write beyond these roles and to explore the problem of agency among black youths, in particular. Most strikingly, he suggests that the social 'victim' is often also in another context the aggressor. For him the black British subject must take responsibility for his or her actions, even when encouraged not to do so by just these categories of 'problem' or 'victim' that are imposed by white liberal society—a society of which the theatre has historically been part. The new characters identified by Rubasingham put issues of responsibility and identity centre stage so that Williams' theatre asks questions about the black subject on his or her own terms.

The renunciation of political and social agency on the part of the post-Thatcherite, politically disaffected subject is an issue to which theatre has insistently returned. Aleks Sierz has written of contemporary British theatre that 'by emphasizing such troubling notions as the complicity of victims in their victimization, provocative drama became more complex, less ideological... theatre offered grey areas and ambiguous situations' (Sierz 2000: 21). Sierz identifies this phenomenon in particular with sexuality, the masochism that the passive, infantilized generation in plays such as Ravenhill's *Shopping and Fucking*, or Kane's *Blasted* and *Cleansed* embrace. Roy Williams, too, looks at how social issues are so often displaced onto sexual behaviour, showing in his work that in a different context it is sexual aggression and social victimization that are intimately linked. Williams also examines the phenomenon of victimhood in a wider context, however, in exploring the appropriation and reinforcement of negative stereotypes of black youth by the black population itself. This is exemplified by the character of Joe in *Fallout*, who as a black policeman jaded by dealing with decades of interracial conflict voices some of the most racist views in Williams' work—'You liked him? That Zulu warrior who's black as coal? Who thought he smarter than the lot of you?'—and uses the term 'nigger' with abandon, or Mal in *Lift Off*, who prefers the punctual white drug dealers to Spencer who 'acts like he juss come off the plane from Jamaica' (Williams 2002: 176).

For Williams, as for his de-politicized 'In-Yer-Face' contemporaries, it is in the arena of sexual politics that social tension most often finds expression. In Williams's case, however, this expression takes a very specific and consistent form. Williams' work shares with that of his mid-1990s contemporaries a renewed preoccupation with the male voice in the wake of the feminist challenges—in and outside the theatre—of the 1970s and 1980s. David Edgar notes that one of the main reasons so many new plays emerged in the 1990s was precisely because 'writers found a subject... these plays address masculinity and its discontents as demonstrably as the plays of the early 1960s addressed class and those of the 1970s the failures of social democracy' (Edgar 1999: 27-8). However, what differentiates Williams is that he specifically addresses the complex relationship between this masculine identity and the racial identity of his black male characters, and examines how their particular struggle for status and cultural representation in British society is often expressed in sexual terms.

Lift Off, Williams' first play to address the black experience in urban London, examines the friendship between two young men in their early twenties: Mal, a seemingly self-confident, tough, virile black male, and Tone, his life-long white friend, who desperately wants to be as tough and cool as Mal. The play, first produced at the Royal Court Upstairs in London in 1999, was performed on a raised concrete stage that resembled a boxing-ring, as several reviewers pointed out, providing a fitting space for the dissection of the aggression and competitiveness of the male community that Williams presents. The play interleaves scenes depicting the two men as youngsters, in which they interact with a more peaceable and reserved black boy called Rich, and the later scenes, in the play's present, when they also encounter Tone's sister Carol and others. At the heart of these earlier scenes is Young Mal's struggle to establish his racial identity amidst the pressures that come from his gender, burgeoning sexuality, and contrasting friendship with both Tone and Rich. Williams told Dominic Cavendish that he too felt the difficulties felt by Young Mal when he was the character's age, as he asked himself: 'What is being black? How 'black' should I be?' (Cavendish 2004).

During the course of the play Young Mal chooses between the roles that Tone and Rich offer. Mal has some fondness for Rich, which leads him to try and persuade Rich to emulate the aggressive stance that he and Young Tone habitually take. At one point when Tone is picking on Rich, Mal provokes Rich: 'Yu juss gonna let him do this? Fight him man!' (Williams 2002: 200). In another instance, he tries to initiate Rich into the linguistic customs of the other boys. Lost amidst the vernacular of their insults, Rich is beaten after inadvertently directing sexual insults at Tone's mother in slightly the wrong fashion. Young Mal explains: 'I told yu to say, '*and* yer mum'. Yu don't call his mum a slag right out' (Williams 2002: 202). In contrast to Rich, Young Tone is felt to be far superior to Young Mal on the young boys' terms. In their wrestling matches Tone dominates Mal and with his domination comes a surprising claim of superiority of race, the white Tone identifying the condition of toughness with 'blackness':

Young Tone: I'm blacker than yu Mal.
Young Mal: Yer wish. (*Falls to floor.*)
Young Tone: Winner! (Williams 2002: 171)

Not only does white Young Tone lord his superior brand of 'blackness' over Young Mal in their physical fighting, but he also catches the eye of Delroy, leader of an all-black gang, who wants Young Tone (but not Mal) to join them as their first white member.

It is precisely this rejection by members of his own race that provokes Young Mal to choose Tone over Rich.

Rich: I'm not a loner.

Young Mal: Yes yu are. And I'm a bloody loner as well for hangin' out wid yer. Why d'yer think Tone isn't hangin' round wid us? He's got better things to do than fly stupid aeroplanes man.
Rich: My planes ain't stupid right.
Young Mal: He's hangin' round wid Delroy's gang, the only white kid there man. That ain't right. And yu know wat Delroy said to me, if we ain't better than white kids we aint nuttin'. (Williams 2002: 191)

The friendship between the two boys grows more strained and eventually due to Young Mal's hectoring and insults, Rich grows despondent and commits suicide.

Mal's betrayal of Rich is a result of his unease about his own 'blackness', an epithet which has detached itself from skin colour and become a set of attitudes and attributes connected to physical strength and pugnacity. It also becomes identified with a certain related attitude to sexual behaviour. Mal's desire to be seen as sufficiently 'black' leads to him sleep with Tone's younger sister Carol and then deny paternity when she becomes pregnant. In another instance, after being rejected by a white female clubber he vents his frustration by abusing an employee and customers at a fast food restaurant. In disavowing his friendship with Rich, he has committed himself to being a hard 'bwoi', a tough customer who only sees females in terms of their sexual availability. Mal tells Tone, in defending his sleeping with Carol: 'When pussy's on offer yu tek it! Fuck wat matters thass it' (Williams 2002: 231). Mal recognizes but cannot resist these stereotypes of black machismo.

Complicating this identification with the most negative aspects of his racial identity is Mal's discovery that he has leukaemia. Facing death makes him re-evaluate the choices he has made: ten years on he now finds himself as the lone black figure struggling to define himself amidst white faces, and being 'black' does not now carry the same cultural cachet as it did when he was younger. In a heated argument with Carol, Mal reveals the crux of his situation. He needs a bone marrow transplant, but 'from anoder black guy....There ain't enough black on the register dough Carol, there ain't enough. Cos they don't give a shit' (Williams 2002: 217). And with this admission about the lack of support within the black community, Mal makes a statement that will echo throughout Williams' other London plays:

Mal: I wanna be white.
Carol: White? Wat yu talking about?
Mal: Yer so lucky.
Carol: Lucky?
Mal: Can't yu see that? (Williams 2002: 218)

Ironically, Young Mal chose Tone over Rich because the white Tone was 'blacker'—stronger, more powerful—than Mal was, and he wanted to regain his racial identity, but as he has grown older he no longer embraces this identity, and indeed recognizes the cost of the attitude of studied irresponsibility and machismo that his black peers affect. In one sense, Williams suggests that Mal's predicament stems from this culture of apathy in his community, but on a more personal level Mal's situation is of his own creation and brings home to him the consequences of his actions.

Mal struggles with his own impulses in relation to the societal expectations of behaviour associated with his skin colour. In the final scene of confrontation between Tone and Mal, Mal recognizes the contradictions of his own identity and accepts the epithet of 'nigger' even when some of his actions in the play have also disavowed it:

> ...niggers don't care Tone, it's not in us. I mean we'd rather stuff our faces wid fried chicken, go out and tief, fuck whoever we like, than give blood to one of our own who badly needs it—who would die if he don't get it....We do wat everyone thinks, wat everyone expects, so give 'em wat they want, go for the pussy' (Williams 2002: 232)

Williams' ability to show Mal as an aggressor as well as a victim places him firmly in the fold of the writing of his 'In-Yer-Face' peers, 'emphasizing', as Sierz put it, 'such troubling notions as the complicity of victims in their victimization'.

Mal's last injunction to Tony—'Hate me!'—seems to recognize that his machismo and sexual aggression are not a good model to follow, but where his own models should have come from remains an open question at the end of the play.

Williams' follow-up play at the Royal Court Theatre Upstairs was *Clubland*, which earned him the *Evening Standard* Charles Wintour Award for Most Promising Playwright award. As in *Lift Off*, Williams once again tackles the issue of interracial male relationships, but in this instance the focus turns from estate toughs to Kenny, a black bank manager woefully inexperienced with females, and his friendship with Ben, a misogynistic, married but unfaithful white friend from school, who constantly berates Kenny about his nonexistent sex life:

Ben: So wat happened?
Kenny: Didn't fancy it. I had a feeling she was a kid.
Ben: Shut up, man, I saw yer, yer tongue was on the floor dread, nuttin happened cos yu were boring the arse off her about yer job. Who gives a fuck about pensions? Yu think she wants to hear that? She was waitin' for the jump, man. (Williams 2004a: 17)

Clubland overlaps with the lad plays of the mid-1990s, which were written by Nick Grosso, Patrick Marber, Jez Butterworth, Simon Bent and others and presented male characters who, in a show of post-feminist misogyny, live in a world wilfully blind to the progress in gender relations in the last twenty years. Ben's vitriol prompted Charles Spencer in his review to write that the male characters in *Clubland* possess 'attitudes that make Jimmy Porter seem like a passionate feminist.'

Kenny's friendship with Ben contrasts with his relationships with the play's other black and white figures. Like Mal before him, Kenny is questioning the decision he made in school, when he opted to side with his white friends and not protest when they beat up and taunted Ade, a young African immigrant new to their class, with racial insults: 'Kunta, Kunta Kinte! ([Kenny] *Pretends to crack a whip*.) Yer name is Toby! Kunta Kinte!' (Williams 2004a: 5). A number of encounters force Kenny to reconsider his friendship with Ben: a club conversation with Ade, now a muscular Adonis whose performance on the dancefloor draws rapturous sighs from many of the white female clubbers; an offer to be a godfather of the daughter of Nathan, a white school friend who, unlike Ben, is now happily married; and a challenge by Sandra, Ade's (black) former girlfriend, tired of his one-night stands with white women. Kenny struggles with his identity as a black man under the pressure he feels from Ben, Nathan, Ade and Sandra, all of whom want him to be or represent something different from what he currently is, ranging from a tough 'bwoi' (Ben) to a respectable family man (Nathan) to a strong-willed, self-confident, sexually successful black man (Ade). He must answer the question Williams tries to pose in all his drama: 'Where do I fit in?' As Winsome Pinnock observes, the second-generation immigrant such as Williams writes in order to explore 'the idea of being trapped between certain dualities: migrant/native, 'black' culture/'white' culture; being caught between two cultures and belonging to neither' (Pinnock 1999: 31).

Ultimately, Kenny does begin to make choices, some successful, others less so. He opts to be a godfather for Nathan's daughter. After numerous rebuffs, Sandra takes pity on him and sleeps with him on one occasion, which prompts him to ask her to marry him, but their relationship ends quickly thereafter. Kenny also realizes that he cannot compete with Ade in terms of Sandra or on the dance floor at the club. ''Being black'', as Rubasingham writes in her introduction to Williams' work, brings with it expectations in this context: 'speaking 'black', dressing 'black'', being hard (Williams 2002: xx). Kenny is challenged to decide, as the young Williams was, how 'black' he wants to be. Ade ridicules Kenny not only for being aroused as he stares at the white female clubbers, but also for his decision to befriend the white boys rather than him at school. In a gesture of fraternal loyalty familiar in Williams' work, however, Kenny still opts to remain Ben's friend, despite Ade's comments about this friendship as a rejection of his racial identity, and Nathan's attempts to turn Kenny away from Ben's misogyny and aggression. Yet the play's final scene suggests that changes have occurred in both men. As Ben expresses a surprising degree of contrition after his wife leaves him and he loses his job (his wife's father was his boss), Kenny becomes more confident about himself. He shares with Ben the fact that, for the first time, a white woman gave him her phone number. The play ends then not with a major dramatic revelation in terms of Kenny's character, but instead with small moments showing his negotiation of the roles offered by the other characters in the process of finding his own identity.

This adaptability becomes even more striking in contrast to Ade, whose own masculine and racial identity is challenged by Sandra, who argues that his constant need to sleep with white club girls stems from his failure to overcome the white boys' choice of Kenny over him in school. Sandra observes that this earlier humiliation diminished Ade's masculinity as well as his racial pride:

> Sandra: Look me in the eye. Tell me yu weren't lyin on the ground yeah, getting kicked around, thinking to yerself, 'Choose me, choose me, I'm better than he is, choose me!'
> Ade: No
> Sandra: True, ennit?
> Ade: Fuck off.
> Sandra: Knew it. (Williams 2004a: 58)

Every night Ade tries to undo the harm done to him in school as he takes his anger out on the white women in the club and, in turn, the white males who see him sweeping the girls out of the club night after night. While Ade unhappily battles against the white faces around him, Kenny has found more self-assurance by identifying with aspects of both black and white culture, and, unlike the others in the play, he successfully navigates both worlds.

The idea of such a balanced cultural identity in either the white or black characters in Williams' work would be dramatically challenged in his next play. As part of the Transformation season, the Royal National Theatre converted the upstairs lobby of the Lyttelton Theatre into a one hundred-seat space to feature new writing and entice younger theatregoers to the South Bank. The National commissioned Roy Williams for the experiment and his play *Sing Yer Heart Out for the Lads* opened the season. Williams' piece was based on an experience he had in 2000 in a Birmingham pub watching England play Germany in a World Cup qualifying game, where the reactions of the xenophobic fans to England's loss ultimately forced him to leave. Williams told Charlotte Cripps, 'As England are losing 1-0, it becomes less about football and more about nationalism.' Having seen the football hooliganism by English fans during the European Cup 2000, Williams wanted to explore what would drive English fans to such violence and vitriol. 'Some of them just can't get enough of kicking people's heads in, but it is also a lack of self-worth,' he continued to Cripps. 'The England they feel they love is falling apart in front of their eyes. They are still holding on to the past and they can't let go.' The play examines the relationship between the xenophobia of the football fans and the racism between the various 'British' identities.

In *There Ain't No Black in the Union Jack* Paul Gilroy notes the contradictory nature of the very term 'Black British' itself (just as Jatinder Verma is at pains to point out in his writing on British theatre that the term 'black theatre' only makes sense at all in a (white) British context). Awam Amkpa, quoted in Gilroy's study, writes that 'the semantics of 'Black British'… make concessions to hybrid identity by accommodating the history of empire. 'Black British' is simultaneously an identity of resistance, for it shapes the grounds for asserting agency and citizenship by those who are touched by Englishness but are deprived of the right to claim it' (Gilroy 1993: 179). Tellingly, it is often when the white characters begin to copy or appropriate black culture that this dilemma is most evident. When Glen, the pub landlady's white son mimics his black peers, his mother unwittingly brings these tensions to light:

Jimmy: I can't even understand half the things they're saying.
Glen: Ca you ain't wid it guy.
Gina: English, Glen, we speak English in here. (Williams 2004a: 135)

Williams' play highlights the contradictory nature of the 'Black British' identity in the context of the rampant hatred and disgust for the racial other evident in the phenomenon of British football hooliganism, setting his play during the same match in 2000 where England lose to Germany, in an East London pub called, fittingly, the St. George.

Sing Yer Heart Out for the Lads is Williams' most ambitious play, as he moves from writing for a cast of five to fourteen. He keenly dissects character while juggling simultaneous conversations as characters not only react to the football game on television but also talk at the bar, a pool table, and in the men's toilet. In the midst of all these characters is Mark, black, recently returned from serving in the British army, and former drinker at the St. George pub. He previously had a relationship with the white owner, Gina, and used to play for the pub football team, to which his brother Barry now belongs. On this day, he has returned to his old haunt to collect Barry in order to take him to see their sick father. Barry, though, refuses, wanting to bask in the glory of having scored two goals in the pub's football match earlier that day and to watch the England match with his white teammates.

Unlike *Lift Off* and *Clubland*, racial tensions dominate the entire work. Examples range from off-hand comments about the colour of the referee during the pub match that day:

Lawrie: They love stickin together them lot.
Gina: Let me guess, the ref was black?
Lawrie: As soot. Never seen anything so dark. (Williams 2004a: 153)

to larger philosophical statements by Alan, who shows his staunch support of Enoch Powell by quoting from the politician's 'rivers of blood' speech and expressing his own ideological agenda at every opportunity:

Alan: If they want to practise their black culture and heritage, then they should be allowed to do it in their own part of the world. By all means.
Gina: So whites are superior to blacks?
Alan: Yes, if you like.
Gina: Bollocks. (Williams 2004a: 188)

In addition to the blatant racist statements by Alan and Lawrie, who is Alan's sidekick, Williams' play also features liberal characters that see and protest at the wrong inherent in the racist notions of Alan and Lawrie, and yet at the same time articulate their own racial prejudices. Gina's anger over two black boys roughing up her son Glen and stealing his coat and mobile phone provokes the following outburst:

Gina: Leave him alone. I'm gonna kill the little cunt.
Mark: You mean black cunt? (*To Barry.*) You getting this?
Gina: Come on, Mark, they were a couple of wrong uns you saw 'em yerself, even if I was thinking it, can you blame me?...Would they have nicked his stuff if he was black? (Williams 2004a: 183)

Moreover, Lee, a policeman, brother to Lawrie, and one of the more level-headed characters in the play, tries to balance his own conflicting feelings about his friendship with Mark and the fact that a black man stabbed him when he tried to break up a scuffle at a club. He is disturbed that since the attack his thoughts might have become prejudiced against the black community members he comes into contact with through his work. While the inside of the bar grows more tense because of England's poor playing and the escalating racial tensions fostered by Alan and Lawrie, there is also growing unrest outside the bar (in a scene with strong similarities to Spike Lee's film *Do the Right Thing*, a cherished influence on Williams' work) as the black locals protest at the way the pub regulars and police behave towards Sandra, a black woman who confronted Gina about the way the pub customers treated her son.

The complexity of the racial issues outside and inside the pub parallels Mark's own internal struggles over being a black man in a xenophobic and racist England. Mark now realizes the difficult situation of the black Englishman, where the xenophobia of the nation is embedded in an 'us versus them' mentality where black faces are always cast in the role of 'them'. As a younger man however, Mark fully identified himself as English and believed that all the privileges afforded a white man were also his. He had the English flag tattooed on his body, dated a white woman, played football with the all-white pub regulars on the football team, and joined the army. He also supported England at matches, even to the extent of involving himself in some low-level hooliganism. With his newfound awareness, learned in the army when he encountered racist superiors, he now is trying to also show his brother that the men at the bar are not his friends: 'They don't want us here, Barry' (Williams 2004a: 210).

However, as with Williams' depiction of Lee and Gina, Mark is also a complex figure in terms of his perception of prejudice. He looks for racism in every comment made by the pub patrons. At one point he accuses one of the regulars of racism because he applauded a black player being sent off the pitch, when in reality the player was playing poorly. Later he confronts Gina, claiming that she broke their relationship off with him because of his skin colour. Gina responds: 'I finished wid you cos you were boring. You were boring in bed, and you were boring to talk to. If you woke up tomorrow as white as I am, you'll still be boring' [sic] (Williams 2004a: 208). Williams' developing theatrical maturity is apparent in the complexity of Mark's character. He refuses to glorify Mark by putting him on a pedestal above the xenophobia and racism around him. Mark too has the same issues and prejudices to confront, but unlike the men in the bar, he has progressed beyond their limited perspectives, wherein the only answer is violence and hatred.

Sing Yer Heart Out for the Lads, then, is a balanced and complex play about race that ultimately ends in Mark's attempt to prevent the hatred between blacks and whites from continuing into a new generation. Gina's son Glen wants to get even with the black boys who stole his coat and mobile phone and, in the process, embarrassed him in front of his mother's customers. In the pub toilet Mark discovers that Glen has a knife and he tries to convince him to turn it over to him, so that the anger and violence outside and inside the pub is not further exacerbated. In a shocking moment Glen stabs Mark to death. This act, which is so quick and brutal, echoes the death of Toledo at the hands of Levee in *Ma Rainey's Black Bottom* by August Wilson, one of Williams' inspirations for his own playwriting. And as in Wilson's play, this fatal act results in the halting of progress. Toledo possessed great intelligence and Levee great artistic talent and both had the potential to make a change in their own lives and those of other African-Americans. But because of Levee's anger, both would have no impact on others. Here too Mark, despite his own faults, possesses the emotional stability and power of speech to educate his brother and others about English racism, and so to combat the likes of Alan, with his bigoted philosophies, and Lawrie, with his over-eager fists. Mark's death, at the hands of the youngest white male character in the play, only shows the continued impact of racism and brutality. If England's youngest generation continues to enact the ideology of Enoch Powell's 'rivers of blood' speech, as the fascist Alan observes it to be doing at the end of the play, then the outlook is bleak.

Strikingly, the last image of the play is that of Barry, who has remained apolitical amidst all the racist comments directed his way. He realizes his apathy led to his brother's death and with that realization he wipes the painted English flag—displayed proudly throughout the match—off his face. With this act Barry announces that he has taken Mark's place, the rational, philosophical brother replaced by the much more aggressive, physically inclined one. The play closes with a warning. Lee pleads with Barry: 'Don't lose yerself' (Williams 2004a: 235). Don't disappear, in other words, under the mask of the racist, the absolutist thinker who is consumed by the simplistic positions of prejudice. This final image of Barry makes a stark and powerful contrast to the final images of Mal and Kenny, who challenged but finally settled peacefully into their interracial friendships.

Two months after the premiere of *Sing Yer Heart Out for the Lads*, Joe Penhall told the *Guardian*: 'The West End is still so monocultural and parochial it's practically Victorian. Go to the West End and the only black or brown faces are the ushers. It's a joke' (Penhall 2002). However, Penhall overlooked some significant changes in the West End. A year later Roy Williams' fourth London play *Fallout*, about the investigation of the murder of a college-bound black youth, premiered at the Royal Court Theatre Downstairs, a significant venue shift for Williams, moving his work from black box theatres to a main London stage. Williams was not the only black writer to have benefited from the explosion of new writing in the mid-1990s. Tanika Gupta had *The Waiting Room* produced at the National Theatre in 2000, and *Sanctuary* produced in the Cottesloe as part of the Transformation series in 2002. Another regular writer at the National Theatre is Kwame Kwei-Armah, whose fifth play *Elmina's Kitchen* received critical acclaim in the Cottesloe Theatre in the summer of 2003 and has toured Britain in 2004-5; his next play *Fix Up* had its première there in December 2004. DeObia Oparei's very first play *crazyblackmuthafuckin'self* also premiered at the Royal Court in November 2002.[21]

Williams' work, like that of Oparei, is significant in particular for its dialogue. Its linguistic idiom makes an important contribution to twenty-first century theatre, employing the energies and distinctive rhythms of contemporary black British speech but also exploring how this language is coming to dominate British youth culture both black and white. The balance of economic and social power may not

---

[21] For more on the playwrights mentioned, see Deirdre Osborne, 'The State of the Nation'; Samuel Kasule, 'Aspects of Madness and Theatricality in Kwame Kwei-Armah's Drama' and Kathleen Starck on Tanika Gupta's *Sanctuary, Skeleton* and *Inside Out*, in this book.

be shifting but the dominance of white culture is being challenged by the prevalence of the black British idiom in the speech of a generation of urban young people. The huge popularity of 'Ali G', the persona of white Jewish comedian Sasha Baron-Cohen, demonstrates how established the phenomenon of white youth imitating black youth is, not only in speech patterns and lexicon but also in the arenas of musical taste, dance, and sport.

In *Little Sweet Thing*, Williams returns to this phenomenon. The white youth, Ryan, imitates his black friend, Kev, and tries to establish a territory that they can both inhabit, both literally in the form of 'their' basketball court in the local park, and conceptually in the fraternity he tries to create by linguistic imitation. He speaks in an idiom indistinguishable from the black characters—'Bwoi thinks he's man now. Top shotter. You gotta tek him Kev, get your throne back. Believe!'— and they automatically refer to him as another 'bwoi' in the gang. In a reversal of the 'Guess Who's Coming to Dinner' scenarios of early 'race relations' theatre, it is the white character who is pictured here negotiating a community not his own. This play also marks a turning-point in terms of social theatre history, having achieved in a mainstream London theatre an audience that was over sixty per cent non-white.

As David Edgar has written, 'the idea that emulating black urban culture can turn weak, nice people into strong, nasty ones is a pretty brave notion for a black writer to express' (Edgar 2003). The play ends with a shock act, reminiscent of the In-Yer-Face theatre of Sarah Kane or Martin McDonagh, in which Ryan breaks Kev's neck. This is an action far more disturbing even than the impulsive stabbing of a black man by a white boy that ends *Sing Yer Heart Out*. It is also, however, a much more ambivalent action—and all the more chilling for this. Here the white character is failing and desperate, clinging to Kev and embracing him at the same time as murdering him, an image with homosexual, or at least homosocial overtones reminiscent of the ending of Amiri Baraka's 1964 *The Toilet*, in which a black gang leader is cajoled into beating up the white homosexual who has made advances towards him, but whom he cradles lovingly and sorrowfully at the end of the play. Williams reverses the racial dynamic, but explores similarly conflicting impulses of difference and desire: Ryan wants to be Kev as well as to destroy him.

Despite this last image of the abject figure of Ryan, however, the emulation of black culture by white youth is far from being a simple reversal of power in this play. The white Zoe may be both envious and terrified of her black schoolmate Tash, but both the latter and her brother Kev die violent and, as one reviewer put it, all-too-credible deaths in the course of the play. Supremacy in linguistic sparring and dance competitions cannot mask persistent social inequalities and discrimination against blacks in the adult world. Just as sport is intended to diffuse and displace feelings of violence and conflict, but so often incites them, Williams suggests that the dominance of a certain kind of black English culture, apparently uniting the urban youth of every ethnicity, in fact encodes the harmful values of aggression and sexual predation that will divide them.

After the vigour and linguistic sophistication of the naturalism in Williams' other 'urban' plays, some of the dramatic techniques in *Little Sweet Thing* feel dated. The black hooded emanation of Kev's psyche, while oddly prescient in foreshadowing the British government's interdiction on 'hoodies' in 2005, is a somewhat clumsy dramatic device in comparison to the subtle evocation of interiority in Williams' earlier plays—the childhood memory-sequences in *The No Boys Club* and *Lift Off*, or the invisible film set in *Starstruck* that symbolized so many aspirations and desires. The graffitied walls of the stage set are also perhaps an over-familiar image of 'alienated urban youth'. In the techniques that Williams and his director Michael Buffong borrow from film, however, such as the slow-motion shooting scene in the club, the physicality of this theatre draws out the proximity between dance, sport, sexuality and violence that underpins Williams' work.

Despite the impeccably naturalistic dialogue, Williams and his directors draw in this respect, whether inadvertently or not, on one of the principles of radically 'black' theatre identified by the director Jatinder Verma. The role of the body in both communication and identity is reinforced in the physical rituals of the club or sports court or, indeed, the gang fight, as they are choreographed in Williams' theatre. English naturalism has been described by Jatinder Verma as 'acting from the neck up' (Verma 1996: 12); Williams and his directors use the trend towards physical theatre to revitalize the naturalist form and—for all Williams' attention to language—to underline how prominent physical prowess is in the culture which he presents.

Little Sweet Thing and the 2003 *Fallout* were, as we have suggested, remarkable in changing the racial constituency of the London theatre audience. Williams, with these plays and in his work specifically for schools and young people, has also reached out to a younger audience. His work with the Young Apprentices writing and theatre group in London demonstrates his commitment to involving young people in the creative process, writing not just for them but also with them. He has not relinquished his prominent position in the renaissance of British writing for the theatre that emerged in the 1990s, but his theatre is one of social intervention, a theatre where theatre is perhaps most needed.

In its responsiveness to the contemporary situation, Williams' work has also been on the cusp of an important new trend in British theatre. In describing *Fallout* as 'part police procedural' in his review in the *Daily Telegraph* on 19 June 2003, the critic Charles Spencer indicated the proximity of Williams' work to a new kind of theatre, called 'verbatim theatre' or 'docu-drama', an art-form with a particular relationship to current events. *Fallout*, with its exploration of racism in the police force and its staging of an investigation of the killing of a young African, and in

Dimple Godiwala

particular with the detail of an unreliable female teenage witness, drew deliberate parallels with the Damilola Taylor case, and also the trial of Stephen Lawrence's killers, itself already dramatized at Tricycle Theatre in London (and later in the year at the National Theatre) as *The Colour of Justice* in 1999. Although Williams does not use material from real transcripts or interviews, this proximity between theatre and life has meant that his theatre has had a particular social relevance. He treats issues that concern white as well as black young people, and that are indeed the focus of the government policy reported daily in all types of news media. Balancing the brutality and stylized violence of In-Yer-Face theatre with the social complexity and emotive power of docu-drama, his is theatre that focuses on the drama rather than the documentary, but does not simplify the topical issues with stereotypical characterizations or neat dramatic resolutions.

Writers such as Williams and his peers indicate that the British theatre is on the cusp of a powerful movement of playwrights challenging the accepted mainstream characterizations and themes of the London stage. These writers have already garnered the support of the West End artistic directors, have proven financially and critically successful, and have enticed an increasing number of young and black audience members to the theatres. In essence, Williams and his peers now have the attention of the British theatre world, and with it will come the ability to make a dramatic change in the way we talk about the nature of British theatre. The next step entirely resides with them and the quality of the plays they produce. As Michael Billington noted in his 2002 article on the state of British ethnic theatre: 'the real motor of change is the writer, who, by offering us an image of the confused Britain in which we actually live, can turn cultural diversity from a *bien-pensant* ideal into a living reality. In the beginning, and the end, is the word.' If the work of Williams is a gauge, then the first decade of the twenty-first century may soon become recognised as the period when black drama in Britain emerged as a dominant mainstream force.

Works Cited

Dahl, Mary Karen (1995), 'Postcolonial British Theatre: Black Voices at the Center,' in *Imperialism and Theatre: Essays of World Theatre, Drama and Performance*, (ed.) J. Ellen Gainor, London: Routledge.
Edgar, David (1999), 'Provocative Acts: British Playwriting in the Post-War Era and Beyond,' in *State of Play: Playwrights on Playwriting*, (ed.) David Edgar, London: Faber and Faber.
Gilroy, Paul (1993), *There Ain't No Black in the Union Jack: The Cultural Politics of Race and Nation*, Chicago: Chicago University Press.
Pinnock, Winsome (1999), 'Breaking Down the Door', in *Theatre in a Cool Climate*, (ed.) Vera Gottlieb and Colin Chambers, Oxford: Amber Lane Press.

Rubasingham, Indhu (2002), Introduction in *Roy Williams: Plays: 1*, London: Methuen.

Sierz, Aleks (2000), *In-Yer-Face Theatre: British Drama Today*, London: Faber and Faber.

Verma, Jatinder (1996), 'Toward a Black Aesthetic', *Black Theatre in Britain*, special issue of *Performing Arts Today*, 1: 2.

Williams, Roy (2002), *Plays: 1 [The No Boys Cricket Club, Starstruck, Lift Off]*, London: Methuen.

---------------- (2003), *Fallout*, London: Methuen, 2003

---------------- (2004a), *Plays: 2 [The Gift, Clubland, Sing Yer Heart Out for the Lads]*, London: Methuen.

---------------- (2005), *Little Sweet Thing*, London: Nick Hern Books, 2005.

Newspapers

Billington, Michael (4 December 2002), 'Life in a Box,' *Guardian*.

---------------------- (17 December 2003), 'Hello Cruel World', *Guardian*.

Cavendish, Dominic (19 April 2004), 'Man of the Match,' *Daily Telegraph*.

Cripps, Charlotte (20 April 2004), 'It's much more than a game,' *Independent*.

Crompton, Sarah (9 July 2003), 'Black British Drama Takes Centre Stage', *Daily Telegraph*.

Curtis, Nick (30 November 1995), 'Spotting a real winner,' *Evening Standard*.

Edgar, David (18 May 2003), 'Attack!' *The Guardian*.

Penhall, Joe (6 July 2002), Interview, *The Guardian*.

Spencer, Charles (21 June 2001), Review of *Clubland*, *Daily Telegraph*.

Williams, Roy (2004b: 29 April 2004), 'Shades of Black,' *Guardian*.

CHAPTER FOURTEEN

ASPECTS OF MADNESS AND THEATRICALITY IN KWAME KWEI-ARMAH'S DRAMA

SAMUEL KASULE

Synopsis:
This chapter is concerned with the development of Kwame Kwei-Armah as a credible black British playwright whose theatre shows a strong awareness of issues affecting multicultural Britain. In it I consider the notions of 'madness' and 'possession' as a key to an understanding of the consciousness of the characters represented on stage. Readings of selected plays informed by the playwright's occasional essays are offered in order to enable in-depth interpretations of Kwei-Armah's corpus of plays.

Since the 1980s Black British theatre has developed parallel to beat poetry, hip hop, gangsta rap and garage music, the 'symbolic voice of black urban males' (Rose 1994: 126) within African American and Black British communities. Black music constructs a false image of manhood that connotes violence, aggressiveness and glamorous wealth. Tupac Shakur's 'Shorty Wanna Be a Thug' (Shakur, 1996), for example, evokes Shorty's ambitions of leading a thug life, characterized by fearlessness, hustling and criminal behaviour, defining marks of manhood among the Black British youths who, taking it literally, emulate the lyrics. The rap's title however, is a cynical statement about Shorty's ambition. 'Shorty Wanna Be a Thug' is a verbal address and the last verse articulates Shakur's message voicing the concern of the community about the antisocial criminal behaviour of the young black male:

.

You little bad ass nigga, to the young niggas
Gotta stay sharp nigga, play your part
You got plenty of time (you bad mutha fuckas)
You only get three mistakes, then thats life,
Big baby (niggas craaazy)
Watch the signs
Damn, you ain't but sixteen nigga?
Sixteen? !? !
That's a bad muthafucker ('Shorty Wanna be A Thug')

The subtext of the song is a hidden political response challenging the authorities to save the endangered generation of young black youths damaged by dysfunctional state and parental systems. This chapter discusses Kwame Kwei-Armah's plays, *Elmina's Kitchen* (2003) and *Fix Up* (2004), which engage with the problems facing urban black youths such as criminality, identity, materialism, institutional racism and schizophrenia. Kwei-Armah's plays are a demonstration of his critical attitudes: for example, his disgust with violence is expressed when he comments about 'the rise in inner-city gunplay – people using guns as if they were in movies'(Cavendish 2003). As well as interrogating and contesting the myth of a tranquil black British community, he offers an alternative history of the black experience to that visualised in the Windrush celebrations of 1998.

The performance of *Elmina's Kitchen* in 2003 seems to have broken, for the first time, the belief sustained in literary circles that black British communities had no credible playwright. The difference between black and white British theatre was for the first time perceived as not so great, indeed, that any consideration of British theatre would have to include black British writers, performance artists, and their claim to professionalism. It is evident that Kwei-Armah's work has created a large interest in black British theatre due mainly in part to the quality of acting of black actors but also to the increased awareness of race issues, and the destructive effects of criminal gangs in inner cities that the play challenges. In reviewing *Elmina's Kitchen* on its first performance at the National Theatre, Cottesloe, Mark Shenton, theatre reviewer of Radio Four commented, 'Black audiences and black voices have been dismally served here until now, with only two August Wilson plays from America and one black and British-written play transferring to the stages of the National Theatre in the last 25 years or so.' Described as a 'bright and blistering blast of a play' (Shenton, 2003), it is not surprising that it became the first play by a contemporary British-born black writer to be staged in the West End. Also an actor of some repute, Kwei-Armah's performance in *Casualty*, a BBC One hospital drama, and *Celebrity Fame Academy* are unforgettable because they conjure up a complex character. With a powerful stage presence, his formidable stage persona belies the powers that are seen in his work as a

316   Dimple Godiwala

playwright and social critic. The exchanges of his media conversations/interviews underscore his credibility as a black playwright. For example, in his interview with Barbara Ellen, Kwei-Armah observes that his main interest lay with 'investigating humanity through the 'cultural lens' (2003) of the black experience. Kwei-Armah's statement is the crux of the matter for clearly his concept of theatre is both functional and political, and he demands an understanding of race and culture; a challenge to the audience from a theatrical performance. The pessimism expressed with a humorous perception in both plays embraces not just the young generation but also the middle aged who believed in Pan-Africanism[22].

The analysis of Black British plays is grounded in specific historical and cultural situations in which 'Black' is construed as different from 'White' and, in particular contexts, may be different from 'Asian' and 'Chinese'. Kwei-Armah's theatre would fall into the category of the 'Binglish' (Verma, 1996: 193-202; see Hingorani in this book) theatre form as described by Jatinder Verma. This is multicultural theatre that, apart from being written by a black British writer, overtly draws on the experience of the black British community and engages a cross section of black performers. The 'otherness' of this theatre is informed by the uses of language, rhythms, and music. The performance text shows a versatility with 'Blinglish' (Doward, 2004), language aspects, grammar, syntax and neologisms that incorporate patois, and English, reflecting the performers' dual/multiple heritage.

I wish to focus on *Fix Up* and *Elmina's Kitchen* because, as the best examples of Kwame's writing, they celebrate twenty first century black British theatre, address the problems in black communities, and have a rich variety of characters and intriguing conflicts. The underlying message is the contention that the contemporary plight of black British people has been influenced by a history of slavery, migration and deprivation. *Elmina's Kitchen* is a provocative comment on the gang warfare fuelled by 'Yardies' in three of Britain's largest cities, Nottingham, Birmingham and London. It indirectly refers to the shooting of the two black girls Charlene Ellis, 18, and Latisha Shakespear, 17, outside Uniseven Studios in Aston, in Birmingham on 3 January, 2003, as a marker for the effect of black on black violence in inner city communities. *Fix Up* focuses on capitalism as

---

[22] Pan-Africanism is an idea that developed as a result of the 19th century campaign to end slavery. Black people in the African diaspora remained oppressed just like the Africans labouring under colonialism. Several Pan-African Conferences were organised such as those in London (1900), Paris (1919), London (1923) and New York (1927) which aimed at mobilising black people to work together to solve the shared problems of slavery, colonialism and racism. The meetings also promoted togetherness and the belief in a shared heritage of history and culture. The most influential leaders were Sylvester Williams, W.E.B. Du Bois, Marcus Garvey, and Kwame Nkrumah.

well as cultural identity, allowing people of dual heritage to present their views and, not surprisingly, this ruptures the relationships in the bookshop community. The style and language of the play invite the audience to engage in the discourse of language and politics that pervades the black community. Previously, the voices of people with dual heritage, particularly women, have been subsumed into the black narratives, so the essence of *Fix Up* is its focus on this issue, specifically its representation of Norma, Kiyi's best friend, and Alice, his daughter from a racially mixed relationship. In the world of Digger, the murderous Yardie in *Elmina's Kitchen*, mixed race relationships, or acquiescence with white people is a betrayal of the black people. He spites Deli's sister because 'she loves too much blasted Englishman' and every time her picture appears in the papers 'she have a rhated white man on she hand' (*Elmina's Kitchen*, I, i, p. 5). Edward Said's comment that 'all social situations -- and, hence, all populations, states, and groupings -- are *in fact* mixed. Thus, there cannot be any such thing as a pure race, a pure nation, or a pure collectivity, regardless of patriotic, ideological, or religious argument' (Said, 1985: 38-58) is useful in our understanding of Kwei-Armah's interest with critical issues of race, hybridity and multiculturalism. In conversation with Aleks Sierz, Kwei-Armah acknowledges the problems posed by dual heritage identities within the black communities arguing that it is not a matter of 'being half of one and half of another' (Sierz, 2004) because some families have been mixed race for generations.

Kwei-Armah weaves aspects of black British identity and values into the dramatic fabric as exemplified by Anastasia, a sharp-tongued woman, who enjoys reading and appears better educated than the men.

> Although black British, she too swings into authentic, full-attitude Jamaican at the drop of a hat. She speaks with confidence if not a little attitude. (Elmina's Kitchen, I, i, p. 15)

The plays raise the debate on the relationship between colour, identification with black cultures and success that underlies the dilemma facing black people aiming to challenge the stereotype perceptions. The significance of this issue is underscored by celebrities like Trevor McDonald and Lenny Henry who are engaged in a process of rearticulating their identity, achieving a recognition at the 'centre' which they would have been denied had they remained 'too conspicuously black' for, to do so means failure (Kwei-Armah, 2004).

Kwei-Armah conjectures complex seeing for the audience to examine the impact of slavery and migration on the Black community. *Fix Up*, for instance, dramatizes the complex tension of race and colour, revealing the ambiguous perception of the notion of 'shadism' or 'pigmentation' obtaining in Britain but rooted in the legacy of the slave trade. Alice, a troubled mixed race teacher, prefers to be called a person of dual heritage and, unlike the rest of the group, sees no definite binaries of black and white. When Brother Kiyi asserts that the only customer to have bought a 'book of substance' in weeks was not black he sparks off a heated exchange between himself and Alice over colour gradation.

Alice: She was white?
Brother Kiyi: No, she was mixed. (He stops himself.)
Alice: I believe the term is now person of dual heritage.
Brother Kiyi: I'm sure it is.
Alice: Shouldn't you be up-to-date on that sort of stuff? Being a leader of your community an' all?
(*Fix Up*, Scene ii, p. 39)

Her total action is to challenge the social and cultural binaries and it is in that spirit that she rebukes Brother Kiyi's selective discrimination of black people. The destruction of the bookshop is a conscious rejection by Kwei-Armah of the concept of a black British identity based on the recovery of African ancestry.

The notion of madness is portrayed dramatically in terms of individual psychology and social manipulation. In the history of theatre, playwrights such as Shakespeare have explored the trope of madness specifically because of the theatrical elements inherent in the condition. In the real world the mentally ill are individuals whom society has positioned by means of designation and the operation of language and labelling as those who resist any links with rational thinking. When theatricality and madness meet in the area of performance, theatrical aspects of madness are suggested by such words as 'mask', persona, utterance, dissembling and concealment, violence and discovery. As Tim Shields states: 'Exterior manifestations (behaviours) are our only guide to interior workings (psychologies). (Shields, 2003: 37 – 47) My reading of *Fix Up* and *Elmina's Kitchen* draws its inspiration from Elam Jr's essay 'August Wilson, Doubling, Madness, and Modern African-American Drama' (Elam Jr, 2000) an examination of plays by African American playwright August Wilson. What Elam describes as August Wilson's notion of 'racial madness' developed in a number of his plays including *The Piano Lesson* (1990), and *Fences* (1987) is evident here. No study of these can ignore Harry Elam Jr's exegesis of August Wilson's theatre and the notion of 'racial madness' that pervades the characters. He states that they 'appear mentally impaired, besieged by madness, unable to grasp the reality of the world around them' (Elam Jr 2000). He continues: 'They represent a connection to a powerful, transgressive spirituality, to a lost African consciousness, and to a legacy of black social activism' (Elam Jr 2000). His model relates to the African American description of madness as a state of mind within these characters that functions at both 'symbolic and literal planes' (Elam Jr 2000); a trope that is used in literary creation and cultural theory to explain the mental illness of black people; and a double consciousness that is the result of racism, oppression and the 'struggle for black liberation' (Elam Jr 2000). Elam takes the view that however we conceive madness and possession, it needs to be healed.

One major aspect of his model is its adoption of Du Bois' concept of 'black modernism' (Elam Jr 2000) which, in emphasising the notion of 'double consciousness' (Du Bois 1993: 45), presupposes the need for the black person to return to, or, 'renegotiate' (Elam Jr 2000) his past. It is imperative that we understand that the black people's state of 'double consciousness' comes about as a result of the ruptures initiated by the original separation (of their ancestors) from the African continent, the horrific experiences of slavery and the 'middle passage' (Elam Jr 2000), and colonisation. Elam Jr argues that 'racial madness' is not a mental or social *condition* but a mental state that requires a holistic approach to healing: spiritual, psychological, social and medical. In order for healing to take place there needs to be a definite attempt to enable the people to reconnect or negotiate their past, for them to come to terms with the horrific experiences of their ancestors and the power of the impact of slavery. Personal and communal history affects the person's present condition and despite the long severed relationship, there is evidence of an African and African-Caribbean sensibility among Kwei-Armah's characters. Digger, insane and possessed, is a form of character that Kwei-Armah develops albeit on a different plane of madness. In his deluded world he rejects what he calls the 'British black' identity although he only spent his first fourteen years in Grenada.

Digger: (shoots out) Never! I was born in Grenada and I've lived in jailhouse all over the world. I know who the fuck I am, don't you ever include me in all you stupidness. (*Elmina's Kitchen*, I, i, p 15)

Possessed by a self-centred need to control other people, he is oblivious to their emotions. Similarly, Brother Kiyi is mad and possessed, self-centred and blinded by an ambition to collect books on Africa and its diaspora.

Kwei-Armah uses the restaurant, *Elmina's Kitchen*, as an evocative presence in Deli and Ashley's search for economic freedom, and self-realization. The cost of achieving both goals is high and Deli is in a dilemma whether to surrender respectability and the memory of his mother. His renovation of the restaurant is a desperate effort at self-realisation and economic freedom. In the play his son becomes the victim of his decision. The restaurant named after Deli's mother is a physical reminder of the slave trade. Elmina's Castle, built by the Portuguese in 1482 to protect their gold and ivory trade, was captured by the Dutch in 1637 and used as a fort for slaves being transported to America. The dungeons held the slaves below while Europeans worked in the immaculate offices above and a staircase from the women's dungeon led to the Governor's office ensuring that he picked his concubines at will. The presence of Digger constitutes, in the minds of

the audience, a second metaphorical enslavement which Baygee rejects and, to a
limited extent, Deli flies from. Throughout the play Baygee obstinately challenges
the disgraceful behaviour of Digger and his fellow Yardies giving us an insight
into the waves of the criminal gangs migrating to Hackney:

> Baygee: (*prodding Digger*) Eh, I see a couple of wild Yard boys driving up
> a one-way street yesterday. When a man show them the sign, the youth
> don't just take out he gun and threaten to kill him!
> Digger: *doesn't reply!*
> Baygee: Figure it must be one of the new set of Yardies that eating up
> Hackney. They giving children BMWs, who could compete with that, eh?
> Hmm! People should always read street signs, don't you think Digger? I
> gone. (*Elmina's Kitchen*, I, ii, p 23-24)

This scene shows that in Kwei-Armah's plays there is a consistent rejection of
elements of violence and criminality that pervade the black community. It is also
intriguing to see how, in specific contexts, in his exploration of 'racial madness',
he does not draw the lines between sanity and insanity.

The play introduces characters such as Anastasia, the voice of reason, Baygee
and Clifton, voices from the inner city. Clifton has come back to Britain to bury his
son, Dougie, killed on the day of his release from prison. Kwei-Armah is insistent
on reminding black people of their colour. Apart from Anastasia's action of giving
her son's jacket as a present to Ashley, there is no other specific point when
characters return to sanity.

> She moves to the table and opens the bag. She begins to take out some clothes. The first
> thing is an Averix leather jacket.
> Anastasia: (*ignoring him*) ... This belonged to Marvin, my son. I know kids don't like
> wearing other people's clothes but I figured Ashley might like this ...
> Deli: *is unsure why she is doing this.*
> Deli: That's a wicked jacket, doesn't Marvin still ... (wana wear that).
> Anastasia: ... Unless you think it's bad luck to give him dead clothes?
> Deli: *stops in his tracks. He stares at her first not understanding then, understanding.
> There's a long pause while they speak to each other without words. Anastasia finally
> answers the question Deli has been trying to articulate.* (*Elmina's Kitchen*, II, iii, p. 75)

This action provides a closure for Anastasia's suffering and madness. It
initiates the process of healing for her, while for Deli it is the dawn of a new
reality of madness. Each of these characters displays a specific type of
'madness' that evokes a fragmented identity. Individual characters are
haunted by the memory of past legacies as well as the present social
condition.

Kwei-Armah interrogates the phrase 'keeping it real' (Kwei-Armah, 2003) which evolved because:

the black communities felt that some black people were becoming successful and dropping their black cultural habits and imitating those of the power-broker – the white community. So then you got: 'I,m keeping it real, I'm not trying to be like those who reject, or eject, our culture.' The flip side was that 'keeping it real' began to mean acting like a thug acts, behaving like someone who's involved in some form of criminality. Suddenly that is what equalled 'keeping it real', that's what equalled black.

The immediate target of *Elmina's Kitchen* are people who are possessed with the acquisition of material wealth in pursuit of an identity, specifically the Yardies plaguing the inner city streets and estates. Digger is a psychopath who haunts the stage. In the first scene Armah analyzes different aspects of criminality and violence, as exemplified by the Yardies. Digger's attitude and behaviour illustrates the type of character described above:

Sitting on a stool close to the counter is Digger (mid-thirties). He is very powerfully built and looks every bit the 'bad man' that he is. (Elmina's Kitchen, I, i, p. 4)

And later he graphically gives as an image of the 'nastiness' of the Yardies:

Deli: I knew that motherfucker had to be dealing. How else could he move from one fucking blow-dryer and Sat'day girl to employing twelve fit woman in under nine months?
Digger: I thought you doesn't watch odder people tings?
Deli: Shut up. How much was he down for?
Digger: Nothin' real big. Twenty.
Deli: Twenty?
Digger: Well, he owe Matic dem fifteen and once I put my fee pon top…
Deli: … Tweny? Damn.
Digger: When I put de gun by he head, you know what he do?
Deli: What?
Digger: He offer me his fifteen-year-old daughter?
Deli: To do what wid?
Digger: To fuck of course.
Deli: (outraged) You lie?
Digger: I buck him with me pistol. Who the hell you take me for Rodent?
Deli: Rodent?
Digger: The Yardie bwoy that rape all them people dem pickney when he was collecting. Motherfucker gave the trade a bad name. (*Elmina's Kitchen*, I, i, p. 9)

The concentration on material wealth for its own sake is the obsession raised to insanity in the play that climaxes into a grisly catharsis when Ashley, having failed to kill his father is killed by Digger in front of his eyes:

Digger: Alright, now point the gun at your punk-arsed dad. The one that gets beat up and does nothing, has his business near taken away and does nothing, but then informs on a brother man to the other man for what? A piddling fifty grand! I could ah give you that! Is this the type of people we need in our midst? Weak-hearted, unfocused informers? No, I don't think so. Do you, Ashley?
Ashley's hands are shaking a little. After a beat.
Ashley: Digger, I don't think...
Digger: (*screams at him*) Is this the type of people we need in our midst?
Ashley: No.
Digger: Ok then, raise the gun, point it.
Ashley does.
Digger: Good. Is your finger on the trigger?
Ashley: Yes.
Digger: Good.
Digger pulls out his gun and shoots Ashley dead. (*Elmina's Kitchen*, II iv, p. 91)

Ironically Digger repeats the behaviour of the African slave traders who were instrumental in the operation of the murderous trade. His unpredictable behaviour in this scene confirms Shields description of madness as 'anarchic and transgressive', a state that 'displays human behaviour in excess, in *extremis*, on the edge' (Shields 2003: 37-46). This clearly refers to the unpredictable contemporary world of inner-city gangsters rather than a stable community, a representation of an irrational material world of *Elmina's Kitchen* inhabited by characters whose range of behaviour on stage illuminates their inner worlds.

Elmina's Kitchen marks Kwei-Armah's exploration of the self-destructive character that he also develops in his drama *Fix Up*. Brother Kiyi is mentally sick, plagued by a type of madness that makes him oblivious of the damage he is inflicting on his community, and daughter. *Fix Up* is structured around events leading to the demolition of a specialist black bookshop to make way for the building of a luxury block of flats. The bookshop community is a mix of black and dual heritage customers. The female customers are critical of the way Brother Kiyi, the proprietor, runs his business as well as his attitude to 'pigmentation'. Brother Kiyi, possessed by 'strange passions', (Davis, 1993: 175-190) the search for the truth of his roots and true identity, exhibits abnormal behaviour which may be described as 'possession' (Kasule 2004), a condition verging on madness in African theatre performance. He will not stop buying books. It is the horrible confrontation between daughter, Alice and father, Brother Kiyi that stretches the play to the utmost limit of insanity leaving no room of disengagement for audience.

Brother Kiyi is an embodiment of a madman who is possessed, and whose condition has prevented him from seeing reality. Although he regards himself as the father of the community his madness leads to his exclusion. In moments of emotional excitement Brother Kiyi reconnects with his past through singing and dancing to slave songs thus exhibiting his 'madness'. Inferring Mark Rocha's statement that 'absence – the inability to render presence – is what incites black madness' (Rocha, 1993: 191 – 203), one may conclude that the absence of Brother Kiyi's daughter is the source of his madness and possession. Ironically her presence causes rupture which culminates in the disbandment of the bookshop community. Alice does not only challenge the chauvinistic and racist attitudes of the bookshop inhabitants but also the old black writers for excluding women from 'participating in 'the struggle'' (*Fix Up*, Act I ii, p 33). Like *The Piano Lesson, Fix Up* is a 'contest of madnesses' (Rocha, 1993), a competition between beliefs as exemplified by Carl, Brother Kiyi, Alice and Norma.

Fix up, like *Elmina's Kitchen*, is on one hand about multiculturalism, mixed race experiences and identity, and contemporary black British culture but simultaneously it is a text that examines the tensions between being black and British. It interrogates the dynamic relationship within this community while at the same time exposing the fissures in British identity and class. Alice dismisses the talk about West Indians and Yanks by stating to Kwesi that she is from Somerset. The split identity of the characters in both plays is symbolized by the variety of Englishes that they speak, especially Deli in *Elmina's Kitchen* who traverses Hackney, Hampstead and West Indies accents, Brother Kiyi who speaks patois and Naomi who mixes standard English and patois.

Kwei-Armah conjectures a complex way of looking at black British history and identity when he structures multiple narratives in *Fix Up*. First he creates a narrative that focuses on the discourse of 'shadism' by allowing Alice to confront Brother Kiyi, her father, and his friends in the bookshop. This is superimposed upon by a narrative of mythical voices of Black ideologists experienced through audio playbacks or readings of James Baldwin[23] and Marcus Garvey[24] and Claude

---

[23] James Baldwin (1924-1987) is one of the most influential black writers of the 20th Century, whose writings critique America's racism and separatism who believed that race was an impediment to growth and moral development for all human kind.

[24] Marcus Garvey (1887-1940), widely admired as a hero in Jamaica and all black communities in the world, coordinated the the black nationalist movement of the 1920s in the United States. From 1919 he recruited followers for the Universal Negro Improvement Association that aimed to unite all black peoples through the establishment in Africa of a country and government of their own. An outstanding orator, his views on economic independence, pride of race, and the need for black Americans to return to Africa were published in his newspaper, *Negro World*. He coined the phrase, 'black is beautiful' and aimed to liberate black people from a psychological bondage of racial inferiority.

McKay's[25] writing. Secondly, he uses the old slave narratives from a selection of texts in the bookshop, and old slave chants of call and response to confirm the oneness as well as the heritage of abuse and slavery experienced by people of African descent. It is this haunting past that is the cause of insanity within the Black British person. He coalesces issues of capitalism, gender, a fragmented community, society's obsession with wealth, and insanity, so that Brother Kiyi's story becomes a metaphorical narrative by itself. Blackness. The frustration of redefining blackness is at the centre of the play, articulated by the narratives and the books in the bookshop. For Alice, her life constitutes a narrative of experience shared by people with a dual heritage. Advocating for society's acknowledgement of persons with dual heritage he states, 'We talk about people of dual heritage being half of one and half of another–white society sees them as black, and blacks see them as close to white. But in places such as Liverpool, there are people whose families have been mixed race for generations, so they can't just be half and half.' This is the generation that refer to themselves as 'Generation M' or the 'remix generation' (Kwei-Armah, 2004). To articulate the issue of 'shadism' he creates a confrontation between Kwesi and Alice as a reminder of the issue of miscegenation and mixed race relationships first raised in *Elmina's Kitchen*. Carl, quoting from James Baldwin's Notes on a Native Son states:

Neither white nor blacks for excellent reasons of their own have the faintest desire to look back. But I think that the past is all that makes the present coherent... (Fix Up vi, p. 78)

The undercurrent of the play is the question of identity of the contemporary Black British person. Throughout the play the books become the touchstone by which each person may seek to define their roots and identity. The contradiction arises when Alice, a mixed race customer, insists on the acknowledgement of her dual heritage. In a struggle to assert her identity and her being, she attempts to force Brother Kiyi admit his position as her father, his existence in a multicultural society, and the emergence of a new generation:

Alice: ...You're wrong, 'cos we are the future. We are where it's at. You're borrowing from us and you don't even know it. (*She runs to the shelves and starts pulling down books.*) See, Bob Marley, mixed race. Alexandre Dumas mixed, and she's mixed an' he's

---

[25] Claude McKay (1890-1948), one of the poets of the African-American Harlem Renaissance, was born in Jamaica but moved to the United States in 1912. He attended the Tuskegee Institute in Alabama and Kansas State University. He lived in England from 1919 to 1021 after which he travelled throughout Europe. His extensive work as a poet is credited with having made great contributions to the 'Negro Literary Renaissance'.

mixed. Most of your so-called black heroes are mixed. All of us are mixed! (*Fix Up*, v, p. 75)

[*Fix Up*, National Theatre 2005 ©Catherine Ashmore]

In *Fix Up* Armah conflates the philosophy and attributes of James Baldwin and Marcus Garvey to write a play on issues of cultural identity. The two were influential in the Civil Rights and Counter-Culture movements in America that in turn influenced Black British activists. The play reminisces about the memory of the intensity with which, the black community searching for identity in a hostile country, embraced Pan Africanism. Present time is frequently interjected with memories and narratives of the past; James Baldwin, Marcus Garvey and Claude McKay emerge from the past to intrude into the life of Brother Kiyi and his customers. Juxtaposed with their voices are the Slave narratives. Combined, these draw our attention to the importance of the past to the African slave descendants as well as the contradictions of their present condition. The divergence of Brother Kiyi, Carl and Alice's attitude towards the bookshop indicates their specific relationship with their roots, a common ancestry, and the future.

Music in *Elmina's Kitchen* is not merely used for its entertainment value but is a connection with the past, an essential route for dealing with issues concerning the history and presence of black people in Britain. It functions at a spiritual level at the beginning of Act Two during the funeral of Duggie when the characters sing the blues, *You Gotta Move On*. Drinking during the opening of the refurbished Elmina's Kitchen, Clifton urges Ashley to pick a topic to which he can extemporise. Ashley picks football and is warned in turn to be 'prepared to get teach' (*Elmina's Kitchen*, II i, p. 53). As he begins to sing against Baygee accompaniment of '*an old-time calypso rhythm*' (*Elmina's Kitchen*, II i, p. 53) he delivers a lesson on the history of racism in football, the love and hate relationship between football crowds and black players underlined the issue of colour because you cannot disguise your colour.

Clifton: Here we go. They use to call me culture master. Be prepared to get teach (*Sings*)

History is a funny thing,
History is a funny thing,
Listen to me, people,
Cos is about football me ah sing.
Clive Best the greatest,
Baller West Ham ever had,
But from the stands they'd shout each game,
Go home you black bastard.
Deli: Oh here we go!
Clifton: (*sings*)
Oh England, what a wonderful land,
In England what you must understand,
Is whatever you do, whenever you rise,
Please realise, you could never disguise.
You's black man in a cold cold land. (*Elmina's Kitchen*, II, i, p. 53)

In Clifton's carefree world he associates music, reggae and calypso, and alcohol with boundless romance hence he begins to 'sex' Anastasia. Clinton personifies the racial stereotype of that equates black manhood with sexuality. The song particularly focuses on thematic aspects of colour, race, identity, and history. The effect is a spontaneous coming together of the people gathered to celebrate the opening of the new 'ELMINA'S PLANTAIN HUT'.

Conclusion

In considering Kwei-Armah's impact on theatre in Britain, it is apparent that several developments are taking place the direction of which may be attributed to him. Firstly, there is a new awareness for the theatre going community, of a multi-skilled Black British artist who combines writing, television and stage acting, directing, singing, and theatre criticism. Secondly, in contemporary British theatre, Kwei-Armah has influenced performances that show awareness of social/political issues within Black communities without preaching to their audiences. The plays are in many ways a response to contemporary Britain. They stress the need for the state to reengage with the inner cities and the ethnic communities. Kwei-Armah is asking the audience to recognise the significance of race and colour, identity, and education in understanding the condition of the black British person. That he is finding a positive response from both black and white audiences is a positive sign that his drama is engaging their attention.

Acknowledgements: The photograph that accompanies this chapter is of Kwame Kwei-Armah's *Fix Up* at the Royal National Theatre, 2005. Photo by Catherine Ashmore. Courtesy: NT.

Works cited:

Davis, Jim (1993), 'A Play for England: The Royal Court Adapts *The Playmaker*' in P. Reynolds (ed.), *Novel Images: Literature in performance*, London: Routledge.

Du Bois, W.E.B. ([1903] 1993) *The Souls of Black Folk*, New York: Knopf.

Kasule, Sam (2004), 'Climates of performance: ethnicity, folk performances, language and theatre in a post-authoritarian state' in E. Wamala et al (eds.), *Africa in World Affairs: Challenges to Humanities*, Kampala: Faculty of Arts.

Kwei-Armah, Kwame (2003), *Elmina's Kitchen*, London: Methuen.

-------------------------- (2004) *Fix Up*, London: Methuen.

Rocha, Mark, W. (1993), 'Black Madness in August Wilson's 'Down the Line' cycle' in J. Redmond (ed.), *Madness in Drama*, Cambridge: Cambridge University Press.

Rose, Tricia (1994), *Black Noise: Rap Music and Black Culture in Contemporary America*, Hanover: University Press of New England.

Said, Edward (1985), 'An Ideology of Difference' in H. L. Gates, (ed.), *'Race' Writing, and Difference*, Chicago: University of Chicago Press.

Shields, Tim (2003), 'Theatricality and Madness: Minding the Mind-doctors' in Daniel Meyer-Dinkgrafe (ed.), *The Professions in Contemporary Drama*, Bristol: Intellect.

Verma, Jatinder (1996), 'The challenge of Binglish: analyzing multi-cultural productions', in P. Campbell (ed.), *Analyzing Performance: A Critical Reader*, Manchester: Manchester University Press.

Newspaper reviews

Cavendish, Dominic (24 May 2003), 'Getting on Famously', *Daily Telegraph*.

Doward, Jamied (22 February 2004), 'Yo, Blingland! Hip-Hop culture rules for British teens', *Observer*.

Ellen, Barbara (23 November 2003), 'Songs in the key of Kwame', *The Observer*.

Kwei-Armah, Kwame (11 May 2004), 'How black can one be?', *Guardian*.

Sierz, Aleks (6 December 2004), 'Read your roots: as a child in the 1970s, he was called Golliwog and Sambo. Kwame Kwei-Armah talks race and history with Aleks Sierz', *The New Statesman*.

Websites

Shenton, Mark (2003), 'First Night: *Elmina's Kitchen*',
http://www.bbc.co.uk/london/entertainment/theatre/elminaskitchen_300503.sh
tml

CDs

Shakur, Tupac (13 February 1996), 'Shorty Want to be a Thug', on *All Eyez On Me*, Polygram Records.

CHAPTER FIFTEEN

KALI: PROVIDING A FORUM FOR BRITISH-ASIAN WOMEN PLAYWRIGHTS

DIMPLE GODIWALA

Synopsis:

This chapter traces the first phase of Kali Theatre with founder-members Rukhsana Ahmad and Rita Wolf at the helm of the company. It performs a close reading of a few of the plays Kali staged in its early years, and includes extensive material from my interviews with Rukhsana Ahmad and Bapsi Sidhwa. The plays analyzed are: Anu Kumar's The Ecstasy, Rukhsana Ahmad's Song for a Sanctuary, River on Fire and Kali Shalwar, Bettina Gracias' Singh Tangos, and Bapsi Sidhwa's Sock 'Em With Honey based on her novel An American Brat.

Kali. In Vedic and later Hindu myth, she is the creator and wife of Shiva. Goddess of time and an early war goddess. Later she represents sex, eroticism, death and power. In common parlance (Hindi) *Kali* also means black woman. In Bengali, *Kali* denotes black ink.

Rukhsana Ahmad, founder member of *Kali* theatre company says: The goddess conjured up the idea of 'female power, regeneration, fertility and strength' (Ahmad 2004). All these notions, of creation, of blackness, of writing, go into the formation of Britain's *Kali* Theatre Company. The space it occupies within the locus of British theatre companies is a singular one: dedicated to the performance of women writers of Indian and other subcontinental origins, *Kali* has a focus currently shared by no other Asian theatre company in Britain. Based in London, playing to mixed audiences which are, however, largely Asian, *Kali* provides the theatrical space much needed by both fledging and experienced Asian women writers.

Set up in 1990 by actor-director Rita Wolf and writer Rukhsana Ahmad, the company had strongly feminist goals at its inception. Wolf wanted to create a space which would include women as theatre managers, technicians, and administrative staff, while she directed their first play, *Song for a Sanctuary* written by Rukhsana Ahmad.

Rukhsana Ahmad was born and educated in Karachi, where she studied Eng. Lit. and Linguistics. In Britain she has freelanced as a writer since 1985. She has written drama, fiction and translated from Urdu. Besides being the Artistic Director of Kali Theatre Company, she is a founding member of Asian Women Writers Collective and a founding trustee and current chair of the South Asian Diaspora Literature and Arts Archive. She was writer-in-residence at Middlesbrough, Newcastle and Harrow.

About the setting up of *Kali* Ahmad says: 'We were both definitely political and very committed to feminism. I think our focus was on content rather than on ethnicity. We wanted to encourage new texts (get them written and produced) that would reflect our realities and culture and would, therefore, be more interesting for us' (Ahmad 2004).

This need to address issues of both, ethnicity and gender, is reflected in Kadija George's introduction to *Six Plays by Black and Asian Women Writers*, where she describes it as, '[a]n age old problem as the cultural meaning and tradition of classical theatre in schools has meant the isolation of Black people, especially Black women. Young Black women will now have models to look towards, reinforced by Black actresses and writers-in-residence going into schools' (George 1993: 5).

In the early years *Kali* was project based, having to raise funds for productions. Rukhsana Ahmad recalls: 'We tried to develop workshops at first, then gave support to Tanika Gupta for *Tilak's Revenge* and then moved on to delivering writing workshops before we chose another play' (Ahmad 2004). The second production was Joyoti Grech's *Natural World* in 1995 followed by the well-known double bill in 1999: Anu Kumar's *The Ecstasy* and Rukhsana Ahmad's *Kali Shalwar*, an adaptation of Manto. Ahmad's *River on Fire* followed in 2000. 2001 saw the production of Bettina Gracias' *Singh Tangos*, and in 2002 Bapsi Sidhwa's *Sock Em With Honey* based on her novel *An American Brat* was staged. After 2002, Janet Steel took over from Ahmad as Artistic Director, and currently *Kali* follows a similar trajectory of providing a forum for drama written by Asian women. This chapter will focus on *Kali*'s first phase with Rukhsana Ahmad on the Board of Directors.

Song for a Sanctuary

Ahmad's *Song for a Sanctuary*, produced in 1990, was about women's refuges. Written around the time that Ken Livingstone's GLC[26] was funding and supporting the self-organization efforts of black women, and separate Asian women's refuges were being set up, Ahmad's sanctuary is a multicultural refuge, making the point that violence to women is not an ethnic or a minority issue. The women in the refuge, both residents and refuge workers, are battered women who have escaped from their violent spouses.

The series of incidents in the mid-80s which brought into focus the domestic violence faced by many Asian women: the suicide of Krishna Sharma in the wake of continued domestic violence, Kiranjit Ahluwalia's imprisonment for the murder of her violent husband, and especially the murder of Balwant Kaur in a refuge by her own husband, led to the formation of a coalition of groups called the Network of Women (Sahgal 1992: 186). However, what *Song for a Sanctuary* brings into focus is that domestic violence is a fact that many women, of differing ethnicities, have to live with. Although the cultural codes that govern patriarchal Hindu family life seem different, the impulses that lead a battered woman to leave her partner, and also, later, to desire to return to him in spite of the knowledge that the violent patterns within which their relationship is constituted will not change, are here depicted as a behavioural pattern which cuts through class and ethnicity despite the differing cultural norms which govern the women.

Eileen, who has worked as a refuge worker for eleven years, was initially a battered resident. Sonia, a resident, is a prostitute who is frequently battered by her boyfriend, from whom she escapes from time to time by going to a women's refuge. Rajinder is a middle class Punjabi woman with three children who has escaped the tyranny of her abusive husband. Kamla, a refuge worker, born in the Caribbean, is ethnically from an Indian background, but insists she has nothing in common with Rajinder: 'I'm not going to be sentimental and gush over her just because she is Indian.' (I, iv). Kamla is modern but comes across as harsh, insensitive to the plight of the women in the refuge, and even racist in her internalization of the prejudice against non-white women. She believes in the power of the bureaucracy and the need to prescribe rules, which the gentler Eileen rejects as too severe an attitude. Eileen's attitude is more humane, as she regards the people they deal with as women who have suffered, not mere 'case-histories'. However, it is Kamla who is the political voice of the Asian woman in Britain. She represents the women 'who had been politicized through the anti-racist movement

---

[26] For more on the GLC and funding for black arts see Alda Terracciano, 'Mainstreaming African, Asian and Caribbean Theatre: The Experiments of the Black Theatre Forum' in this book.

[who] regarded an Asian women's refuge as a necessity because [...] [t]hey were fighting for women to be able to make truly autonomous decisions.' These refuge workers 'refused to organize reconciliations, saying they would not reproduce the family pressure from which women had escaped' (Sahgal 1992: 173).

Rajinder's ideas concerning the upbringing of her children are conservative in the need to preserve an ethnicity she sees as endangered in the west. Her words pose a direct challenge to the anglicised Kamla: '[W]e've taken refuge here but that doesn't mean my children have to be taken over and re-modelled into something that belongs neither here nor there' (I, v). Ironically, Rajinder's decision to leave her husband is seen as selfish by her older sister Amrit. It comes under 'the self-indulgent, sick ways of the West.' (Amrit, I, vi). Endorsing the passive compliance of the prescriptive notion of the model of suffering, traditional Indian womanhood to the patriarchal authority of the husband, Amrit prefers 'honour' to 'disgrace':

Rajinder: Would you rather I set myself alight in the back garden?
Amrit: Honour is always preferable to disgrace, but the choice of course is yours (I, vi).

The complex relationship between Kamla and Rajinder comes to the fore in II, i. Kamla's standpoint that the women in the refuge should not be allowed to return to violent relationships is read by Rajinder as 'this passion that you [Kamla] put into destroying other people's marriages.' Kamla, who is a modern, rational hybrid of east and west is not able to conceptualize the codes which prescribe *sanctity* of the marital bond as practised in India, which prohibits her from empathising with the enormity of Rajinder's decision to leave her husband, and her need for the right to privacy about the details of her marriage. Unaware of the sacrality of marriage, for Kamla, marriage is an institution, entered and left at will, rather than a sacred bond. This misrecognition of the social ideology of the Other leads to the continued lack of empathy between Kamla and Rajinder (and, ironically, highlights the need for separate refuges for Asian women). Their exchange brings to the fore the differing norms and values that govern marital and family bonds in the eastern and western worlds. For the traditional Indian woman, the act of leaving her husband is a statement made in extremity, often unsupported by the members of her own family. As Gita Sahgal explains it, 'A key concept is *izzat* – the notion of honour. While *izzat* is a code which affects men and women in different ways [...] the idea is commonly understood. Most women who have escaped from violence in the family have broken one of the codes of *izzat*: that the honour of the family rests on the woman's behaviour' (Sahgal 1992: 187). For the Hindu woman to leave a marriage for any reason whatsoever, however extreme, is to bear the cost of lost honour and family support. Separation in Indian marriage is of necessity, here represented as because of constant physical abuse and damage, differentiating it from the contemporary western familial model which is subject to breakdown from factors as superficial as losing the initial fizz. [27]

Furthermore, the ideal Hindu wife is passive and submissive, and her *dharma* (duty) consists of regarding her husband as a god (*pati-dev*). Sahgal points out that the notion 'of service [*sewa*] to your husband as if he were your god is embedded in the language itself' (Sahgal 1992: 189). These are ideas alien to the feminized Kamla, who, though ethnically Asian, is unable to engage in an empathic dialogue with Rajinder. It may perhaps have helped if Kamla could aid Rajinder to come to terms with the ideas understood as natural within the discourse of a traditional Hindu marriage in order to help her circumvent them and emerge autonomous; after all, Rajinder had herself taken the first step of leaving her marital home.

The relationship between Rajinder and her teenage daughter Savita is marked with the ambivalence which characterises the products of violent homes. Savita's feelings toward both, her abusive-paedophilic father, and her harsh-disciplinarian mother fluctuate between love and hate. Again, ambivalence dictates Savita's desire to fit into the western outer world, which elicits constant rebuke from her mother who disciplines her with violence.

The silent figure of Rajinder's husband, Pradeep, which looms constantly in the shadows of the refuge represents, in this play, the threatening and violent power of patriarchy. The power of the orthodox Hindu husband, maintained and reinforced through the powerful discourses of religion and family values as practised in the network of societal relations, is perhaps more potent than post-feminist Western patriarchy within which contemporary women have more agency. Rajinder's words spoken early in the play: 'You can get away if you really want to' (I, iii) are belied by the violence of the ending, when Pradeep infiltrates the refuge and stabs her violently in the presence of his daughter. It is the violence of orthodox Hindu patriarchy which has the last word in this stark, almost defeatist drama. Yet, constituted in the discourse of western patriarchy, the women of the refuge, whether White or Asian, seem to have neither power nor choice within the bureaucracy of the system which determines their futures. The refuge workers' lives are similarly determined by the strongly patriarchal and capitalist western system, whether, like Kamla, they think they live 'outside' it, or, like Eileen, they have been damaged by it.

The play enacts the dialectical relationship between women who are constituted within the framework of Western patriarchy and orthodox Hindu patriarchy. The resolution emphasizes the similarities of the two systems as we become aware of the differences in terms of social and cultural codes and conduct.

---

[27] Thus, according to the Hindu code, Krishna Sharma preserved notions of familial honour – *izzat* – by hanging herself.

The Ecstasy

It would be easy to describe Kumar's play *The Ecstasy* as a gay play. Instead of working through the usual dilemmas of societal censure and soul searching which accompany 'coming out' plays, *The Ecstasy* takes gayness as a fact, and Amit and Sanjay's relationship is posited as 'normal' as a heterosexual one. What is also refreshing about this play is that the relationships it charts are about openness and a coming to terms with emotional ties on the part of the characters. Kumar writes with an undeniably Indian use of the English language, making the characters ethnically Indian.

Amit, the accountant turned sculptor, comes from a privileged class background. He and Sanjay are Indian professionals living in London. That Jackie, the Liverpudlian, is also from an elsewhere, like Amit, is a metaphor for the groundlessness felt by both. This groundlessness is an emotional rather than a geographical deterritorialization: a psychic rather than physical upheaval. Jackie has lost her 19 year old son in an accident; Amit has lost his mother in the act of being born. Both feel their loss keenly and function as surrogates for each other in spite of their cultural, class and ethnic differences.

Jackie, who meets Amit to sit for him as a nude model, ends up looking after his domestic needs. Although this tires him, along with her incessant chatter, he puts up with Jackie, although he is never able to finish the sculpture modelled on her. It is not until he meets Sanjay, an embryologist, that Amit feels that Jackie is in the way. Sanjay is more empathetic of the lonely Jackie, and offers her the warmth of understanding.

Amit's unfinished sculpture of Jackie is highly naturalistic in that it reveals all her scars and blemishes. She tells him about her invisible scar: the hysterectomy where 'they turn your womb inside out and pull it out of your [...] vagina. It's like a joke isn't it? I mean having a baby and then delivering your own womb' (Scene vi).

Sanjay and Amit's developing relationship leaves no space for Jackie. Telling her he doesn't need her to model for him anymore, he dismisses her. However, in the space of this time she has become more a part of Amit's life, and, also having met Sanjay, she is more a friend than an employee.

In spite of the many scenes of intimacy between Amit and Sanjay, including those where he paints him nude, *The Ecstasy* is more about maternal bonds than gay relationships. Oddly, it is Jackie, as herself and as a symbol of Amit's maternal loss, and also perhaps as a figure which represents the absent feminine in Amit and Sanjay's relationship, who is the centre of the play. From the unfinished sculpture to her finding the tiny clay figure representing her in his garden, Jackie is more a symbol and a metaphor of womanhood than an individual in her own right. A trope for the necessary feminine who, as the male characters do, needs to find a meeting point within the space of the differently gendered Other, the play ends with her discovery of her representation lovingly sculpted by Amit. And thus, it is finding the sculpture which finally grounds her.

It's a lovely place that garden with those mossy little walls. I could hear the water and all the flowers were so pretty and smelt so nice and then I saw it. When I saw it, I was surprised that you'd managed to make it so small. At first I didn't recognise myself, then I thought, he's made me dead on a chair, naked and I knelt down and looked at it and I looked, and as I looked I could see what you had done, you'd put poppies and cornflowers and daisies in my hair and then I thought, no it's not dead it's asleep and I looked more and I thought it was a robe all those folds but it wasn't it was a flower, a flower coming out of my womb and then when I looked again at the face, I saw my eyes open and I just looked peaceful. It was like watching myself come to life and I thought what a clever man you are Amit. (Scene xii. The End)

In the making of the sculpture, Amit comes to terms with all that is positive in women: their fertility, their beauty, and the hope they represent. Jackie's closing monologue is about the transformation of the childless, wombless woman into a symbol of fertility and joy. By inscribing her clay form with poppies, cornflowers and daisies, making her womb come alive with flowers, Amit is honouring both, his dead mother as well as the ageing Englishwoman, and through them, the essential feminine, which does not know the barriers of class or culture.

Anu Kumar succeeds in transcending all cultural barriers which determine relationships in an Indian or English context by celebrating the very slippery tropes of masculinity and femininity in many aspects of the way that relationships can be played out. Ultimately, the play is an abstract celebration of the contradiction of gender identities which are resolved by a reconciling unity made material, visible, palpable in an immediate way that only theatre can accomplish. *The Ecstasy* is an abstract work of art concretized on the space of the stage.

Kali Shalwar

Rukhsana Ahmad's adaptation of S. H. Manto's short story is set entirely in India. Charting the life of Sultana, a prostitute in the town of Ambala, one of the first things Ahmad has her protagonist say is: 'we are *all our own women* round here. We sell our time not ourselves' (I, i) It is this agency demonstrated by Sultana which is the pivot of the play. Set in colonial India, it depicts a woman from a small town who has the independence and will to forge the path of her own life. It is Sultana's emotional attachment to a man which leads to her material downfall, but the end shows her preparing to return to her village, independent once more.

Sultana and Khuda Bhuksh's first encounter is unusual in that he is in search of another woman (Zohra) who he describes as '*kashmir ki kulli*' (or 'the rosebud of Kashmir') 'a real lady'. Drawn to Sultana, as 'there's something about you which is very... like her...' he ends up living with her. Sultana has fallen deeply in love with Khuda Bhuksh:

I lived in the hope that one day I might become his Zohra. That he'd love me and never leave me - and if I ever left him he'd go up and down the country looking for me - like a real twentieth century Mujnoon - driven insane with his longing for me. (sc i)

Sultana continues to practice her profession in the British cantonment town of Ambala. Although this drama is clearly set in the colonial period, the English merely occupy a periphery which is introduced into the play only by means of a casual verbal mention, as in their exchange when Bhuksh intends to pursue photography:

SULTANA: Do you know how much a camera costs? Must be at least forty rupees if not more...?
K. BUKHSH: We'll soon find out, won't we? You have to see it as an investment. It might be the making of us.
SULTANA:Or a total waste of money.
K. BUKHSH: Once I get to know some of the *goras* I could even pick up business for you. (sc. ii)

Or when Sultana recounts her source of income:

Night after night the goras came - mostly soldiers from the cantonment. They paid very good money. If any one ever tried to haggle I pretended not to understand him (sc. iii).

Whilst Bhuksh struggles to find a source of income, Sultana can afford to indulge in luxuries: 'Sofa set last month, gold bangles the month before, and now, a new silk suit...' Although Bhuksh is dismissive: 'Anyway, what's twenty five rupees, for you? You make that in a couple of good nights, don't you, just lying on your back', he is eager to make his way in the world. *Dilli* beckons him with all the seductions of a big metropole. *Dilli* however, holds for Bhuksh more than mere economic glamour: it is a cultural paradise, beside which the small Ambala appears shabby and dull. After his first return from Delhi, Bhuksh plays the harmonium for Sultana, and recites Amir Khusro's *qawalli*, excitedly describing his experience of the city's culture:

K. BUKHSH: When I close my eyes I can still hear it in my head so clearly - I wish I could play it for you, sing it to you. They were so good. We sat up all night listening to them, men in whirls of ecstasy, women, slapping the floor, beating their breasts - every one in a trance. It was magical!

SULTANA : They've cast a spell on you, haven't they?

K. BUKHSH: You'd fall in love with it too, I know.

SULTANA: I would love to see it all, hear it for myself.

K. BUKHSH : You must. You will.

SULTANA: Hum.

K. BUKHSH: Listen to me, Sultana. Let's leave all this hustling, this shabbiness behind, just up and go. Let's go to Dilli (Scene v).

Paradoxically, the metropole also serves as a spiritual paradise for Bhuksh, as he seeks the advice and blessings of several religious leaders. Sultana's deterritorialization into a big city is physical at first: getting lost in the big streets and learning to use the English toilet. (Scene vi). Quite soon it is economic: the lack of clients in the new city is depressing for Sultana, who used to make a grand thirty rupees a night from the English soldiers in Ambala. It is the onset of *Moharram*, the Islamic period of mourning which begins the year, that sees Sultana desperate for the new black clothes she cannot afford. Her descent from material comfort to poverty is complete when she barters her earrings for a pair of the highly coveted black satin *shalwar* with the help of the slimy Shanker. Shanker, who has brought her a few moments of distraction is a creature of means he describes as very like Sultana's profession. Pleasuring more than one woman at a time, he lives on the payments he receives.

As Bhuksh leaves to follow his spiritual master to Jammu, Sultana makes preparations to go back to her economic paradise as the play ends.

Although the play demonstrates the agency of the woman in a comparatively rural backwater, where stereotypically it would be imagined that the woman must be economically dependant, it does not comment on the hardship and difficulties faced by the average prostitute. It assumes that prostitution is a choice, and having sex with several men a night is not problematized as a physical difficulty. On the contrary, Sultana is depicted as utterly in control of her life making her emblematic of an independent and strong woman who knows her priorities, apart from the one emotional attachment (to Bhuksh) which nearly leads to economic destruction. Her clients are never a physical threat, and she does not seem to incur societal censure. Unlike Bhuksh she does not lean toward the spiritual, and, regarding body and soul as one leads her to desire only the material. Her slight learning of classical poets is used only to entertain her clients and never forms food for the soul as it does Khuda Bhuksh, and did traditional courtesans in India.[28] The play does not really

---

[28] With the onset of British colonial rule, many independent women, accomplished in the arts, poetry and literature became penniless. Previously sponsored by generous rulers who

succeed as a piece depicting the agency of women. It is rather more successful when seen as the dichotomy of the spiritual (Bhuksh) and the material (Sultana), and that perhaps a little of both are needed to survive and live gracefully.

River on Fire

The play opens in a private hospital in Bombay during the Ayodhya riots[29]. Bobby has arrived from London to see his ill *amma* and his conversation with his half-sister Zara reveals the economic and social mobility experienced by him in England. Bobby and his sister Kiran hail from a poor neighbourhood in India as do most British Asians. Bobby's father's family home was:

> On Mohammad Ali Road - an old ruin. Lots of families lived on pavements and railway tracks near us! Growing up there would have been tough! We were dead lucky Kiran and I - to grow up in London. (River on Fire, I, i)

The scientist from the west (Bobby) is juxtaposed with the religious and ritualistic Zara from Bombay. This reflects the Bollywood script penned by their mother Seema which is being filmed in Bombay. In enacting the disorganised ad-hoc world of Bollywood film-making, Ahmad tries in vain to convey that Bollywood plots educate as well as entertain. King Akbar's wisdom mingles with his minister Birbal's humour as Akbar demonstrates that different religions worship aspects of the same god. Meanwhile the director of the film instructs the London-based Kiran in the shastras of Bollywood emotion apparently influenced by the ancient performance classic *Natya Shastra*: 'we go for the *rasa* full on in India - we allow ourselves to feel the emotion, to wear it, show it - in every muscle, every pore. You need to make things BIG!' (I, ii). The conflict between religious beliefs is brought to the fore even as the Muslim king of the film orders a burial for a prince raised as a Hindu by his mother, replicating the religious tensions felt in

---

were patrons of their art, these women, who sometimes functioned as state courtesans, now had to resort to prostitution to survive. Sultana does not occupy this category of women; she is, instead, a common prostitute with little or no learning (see Godiwala 2005).
[29] Ayodhya, the mythological birthplace of the Hindu king and god Rama, had a mosque torn down to make space for a temple as the Hindus fanatically claimed the site as sacred. Traditionally, pre-colonial India was a place of religious tolerance which saw rulers and empires of several faiths, Hindu, Muslim and Buddhist. However, the religious divide and rule policy of the British has left long lasting scars in the psyche of a country divided into the Islamic East and West Pakistan (later, Pakistan and Bangla Desh) and the secular ideal that India represented post-1947. Over time the rise of Hindu fanaticism has claimed the always-religiously-plural India as a nation of and for Hindus (Hindustan) giving rise to sporadic violent riots through the country.

India during the riots which followed the destruction of the mosque in Rama's birthplace. Misrepresenting history, the film itself is a typical blockbuster entertainer with the mandatory Bollywood rituals of song and dance.

The tensions that attend the funeral preparations for the dead mother reflect in turn the Bollywood theme as well as the riots and curfews in the city. Religious dissensions arise within the family: born Hindu, married into a Hindu and later, a Muslim family with her children belonging to diverse faiths, Seema in death represents an ideal hybridity of belief, which almost verges on the secular ideals of Independent India. However, her elder daughter Zara and husband Ashok discuss her funeral arrangements: is it to be a cremation or will Zara's half-siblings want a burial? Seema's prosopopoeic presence haunts the play commenting on her children's attitudes and on her filmscript. Hovering about the filmset after she is dead, she has never adhered strongly to either faith, leaving no instructions to her children about her last rites. Politically active, a humanitarian in life, she was a successful novelist and screen writer. In life as in death, religion is not an issue. The film script 'was a story about power and politics not faith' (Seema, I, iv). And yet, it is the clash of faiths and the violence it produces which circumscribes the three concentric circles this play is framed within: the city torn by religious dissension, the Bollywood script which echoes the country's violent division between the Hindus and the Muslims, and the family itself which is comprised of both faiths which fall out over the funerary rites of the dead mother who, ironically, was more a rational atheist than believing. As Seema appears on stage after the cremation she reflects on religious divisions within the family and in the city:

For me the worst of it was not the fire - that never touched me somehow - but the pain of watching my three live through the traumas of that day. Zara - so alone! Kiran bristling with rage and, my poor Bobby, out of his mind with anxiety. It's been like this all over Bombay... crackling with tension. Neighbours are edgy with neighbours, friends with age-old friends, families with each other. But let's not lose hope. (II, i)

Things get ugly at the cremation as Kiran loudly chants an Islamic prayer which over-rides the funerary chant of the increasingly angry Hindu priest. The violence the country is experiencing spills over into a family feud as Ashok hits Kiran and then Bobby. The dead Seema laments that she can comfort neither Zara nor Kiran: 'Whom do I comfort first - and how? You – my first-born – whom I tried to forget for years on end, whose tears never stopped chasing my dreams. I desperately need to make my peace with you. Or, you, my precious baby – whose love and laughter helped me through my worst sorrows' (II, i).

The play is over-long and the second act sinks into murky Bollywood kitsch as the filmscript is changed from the original plot of the heroine dying for romantic love to dying in defence of religious fanaticism. The theme of capitalistic exploitation is woven into the main threads that spell religious dissent, as Ashok the Hindu, already depicted as a violent religious fanatic, is villainized to represent the exploiter. The play ends as Zara goes to the ironically named Shantinagar (town of peace) to look for her half-siblings and make her peace with them. The melodramatic twist has Zara killed by Muslim snipers.

River on Fire certainly makes its point about the religious divisions with which post-Independence India has been riven, especially in the wake of riots following the Ayodhya conflict. The play achieves this with the threefold threads that form the warp and woof of the first act: the Muslim and Hindu hatred in the city, in the family and in the Bollywood film. However, this point seems laboured by the inclusion of the mostly extraneous second act which adds almost nothing to the piece. The end, rather abrupt, and attempting to backtrack into depicting that Muslims also retaliated with violence, serves to emphasize that peace amongst the religious extremists of either side may be a dream shattered by the very real bloodshed in the cities.

Singh Tangos

Bettina Gracias' play is set in the 80s and negotiates the attempt to acculturate and engage meaningfully with the host culture by the Singhs, a Sikh couple who have lived in England for ten years. Their attempts to befriend 'English people' since they have been in England seem to have met only scorn:

Mr Singh: I came here to find culture
Mrs Singh: I tried saying hello
Mr Singh: The land of Shaw and Shakespeare
Mrs Singh: But they ran away. (Sc i)

But Mr. Singh perseveres, as his idea of 'culture' is to be intercultural, to engage with the host culture:

Mrs. Singh: They look so hard and cold
Mr. Singh: The fish and chips?
Mrs Singh: The people
Mr Singh: This is England you'd better start mixing with them
Mrs Singh: They're not very friendly. (Sc i)

The naïve views of Mr. Singh contrasts with the insularity of Mrs. Singh:

Mr. Singh: We came here to be educated
Mrs Singh: I thought we came to make money. (Sc i)

But Mr. Singh, over-riding all his wife's objections, hits upon a plan: 'Ballroom dancing'. If they learned 'western' dancing they would meet the English on their own turf. It's no use attending Kathak classes, after all, 'the English won't learn Kathak'.

Change your sari and put up your hair. We're going to find a dance class with cultured people. It's time to integrate, we're moving to the suburbs. And for god's sake don't wear those bloody chappels. (Sc i)

This furious need to integrate is enacted as a comedy, but the play is informative in its encouragement to the primarily Asian audiences that the structures of society may have transformed enough to allow them to integrate if they have a need and a wish to do so. Mrs. Singh's transformation from the insularity of preferring the art and performance styles of her own culture to a rapid appreciation of and expertise at the cultural production of the Other is at once funny and serious.

Mr. Singh: Let's go to bed.
Mrs. Singh: But my feet want to move, even though you bruised them.
Mr. Singh: Let's move them to the bedroom.
Mrs. Singh: Thank you for forcing me to go [to the dance class]. You're the sweetest, cleverest, husband in England. (Sc ii)

Within Mr. Singh's strategy to acculturate comes the desire for 'authentically English' food. Ironically, it is his teenage daughter Cassie who objects, preferring a biryani to 'that plastic pizza-schmizza rubbish with no flavour.' Living typically, as the British-Asian does, in Indias-of-the-mind, claiming to belong to a home they have never seen, Cassie pretends to know how things are done in India:

Mr. Singh: You can't drown a delicate meal with whiskey
Cassie: They do in India
Tej: Rubbish. You haven't even been there. (Sc iii)

For Cassie, her need to establish her identity as authentically Indian comes from clothes, a strongly voiced belief in arranged marriages, a thorough rejection of the 'western music and dance' her parents are learning in a futile attempt to assimilate. She accuses her father of being ashamed of his roots as he does not wear a turban (they are Sikhs). At this point in the play Cassie's strenuous assertion of an 'Indian' identity is merely an assertion of 'roots'. It does not make one 'more Indian', especially in large cosmopolitan cities such as Bombay, to display a need to wear a salwar khameez or a sari. The younger generations are equally comfortable in jeans and minis as they are in Indian clothes, and this

eclecticism does not, in India, take away from one's sense of Indianness. Cosmopolitan Indians born and brought up in the metropoles by and large alternate easily and fluidly between eating spaghetti, chicken tikka and Mongolian chicken. Metropolitan identities are interstitial and the love of jazz does not clash with an appreciation of the ghazal. The insistence of the deterritorialized Asian to display her difference comes in part from the exclusions practiced by the host culture.

The determination of the Singhs to appreciate and partake of things western do not seem to meet with any success as they have not been able to befriend any English person in their dance class. Although they excel at their newly practiced hobby, their primary intention seems thwarted. Mr. Singh is honest: 'I came to this country to be comfortable, I made money so we could have an easy life' (Sc v).

However, the teenagers' idea of India is stereotyped. When Cassie voices a desire to marry a man in India, her brother cautions her: 'I'm serious Cas, how long do you really think you could stand it in India? You'll be going back in time. The women out there are expected to cook and clean and look after their husbands [...]You won't have the freedom to go out when you want, wear what you want.' Cassie's response is constructed within the discourse of the racism she has experienced:

What sort of freedom do you think I have here? Do you think I feel comfortable going out on the streets waiting for some fucking skinhead to spit at me? [...] And all the girls at school: 'What sort of food do you eat at home? Are you allowed out after dark? Is your dad arranging your marriage. Will you meet him first? Are you a virgin? They're so ignorant they don't realise they've had more curries than I have. I can do what I fucking want. I have more freedom than they do. But they can't see it. All they see is that I'm different because I'm Asian. Well I'm fed up with being different, I'm fed up with all those stupid questions. I want to be somewhere where I fit in. I want to be invisible (Sc viii).

However, India is a romantic fantasy in Cassie's mind. To be 'invisible' occupying a non-identity in a non-place like her imagined India is her ideal, somewhat close to her need for self-annihilation. She obviously has no idea of the changing structures of a country she has never seen:

We'll go to India together where we belong. I know you're not happy here. I can feel it. We'll live like kings with our people, in our home country. We'll learn the languages and the cooking and wear long flowing colourful clothes. We'll meet all our relatives, hundreds of aunts and cousins who'll take us in to their family. And we'll laugh, we'll sit in the sun and laugh. (Sc xv)

India becomes a fantasy as it offers a non-racist context for the British-Asians:

In Britain, racism to someone like me is a [constant] background noise [...] It switches off in India and you never have the idea that the cab didn't stop because of the colour of your skin, the service in the shop was bad because of the colour of your skin (Samir Shah, BBC Deputy Editor of Television News in Gifford 1990: 70).

The central gest of the play is the Singhs' need to be accepted and appreciated by the host culture. It informs all their actions, from the parents' classes in ballroom dancing to Cassie's longing for a space she can be herself in. Mr. Singh's monologue towards the close of the play accentuates this longing to be part of a culture which has continually rejected them. His history in England has been one of painful rejection:

My step was so light with anticipation I almost flew off the plane .... Only to land with a bump. All my education, years of study, sitting in semi-darkness reading on my own instead of running free and wild counted for nothing. The cigars and chandeliers of Gentlemen's clubs were barred to me. I realised that the only way I could show these ignorant people was not by wit and intellect but through my pocket. I built my own Empire. I was the king of the Singh factory. But the doors remained tightly shut. It was Minnie [his wife] that showed me, poor, sweet, innocent, little Minnie showed me the looks on their faces when we won. I saw respect, I saw envy. I saw them reaching out desperately trying to grab a piece, not of my well developed mind, they're too ignorant to appreciate that, but of my body. My graceful, flowing body. (Sc xvi)

This is a bitter-sweet play in which the desire to be appreciated for themselves is such a keen need that winning the dance competition is a very important victory, symbolising as it does to the Singhs that they are not merely the equals of those in their adopted land but head and shoulders above them. This victory liberates in them, momentarily, the need to engage with aspects of English cultural codes as they are now, symbolically, free. The play ends on the Singhs' taking comfort in rituals signifying Indianness:

Mrs. Singh: I haven't made [biryani] for years
(*exiting*) I'll need some good basmati rice, tomatoes, chicken
and saffron.

(*Making sure she's gone [Mr. Singh] gets up puts an Indian record on takes off his jacket to reveal a Nehru shirt and dances freely*) (Sc xvi).

As comic and serious as Gracias' play is, it displays the contradictory space the British-Asians found themselves located in and constructed by when they arrived in England in the 60s. It is a play about strangers in society, their need to belong and feel part of the larger culture and their attempts to do so. *Singh Tangos* is a drama of hopes, desires, frustrations, exclusions and haunting sadness.

Sock 'Em With Honey

The opening years of the 21st century saw the production of Bapsi Sidhwa's play, *Sock 'Em With Honey*[30] in London and New York. The Indian mother who travels to London to meet her daughter's English-Jewish fiancé, is fluent in terms of language and modern attitudes – western cultural performatives – to be able to engage meaningfully with her daughter's white English friends, but simultaneously displays a fierce pride in Parsi tradition and customs.

[*Sock Em With Honey*: A toast. Photo credit: Robert Day]

The play opens in Zareen and Cyrus's bedroom in Lahore. It is an upper middle class family home (air conditioner; tea trolley). Ostensibly, the family is traditionally Parsi: they speak in a hybrid form of English and furiously object to the impending marriage of the daughter with a non-Parsi. Their prejudices are clearly laid out in the opening dialogue:

Zareen: *[crying]*
Oh, Mumma … She wants to marry a NON.. Some non-Parsee boy she met in London!
Mumma:*[Thumps hand on heart and staggers.]*
O Khoda! O mahara baap!

---

[30] Based on her novel *An American Brat*.

Zareen: *[Escorts Mumma, in her sari-petticoat and blouse, to sit on the bed. stacks pillows behind her]* There! Comfortable?
[Mumma mutely refuses. Zareen begins folding Mumma's sari.]
Mumma: A WHITE Non, or a BLACK Non!?
Zareen: He's white! O God Mumma! Don't make it sound any worse than it is.
[…]
Mumma: I begged you: 'Don't send the child to England. What's the use of all this study-shudy?' You and that quack have only yourselves to blame. (I, i)

The daughter Feroza lives in London with her lesbian flatmate Sheila and her Jewish-English boyfriend. David's opening words display a linguistic hybridity, comfortable with Parsi and English: 'Good morning everyone … How are you luv? Mmm … You smell nice, don't you … Come with me … let's go to my room and mess around – a little kissy-koty?' and so is Feroza: 'Let her be, she's having a bad day. I'll get you coffee, jaan.' The couple displays a linguistic performative which indicates their identification with and assimilation of each other's culture and language. This is a new generation of intercultural marriages which do not cater to the cultural hegemony practiced by past generations which privileged a hierarchy of colonial languages and cultures over the east within a mixed family.

The play has Feroza's family accept David in a typical liberal-Parsi fashion, even though the beginning seemed to indicate a sense of fixed traditions. The hybrid langue of the Parsis indicates a cultural mixture which enables the family to accept a 'non'. The 21st century has given us drama such as Sidhwa's which has Britons delight in aspects of Indian cultural production such as exhibitions of Moghul miniatures, and drama about Indians on the West End. The Indian characters, mother and daughter, employ a linguistic hybridity, a performative versatility, as the daughter's fiancé is also brought into this dynamic orbit. The daughter's Jewish-English fiancé fluently uses Indian terms of endearment and the daughter, far from being a mimic man displays various linguistic and performative signs of being of a culture which does not hegemonically bow to the imagined and imposed superiority of western ways (see Godiwala forthcoming). Sidhwa herself feels that she inhabits a fluid identity: 'I come from Lahore in Pakistan, although for a short time I became an Indian citizen and now I'm American. So borders for me have become fluid and I feel I belong to all these countries simultaneously'. Sidhwa says her play is 'funny and at the same time tackles the subject of gender and perhaps ethnicity and religion rather than race' (Sidhwa 2004).

∇

Rukhsana Ahmad resigned from the Kali Board of Directors in 2002. In an interview she said to me: 'I enjoyed my changing role at the company but I became a victim of its success. The Arts Council chose us for revenue funding which meant that our work was growing at an exponential rate. I had managed to raise its profile as a company and it was attracting more and more women. I really could not envisage getting any time for my own writing if I had stayed. And I also honestly felt the company would be served better by a working director who could assist more writers with more productions. I am primarily a writer and was not interested in becoming a director.

'I don't think its agenda has been hijacked in any sense. It is delivering Kali Shorts and Kali Futures – two tiers of writing developing over time in the way that I had set them up. Janet [Steel] does some workshops for writers but I think it's inevitable that the artistic director of a company will have an impact on its future. Since I am a writer my focus and emphasis was on the basic skill of writing for the theatre, now that Janet is running the company she is quite interested in building other possibilities within that (e.g., using more actors and devising).

'The only other way in which I am definitively different from the present team is the fact that I am multilingual. It meant we could seek to do and successfully deliver community projects with a genuine grassroots connection. Hence the success of the *Meri Kahani* [literally, 'my story'] programmes that we delivered for Southall Black Sisters. That imperative is now a little lost.

'The people on the Board to whom that kind of work mattered the most have also left. The present team's focus is on achievement on the boards [in terms of form and style rather than the previous emphasis on content] and that perhaps has a clarity which will be very useful in strengthening the company's profile and image in the years ahead' (Ahmad 2004).

Kali is arguably the most important forum for the staging of Asian women's theatre in Britain. With its current focus on theatrical excellence and the continued emphasis on plays which explore the interconnectedness of the identities of gender, race, sexuality and class makes this theatre company appeal not only to Asian audiences but also to majoritarian spectators.

Acknowledgements: I am grateful to Kali Theatre Company and playwrights Rukhsana Ahmad, Anu Kumar and Bapsi Sidhwa for providing me with unpublished playscripts and photographs.

Works cited

Ahmad, Rukhsana (1993), *Song for a Sanctuary*, in *Six Plays by Black and Asian Women Writers*, (ed.) Kadija George, London: Aurora Metro Press.

Ahmad, Rukhsana, *Kali Shalwar,* unpublished. Courtesy Rukhsana Ahmad.

Ahmad, Rukhsana, *River on Fire,* unpublished. Courtesy Rukhsana Ahmad.

Gifford, Zerbanoo (1990), *The Golden Thread: Asian Experiences of Post-Raj Britain,* London: Pandora.

George, Kadija (ed.) (1993), *Six Plays by Black and Asian Women Writers,* London: Aurora Metro Press.

Godiwala, Dimple (2005), 'The Sacred and the Feminine: Indian Women Poets Writing Since 600 BCE', *LinQ.*

Godiwala, Dimple (2006), 'Postcolonial Desire: Mimicry, Hegemony, Identity', in *Reconstructing Hybridity,* (eds.) Joel Kuortti and Jopi Nyman, Amsterdam & NY: Rodopi.

Gracias, Bettina, *Singh Tangos,* unpublished. Courtesy Kali Theatre Company.

Kumar, Anu, *The Ecstasy,* unpublished. Courtesy Anu Kumar and Kali Theatre Company.

Sahgal, Gita (1992), 'Secular Spaces: The Experience of Asian Women Organizing', in *Refusing Holy Orders: Women and Fundamentalism in Britain,* (eds.) Gita Sahgal and Nira Yuval-Davis, London: Virago.

Sidhwa, Bapsi, *Sock Em With Honey,* unpublished. Courtesy Bapsi Sidhwa and Kali Theatre Company.

Correspondence:
Ahmad, Rukhsana to Dimple Godiwala, 14 July 2004.
Sidhwa, Bapsi to Dimple Godiwala, 24 June 2004.

CHAPTER SIXTEEN

'THEY CALL ME AN "ASIAN WRITER" AS WELL'[31] – TANIKA GUPTA'S *SANCTUARY, SKELETON* AND *INSIDE OUT*

KATHLEEN STARCK

Synopsis:
This chapter looks at the labelling of Tanika Gupta as an 'Asian Writer.' Gupta herself rejects this categorisation and claims that even if the subject matter of some of her plays is Asian, it does not mean that that is all she can write. In addition, she questions the idea of separate awards for 'Asian' and 'mainstream' work. Supporting this view, I prove in my analyses of three of Gupta's plays that she addresses topics which are not merely accessible to non-Asian audiences, but, instead, are of relevance across national or cultural borders.

Although Tanika Gupta's play *Sanctuary* was produced as part of the London based National Theatre's 2002 *Transformation* season which was designed to promote new writers, Gupta is not exactly a new writer. In addition to writing for BBC radio 4 and 5, she has worked extensively for television – writing for *East Enders, Grange Hill* and *The Bill*, was writer-in-residence at the Soho Theatre from 1996 to 1998 (where her play *Skeleton* premiered in 1997), and had *The*

---

[31]Tanika Gupta in 'Between the Sheets.' Interview with Dominic Francis. www.nationaltheatre.org.uk/?lid=2551. 16.06.2004.

Waiting Room produced at the National Theatre in 2000 where she was writer-in-residence in 2001-2. She further wrote the plays *Inside Out* (2002) in collaboration with Clean Break Theatre Company, and *Fragile Land* (2003) which was the opening production of the Hampstead Theatre's new theatre studio (which is dedicated exclusively to young people's theatre (Sierz 2003), the Space. Her latest work is a rewriting of Harold Brighouse's 1915 comedy *Hobson's Choice* (2003), which she has set in an Asian community. In addition, she has collaborated on a project with musician Nitin Sawhney (Sawhney.www.Cgi.bbc.co.uk/later/interviews/nitinsawhney.shtml).

In spite of having started writing with the resolution of 'not going to write about being torn between two cultures,' Gupta at the same time admits that 'inevitably, everything you end up writing is about trying to get that character to search out their roots, [i]t's always about confusion and identity crisis' (Gupta in Stephenson & Langridge 1997: 117). On the other hand, despite the fact that she was a member of the now defunct Asian Women Writers Collective and received the 2003 Asian Women of Achievement award for arts, Gupta dislikes being pigeonholed as an Asian writer. Likewise, she criticises the idea of separate awards: '[...] but then we don't get nominated for mainstream awards. It still feels very much as if the theatre industry and TV and film really take only their own work seriously – meaning white work' (Marlowe 2003). Talking about *The Waiting Room* in an interview with Dominic Francis at the National Theatre Gupta argues: '[...] they would never describe Harold Pinter as an 'English' or 'White' writer, would they? Maybe the subject matter of *The Waiting Room* is Asian, but that doesn't mean that's all I can write' (Gupta 2004). This is a point I would like to illustrate with an analysis of *Sanctuary, Skeleton*, and *Inside Out*.

Sanctuary

Sanctuary was produced during The National Theatre's 2002 *Transformation* season which was hosted in two new theatre spaces, with special low ticket prices. It was director Trevor Nunn's declared aim to reach new audiences by introducing to them a new generation of theatre makers. Talking about his idea of the National Theatre he says:

> We must draw on our heritage, on our recent past, and on the talent of the next generation. I want a thriving new audience, including a body of young people under 30 with a theatre-going habit, a new generation of artistic and administrative talent committed to taking the National [Theatre] forward and a realization of the varied potential within this glorious building. (Nunn 2002)

Although *Sanctuary* at times seems somewhat overloaded by its 'assorted' colonial and postcolonial issues, it is daring in what Michael Billington describes as 'rub[bing] our noses in global reality' (2002). It is a biting comment on the British government's reception of refugees as well as a challenge to the construction of global racial hierarchies which underlie much of Western politics. When questioned on *Sanctuary*, Gupta remarks on the British government's line on asylum seekers:

> It stinks. Guilty until proven innocent. I detest David Blunkett's language where he intimated that refugee children were 'swamping' the schools. I abhor the attitude that all refugees are 'bogus' asylum seekers (perpetuated by the tabloid press) and I am disgusted by the detention centres and the fact that most of those traumatised refugees are sent back to the countries they are trying to escape. The Government on this issue are unsympathetic, inhuman and downright racist. (Marlowe 2002) [32]

Sanctuary tells the stories of three men of Asian, African and African-Caribbean origin who for different reasons find their particular kind of 'sanctuary' in the graveyard of an English church. Kabir, the gardener, was forced to witness the rape and killing of his wife in Kashmir. The shame of not having been able to help her led him to flee his country and prevents him from ever returning there. Sebastian is a journalist with a drinking habit who in the course of his working life has witnessed horrible war crimes. The third main character, Michael, is a Rwandan priest who escaped the war in his country under mysterious circumstances. What these men share is their friendship with Jenny, the vicar of the church, as well as their enjoyment of the peace and quiet of the churchyard. Their haven, however, is threatened by the imminent conversion of the church into a health centre. This functions as a metaphor and as a catalyst at the same time. The vision of 'his' garden being turned into a swimming pool, causes Kabir to literally start destroying the place which in turn triggers off his and Michael's revelation of their respective traumas and finally leads to the destruction/killing of Michael.

Set in an Eden-like English churchyard, *Sanctuary* contains several layers of metaphor. The National Theatre's set was dominated by multiple television screens showing luscious and luminous exotic flowers. The notion of Paradise is unavoidable, particularly when one considers the events which cause the characters to be driven out of 'Paradise'. Moreover, the Old Testament comes to mind when Kabir foresees the churchyard's future as a swimming pool: 'It's going to be flooded' (*Sanctuary* 71).

Whereas Jenny might function as a God-like figure, providing comfort and shelter (even if she is not sufficiently powerful to prevent eviction), Michael could be seen as the embodiment of evil. He sneaks into Paradise in the disguise of a smartly dressed Rwandan priest, but in the course of the play is exposed as a war

---

[32] Gupta's comments are very similar to those of Kay Adshead in the 2000 Edinburgh Fringe Festival programme to her play *The Bogus Women*.

criminal. Furthermore, when Kabir talks of his experience of seeing the devil, which Sebastian doubts, Michael responds with 'I believe you!' (50).

Sebastian, on the other hand, is a fool-like character. With his dishevelled appearance and continuous drinking he seems to be incompetent and the other characters do not quite know whether to believe him when he says that he formerly had a career in photography. However, it is Sebastian who has apparently been following Michael in order to bring him to justice. Not only that, but he also reveals Michael's identity. When he begins his disclosures, the other characters react with 'He's pissed,' 'Stop it,' 'You are being ridiculous,' 'You have been drinking too much again,' 'Sebastian, stop this nonsense right now. You're imagining things,' and, finally, Michael's 'He's gone mad' (91-93). Thus, it is the mad, blinded-by-drink fool telling the truth.

The setting of the graveyard also evokes the idea of death. On a metaphorical level, Kabir, Sebastian and Michael *are* dead. Since they cannot go back to their former lives they are dead to their countries, dead to their past, their former identity. What is more, it is difficult for them to find a new life and identity in the 'Paradise' of a British graveyard. Their attempts at building a new life are not successful and – like the dead – they have no prospects: Kabir has to leave 'his' garden, Sebastian is an alcoholic with a lost professional career and Michael is literally dead at the end of the play.

Similarly, these three characters can be seen as the washed-up bodies of the colonial past. This past is embodied by Jenny's grandmother Margaret, who clearly stands for colonialism. With her government-employed husband she stayed in different parts of the empire and throughout the play puts the audience in the ambiguous position of not knowing whether to be amused or disgusted. Many of her remarks are outrageously racist, yet delivered in such a comic 'sweet-old-lady' manner that one is tempted to forgive her. Thus she says things like 'The English language – murdered by illiterates and foreigners' (34). She obviously lives in a world of strict division between colonial *Self* and (post-) colonised *Other* which is proven when she complains to Sebastian in response to his ironic comment about there being too many black people in Trinidad: 'I never understood why it's so difficult to have a simple conversation with *you people*. You always take offence and turn aggressive' (55). [my emphasis] When the schoolgirl Ayesha tells her about her plan to travel in India, Margaret objects: 'Don't you want to go somewhere civilized like the States or Australia, New Zealand – what about Europe?' (58).

Kabir and Sebastian are the personified aftermaths of British colonialism. It could be argued that, since the British have refused to deal with the legacies of their empire, this has become unavoidable now with the past literally turning up on their doorstep. Kabir explicitly states this when he challenges Jenny: 'You are collecting money in your church to ease your own little conscience when it is your Church that caused the fuck ups in those countries in the first place!' (81).

By creating a Rwandan character, Michael, Gupta goes beyond the issue of British colonialism. As a result of World War I, Rwanda came under Belgian rule before it gained independence in 1962. Moreover, not only the postcolonial condition but also the Euro-centrist attitude of the West and the ongoing reproduction of colonial thinking in racial/racist hierarchies is harshly criticised when Sebastian describes the Rwandan genocide in his disclosure speech:

> My people – my ancestors – people I honoured and respected – capable of such depravity. Children in the classroom, their arithmetic still chalked up on the board, mothers with their babies hacked to pieces in their arms, pregnant women with their wombs ripped out...and no one cared. No one did anything. [...] One million people in hundred days. Africans killing Africans and the world stood back and watched. Because our sorry black faces aren't worth shit to them. (93)

Although it would be mere speculation to discuss the extent to which Belgian colonialism might have encouraged or even provided reasons for the Rwandan genocide, it is evident that in creating Michael Gupta draws attention to the role Belgium, the United Nations, France, and the USA – and possibly the whole international community – played in facilitating or not preventing the crimes which took place in this African country. According to the organisation Human Rights Watch, the Rwandan (paramilitary) opposition Rwandan Patriotic Front (RPF), which consisted of Tutsi, had warned foreign observers of preparations for the massacres to follow months before they were carried out.[33] In fact, officers opposed to Colonel Bagosora, who had taken control of the Hutu government, appealed to representatives of France, Belgium and the US not to desert Rwanda[34]. These were not the only warnings.

> The warnings of catastrophe multiplied, some public, like assassinations and riots, some discreet, like confidential letters and coded telegrams, some in the passionate pleas of desperate Rwandans, some in the restrained language of the professional soldier. A Catholic bishop and his clergy in Gisenyi, human rights activists in Kigali, New York, Brussels, Montreal, Ouagadougou, an intelligence analyst in Washington, a military officer in Kigali – all with the same message: act now or many will die. ('Leave None to Tell the Story. Genocide in Rwanda', 2003. www.hrw.org)

---

[33] A chronology of the events in Rwanda and of the warnings issued by a variety of official and unofficial sources can be found on the Human Rights Watch websites.

[34] The troops were present due to the peace treaty of 1993, a result of the former civil war in the early 1990s.

In spite of this, foreigners were evacuated by French, Belgian and Italian troops who then left. On top of this, the Belgians withdrew their troops from the UN peacekeeping force.

By making this world-wide ignorance one of the central issues of *Sanctuary*, Gupta seems to create a new form of postcolonial drama. It is not so much the quest for an identity that is placed at the play's centre, as is often the case, but the question as to whether anything has actually changed in our perception of a postcolonial world. Divisions between centre and margin are evidently still very much in place, in spite of the coming of age of the 'postcolonial condition' as well as postcolonial studies. When a civil war rages right outside our front doors, as in the former Yugoslavia, we – the 'White Western Community' – are shocked and demand action. If the same atrocities are carried out in a former colony and, above all, on the 'dark continent', 'their sorry black faces aren't worth shit to us' as Sebastian puts it.

Apart from challenging the construction – and worse the upholding – of a racial hierarchy, *Sanctuary* deals with concepts of guilt, revenge and justice. Outraged by his discovery of Michael's deeds, which forces him to relive his own trauma, Kabir first mutilates and then burns the Rwandan. Although the audience clearly sympathises with Kabir and detests Michael for his crimes, this does not prevent the spectators from feeling agony as they hear Michael's 'blood curdling screams' and 'the sound of a machete' (106) coming from Kabir's garden shed. Kabir explicitly voices his idea of 'justice' when he says: 'An eye for an eye, a tooth for a tooth' (106). The issue is taken further when Sebastian understands what has happened and argues:

> I've searched for him for eight years and you…you've just murdered him? I was going to take him back, to face his accusers. What about justice? […] [w]e have no right to act as judge and executioner. What about the survivors? The families of his victims? (109)

While the audience is brought to believe that Sebastian is the real advocate of justice in the play, his interests became slightly questionable when he says 'As long as he was alive he would have suffered but now…he's been released' (109). Thus, revenge comes into play. Whereas Kabir's nighttime deed might be seen as caused by an urge to belated take action against war criminals – something he had been unable to when his wife was murdered in front of his eyes – it becomes clear in the next scene that he believes Michael deserved his fate. It takes place in broad daylight with almost all the other characters present. When they have dug a pit and thrown the remains of Michael's charred body into it, 'Kabir smashes the scull with the machete and then collapses weeping' (112). Concerning the question of who should be authorised to make decisions about the (in)justice of sanctions, what is possibly the most interesting statement comes from Kabir when he claims that only he could have punished Michael because he was his friend (110). Authorised or not, it is certainly remarkable that Michael's persecution as well as his sanctioning/killing are carried out by non-white postcolonial subjects. The white characters remain ignorant and/or inactive until there remains nothing to do except dispose of the evidence. This situation once more suggests parallels to the international treatment of the Rwandan genocide.

Having said that, all characters, with the exception of Ayesha, help dig the pit for Michael's body. They therefore seem to have agreed that in a way he received what he deserved. Moreover, Jenny refuses to say a prayer by the grave and, instead, Kabir reads out a letter Michael had hidden. This letter had obviously been written to him by Rwandans pleading for help from him, their Pastor. Help which the audience knows he denied. The letter ends with the words 'We give respect to you' (112). In the play, these are the last words spoken on the matter of Michael. Thus the notion of Michael's guilt is emphasised while, at the same time, the idea of paying someone like him respect is mocked. The character of Michael is shown as completely evil, not only having committed terrible war crimes but also deceiving his 'friends' so that they hide him. In fact, a bad, devil-like character. It would certainly have been interesting to see how the dynamics of the play would have changed, had Michael been forced to partake in the genocide instead of believing in and defending it.

Sanctuary ends with an air of hope. It is Margaret who initiates the burial of Michael in order to save 'Gunga Din' as she used to call Kabir. Further, the last scene shows a reformed Margaret in conversation with Ayesha. If the old woman stands for the colonial past, then the schoolgirl Ayesha embodies the postcolonial hybrid present and future. Ayesha is of British-Turkish descent with some of her family roots going back to Scotland, Ireland and Norway. Although the two women and the realities they personify seem to be strongly opposed to each other, they strike up something resembling a friendship. What is more, Margaret hands Ayesha the diamond which had been in Michael's possession and which was 'found' by Kabir. This will enable her to travel around as she is planning. No further mention is made of preferring 'civilised' countries. Finally, past and present reconcile as Ayesha kisses Margaret to thank her for the gift. The play ends with only Ayesha on stage, chucking the diamond in the air, smiling and then exiting – into her (financially) bright future. So the pessimistic statement about Western postcolonial perceptions, as still filtered through the margin-centre lens, is somewhat lightened by this optimistic outlook. Likewise, Gupta's critique of the treatment of refugees in Great Britain is counterbalanced by the impression that things are, if slowly, changing for the better.

Skeleton

The subject of migration is also at the centre of Gupta's first fully produced play *Skeleton*. However, in this case the migration is neither forced nor does it include the experience of a foreign country. Instead, the main character, Gopal, has left his home village to study medicine in the city of Calcutta. He returns to his father's house for a holiday and finds it impossible to 're-settle' in his old environment. Griffin calls this a

> map[ping of] geographies of unbelonging and liminal states as [the] characters seek to come to terms with the alienation that migration, even within one country, entails, signalled by the impossibility of a return to the place left behind. (2003: 9)

Skeleton was inspired by one of Rabindranath Tagore's short stories. Tagore was the first Bengali writer to establish the short story as a serious art form, but is best known for his poetry. He was awarded the Nobel Prize for literature in 1913 (the first Asian to receive it) and was knighted in 1915. Gupta grew up in an environment which introduced her intimately to this writer since as a child she performed Tagore dance dramas in her parents' group 'The Tagoreans' (black information link, www.blink.org.uk/print.asp?key=895).

Most of the events in *Skeleton* are triggered by a female skeleton which Gopal receives as a present from his father, Prasad. Nightly, the skeleton comes to life and has lengthy conversations with Gopal. It appears in the body of a beautiful woman named Nayani. She slowly tells her story to Gopal, step by step, each night revealing a bit more. Thus, the inclusion of magic in the form of a ghost – which Griffin has found a frequent device in plays by Asian women and which she sees as part of their frequent addressing of the issue of spirituality (10) – is amplified by the introduction of a fairy tale element, reminiscent of *The Book of One Thousand and One Nights*. In this piece of classic Arabic literature, a frame tale is employed in which the clever Scheherazade outwits her husband, the king, by telling him a new story every night, always ending with a cliff-hanger. Thus, the king every morning postpones her execution in order to hear the rest of the tale (BBC, www.bbc.co.uk/orchestras/philharmonic/education/workingwithus/prognote03100 2.shtml).

When Nayani first comes to life, Gopal is thinking and speaking of his secret love, a young girl in the city. Just before his departure he has written a letter to her in which he proposed. Now he longingly and restlessly waits for a reply. In his daydream he imagines the skeleton to be his bride and talks to and caresses it. In response, 'he hears a strong heavy breathing' (*Skeleton* 21). After the skeleton has transformed into Nayani, 'The woman stretches and then takes Gopal's hands in hers and guides them over her face and then down to her breasts' (22). Thus, from the beginning, Nayani is associated with sexual desire and longing. She is a temptress who bewitches Gopal with her stories and her beauty and throws him into an ever growing confusion.

Gopal is engaged to the village girl Anju, yet is planning to break the engagement in favour of his city love Mukti. However, Nayani succeeds in driving Mukti, at least temporarily, from his mind:

Nayani: Say my name.
Gopal: Nayani.
Nayani: Again.
Gopal: Nayani... [sic]
Nayani: Now, as you said Mukti's name – with longing. (23)

Later Nayani cites poetry (Tagore) for Gopal and agrees to tell the end of her story only if Gopal is ready to join her in the realm of the dead. It is revealed that she poisoned her two husbands and herself due to her fear of losing her beauty. When she offers him the poison, Gopal finally 'wakes up' and not only refuses to take his life, but also orders Nayani to leave him alone.

This is followed by the turning point of the play, Gopal's breakdown and subsequent restoration of his relationships with his father, best friend Biju, and former fiancé Anju, and finally, by the arrival of a letter from Mukti who would like to get to know Gopal better.

On the surface it seems it is Nayani who brings about Gopal's crisis. Yet, I would suggest that Nayani is merely a symbol of something else. She is the embodiment of Gopal's confusion brought about by his move from a rural to an urban life and the discovery that he is unable to easily readjust to his old home. His (ex)fiancé observes this early in the play:

Anju:Ever since I can remember I've loved Gopal. I can't remember my life before I
knew him. [...] But when I saw him yesterday, it was as if he were a
stranger. He stood looking at the river as if it were a ditch. He kicked dirt from
the bank with his feet into the water. He stood there with a haughty air and
then dipped his ankle in for a second.
Mishti:What would the old Gopal have done?
Anju:Pulled off his clothes, jumped in and gone for a swim. (30)

In a similar way, an earlier conversation with his best friend illustrates how much in awe Gopal is of the city:

Biju – it's so ... [sic] so vibrant. Everywhere there are people – hundreds – busy people.
At night there are lights on the street, trams, Sahibs in horse and carriages and palanquins
hiding beautiful women. [...] when I first got to Calcutta I didn't fit in – I wanted to turn
right around and come back. I felt like the village idiot. At night I'd stand for hours
looking at the street lights – they looked so beautiful to me, so modern. (12-13)

In response, Biju makes the same observation as Anju: 'Sounds to me like the city's turned your head' (13). So Nayani is not the origin of Gopal's confusion and estrangement, she merely makes it visible and amplifies it. Nayani embodies Gopal's longing to leave the liminal space somewhere between his past in the village and his present/future in the city. Thus, when, at the end of the play, Gopal drowns Nayani's skeleton in the river, this can be seen as a drowning of Gopal's crisis.

Interestingly, the scene is paralleled by the drowning of the 'Protima', the image of the Goddess Durga. *Skeleton* is set against the background of the approaching Durga Puja. In Hindu mythology Durga, which in Sanskrit means 'the Inaccessible', is the Divine Mother, the wife of Shiva. Created for the purpose of slaying the buffalo-demon Mahisasura by Brahma, Vishnu, Siva and lesser gods, the ten-armed Goddess is equipped with the special weapons of these gods. Durga is both, beautiful and a fierce menace to her enemies, a statement that to an extent holds true for Nayani in *Skeleton*, too.

During Durga Puja, Durga's visit to her parents' house is commemorated. Her mother had longed to see her, however, Lord Shiva granted them only nine days. Thus, the tenth day, the Vijaya Dasami day, marks Durga's return to Mount Kailas to be reunited with her husband. This is symbolised by the sinking of the Protima in a river or pond.[35]

Nayani likewise stays for a few days only and then is returned to her husband(s), to the world of the dead, by being sunk in a river. Moreover, the context of Durga Puja adds an element of spirituality to the magical one of the ghost and the fairy tale one of 1001 nights and thus contributes to a mystical atmosphere. This is further aided by Gupta's use of poetry, dance, music, the carving and decorating of the Protima on stage and the way Nayani tells her story. Whenever she talks about her past, she conjures up the respective protagonists who then act out the flashback scenes. Sometimes, however, Nayani is present in both, her conversation with Gopal and a scene from her past, for example when she describes/acts out the wedding night with her first husband:

> *Pradip carefully takes Nayani in his arms and holds her. He looks afraid. Nayani looks*
> *disappointed. They lay together in Gopal's bed [...] Gopal turns away embarrassed.*
> *Nayani pops her head out from the net.*
> Nayani: It's alright, you needn't look away. Nothing happened. My husband
> was so dazzled by my beauty, he couldn't make love. He was afraid. (40)

Nayani is physically part of the past, as she is lying in bed with her husband. Yet at the same time, at least her head is likewise physically part of the present

---

[35] Most information taken from: Sri Swami Sivananda, *Hindu Fasts and Festivals*.

when she looks out from the net and talks to Gopal. In this way she also mirrors Gopal's entrapment in a state of 'unbelonging', caught between two places, unable to return to what he left behind.

A possible explanation for creating such a strong mystical atmosphere in *Skeleton*, besides Gupta's declared interest in magical realism (in fact, there are ghosts in *Sanctuary* and *Inside Out* as well) and Hindu mysticism (Gupta in Stephenson & Langridge 1997: 118), could be provided by Tagore's initial reception in the West. Since translations were often bad, he sometimes was seen as an over-rated writer, 'an icon for the Bengalis whose time is over' (Mukherjee 2004). As a result, he translated his stories himself, however, 'leaving out details of Indian life that he thought would be too foreign to non-Indian readers' (Chanda 2004). Gupta now, by reintroducing these elements, could be said to emphasise the value of Tagore's original writing.

Inside Out

'Mystical' is probably the last word that comes to mind in connection with the realist *Inside Out*. The play has been called 'harrowing' (Marlowe 2002), 'gritty' (Khan 2002), is said to have 'wrung tears from its audiences' (Marlowe 2002) and had people 'visibly flinching' (Khan 2002) at some of the scenes. According to Gupta, it is 'at heart [...] simply a story of two sisters' yet it evolved from Gupta's three-month research, running writing workshops, at Winchester Women's prison. This experience taught the author that more often than not women prisoners come from a poor background and that a disproportionately large number of black women are imprisoned for relatively minor offences (Gupta 2002: 7-8).

Inside Out tells the story of the teenage half-sisters Di and Affy and the devastating effects their dysfunctional family background has on their lives. Di who is of mixed race and Affi who is white live with their 'pathetic and dependant [prostitute mother] Chloe, who is much more of a child than either of her daughters' (Gardner). Apart from Chloe, who might be seen as the real source of the family's problems, there is her violent partner Ed, 'Godzilla,' as the girls call him. He threatens, intimidates and abuses the women until after yet another beating Affi decides to leave and live with her real father. Di and Chloe, prompted by Affi's father's alarming the police, get out an injuction against Ed. However, after a while Chloe allows him back into the house. This leads to Di's decision to finally leave her mother to fend for herself, Chloe's attempt to forcefully prevent this with a kitchen knife and her subsequent stabbing by Di. The play ends with Di's release from prison after five years, a tentative re-uniting of the sisters and Di's making plans for the future.

The relationship between the sisters is shown to change from great intimacy and mutual support to disappointment and mistrust and is finally put on a halt when

Di is imprisoned. At the beginning of the play Di comes looking for her little sister and tries to find out why she is playing truant from school. In spite of their bantering and verbal abuse it is clear that Di feels protective:

Di: You ain't been bunking off again have you?
[...]
Is it that fat face cow again? 'Cos if it is, I'll smash her face in for you.
[...]
So, it is fat face? She been nicking your dinner money again? (*Inside Out* 13-14)

On the other hand, Affy is so eager to prove loyal to her sister that she physically attackes another girl at school who has 'nicked' Di's boyfriend, Jake.

Affy: Pretended to go for the ball but whacked her instead. She fell over, landed on her face and bit her tongue. Blood everywhere. [...] She won't be sucking cocks for a while. I got sent home to 'cool off'. (26)

In addition, she slashed the tyres of Jake's car because she heard him call Di a 'nigger'. After the beating which is to change Affy's life, it is once more Di who goes in search of Affy to comfort her and take her home. As well as this, the sisters have planned to leave home and live together once Affy turns sixteen.

When Di learns of Affy's plans to live with her father, she feels not only excluded, but the situation is somewhat a continuation of their mother's life-long preference for her white daughter, which I will analyze below. First of all, Affy is able to break free from her violent home, however, at the same time she is given the chance to leave behind her class. Her real father is a teacher and life with him offers the pleasures and securities of a middle-class home. However, the sisterly bond is strong enough for Di to steal a camera as a farewell present for Affy. Moreover, when Affy visits her mother and sister she admits that although she was the one who left and although her father is 'bent over backwards' (64) to get her on her feet, she misses her sister and mother. This is also the only scene which still bears an echo of a functional family life and where some kind of bonding between mother and daughters is visible. Chloe improvises a meal of bread and cheese which she presents on a tray full of lighted candles and the three women fantasise about a better life:

Di: You could get a really good job. People with degrees get paid loads.
Chloe:Eh – Affy – Me and Di'll be knocking on your door every day goin' – 'Lend us a fiver.'
Affy: I could buy us all a big house to live in.
Chloe: With a swimming pool...
Di: And a butler...

Affy: And a huge tank with tropical fish.
Chloe: And I want a really fit toy boy to rub sun tan lotion into me back…and maybe my front too.
Affy: So you're not angry with me anymore. I am sorry. It's just, I couldn't…
Chloe: You did us a favour. It was a bit of a shock what you did, but in the end Ed's gone and I'm never letting him back in here again. And it's all thanks to you
Affy. (66)

Considering the strong sisterly ties, it comes as a surprise when in act three it is revealed that Affy neither visited nor wrote to her sister during the five years she spent in prison. In a long conversation, after Affy's initial refusal, they work through the reasons for their estrangement. Once more it becomes clear to what extent their dysfunctional family has shaped their lives:

Affy: You don't know what it's been like for me. Keeping everything together – don't want anyone to know – about my family. I got kids now. Gotta protect them. […] From the past. My mum the fucked-up tart who was murdered by my sister. […] I couldn't cope – not with you on the inside and me outside – couldn't even finish school. I was a mess. (95)

What Affy is not aware of, however, is their mother's racism. Not only is the young Di faced with the violence of her mother's partner and is sold to his friends as a child prostitute by her own mother, but she is constantly ascribed an inferior status due to her mixed race. At the beginning of the play this still takes the comparatively mild form of comments such as the one on the programme 'Blind Date': 'He'll crap his pants when he sees she's coloured' (50). It becomes more visible when she tells Di to forget about her exams and earn money instead: 'What's the point of exams? If you strutted your stuff a bit more, we could get some proper cash. Men pay well for black pussy' (60). Downright hostility is displayed when Di decides to leave and tells her mother that she does not want to end up like her. Chloe replies: 'At least I'm white you bag of shit' (71). This clearly reveals two things, Chloe's helplessness and a value system based on a racial hierarchy. Chloe has nothing left to say which might discredit Di's claim that her mother is disgusting. She cannot deny that she is poor, unemployed, dependent on her violent partner, not fit to be a mother and selling her body to make a living. Yet, there is this one thing her daughter can never 'achieve' – whiteness. So no matter what her status within a white society, her skin colour will always secure her superiority over Di.

Chloe's racism culminates in her last words before her death: 'My mum threw me out because of you. Half-caste, frizzy haired, bastard. I should have chucked you in the bin the day you were born. My whole life ruined – because of you' (73). These racist, hateful words are the last thing Di ever hears from her mother.

The effects of a violent family history on an individuals' life can, to a certain extent, also be traced for Chloe. Not much is said about her background, however, she tells one story which is quite revealing:

Di:Apparently she's [Cilla Black] rolling it in.
Chloe:Reminds me of my great aunt Sarah. Used to babysit for us. Right up until she was eighty years old, she had hair same colour as Cilla. Your uncle Dan said it was a wig [...] I believed him and tried to pull it off once. [...] She beat the living daylights out of me. Had this walking stick she used.
Di:How old were you?
Chloe:Only little. Dan thought it was a great laugh. But it hurt you know? *She was always doing that*. (48-49) [my emphasis]

Repeatedly the stage directions require Chloe putting her thumb into her mouth for comfort, she keeps losing her keys, cannot find or hold down a job, and is unable to free herself from her violent relationship with Ed. A common pattern emerges when it becomes clear that she is in no position to acknowledge her situation and the need for a change:

Di:Please mum...get rid of him.
Chloe:How can I?
Affy:It's easy.
Chloe: I love him. He's the only bloke who's ever loved me back.
Affy:What about when he beats the shit out of you? Is that what you call loving you back?
Chloe puts her hands over her ears.
Chloe: Stop it.
She rocks backwards and forwards on her haunches.
It's my fault he gets angry. It's all my fault. I egg him on and then he loses his rag and takes it out on my girls. (35)

This pattern of self-blaming brings to mind other plays on violent and also sexual abuse such as Anne Marie di Mambro's *The Letter-Box*, Clare McIntyre's *Low Level Panic* and also in Roddy Doyle's novel *The Woman Who Walked into Doors*. This corresponds alarmingly to findings of organisations dealing with domestic violence who in their 'guidelines' place much emphasis on the issue of self-blaming. *Refuge*, for example, tells women:

Domestic violence is a crime. You, and your children, have the right to be safe. The violence is not your fault. The abuser is responsible for his behaviour. He alone is responsible for his actions. You do not have to live with abuse. (Refuge. www.refuge.org.uk/safety.htm)

However, Gupta's Chloe is not able to seek and accept help. She has not learned to stand up neither for herself, nor for her children. On the other hand, this character is quite a challenge as the pity one might feel for Chloe easily turns into disgust when faced with her deeply ingrained racism. Thus, her death leaves the audience with ambiguous feelings. As a consequence, not only the characters, but also the spectators are 'turned inside out'. As Shamaila Khan puts it: 'It also makes you question how fragile they [relationships] really are, especially the bonds that you take for granted, like unconditional love from your family' (Khan).

What becomes clear from the analyzes of the examples of *Sanctuary*, *Skeleton* and *Inside Out* is the fact that Tanika Gupta's work defies the label 'Asian'. Although *Skeleton* is explicitly set in India and *Sanctuary* contains an Indian character, the subjects Gupta addresses go beyond the label 'Asian'. Postcolonial global (individual and collective) guilt, revenge and justice, the consequences of forced and voluntary migration, and the effects of domestic violence and racism are not issues restricted to the Asian community.

Works cited

Griffin, Gabriele (2003), *Contemporary Black and Asian Women Playwrights in Britain*, Cambridge: Cambridge University Press.
Gupta, Tanika (1997), *Skeleton*, London: Faber and Faber.
Gupta, Tanika (2002), *Sanctuary*, London. Oberon.
Gupta, Tanika (2002), *Inside Out*, London: Oberon.
Nunn, Trevor (2002), Introduction to *Sanctuary*, Tanika Gupta, London: Oberon.
Stephenson, Heidi & Natasha Langridge (1997), *Rage and Reason. Women Playwrights on Playwriting*, London: Methuen.

Newspaper reviews
Sierz, Aleks, 'Fragile Land.' *The Stage*, 3 April, 2003.

Websites (BBC)

http://www.bbc.co.uk/orchestras/philharmonic/education/workingwithus/prognote0 31002.shtml, 28 June, 2004.
Billington, Michael. 'Sanctuary' in *The Guardian*, 31 July 2002. http://www.guardian.co.uk/reviews/story/0,3604,765843,00.html, 20 June, 2004.
Black information link. http://www.blink.org.uk/print.asp?key=895, 16 June, 2004.
Chanda, Rajat, 'Selected Short Stories of Rabindranath Tagore. Review' http://www.parabaas.com/translation/database/reviews/tagoreshor..., 16 June, 2004.

Gardner, Lyn. 'Inside Out,' in *The Guardian*, November 20, 2002. http://www.guardian.co.uk/arts/critic/review/0,1169,843499,00.html, 23 June, 2004.

Gupta, Tanika. in 'Between The Sheets,' Interview with Dominic Francis. http://www.nationaltheatre.org.uk/?lid=2551, 16 June, 2004.

Khan, Shamaila. 'Inside Out Review.' *BBC Manchester Masti*, 24 October, 2002. http://www.db.bbc.co.uk/manchaster/masti/2002/10/24/inside_out_revi..., 18 June, 2004.

Marlowe, Sam. 'Gupta's Choice.' in *The Independent*, 26 June 2003. http://www.Independent.co.uk/theatre/interviews/story.jsp?story=418975, 20 June, 2004.

-----------------'Tanika Gupta: From Kashmir to 'Grange Hill.'' 28 July 2002. http://www.Independent.co.uk/theatre/interviews/story.jsp?story=319636, 23 June, 2004.

'Leave None to Tell the Story. Genocide in Rwanda.' 02 July 2003. http://www.hrw.org/reports/1999/rwanda/, 24 June, 2004.

Mukherjee, Meenakshi. 'Review of *Yogayog* by R.Tagore.' http://www.parabaas.com.rabindranath/articles/brMeenakshi.html, 21 June, 2004.

Refuge. A National Lifeline for Women and Children experiencing Domestic Violence. http://www.refuge.org.uk/safety.htm, 25 June, 2004.

Sawhney, Nitin. http://www.Cgi.bbc.co.uk/later/interviews/nitinsawhney.shtml, 18 June, 2004.

Sri Swami Sivananda. *Hindu Fasts and Festivals*, Divine Life Society. 1983. http://www.sivanandadlshq.org/religions/navaratri.htm, 21 June, 2004

CHAPTER SEVENTEEN

'SHAMELESS' – WOMEN, SEXUALITY AND VIOLENCE IN BRITISH ASIAN DRAMA

VALERIE KANEKO LUCAS

Synopsis:

This chapter examines the relationship between sexuality, agency and female desire in four British Asian plays: Deepak Verma's Ghostdancing, Behsharam (Shameless) and Behzti (Dishonour), both by Gurpreet Kaur Bhatti, and Yasmin Whittaker Khan's Bells. The texts' critique of patriarchal cultural values reveal a deep-seated anxiety and ambivalence regarding women as objects of exchange between men, and considers the suppression and policing of female agency and sexual desire.

Deepak Verma's *Ghostdancing*, produced by Tamasha Theatre (in association with the Leicester Haymarket Theatre) in 2001; Gurpreet Kaur Bhatti's *Behsharam (Shameless)*, produced by the Birmingham Repertory Theatre and Soho Theatre Company in 2001 and her *Behzti (Dishonour)*, produced by the Birmingham Repertory Theatre in 2004; and Yasmin Whittaker Khan's *Bells*, produced by Kali Theatre for the Birmingham Repertory Theatre in 2005 are set in communities whose gender ideologies are (by Western standards) conservative. Nonetheless these plays exhibit a deep-seated anxiety and ambivalence regarding women as objects of exchange between men, and expose the psychological and physical damage which results from these practices. In Verma's *Ghostdancing*, a wife's illicit sexual desires lead to the murder of her husband and the collapse of their family. In *Behsharam (Shameless)*, the punishment meted out to a wife who has failed to produce a son lays the foundation for the psychological damage of her two daughters, whilst in *Behzti*, a mother's search for a good arranged marriage leads her daughter into the lair of a rapist. *Bells*, set in a butcher's shop turned bordello, looks at the buying and selling of female (and male) flesh. In analyzing these plays, I consider the means by which female agency is thwarted and sexual desire is variously policed, bartered or repressed, often by an older generation who exploit the young people under their care.

Ghostdancing

Based upon Emile Zola's *Thérèse Raquin*, Deepak Verma's *Ghostdancing*[36] sets this tale of doomed lovers in an urban Indian setting. Of the four plays discussed in this chapter, *Ghostdancing* is the most conservative (and indeed misogynistic) in its representation of polarized gender roles within a patriarchal culture, where women are wholly dependent upon men, both financially and psychologically. Like Zola's Naturalist originals[37], Rani and Nitin engage in a fatal passion; in this respect, knowledge of the source text predisposes the reader to view *Ghostdancing* as simply another cautionary tale about unbridled sexuality. Yet, embedded within this play is a telling critique of masculinity in crisis, established by the opening scene where 'Rani comes into the room carrying Raj. She puts him down on the sofa. Raj is coughing violently. His fit gets gradually stronger' (Verma 2001: 3). Raj, the master of the house, is no potent patriarch, but a desperately ill man, infantilized by his mother Leila and nursed by his wife Rani. When his boyhood friend Nitin visits, his appearance sparks Leila's unfavourable

---

[36] *Ghostdancing* was first performed on 8 October 2001 at the Lyric Theatre Hammersmith; it was directed by Kristine Landon Smith and designed by Sue Mayes for Tamasha Theatre in association with the Leicester Haymarket Theatre. The cast were Shammi Aulakh (Raj), Anjali Jay (Rani), Sameena Zehra (Leila), Simon Nagra (Doctor) and Rehan Sheikh (Nitin).
[37] In his preface to his novel Thérèse Raquin, Zola suggested that the human being is driven not by morals, but by primal impulses: 'I hope that by now it is becoming clear that my object has been first and foremost a scientific one. When my two characters, Thérèse and Laurent, were created, I set myself certain problems and solved them for the interest of the thing. I tried to explain the mysterious attraction that can spring up between two different temperaments, and I demonstrated the deep-seated disturbances of a sanguine nature brought into contact with a nervous one. If the novel is read with care, it will be seen that each chapter is a study of a curious physiological case. In a word, I had only one desire - given a highly-sexed man and an unsatisfied women, to uncover the animal side of them and see that alone, then throw them together in a violent drama and note down with scrupulous care the sensations and actions of these creatures.' (Zola 1868:22-23)

comparison with the sickly Raj: 'Now we have a real man in the house....Nitin is a bull of a man and look at those big hands!' (Verma 2001: 12). As the play progresses, Raj's failure to fulfil the traditional role of provider becomes more marked: he is passed over for promotion in favour of a boy 'hardly out of his mother's lap,' tricked into accepting an increased workload without a salary rise, and cuckolded in his own house by his so-called best friend (Verma 2001: 5, 36, 30). Raj's failures as a male are finally symbolized by behaviours stigmatized as effeminate. Preparing for a holiday *à trois* in the Kullu Valley, Raj speaks to Nitin like a coquettish woman: 'Do you think I should have something done to my hair? It's all the fashion these days to have curls...' Nitin eggs him on: '...curls would suit you down to the ground. And, you know that putting powder on your face is all the rage these days?' When Leila objects to Raj's transformation: 'I'm not having you look like a fop. A hijra...' (Verma 2001: 37), this reference is significant, associating her son with an effeminate, cross-dressed prostitute, and, more importantly, a castrated male.[38] And indeed, in the next scene, Raj behaves flirtatiously, throwing his arms around Nitin, declaring 'You know I love you, Nitin. Love you. Like a brother' (Verma 2001: 43). With this final declaration (despite its qualification) it would seem that Raj's emasculation is complete.

Masculinity and femininity, as socially constructed, have a particular resonance in this Indian setting: more than any of the other plays discussed, the feminine is configured as lack: lack of power, lack of knowledge, lack of agency. Alone for the first time with Rani, he senses her discontent with the restrictions of her married life:

Nitin:Go on. Be brave – tell me . . .
Rani:I am suffocating . . . drowning ... in an abyss of time. The same . . . day in and day out. . . There is no world out there – I am a slave.
Nitin: Did you choose to do what you are doing at the moment? Did you choose any of it?
Rani:It's what I know. What I have been taught...
(Verma 2001: 21).

Rani is a sheltered young woman, married to her cousin; her life, thus far, has been shaped by the submission and duty deemed appropriate to her sex. When Nitin tempts her with brandy, she refers to the cultural constraints upon her gender:

Rani:I don't know any women who drink.

---

[38] The complex identity of the *hijra* as intersex, eunuch, sacred and outcast is detailed in Serena Nanda's 1998 study, *Neither Man nor Woman: the Hijras of India*; a comical view of the hijra is found in Ash Kotak's 2001 play, *Hijra*.

Nitin:Is it wrong for a woman to do what men spend their entire life doing?
Rani: It's what some women are used to. (Verma 2001: 18).

In contrast to Rani's husband, who is a railway clerk, Nitin comes from a background of privilege: he has a wealthy father who sent him to university; in his current Bohemian life as an artist, he has travelled widely, with ready access to sexual escapades with European women. His self-presentation, however, is not that of a debauched seducer after another man's wife, but of a gentle pilgrim in search of truth. He tells Rani how his guru has taught him the hard-earned art of ghostdancing, the freeing of the spirit: 'Our bodies are the manifestation of our souls. If the body is free, then the soul shall also be free' (Verma 2001: 20). Nitin's proposal cleverly conflates spiritual liberation with sexual license, packaging adultery as spiritual development: 'You can take control – by actively seeking what you desire. Your being has atrophied . . . bring it back to life. Choose to live. Choose . . .' (Verma 2001: 20, 21). In Zola's original, it is sexual passion which drives Thérèse Raquin into her illicit affair; here, the lure is the tantalizing promise of agency. Such a proposal masks the nature of power relations centring upon sex, in which the 'stimulation of bodies, the intensification of pleasures... [and] the strengthening of controls and resistances are linked to one another' (Foucault 1990: 157). As Rani will discover, she will not be the agent of her destiny, but a subjected being, manipulated and controlled by her sexual desires.

Initially, Rani is shown as the model Indian wife (demonstrated in the first three scenes by her docility, silence, and serving the men). The awakening of her sexuality turns her into the anti-type: she recklessly backchats her husband in front of male guests, gloats about deluding her husband, and schemes for his murder. For her, their affair is 'revenge. For all that they have put me through' (Verma 2001: 22).

After Nitin has conveniently dispatched Raj, Rani creates a gender performance, exhibiting behaviours and actions which 'conform to an expected gender identity' (Butler 1990a: 278)[39] of the 'inconsolable widow.' Rani's ability to do this marks her as duplicitous and corrupt. As widowed women in India, both Rani and her mother-in-law Leila are vulnerable, unless they have a male relative to safeguard their interests and ensure the continuity of the family. Nitin and Rani cleverly exploit this cultural norm to serve their own interests: Nitin creates another gender performance calculated to win Leila's approval: the devoted and concerned friend who is regarded as one of the family. Encouraged by the Doctor,

---

[39] Butler's argument that gender is a performance, selected for particular audiences and effects, is elaborated in *Gender Trouble*: 'There is no gender identity behind the expressions of gender; ... identity is performatively constituted by the very 'expressions' that are said to be its results.' (Butler 1990b: 25)

Leila performs the traditional ceremony in which the 'brother of the dead husband takes the wife to be his own' (Verma 2001: 54); in so doing, she signs over all the financial assets of the two women to Nitin. Once in control of their money, Nitin reveals himself to be a parasite and financial predator, quitting his job so that he can squander the old woman's fortune.

  Ghostdancing is not only conservative, but misogynistic, suggesting that, when women do have agency [particularly in a play penned by a male playwright, Ed.], they will make immoral choices which undermine their marriage and imperil their loved ones. For such a woman, degradation is the inevitable outcome. Rani becomes no better than a prostitute. Nitin follows his wife, and witnesses her 'wearing a flowing sari and she had put on her face the kind of make-up that foreign women wear...I saw her hold the arm of a young man...He took her on his arm and they went into a lodging house. I thought I saw her through the window, with the man's hands on her breasts...'(Verma 2001: 71). The use of make-up links Rani with the 'loose' European women who modelled nude for Nitin, and the lodging house itself is in the D'Souza Marg, the haunt of prostitutes. Stricken by guilt and haunted by the malevolent spectre of Raj, the adulterous pair kill themselves. The wages of sin is, indeed, death.

Behsharam (Shameless)

  In *Behsharam*[40], the crisis of masculinity takes another form: the sins of the father are revisited upon the daughters: the Father's ostracization of the wife who failed to bear him a son becomes the catalyst for his two daughters' psychological damage. Narrated in flashback, *Behsharam* is structured as a thriller, beginning with the 1998 reunion of sisters Jaspal and Sati, and then unfolding the traumatic events which occurred four years earlier. Jaspal, the nominal *behsharam* of the story, lives with Patrick, an aspiring British-born Jamaican boxer. Her younger sister Sati still lives with her Father, her paternal grandmother Beji, stepmother and stepbrother Raj. Both sisters have been failed by their Father, an ineffectual depressive who relies upon Sati and Beji to eke out a living in a corner shop.

  Jaspal and Sati live in a culture where Asian fathers prize sons over daughters, where being female means fated to never being good enough. As Michael Billington noted in his review of the play, Khaur Bhatti's 'real subject, I suspect, is the preoccupation of British-Asian mothers with their male issue, and the treatment

---

[40] *Behsharam (Shameless)* was first performed at the Soho Theatre and Writers' Centre on 11 October 2001. It was directed by Deborah Bruce and designed by Liz Cooke. The cast were Nathalie Armin (Jaspal), Harmage Singh Kalirai (Father), Shelley King (Beji), Rina Mahoney (Sati) and Johann Myers (Patrick).

of daughters as disposable assets.'[41] In the play's penultimate scene, the effects of this patriarchal bias are set forth in a terrifying revelation:

Jaspal: She [their mother] didn't have a boy Sati. And he wasn't satisfied with two daughters, so he had to get a new wife.
Father:Don't listen.
Jaspal:After Mummy Two came you didn't like Mummy did you dad? So you didn't mind when she went and locked herself away listening to her songs while she played with her sewing box.
Beji: Behsharam.
Jaspal: I found her. She was trying to cut up her cunt with a pair of scissors.
Father: No.
Jaspal: She said there was a boy inside her and she was trying to get him out. I found her. Found her with all the blood.
Father: Stop it Jaspal. Please stop.
Jaspal: She's in a home five miles away, she won't come out now. She doesn't want to.
Father: Stop it. Don't listen. (Points at Jaspal.) It was her, she signed the papers. She sent her away. (Kaur Bhatti 2001: 87-88)

This account of the event elides the domestic (the allocated sphere of women) with internalized oppression: the housewife's scissors are used to enact horrific self-mutilation as a desperate woman punishes the maternal body for its failure to produce the longed-for son. For the two young women, this is a defining moment, and one which confirms their despised status. The resultant psychological damage is profound: Jaspal is alienated from her own emotions and incapable of forming a trusting relationship, and Sati escapes into a fantasy life with an imaginary suitor.

For Jaspal, her betrayal of her mother begins a downward spiral of self-hatred and damaging escapism. Cast out from her family, she worked as a prostitute, and develops a drug habit to numb her guilt. Unaware of the reasons for Jaspal's drug abuse, Sati brings a self-help book on addictive behaviours which encourages Jaspal to 'let yourself feel....Once you do that you'll be free'; 'make amends for the past' (Kaur Bhatti 2001: 77;79) However, Jaspal is unable to forgive herself, and is haunted by memories of her mother's torn, bleeding, and despised body.

Jaspal's alienated relationship with her own body is another sign of her psychological damage: she sees her own body simply an object for economic exchange. When Patrick reminds her of her former life, she makes light of her

---

[41] Michael Billington's review of the play appeared in *The Guardian*, 15 October 2001. Billington's review criticizes the play's 'muted realism, and situations take precedence over ideas...Bhatti also is clearly fascinated by tensions between the Asian and Black communities. But instead of boldly confronting these ideas, she simply gives us a soap-style family drama...'

actions: 'Who the fuck do you think you are? Jesus Christ, my saviour? Some knight in shining armour, who came to my rescue cos I used to spread my legs for a few quid' (Kaur Bhatti 2001: 56). Even in her current relationship, she sells her body to Stan in exchange for drugs.

However, most disturbing is Jaspal's inability to reciprocate Patrick's genuine love and care. Scapegoated by her family, she feels that 'No-one ever bothered about me except when they wanted to call someone slag or slut or whore or prostitute.' Although she is verbally abusive and sexually unfaithful, Patrick always has made allowances for her, keeping his 'Faith in you and me' (Kaur Bhatti 2001: 23; 55). The depth of Patrick's commitment is driven home when he recounts the hostilities facing an inter-racial couple (a recurrent motif in plays about second-generation Black and Asian Britons).[42] Patrick is torn between loyalty to Jaspal and the criticism from his own community, who cite Asian prejudice: 'These Pakis man, they look down on us...where's your self respect' and berate him for miscegenation: 'Why you want to pollute your race, man? You is a black man, try fuckin' a black woman' (Kaur Bhatti 2001: 69; 68). Equally, Jaspal knows that her own grandmother sees Patrick as a 'black bastard' and 'some Black people hate Indians as well' (Kaur Bhatti 2001: 45). When Patrick is offered the chance to go to America, he wants Jaspal to consolidate their relationship: 'I want us to think about going....It's our life', but Jaspal's refusal to countenance their joint future provokes Patrick's walking out (Khaur Bhatti 2001: 66).

Sixteen year-old Sati's fantasy relationship with her imaginary suitor forms a comic counterpoint to Jaspal's dysfunctional behaviour, but Sati, too, is psychologically damaged and has accepted her female status as inferior. Her father sees her as a convenient babysitter for his new son, Raju, and his wife, Mummy Two, views Sati as an encumbrance to be married off as soon as possible. Sati is besotted with Ian Wright, a Black football player, and keeps a life-sized cut-out of the Arsenal star as her cherished companion. The cardboard Ian becomes the lonely young woman's confidante, and she endows their imaginary meetings with romance, chivalry, and old-fashioned family values. Fantasizing that Ian plans to abandon his wife for Sati, she chastely refuses, using the clichés of tabloid newspapers to make her case: 'Ian, I've thought about what you said and I can't....I mean you and Debbie, what you have is so great, you've got it all – little

---

[42] Gabriel Griffin has noted 'characters' racial or ethnic identity is stated in the list of characters, indicating that that identity is at issue in the play. This articulation of the characters' racial/ethnic background in the list of characters signals the thematization of intra-racial or intraethnic cross-generational differences' (Griffin 2003: 19). Early 21st century plays focusing upon inter-racial relationships are Georgia Fitch's *Adrenalin Heart* (2003), Tanika Gupta's *Fragile Land* (2003) Roy Williams's *Clubland* (2004).

Stacey, the house in Surrey, the snooker room, I won't let you throw that away Ian' (Kaur Bhatti 2001: 25). To Ian, she can confess the pain of not being wanted, and her perceived responsibility for the break-up of her parents' marriage:

> It's because I'm a girl. That's one thing I know for certain. I heard them all saying things, I remember hearing the fights. If I'd been a boy dad would never have divorced Mummy One, never married Mummy Two. There would be no Raju. Jaspal most probably would never have got a boyfriend and Mummy One would never have gone to India. If I'd been a boy they'd have had more children - another girl, another boy, another girl, another boy. We'd be like an Indian Brady Bunch. (Kaur Bhatti 2001: 51)

Although these scenes of a young girl perched next to a bendy cardboard cut-out are very funny, there is poignancy in Sati's confessions: Ian is the only man who will listen, value and respect her. For Sati, a sense of self-worth is possible only in this fantasy romance.

In *Behsharam*, it may be argued that not only the daughters, but the Father is damaged by his insistence upon male privilege. His new wife sidelines him in favour of cosseting their son Raju with a never-ending stream of dancing lessons, fencing lessons and restaurant meals. His rejection of his first wife alienates him from his daughters, whom he values only when it is far too late to repair the damage inflicted:

> Jaspal: There's always Raju dad. You've got a son. Now there's something to be proud of.
> *She exits. Father sits alone on stage.*
> Father: I can't...I can't face looking at him. (*He looks to where Jaspal has gone. He breaks down.*) I feel shame. So much shame. I want my girls. Where are my girls? I want my girls. (*He looks around and slowly gathers himself together. He opens his book. He takes out his pen. Recites as before*) Tu meri zindagi meh ay... [You came into my life]. (Kaur Bhatti 2001: 91)

Behzti[43]

In her preface to *Behzti*, Gurpreet Khaur Bhatti writes of theatre's role in challenging injustice:

> I find myself drawn to that which is beneath the surface of all that is anonymous and quiet, raging, despairing, human, inhumane, absurd and comical....I believe it is necessary for any community to keep evaluating its progress, to connect with its pain and

---

[43] Also see Anthony Frost, 'Drama in the Age of *Kalyug*: *Behzti* and Sikh self-censorship', in this book.

to its past....And only by challenging fixed ideas of correct and incorrect behaviour can institutionalised hypocrisy be broken down (Kaur Bhatti 2004:17).

Behzti[44] looks at marginalized women, undervalued by their own family and snubbed by their ethnic community. Through their story, Kaur Bhatti exposes sexual abuses engineered by Sikh men, a critique which launched a tidal wave of protest, particularly from the Sikh religious community who were incensed at the representation of sexual abuse in a temple. Sewa Singh Mandha (of the Council of Sikh Gurdwaras in Birmingham) wrote:

In a Sikh temple, sexual abuse does not take place, kissing and dancing don't take place, rape doesn't take place, homosexual activity doesn't take place, murders do not take place. I am 77 years of age and most of my life I have been connected with the institution of gurdwaras and I have never heard of such incidents taking place in gurdwaras' (The Independent 2004).

Much has been written about the *Behzti* furore, ranging from the Sikh community's violent protests at the Birmingham Repertory Theatre, their threats to the author and successful campaign to close down the production[45]; as Anthony Frost has offered a detailed analysis of this controversy elsewhere in this volume, I will curtail my remarks on this play to those specifically pertinent to the themes of gender.

Through the narrative of Min and her mother Balbir, *Behzti* voices the lives of the undervalued; it is a story about becoming visible in a world where women without men are at best grudgingly tolerated and at worst abused. Frumpy but kind-hearted Min cares for her mother Balbir, who has been partially disabled by a stroke. The suicide of Balbir's husband Tej left them 'stinking of his dishonour' (Kaur Bhatti 2004: 45); they lost their home, were moved to a council tower block, and have since been shunned by their Sikh friends. Their link to the outside world is Elvis, a Black carer, who is secretly in love with Min. Although Min enjoys being a carer, Balbir paints a depressing picture of their life, arguing that Min has been 'imprisoned as my nursemaid' and knows no better:

Eating plastic frozen school dinners, waiting for you to wipe my arse, being wheeled about like shopping in a supermarket trolley? You think it is pleasant watching a fat

---

[44] *Behzti* was first performed at the Birmingham Repertory Theatre on 9 December 2004. It was directed by Janet Steel and designed by Matthew Wright; the cast were Shelley King (Balbir), Yasmin Wilde (Min), Jimmy Akingbola (Elvis), Munir Khairdin (Giani Jaswant), Madhav Sharma (Mr. Sandhu), Harvey Virdi (Teetee), Pooja Kumar (Polly).

[45] At the time of this writing, there are one hundred and thirty two separate articles on the *Behzti* controversy.

virgin become infertile? I want to live a life that is something. I want to be seen and noticed and invited by people. I want anything...that is not this. (Kaur Bhatti 2004: 46)

Balbir wishes to secure her daughter's future through a good arranged marriage which will transform their lives, for within this community, a woman's status is determined by that of her husband's or son's. Min's marriage will bring not only a rise in status, but material security and a defined social role. Balbir predicts: 'It will be a big property no doubt and I will have my own quarters. And when you bear your first son...I will be there to guide him through life's rocky road. And what a success he will be' (Khaur Bhatti 2004: 44).

Min, however, is hardly ideal marriage material: already in her thirties, she is so plain and uneducated that even her mother sees her as 'one of Nature's cruel jokes.' Balbir's aspirations for her daughter draw upon mediatized images of feminine perfection from romantic fiction, Bollywood and Western cinema. Balbir tries to prepare her daughter for the visit to the marriage broker, urging her to put on make-up so she will stop 'looking like a bloddy horse' (Kaur Bhatti 2004: 44; 29). She woos Min with a future of basking on the Riviera and drinking cocktails with Richard Burton. Min knows that she is a disappointment to her mother, who had dreamed a Bollywood-style wedding, crowned by Min 'demure and expertly made up, the envy of all womanhood.' Min is content to settle for a mundane life looking after mum, and is highly resistant to the idea of marriage to a stranger. But for Balbir, her daughter is a possession to be disposed of as she wishes: 'your flesh came out of me, it is mine, my property' (Khaur Bhatti 2004: 42, 93).

Min and Balbir (assisted by Elvis) go to the gurdwara [Sikh temple] to celebrate Guru Nanak's birthday and also to meet Mr Sandhu, who supposedly has a list of eligible young men. Balbir badgers the unwilling Min to visit Sandhu in his private office. Sandhu remarks that Min reminds him of her father, a seemingly innocent remark, but prelude to a damning secret: Tej committed suicide because of his homosexual relationship with Sandhu. Sandhu then blames Min for her father's death: 'You watched didn't you...Your eyes met mine. And his....If you hadn't been there, he'd still be here. With me' (Kaur Bhatti 2004: 109). Sandhu then grabs Min and rapes her, pleading to 'possess him. Just one more time' (Kaur Bhatti 2004: 109-110). The significance of Min's childhood gaze is important: here, the intrusion of female presence into male homoerotic desire positions looking (as opposed to being looked at, the classic trope for the female body[46]) as a dangerous and inappropriate act for a woman. The act of rape therefore holds a

---

[46] For more exposition of the claim that the representation of female bodies is configured for a male consumer, see John Berger's 'Naked or Nude' in his *Ways of Seeing* (1972) and Laura Mulvey's 1975 essay, 'Visual Pleasure and Narrative Cinema.'

dual function: Sandhu's punishment of the female gaze and symbolic restoration (through substitution) of his lost love. The truth of Sandhu's avowed passion, however, is open to question; it is later revealed that he is a serial rapist, who has taken advantage of generations of young women (Kaur Bhatti 2004: 125).

Throughout the play, much has been made of Min's virginal status, 'clean and shiny inside. Like a new penny' (Kaur Bhatti 2004: 22). In Sandhu's eyes, his rape enables him to confirm Min's suitability to be his bride: her blood is the outward and visible sign of her virginity. Sandhu's blood-letting is followed by a second blood-letting, this time administered by older women who are complicit in Sandhu's long-standing sexual abuse. When Min emerges, bleeding and dazed after the rape, she is gagged and beaten by Polly and Teetee. Initially, it seems that they have mistaken her for a menstruating woman who has defiled the temple. However, it emerges that they are in collusion with Sandhu, and this beating is calculated to break her will and inure her to marriage to her rapist:

> Min: He put himself inside me (*Indicates her vagina.*) here…and he felt me.
> Teetee: You are expected to say sorry.
> Min: He knows what he did to me. And so do you. And so does God. And you can break every bone in my body and defile me further and bury me here and we'll all still know, because that's what happened. That's the truth. (Kaur Bhatti 2004: 120)

Teetee justifies violence against women, as necessary to the social fabric:

> Our men are cruel to our women but we get used to it and we follow the rules, letting each slap and tickle and bruise and headbutt go by. And at the end of this rubbish life, we write the rules. We find the beauty in our cruelty. My daughter-in-laws suffer just as I suffered. I make sure of it.…Because everything must stay the same' (Kaur Bhatti 2004:101).

In her equation, violence against women is the foundation of social stability, with older women ensuring its continuity for the next generation. This in itself is shocking, even more so when one realizes that Sandhu 'buys' Teetee's silence by promising to get her son a lucrative construction job.

Both Teetee and Balbir have been Sandhu's victims: Sandhu raped the young Teetee, and Balbir finds her daughter has been abused in a similar way. In a rare moment of female solidarity, they unite in an act resembling an honour killing. As widows with no male relatives to defend the family's honour, their murder of Sandhu is an act which is normally the province of males. It is significant that this scene is entitled 'Izzat [Honour],' and the ritualistic import of Balbir's act is heightened by the use of a religious object, gurdwara's *kirpan*, as the murder weapon.

In *Behzti*, the female body is a metaphor for constraint, whether this is the impossible mediatized ideals of female beauty; the cultural constraints placed upon female desire; or women's unwillingness to denounce an abusive man and their collusion in his career of sexual abuse. Min's development – as woman and as human being – is signalled through the transformation of the body: initially the body self-contained and resistant, then silenced and defiled, and finally the body dancing and freed, in spite of sorrow and humiliation. The motif of dancing recurs throughout the play, and expresses Min's wish to be seen and valued for who is she. Her own mother dismisses her dancing as 'rubbish', but Elvis (himself an undervalued cultural outsider) admires her uninhibited dancing at home, and after the rape, embraces her damaged body and dances with her, before releasing her to dance on her own:

Min: Look at me Elvis. Look at me!
Elvis: You're beautiful. See... you're free again.
Min: Perhaps I am. I feel I am. Like it's all begun from now.
(Kaur Bhatti 2004: 137-138)

In considering the centrality of women's visibility in this play, the significance of the *Behzti* controversy goes beyond than the Sikh community's much-discussed attack upon freedom of speech; a secondary (and, in my view, equally important) issue is the silencing of women who criticise male privilege within their own community – a fate experienced by not only by the female characters in the play, but also by Gurpreet Kaur Bhatti herself. Violent protests led to *Behzti* closing midway through its run. Kaur Bhatti received threats and hate mail and went into hiding, but refused to be silenced, defending her duty 'as a writer to think, create and challenge' (*The Birmingham Post* 2005). Similar concerns regarding female agency were voiced by the Reverend John Ray:

My 30 years in India and Pakistan suggest to me that we are witnessing the struggles of the male beneficiaries of shame cultures to preserve their dominance, in the face of the increasing freedom that education brings to young women. Though there is a clear need to respect the leaders of faith communities, yet it is of prime importance for the whole nation to safeguard and strengthen hard-won personal freedoms which are under attack....Though 'God is merciful,' yet in Asian cultures family honour, 'izzat' [the term for honour] so rests upon the woman's purity that whatever misdeeds males may commit are to be hushed up, or if that proves impossible, to be blamed on the woman....the younger generation of British Asian women are making clear their demand for equal social status with men. The story behind Behzti, (dishonour, or shame) has its truth in the many pressured marriages, rapes and varied assaults which are a sad part of the background of so many. Drama is a proper, and often the only, vehicle for this to be brought into the light of day. (Ray 2005)

Bells

First performed in 2005 at the Birmingham Repertory Theatre[47], *Bells* explores the hidden world of a *Mujra* club in east London, where beautifully dressed courtesans perform and pleasure their male audience. For playwright Yasmin Whittaker Khan, her play exposes the sordid underside of these glittering surfaces:

> My research has left me sickened by the hypocrisy, psychological bullying, use of money as power and the seediness of these clubs. Some respectable, even religious men visit Mujra clubs – condemning these vulnerable women in public whilst pursuing them in private. Beneath the exploitation and degradation of the unprotected and sometimes helpless, there are many lonely and pained individuals – both buying and selling the entertainment. (Whittaker Khan 2005: preface)

This seamy reality is underscored by the nature of the venue itself: by day a butcher's shop, by night it is transformed into the Bells Club, touted as 'our own Pakistani Heera Mandi in London' (Whittaker Khan 2005: 118). *Bells* is most explicit in its critique of young women and young men exploited as objects of exchange between men, a point underscored by the scene titles such as '5 lbs. Turkey Breast' or '6 lbs. Chicken Drumsticks.' These jokey titles problematize the proposed seriousness of the play, as does its style, which veers between issue-based drama and sex farce, particularly in the early scenes and in the relationship between club owner Ashraf and the transvestite prostitute Pepsi.

If *Behzti* is about the marginalization of women, *Bells* is a play about young Asians' loss and the search for love in an environment where human beings are regarded as commodities. The narratives of Aiesha and the transvestite prostitute Pepsi demonstrate how an older generation exploits the young, and how the ideology of the brothel as substitute family keeps these young prostitutes in its thrall.

Compared with the other two plays set in Britain (*Behzti* and *Behsharam*), the environment of *Bells* is far more enclosed, both as a spatial location and as a cultural construct. All the action occurs within the premises of the butcher's shop with its upstairs bordello, the Bells Club. Ashraf uses caste as the cultural justification for prostitution, telling Aiesha: 'Your parents didn't want you, darling. We're your family. This profession is built on the misfortunes of lovely girls like you. We are kanjar [caste which undertakes prostitution as their traditional family

---

[47] *Bells* was first performed on 23 March 2005 at the Birmingham Repertory Theatre, The Door. It was directed by Poonam Brah and designed by Matthew Wright. The cast was Damian Asher (Charles), Marc Elliott (Pepsi), Shivan Ghai (Aiesha), Nicholas Khan (Ashraf), and Sharona Sassoon (Madam).

occupation] and you are kanjari [female of kanjar]' (Whittaker Khan 2005:125). Aiesha strives to escape, first by leaving 'Help' notes in the library books which Ashraf brings her and later through her love affair with Charles, but she is reminded time and again that prostitution is the only 'profession' available to her. Moreover, as Pepsi argues, the sex trade provides a safe haven for those who will be despised outside its walls: 'I've been out there and the world is a bastard to the likes of you and me' (Whittaker Khan 2005: 124).

The commodification of the body is clearly set out in Aiesha's narrative: at the age of thirteen, she 'got raped and kidnapped by my father's enemies. Over what, a bit of land in Pakistan?' (Whittaker Khan 2005: 149). Her body had been repayment for her father's debts, so she cannot be readmitted to her family, a pretext which Madam uses to justify Aiesha's enforced training as a prostitute in Pakistan's Heera Mandhi: 'Your family would have killed you just to prove how honourable they were, how they weren't going to allow a soiled girl back into their house' (Whittaker Khan: 166). Madam has brought Aiesha to London as a dancer at the Bells Club and each night sells Aiesha's body to the highest bidder. Like the mince and steak in Ashraf's shop, Aiesha is silent meat on the rack, attractively packaged for sale.

Madam and Ashraf hypocritically style themselves as the protectors of these young people, a sort of perverse mother and father. Outwardly respectable, they perform *Namaz* as devout Muslims, interspersing their prayer session between overseeing the shop and sex trade. Like a proud mother, Madam brags to Charles that she raised Aiesha and trained her in classical Asian dance, but omits the motives behind this training. Ashraf has taken in Pepsi after he has been cast out by his family (who are appalled by his cross-dressing and homosexuality). Affection, however, is entangled with sexual exploitation, and the parental veneer sugar-coats more venal motives. Aiesha counters Madam's 'I love you' with 'For the money I make you' (Whittaker Khan 2005: 166); Ashraf is a mercenary businessman who sees Aiesha as a disposable asset to be cast aside when her visa expires. Not content with trafficking in flesh, Ashraf also samples the goods; he attempts to rape Aiesha and buggers Pepsi, a vulnerable young man who is devoted to Ashraf and sees him as a father figure. Madam and Ashraf are not alone in their hypocrisy. When members of the mosque denounce the Bells as anti-Islam, Ashraf points out that only the appearance of virtue matter to 'our people. They want to look honourable and have a cheap wank' (Whittaker Khan 2005: 160).

However, there are exceptions, and one is Charles, a British-born Asian accountant, who falls in love with Aiesha and wishes to take her away from the Bells Club. This romance reminds Madam of the start of her relationship with Ashraf, who purchased her from her madam; now his initial love has faded and Madam is treated as a business partner rather than as a beloved wife. Her objections to Aiesha and Charles's relationship stem from fears that Charles, too,

will cast off Aiesha once he has tired of her. But Charles is naïve and
inexperienced with women; moreover, he is a cultural outsider whose idealism
grates against Madam's hard-headed cynicism. When Charles proposes to marry
Aiesha, Madam offers a radical critique of marriage as little better than prostitution
– lifelong slavery to a single punter: "you'll have her cooking and cleaning for you
and trapped in a house where she only meets your select friends who'll try to rape
her when you're not around' (Whittaker Khan 2005: 188).

Charles's position as a cultural outsider is itself interesting, given the hermetic
quality of the Bells Club. He is a 'brown English' man from a family 'more
English than the English' (Whittaker Khan 2005: 112, 182), ignorant of his own
roots and initially incapable of picking up the cultural references which mark the
Bells Club as a house of prostitution. His affair with Aiesha opens the way to his
reclamation of his identity as Asian. In Aiesha he sees the embodiment of cultural
authenticity, evidenced by her knowledge of Urdu classics and Asian classical
dance. She is, to his mind, a guide who can help him learn about his own culture.
Declaring his love, Charles asks 'could I not be Majnu and you be my Laila? You
see I remembered...your Laila Majnu...You've filled what has been missing in me
all my life. You're my culture, my Urdu, my poetry, my history and you're my
future...' (Whittaker Khan 2005: 178-179). Charles's romanticization of Pakistan
has more than a touch of Orientalism[48] (and here, he curiously sets himself in the
position of the colonized); this aspect of the play, however, is left unexplored.
Aiesha, in response, recognizes a kindred spirit: 'He was robbed of his rusum aur
ravaage [ceremony and culture] just like you never taught me the customs I should
have had. (Whittaker Khan 2005: 169). Love offers these two the possibility of
recuperation, the restitution of what has been lost: Charles vows that Aiesha will be
re-accepted by her family; Aiesha will help Charles discover his own roots in
India. The happy ending, however, must be secured through female
insubordination (followed, significantly, by restitution of male dominance). As in
Behzti, Bells ends with a woman's avenging her gender through punishment of a
sexually exploitative man. Ashraf intercepts the fleeing lovers, but Madam enables
their escape by viciously whipping her husband. For this transgression, Madam is
punished: the play ends with Ashraf beating his wife as Pepsi cowers in a corner,
bereft and terrified.

---

[48] Note Said's remarks about the Orientalist agenda's 'will or intention to understand, in
some cases to control, manipulate, even to incorporate, what is a manifestly different (or
alternative and novel) world' (Said 1979:12). Said takes the view that the colonization
functions through ensuring that the colonized subject adopts the beliefs, cultural practices
and norms of the colonizer. [**This is apropos Frantz Fanon's *Black Skin, White Masks*.
Ed.**]

I conclude this chapter in the wake of the London bombings of 7 July 2005. Provocative remarks in the popular press about British Asian 'fanatics of al-Quaeda'[49] seem calculated to incite a new bout of Islamophobia. In light of these events, the issues raised by *Behsharam, Behzti*, and *Bells* become even more problematic. Although these plays essentially argue for the rights of the human being (whether male or female) to challenge cultural practices and live free from oppression and abuse, the oppressors are (for the most part) men, and thus the plays may be seen as contributing to the demonization of the Muslim male. So what is at stake in British Asians' articulation of the inequities within their communities? How are those representations interpreted, both within communities and by cultural outsiders? And, given the current climate, what are the dangers inherent in theatrical critiques of Asian cultural practices? As Jatinder Verma has noted, 'It is a very dangerous slope to go down. But for me this is what theatre is about – to excite great passions. When was the last time theatre excited public debate or passions? '[50]

Works cited:

Bhatti, Gurpreet Kaur (2004), *Behzti (Dishonour)*, London: Oberon.
Bhatti, Gurpreet Kaur (2001), *Behsharam (Shameless)*, London: Oberon.
Butler, Judith (1990a), 'Performative Acts and Gender Constitution: An Essay in Phenomenology and Feminist Theory,' in Sue-Ellen Case (ed.), *Performing Feminisms: Feminist Critical Theory and Theatre*, Baltimore: Johns Hopkins University Press.
Butler, Judith (1990b), *Gender Trouble*, London: Routledge.
Foucault, Michel (1990), *The History of Sexuality: an Introduction*, New York: Vintage Books.
Griffin, Gabriele (2003), *Contemporary Black and Asian Women Playwrights in Britain*, Cambridge: Cambridge University Press.
Khan, Yasmin Whittaker (2005), *Bells*, London: Oberon.
Said, Edward (1979), 'Preface to the Twenty-fifth Anniversary Edition,' *Orientalism*, New York: Vintage Books.
Verma, Deepak (2001), *Ghostdancing*, London: Methuen.
Zola, Emile (1868), 'Preface to the second edition of the novel, *Thérèse Raquin'* in Zola, E. (1962) *Thérèse Raquin* (trans. L. Tancock), Harmondsworth: Penguin.

---

[49] See the leader and 'Disciples of Osama' in *The Sun*, 8 July 2005.
[50] Jatinder Verma, artistic director of Tara Arts, is quoted in *The Independent*, 21 December 2004. The article cites the views of Hanif Kureishi, Nicholas Hytner, Corin Redgrave and others on the closure of *Behzti*.

Newspapers

Anon. (21 December 2004), *Independent.*

Anon. (8 July 2005), *Sun.*

Bhatti, Gurpreet Kaur (14 January 2005), 'I Have Nothing to Fear, My Work is Honest', *Birmingham Post.*

Billington, Michael (15 October 2001), Review of *Behsharam, Guardian.*

Ray, Reverend John (31 December 2004), '*Behzti* – What about Women', *Birmingham Post.*

VI: THEATREMAKERS' VOICES

JATINDER VERMA

THE SHAPE OF A HEART

Duality has ruled my life: of Indian parentage, I was born and raised in Africa. As an Indian growing up in East Africa, I spoke Punjabi at home and English in school. In Britain my legal status is that of 'overseas citizen'. It is small wonder, then, that many a time I feel neither Here nor There. Passing my half-century, I have come to understand and accept that duality is at the heart of life for a migrant.

To lay out the facts first: I was born in Dar-es-Salaam, (the 'Gateway to Heaven') in Tanzania, and grew up in Nairobi, Kenya. In 1964, I saw the flag of independent Kenya rise green over the Ngong Hills, staining the Duke of Edinburgh's brilliant-white uniform as he watched the Union Jack come down. In 1968, on a cold and foggy St Valentine's Day, I stepped off an Ethiopian Airlines flight at Heathrow, part of the Asian 'exodus' from Kenya. We were all British citizens by birth, racing to get into the country before 1 March. On that date new legislation, which had just been rushed through Parliament, would deprive us of our status and of our automatic right of entry. I had landed in the country which school life in Kenya had conjured up 'behind the awnings of my mind', to use a phrase of the great Urdu poet Mohammed Iqbal, himself the architect of another imagined country, Pakistan. I knew it as the home of green meadows and red buses, fair play and the Mother of Parliaments. I had also stepped into a country in the throes of savage anti-immigration demonstrations, the country of Enoch Powell (his 'rivers of blood' speech was made in April that year). It took my mother seven months to find a flat where she could freely enjoy the scents of her cooking - the scents that had seen her being refused over and over again by white landlords.

[Photo: Saikat Ahmad, Ravin J Ganatra, Murali Menon, Ashvin K Joshi, Dina Mousawi and Mamta Kash in *Journey to the West* (2002). Credit: Stephen Vaughan]

Living through the tail-end of anti-colonialist struggles, arriving in Britain in that momentous year of 1968 and having a passion for history, it is no surprise that my theatrical career is based on a cause. When we founded Tara Arts in 1977, it was in direct response to the racist murder in July 1976 of a young Sikh man, Gurdip Singh Chaggar. For us, at that time, the need to claim a public space for our own voice had become urgent. Ours was a voice that articulated a new culture that we felt we were forging in our daily lives, a hybrid culture that was neither Indian nor British. The precise nature of its hybridity is elusive: its virtue lies in its flexibility, as I continue to negotiate life in Britain.

Our first production set a pattern for future work: a classic, by the Bengali Rabindranath Tagore, adapted to our modern British experiences. Classic, Indian, Adaptation - Tara and I have sat on this three-legged stool over the years. The unifying thread of the work has been a fascination with making *connections*. Our desire to produce a play by Tagore - we chose his 1917 anti-war play *Sacrifice* - was in part driven by a desire to reclaim him as part of our collective, British, heritage. Tagore had been the darling of the English literati in the early years of the 20th century: championed by W. B. Yeats, he became the first non-European to win the Nobel Prize for Literature in 1913, for his epic poem *Gitanjali*. As quickly as he was fêted, he was dropped, disappearing from the British literary horizon by the 1930s, to the point where, when Philip Larkin was once asked to comment on Tagore's influence, he replied 'Fuck all, Tagore'! It was apparent to us that here was a writer whom we could claim both as 'Indians' and as 'Britishers'.

For a man born in British colonial East Africa, India was the myth of Home (There). When I was transported to Britain (Here), India swiftly became a sustaining myth of identity. My Africanness disappeared from view. This was partly out of expediency - it took too long to explain to white colleagues that, although I looked Indian, I was, actually, African. I was also keenly aware that, in the aftermath of the hurried exodus from Kenya, there was no return possible to the land where I was born: Africa had pushed me irretrievably out of the nest. In order to function, I created a new identity for myself and developed my own myth of being an Indian-in-Britain.

My fascination with history (I read History at York University) helped sustain this myth of being an Indian-in-Britain. My studies drew me along the routes of *connections*: I greedily drank in the knowledge of how intimately connected India has been to Britain in the modern, post-17th century era. And so, as we searched at Tara in the early 1980s for a distinctive aesthetic, for our hybrid voice, our experimentation with Indian forms and dramaturgy became not an end in itself - a deadening 'back to the roots' trip - but a means of making connections with Europe, with Brecht, Grotowski, Brook and others who were or had been on the margins of European theatre ('margins' in the sense of avant-garde, edgy, unconventional). The experimentation was a means to root the vision of Tara not in ethnicity but in an aesthetic: the aesthetic of the migrant/marginal/Black.

It still gives me a thrill when I recall my first reading of the ancient Indian treatise on performance aesthetics, the *Natya Shastra* (compiled c. 4th century A.D.). It defined four elements as key to the art of theatre: voice, gesture, costume and emotion. 'Where are set and props', I remember wondering aloud! The *Natya Shastra*'s emphases on music and movement as essential allies to speech resonated in my heart – which had been fed from an early age with the narrative conventions of popular Indian cinema. Here, I realised, were detailed the means to develop 'total' performers – who could sing, speak, dance a story. How very different this seemed to the 'realistic' conventions that had gripped modern British theatre. Where the Stanislavskian revolution seemed alien to me, Indian aesthetics opened up another route to the same end: the search for truth. A 14th-century Indian critic,

Abhinavagupta, offered a definition of theatre that remains my mantra: 'drama is like a dream: it is not real, but it is really felt'. Perhaps the greatest joy was to realize that, in being inspired by Indian aesthetics, I was following in a long line of European theatre makers – from Edward Gordon Craig to Bertolt Brecht and Peter Brook.

[Photo: Murali Menon in Büchner's *Danton's Death* (1989). Credit: Chris Ha]

In my production of *Oedipus the King* (1991), the dialogue between Indian aesthetics and the European classics materialized in the interpretation of Oedipus as the tragedy of the migrant – where the hubris engendered by having 'made it' leads to a tragic fall. Employing the idioms of classical Indian dance and music, my company became a band of story-tellers, inter-leaving Sophocles' original with their own texts as migrants to Britain. This production formed part of a series that sought, through our 'Indian' dialogue with European classics, to forge an aesthetic that articulated the nature of Tara, and indeed, myself. Cheekily, I coined the word 'Binglish' to reflect the 'not-quite-British' approach of the company, though Robert Lepage's term 'tradaptation' seems to me now to offer a more accurate sense of the process we were undertaking.

[Photo: Murali Menon and Antony Bunsee in *The Government Inspector* (1988). Credit: Carole Baugh]

'Tradaptation' is a combination of 'translation' - in the sense of bearing across from one culture to another – and 'adaptation' - in the sense of shifting forms to suit different conditions or uses. In our production of *The Government Inspector* (1988, directed by Anuradha Kapur of the National School of Drama in New Delhi), we 'tradapted' Gogol's satire to a small town in India. For its inhabitants, Independence had simply not happened, enabling us to focus a critical lens on the Asian obsession with 'all things Blighty', to quote a phrase from the text. Similarly, my production for the National Theatre of Molière's *Tartuffe* (1989), 'tradapted' the text to 17th-century Mughal India, and in so doing, this satire on religious bigotry achieved an acute resonance in the wake of the *fatwa* against Salman Rushdie earlier that year.

Works such as these have allowed me to wrestle a space for dialogue with a tradition of European theatre into which I have, literally, flown. And, crucially, it enabled me to dialogue as an 'Indian-in-Britain', from the margins where I felt I properly belonged.

By the late '90s, however, I had come to feel the absence of Africa as a tangible presence in my life, a feeling prompted by the death of my father in 1995. If the dialogue with European theatre had been inspired by a search for connections between the reality of my life in Britain and my past as an Indian, the death of my father revealed a connection that I had hitherto sidestepped in my work. It took me

a quarter century of theatre work to realize that while I might have flown away from Africa, it continued to score the landscape of my heart.

[Photo: Vincent Ebrahim in *Oedipus the King* (1991). Credit: Hugo Glendinning]

This realization provoked me to embark on what would turn out to be our most ambitious project: a five-year exploration of the East African migrant experience which culminated in an epic trilogy of plays, *Journey to the West (2002)*. The three plays charted the story of Indian migration from India to Africa to Britain during the course of the 20th century.
The methodology of fashioning the trilogy steered us into ways of theatre-making that were quite new to us. It was central to my approach that we should make a piece of theatre that would reflect, as directly as possible, real peoples' experience. By including them in the several stages of development of the piece, they would become a community of creative collaborators. In teams of three we carried out extensive video interviews over several months with three generations of East African Asians living in Britain, from which the text was devised and shaped.

[Photo: Dina Mousawi and Mamta Kash in *Journey to the West* (2002). Credit: Stephen Vaughan]

Having interviewed them – thereby implicating them in the making of our theatre – I was obliged to make them a part of my 'family' of theatre. And so, in the initial years of testing the trilogy, I felt that it was essential that we brought the fruits of their investment nearer to their homes, into spaces with which they had a relationship: schools and community halls. In addition, given that most of the interviewees had never been to theatre and yet had taken us on trust and welcomed us into their homes, we felt obliged to create a welcoming sense of occasion when they entered the theatre space. From this concern emerged our practice of styling foyer-spaces to make each venue as hospitable and sensuous a space as the homes into which we'd been invited to conduct our interviews. By the fifth year this new community was ready to visit theatres around the country, as audience, where the trilogy was staged in its entirety, over one day. The appeal of the experience touched all sections of society: a comment in a Leeds student newspaper reflects the impact *Journey to the West* had:

> more people needed to see this. More people needed to know. This sort of production ought to be compulsory viewing for every one, such is the potential of educational entertainment to deliver important messages without preaching, patronising, or, frankly, boring the arse off all of us. (Juice, May 2002)

The years since the trilogy have been characterised by an acute sense of restlessness. I have made my peace with Africa and made connections between Africa, India and Britain. Over the last 30 years, migrants have become full citizens, products of a changed Britain, emerging from the margins to occupy central roles in British public life. British theatre companies are increasingly reflecting the diversity of the contemporary era in their selections of texts, performers and ways of presentation. Globalization has gone from being an obscure economic concept to a household word. Why then do I continue to search for a space, when it appears that now all spaces are open to me? In previous years my sense of being neither Here nor There afforded me, through 'tradaptations' and dialogues, a way to map the connections between my disparate worlds.

It also helped sustain my sense of being a foreigner in Britain. Now, in an increasingly globalized and diverse world, where the very notion of 'Centre' has been fragmented by an explosion in mass communication (satellite and terrestrial television, the internet, etc), I feel ever-more compelled to explore the Margin. Following the rise of anti-Muslim sentiment post-9/11 and the increasing threat of censorship on religious grounds, there is an urgent need to make connections - not simply between Here and There but also between the Margin and the Centre. There remain a whole host of marginal stories and insights that continue to compel me to make theatre. Stories such as those captured by an obscure 18th-century painting, that illuminate a moment of equality in early Anglo-Indian relations (my production of A Taste For Mangoes, 2003).

Or insights such as those afforded by Shylock's disturbing last words in The Merchant of Venice, 'I am content' – content? How? Why? What does he mean, after the utter humiliation of this marginal/minority/persecuted figure in the final court scene? I have only a series of questions at the moment, since The Merchant is the production I am planning for Autumn 2005. It is in the willingness to pose questions that I feel the drive to 'kick against the pricks' – and it is that drive which provides the reason why I remain in theatre.

[Photo: Soni Razdan in A Taste for Mangoes (2003). Credit: Talula Sheppard]

© Jatinder Verma

YVONNE BREWSTER

A SHORT AUTOBIOGRAPHICAL ESSAY FOCUSING ON MY WORK IN THE THEATRE

[Yvonne Brewster.
Photo credit: Luiza J. Silver]

Early Days

As a child theatre was my grandfather declaiming purple passages from his favourite Shakespearean texts in the morning to his shaving mirror. The sound and fury of Bottom juxtaposed with the quiet introspection of *Othello* had me peeking in at the bathroom door at every opportunity. My grandfather also had ideas on how these plays should be done. He insisted that Cassio as a black man would make Othello's dilemma easier to live with. I listened to this and much more, drinking it in.

Then there were the green boxed Topical tapes which the BBC sent to JBC (the Jamaican version of the BBC). These were meant to bring some English culture to the radio listeners in this far flung corner of the Empire. The station would use these offerings of The Afternoon Play and Mrs. Dales Diary to fill early morning and late night slots of small audiences, none smaller than me at six or seven years old, escaping into other worlds.

In 1956, at seventeen years of age, I landed up as a drama student at the Rose Bruford College of Speech and Drama in Sidcup. I spent three years refusing to be demoralized. I was not a particularly good student, neither were they particularly good teachers but in spite of one thing and another graduated in 1959 with a Diploma, and, belt and braces style, a couple of licentiates from the Royal Academy of Music in Mime and Speech and Drama which had been acquired unbeknown to Miss Bruford. Just in case she failed me which was frequently threatened. I was now ready, I thought, for all comers.

The Sixties

Having been told very early on in my studies in England, on the first day to be precise, that I would never work meant only one thing to me: I must be able to make my own work and not depend on other people's ideas of what I should be allowed to do. Although some people did employ me and luckily continue to do so, this has remained a fundamental pillar of my professional existence.

On my return to Jamaica from England therefore, my father's garage was commandeered into a theatre called the Barn. The idea behind the evolution of this theatre, (which still produces new plays some forty years on), was to give young irreverent Jamaican actors, directors, playwrights a chance to test their wings and wits in a safe place. To see themselves and the society they lived in reflected on the stage. It worked. We, through necessity at first, produced cutting edge stuff from African Americans such as Ed Bullins and trendy Englishmen like Joe Orton until we had written the plays we wanted to do. I was no writer, and certainly not the greatest of actors, so the job of artistic directing and directing fell to me.

Thus, in the tiny space of the Barn Theatre: 144 seats, stage 24' wide and 19' deep, and no headroom to speak of, my directing skills were honed. I think my preference for the non naturalistic began to assert it self there. In such an intimate space it was unrealistic and unimaginative to force naturalism to flourish.

The Seventies

When in the 70's I returned to Britain to live I had had a fair bit of directing experience, not only in the theatre but in television, radio and 'spectacle theatre ('galas' we called them: these events with thousands of participants in stadia performing national celebratory shows for special occasions. Great fun).

In the 70s, in London at least, there was plenty going on. My first toe in the water was helping out with the production at the ICA in the Mall of a play based on the life of the incredibly charismatic Jamaican preacher and intuitive artist Kapo. The play was called *Lippo the New Noah*. It was attempting to draw a parallel between Kapo (Lippo) and Noah. The mainstay of the set was, yes, you got it, an ark. The production was due to open at the ICA and all was not well. It was decided to bring in some local directorial colour (me) to basically calm the nerves of the mainly Caribbean cast and to reassure the duo of English director and writer that the cast would not go on strike. They didn't, and the play had a good run.

In 1972 The Jamaican High Commission supported a London tour of Trevor Rhone's *Smile Orange* to some ten venues. This I was asked to direct. The event turned out to be quite groundbreaking, developing black audiences which began inauspiciously with four lonely souls in the audience on the first night in the cavernous Acton Town Hall and ended four weeks later to sell out performances in Haringey Town Hall and long queues for returned tickets outside Anson Hall in Cricklewood. For the final performances actors who are now highly regarded members of the British Black theatre scene such as Stephan Kalipha, Charles Hyatt and Mona Hammond were all members of the cast. The production demonstrated there was a hungry audience for Caribbean theatre on tour.

The Dark and Light was one of the first buildings in London to be aided by the funding bodies to produce 'black' work. Its artistic director Frank Cousins sensed the need for his Caribbean audience to have a Pantomime at Christmas. *Anancy and Brer Englishman* was not an ordinary English Pantomime; it came out of the Jamaican tradition of hard hitting localised political commentary dressed up in pantomimic clothes. I was asked to direct it. The culturally famished audience loved it and queued up round the block to get in even though it was a cold December in 1972.

Jamal Ali had written a verse play *Black Feet in the Snow* which was socio-politically too hot to handle. Not only was it tackling the racism which people of colour were exposed to on a daily basis but its form was edgy and new, a sort of early tone poem of the type which was to become associated with Ntosake Shange. The multi-disciplined nature of the production employing music and movement as integral aspects of the whole was considered brave. Black directors were not in plentiful supply at the time and I got the job. Jamal's vision had such an impact that the production which was originally staged at the Commonwealth Institute was briefly remounted at the Round House and later filmed for television. An important breakthrough in those days.

Oscar Abrahams created an oasis of Caribbean cultural endeavour in a backstreet behind the Caledonian Road; The Keskidee Centre. There among the falling beams and the graffiti I got the chance to work steadily both as director and adminstrator with other black theatre practitioners and artists such as Rufus

Collins, Linton Kwesi Johnson. Henry Muttoo, Lennox Brown, Pat Amadu Maddy, Emanuel Jegede to name but a few of the young, and not so young, people who got the opportunity to test out their creative skills in an atmosphere of comparative safety.

The Eighties

Carib Theatre Company of which I was a founding member provided the opportunity of directing a number of the company's early shows. I remember vividly a roughly hewn production of the musical version of Barry Reckord's hit of the late sixties *Skyvers* which had mutated in to *StreetWise*. This was poverty stricken theatre in which no one got union rates. Starting off The Abeng in Brixton it toured extensively with great success and produced at least two now well established British actors. Ben Onwookwe and Denise Black who won the Plays and Players Best Supporting Actress that year for her performance in StreetWise. A first for a black production.

However the stress of not only directing the show, but driving the bus, doing the props finally got to me and on the last night of the tour after having driven up the M4 from Bristol and having ferried all six members of the cast home I was unable to find a parking space outside my home in Kilburn. The bus was abandoned, keys in the ignition in the middle of Buckley Road. The hope was that by morning it would have been towed away. But there it remained bright and early Sunday morning sitting pretty.

Ken Chubb founder of the Tricycle Theatre persuaded me that I had to find out how the arts funding system worked if I was to get out of the rut. I soon found myself as the first black woman drama officer at 105 Piccadilly the home of the Arts Council of Great Britain. Two years later I really was more ready for the fray of directing in subsidised theatre. If memory serves me well, on leaving the Arts Council and working as a freelance director I experienced a real whirlwind period of just over a year which included *Fishing* by Paulette Randall remembered for the innovative set designed and executed by Lubaina Himid, *A Raisin in the Sun* for The Black Theatre Co-operative which started life at the Trike with Carmen Munroe as a formidable Mama, two productions *of Two Can Play* with Rudolph Walker as Jim and Mona Hammond and Carmen Munroe as Gloria ,one of which breached the portals of the Bristol Old Vic, *Sticky Fingers* by Michael Ellis at Dan Crawfords' Kings Head, *Moondance Night* by Edgar White, *Blood Sweat and Fears* by Maria Oshodi. *Schools Out* and Earl Lovelace's *The New Hardware Store* and a number of eminently forgettable efforts.

Talawa 1985-2002

The result of my application in 1985 to the soon to be dissolved Greater London Assembly for funding to produce a fully blown presentation of CLR James *The Black Jacobins* which turned out to be the first production of the fledgling company Talawa. For the next seventeen years I was the Artistic Director of this company. Although I worked occasionally for other companies such as the National Theatre for whom I directed *Blood Wedding,* and Teatro Limonaia in Italy amongst others, the bulk of my energies were devoted to leading Talawa. This was never very easy but it was always exciting. Of the many plays I directed for Talawa some stand out in the memory but none more than *The Gods Are Not to Blame,* Ola Rotimi's Nigerian take on the Oedipus story and the way in which the production came together after spending only three weeks in Nigeria researching it. Nigerian Gods and their idiosyncrasies have been the life time study of many academics but the production all came together in a miraculous way. The research was just enough not to get bogged down in ritual, the casting was near perfect, Ellen Cairns' design was inspired in its simplicity and the audiences were supportive and enthusiastic. This production gave meaning to my belief that African/black plays can travel well. Confidence flowed for quite a few people.

The Importance of Being Earnest was rehearsed in Newcastle over a three weeks period. This was the first co-production which Talawa had undertaken and which played in the enormous Newcastle Opera House. I wonder if I would have chosen to direct this play of all plays with an all black cast had I had second sight of the outrage it would cause. Perhaps not. But I did and the company had to survive the often caustic comments in the press. It did so because of the audience reaction which was overwhelmingly positive, even receiving a rare plaudit from Oscar Wilde's only living relative who thought the play has had twenty years taken of it! I learned not to fear the critics too much after that. We found our audiences never read them and that a good vibe in the theatre bar or café, together with positive word of mouth has always been a more essential element in the success of black work.

One Love by Kwame Dawes the Rastafarian musical based on a famous Jamaican novel of the 50s Brother Man is also a production I will not quickly forget. Not the end product so much as the process. One Love was commissioned by Talawa and I was able to work with the playwright from the inception of the idea, which was mine, to the delivery on the stage of England's oldest working theatre the wonderful Bristol Theatre Royal with whom it was co-produced. A have a soft spot for this production because perhaps 'they' said it couldn't be done but it was and the often sold out houses often composed of first time theatre goers testified to its appeal. In fact, many people still tell me it can't be done.

The Shakespeare plays which Talawa produced were challenges of another sort. When working as an actress in the National Theatre's production of The Crucible playing Tituba of course, I happened to be whiling away the long dress rehearsal hours between Act 1 and my next entrance which wasn't for hours, resting in the back of the Dress Circle of the Comedy Theatre when I overheard a conversation between the then Artistic Director and a friend. The thrust of the exchange was that black actors 'just simply could not be expected to 'do' Shakespeare; they simply aren't suited.' I am ashamed to say I did not make my presence known whether it was because I was anxious to keep my job which came with a big photograph of me outside a West End Theatre or perhaps I was too cowardly. However, I knew this belief needed to be challenged.

Thus, during my stint with the company we produced three Shakespeare plays with mainly black casts: *Anthony and Cleopatra . King Lear*, and *Othello*. When national companies started casting 'my' actors in leading Shakespearean roles, as they did with David Harewood whose first big role was Edmund in Talawa's King Lear and who was soon cast as the National's Othello, it was not longer necessary to continue with this programming.

Not that the immense challenge of directing these great plays was not rewarding and enlightening, but to be honest the reasons for their choice were part political and not purely artistic. This truth should be more honestly acknowledged by those who grant the funds. Black theatre, and there is such a thing, does have different constraints from white theatre, apart from agreeing that production values must be high at all times.

An important part of my work in theatre has been to open up, almost by any means possible, the wonderful world of live theatre to as many black people as possible. This was not to the exclusion of whites but surely there were sufficient people working on their behalf?

One way was to encourage workshops which offered with each succeeding play insights into the world of theatre to any group which cared to take us up on the offer. And many did. I think this is now called outreach.

Another way was to market personally: for example I remember walking through the market during lunch breaks in Bristol with Carmen Munroe on one side and Rudolph Walker on the other chatting to, and showering leaflets on, likely prospective target audience members (i.e. any black person we saw). Both actors were often recognised from the 'tele' and that helped take the news into the community. Years later the cast of *The Importance* ran the gamut of the Newcastle market stalls to do likewise very successfully. I guess this doesn't sound very strategic or sophisticated in these digital days. We did this, not because we were total strangers to more accepted marketing methods, but because we were stickling with tried and tested community traditions.

When you are trying to break new ground, when there is no tradition or even expectation of getting black people to believe that theatre has anything to do with them, when they feel that even to enter a theatre, you had almost to bribe people to take part. Once in, they stayed and even returned. No point in doing excellent work to nobody.

Building an audience also from among the young was essential. Talawa's Summer school under the expert leadership of Greta Mendez produced some fine young black actors who now grace national stages in England. The summer schools did more than train successful actors, it trained an audience from which theatre in Britain continues to benefit.

I realised that young black women were not really writing for theatre, and set about securing funding from The London Arts Board for Talawa to run a scheme for Black Women writers to work with established playwrights in order to hone latent skills in this area by giving opportunities of working with distinguished theatre professionals. This scheme has over the years paid decent dividends.

I left the running of Talawa in 2003 because I felt I had done what I could and because of the very real danger of repeating myself. The time was right for a younger, brighter, dynamic director to take over the reigns of the company since when I have been directing outside of Britain for fun, and returning to revamp the Barn in Jamaica, writing books and generally existing in a comparatively stress free but continuing theatrical zone. I had no desire to work in England again but a nice project has just come up and there she goes. AGAIN.

Yvonne Brewster
June 2005

VALERIE MASON-JOHN (AKA QUEENIE)

UNCENSORING MY WRITING

My writing career began at Leeds University. Female students had a lot of fear, we were recovering from the murders of the Yorkshire Ripper. Once he was caught, it gave us permission to vent our anger. The University gave us a women's centre, provided a free taxi service to female students after dark, and financed a women's magazine called Jezebel. I was one of the founding editorial team.

I dropped out of university in the second year, and moved to London. The three things I learnt during my time there, was politics, standing on picket lines in support of the miners strike at 4.30 in the morning, and listening to their difficult stories. I combined the three and became a hard nosed political journalist covering, Broad Water Farm Riots in the 80s, the political upheaval in Nicaragua, and South Africa. I became an international correspondent, covering the Aboriginal Land Rights, and Black deaths in custody, in Australia.

After living and working in Australia for two years I hit a crisis, I asked myself was I a political activist or a journalist, I realised then I had to let go of my job. I realised it was impossible to tell the true stories, the media didn't want the truth, and it was these stories I wanted to tell the world, but didn't know how.

[Photo credit: Michelle Martinoli]

Aged 27 I returned home, and the stage of theatre opened up to me. I had always been fascinated by clowning, mime and physical theatre. And a friend of mine suggested I take a break and go on a clowning course. I did a two week course at City Lit college in London, which lead me to training with the Desmond Jones School of Mime and Physical Theatre for 15 months.

I learnt to tell stories, and the basic structure of putting plays together. I became liberated, I realised I could say anything I wanted in theatre, without it being censored before my audience got to see it. During this time I wrote my first one woman show, *Body Politics*. This explored the themes of sexual abuse, rape, and eating disorders, and how they were dependent upon each other. It was a raw and powerful show, and performers like Bobby Baker, told me I must keep on writing and performing. This show was never performed in a theatre house, and yet it toured through out England and Scotland, and its success was word of mouth. It was very much a play of the early 90s.

While training I had to earn my rent and so continued to half heartedly be a journalist. I was also commissioned to write my first non fiction book. While flying abroad for work I became obsessed by the sea, and felt an overwhelming desire to paint it on canvas. And then I realised although I couldn't paint, I could write, and set about writing a series of poems about the sea. I wrote eight in total and they became the material for my next production *Surfing the Crone*, commissioned by the Institute of Contemporary Arts, in the mid 90s.

I collaborated with the choreographer Delta Streete, and the new era musician Nigel Shaw. Together we created a multi-media choreo poetic play, exploring the themes of strong and courageous women. It was an enjoyable process, but I realised that I needed new input, if I was to continue to write plays.

I attended several courses, and wrote my box office sell out *Sin Dykes*. The title came from the idea of the women behaving badly on the scene. I had grown up as a young adult during the era of lesbian separatism, and black lesbian separatism. The latter culture was vehemently in protest against relationships between black and white women, and the former culture was vehemently in protest against women penetrating their lover with sex toys, and sado masochism. Night clubs had been threatened with axes for having S and M nights, and black women who had white lovers were often ostracised. The debates at conferences were fascinating, and so I dared to write a play exploring these themes.

It began with a rehearsed reading, and the Oval House Theatre investing in the play. Along with private sponsorship, the play was produced. Writing about some of these themes as a journalist would have been almost impossible, but as a playwright I got away with it. Not just in the lesbian and gay world, 40 % of my audience was heterosexual.

The show sold out, in the first week of its run, and there was demand for it to tour nationally. Sadly because I was not known to the now defunct London Arts, no revenue could be found to finance the tour. Interestingly in the past year I've had interest from the USA and Germany about a new production. It seems these issues are still very relevant, in the heterosexual, lesbian and gay communities.

However this show got me noticed by the funders. And I received money for research and development from Diverse Opportunities for my next show. I set about writing a new one woman show. My time in Australia had a huge impact on me. I was often moved by my white Australian friends who told me about looking through the family album and finding heads cut out. After much probing they discovered this was an Aboriginal relative of theirs which had 'blighted' the family.

Coupled with this, I was also interested in Queen Sophia Charlotte, married to King George VI who was half African half German. I used this material along with a picture of an aristocratic French family to tell the story of a black woman who was indeed Queen. The research for this was fascinating as I learned there was a French Queen who also gave birth to a black child, and who they locked up for her entire life.

This material gave birth to *Sweep It Under the Carpet*, a twenty minute piece for the Leading Black Theatre company Talawa. It went on rep at the Lyric Theatre. Critics wrote, 'one of the most startling subversions of racial imagery that Britain has ever seen,' and named me as one of the new most adventurous performers. I realised then that this had to be a full length show.

With the help of some more research and development funding, I rewrote the show and renamed it *Brown Girl In the Ring*. I most definitely know I could never have got away with telling this story as a journalist. Every national paper refused to believe that the Great Great Grand mother of Queen Victoria was half African half German. I even rang up a journalist at the Evening Standard, who said 'what! our Queen?'

It toured nationally and my audiences loved it. My reviews ranged from the sublime to the most hilarious, to lumbering around on stage. After extensive research proving that my fact was right, The Sunday Times eventually printed an article after the show had closed, naming me a political activist. I realised then I was perhaps a little ahead of my times. The British public was not ready for me to tell the truth in 1999 and six years later I feel itchy to bring this play back alive.

This play widened my audience, and I was asked what else I had written. I realised then that I wanted to write for a wider audience. I chucked my job in as the artistic director of London Mardi Gras Arts Festival, and embarked on an MA in Creative Writing and the Arts at Sussex University in the autumn of 1999.

I had also received funding to develop an idea of mine. I wanted to write a fairy tale, which fused the melting pot of cultures that I lived among. I came up with the idea, of re writing a fairy tale, Snow White and Rose Red. What if the protagonists were African and Asian. This opened me up to the world of Anansi the trickster in African Fable, and Kali the Asian Goddess of the night. I had the essence of my fairy tale, and then also lent from the pantomime tradition.

It was a family show aimed at all cultures. It was the first Christmas show of the New Stratford Circus. Writing within this genre allowed me to enter the imaginative world of the child, and share this with an adult audience as well.

Since completing my Masters I have written one play for children *The Totz* exploring gender, power and play, and a new one woman show *The Perfect Road*, exploring abuse in a sequence of classical poetic forms like the sonnet and the villanelle.

I have also completed my debut novel *Borrowed Body* published by Serpents Tail 2005; critics have named it the 'British Color Purple'. A new non fiction book *Detox Your Heart* was published by Windhorse 2005.

I will always write plays. It is my most exciting medium to write in. To see a director take my work, discover all the things I didn't realise I had written, and then see the actors bring the characters alive is a real privilege and joy. Writing is one of my passions, I love to tell stories.

As for my next play, forgiveness is the theme. What if you were five years old in the front passenger seat of a car, with your father driving. He runs a pedestrian over at the zebra crossing, doesn't stop, speeds of into the night, and tells you that you haven't seen anything.

My work as a writer is to enable people to think about issues that concern our lives. I am passionate about writing, and will write without commission or funding. If I have something to say, I am confident it will be heard.

Valerie Mason-John was born on 22 November 1962 in Cambridge. She is a member of the Western Buddhist Order, and works as a writer across genres. She is a trainer in anger management and conflict resolution. Valerie Mason-John won the Windrush Achievement Awards 2000 Arts and community pioneer for her contribution as a writer and performance artist to the Black and Asian Communities.

Produced Plays
Body Politics (one woman show) 1991
(Worked as a performer/actor – 1991 and 1999)
Surfing the Crone – 1995
Sweep it Under the Carpet -- 1997 (one woman show)
Brown Girl In the Ring -- 1998/1999 (one woman show)

Sin Dykes -- 1998
The Adventures of Snow Black and Rose Red -- 2000/01
The Perfect Road – 2003/4
The Totz – 2004

Published Books
Novel – *Borrowed Body*, Serpents Tail, 2005
Collection of plays, poetry and prose – *Brown Girl In The Ring,* Get a Grip, 1999

Published Non Fiction
Detox Your Heart (ways of working with anger, fear and hatred),Windhorse
    Publications, 2005
Talking Black, Cassell, 1995
Making Black Waves, Scarlett Press, 1993

Valerie Mason-John
June 2005

SOL B. RIVER

SERIOUS BUSINESS

I never thought of it as that, a serious business. I never thought that it would become as staid as it sometimes does. The responsibility, the so called success and failure of a life in the theatre. If I would have known, I would have reconsidered. But... I would rather tussle to keep up the vision and feeling that almost commands me to hold on to the dream of the stage. A dream that when fully realized feels like a continual rebirth, one that informs your vocation on earth.

I never thought that my race would become so significant within my career as a writer/director. Phone calls, e-mails, saying, we are looking for a black writer. Why? Because we have to fill a remit. Do you? Yes. Nobody has ever told me that they have to fulfil a remit, but it's on the agenda at the moment and many do not understand why. A friend told me that a mature audience member at our local theatre said, 'They're taking over'.

The remit for diversity should be filled by conscience, acknowledgement and progression. A natural diversity. And above all it should be filled by drama of the highest quality that claims its place in continual moments of theatrical history, a little less obviously than now.

In the first instance my work informed nothing, except that which I thought would make a dramatically entertaining piece but with a social conscience. In the second instance I realized that it would be a good idea to find my voice. In the third instance I thought the best thing would be to find the voice of the people, of the characters. That is the reason for me enclosing groups of plays within what I call albums.

I have to ask myself on witnessing established, mature theatre audiences, what is it they want, what is it they are getting? Are we writers fulfilling our responsibility, are we allowed to? Or is a career like living in a hope? This is a serious business, there is no doubt about that, it has the ability to devastate but also evaluate.

There has to be a certain amount of fantasy about the theatre. There has to be a degree of fantasy concerning life, since that is escapism. The definition of fantasy in theatrical terms for me is in the realization of the work for a live audience. If fantasy is the flight of imagination then you have the opportunity to travel toward realization. The realization that I seek to present is social truth and ideas with a commitment to style, eminence and foundation. There has to be and I have to consider through longevity, the moral and social implications of my philosophical thought process as well as the ethic. My job is to ask characters to inform me and then you of what you might not have had time to consider, and to present work that might hold you by the neck, hand or heart or any other part of the body that the character has chosen. I do this because that's what the characters need to do. I do this because it is not my belief that society should be mute. I have my ear to the ground and I want to tell you what I heard. Old men shall have visions and young men dream dreams.

My cultural background is preoccupied with circumstance, parts of my career has also has been a condition of the same.

So, what would I have been, or what yet might I still have to become? If I hadn't embarked on this social trip of exploration and execution? Nothing. Maybe something. Who would have decided that for me? Be all you can be .. Ask not what your country can do for you. ...

I was allowed to witness for myself formidable alienation. Make yourself a home and then attempt to feel safe within it. Occasionally venture out and witness the society within which you not only have to survive but strive. It is becoming old hat now, isn't it? Talking about what the motherland promised, shouting about the deception while others that look like me (never mind those that don't) say, 'just get on with it'. Get on with what? If I take a pick of a few moments from memory, the instances that captivate moments, I remember the land that as a child I was informed was home. It was indeed home. Born here. Endeavour here. Die here. I remember. But I am not predestined to move in any certain direction, it is not inevitable that I should be conditioned to do what one might ignorantly or stereotypically expect from a young man who is part of the cultural heritage. My cultural heritage consists of a realization enriched by certain experiences that not only help you see yourself in this country, in this world, but also how others see you. In theatre, in writing, the narrative, the character, the subliminal-allegory are some of the instrumental tools of the trade. The conflict, the cause and effect of the conflict should eventually wind its way to telling us some truth. The motivation and purpose + conflict, the cause and effect of the conflict should eventually wind its way to telling us some truth. Truth that bears fruits of longevity, not trivial truth but social truth that expresses the talents. It is at that point of truth that I have found it most difficult.

V

Are we agreed that drama is worldwide? Then we must also be in agreement that it is a catalyst for enlightenment and education. The agenda for dramatic education through the wonder of the stage seems to have been left stagnant. I'm not talking about theatre in education where so many so called ethnic writers are thrust. I'm talking about edification - edu-tainment.

I have witnessed the shadow of the literary managers, the commissioning editors and artistic directors, who have a job to do. His job at times is to find fault where there is none, to pass judgement when God has left the room, to insult his own intelligence by not weighing it against the writer's. Get in or get out. My way, our way or no way, that's the formula. I think there has been a genuine neglect and mistreatment of the theatre writer. Showing an intention to care has not necessarily led to a duty to, and that care could just be understanding. Writers' centres, script readers and reports are futile unless a genuine structure is in place that works in terms of opportunity, production and longevity. The self-congratulatory foolishness – non-progress and still-like vision is what I witness on many a theatrical night. Sometimes I have difficulty in understanding the most basic of drama, since the industry can give the impression that it is too technically difficult for even the practitioner to understand. For the life of me, I have never been able to comprehend that misconception that education was not for life. The definition of education commands that we continue to learn. How be it then that I find myself so consistently surrounded by theatrical individuals who profess to know so much more than I. Maybe they do, each one teach one. But I wouldn't be .... or should I be so arrogant to claim that I am aware of myself too. It is that domination. That, hype of belief. The complacency, the assumption, the misinterpretation and the ultimate failure to listen and attempt to comprehend that prevents our understanding of the sacred stage and who has a right to be on it being fully explored. I mean in a cultural or in any sense. I am not about to define myself or my work according to the title of the book within which this work is contained. I'm more definite than that. But this is the route I have been so often offered with regard to my voice. We have to be specific sometimes, but we have to decide where and why. I thought we were a multicultural society. Who is excluded from that? The majority? The realization should be for anyone described as ethnic, BME, multicultural, black, Asian, migrant or whatever tag is stuck on to your behind, that you are a member of the human race. If you present within the specifics of culture, that is a prerequisite and a prerogative to the understanding of that culture. It doesn't mean it should be so subject to prejudice, individual scrutiny and initiatives that enforce xenophobia and marginalized sub-standard theatre. So it can present itself within itself or, it can cross over. Look in your history books, this has all been said.

I have seen much sub-standard theatre of late, in high-ranking spaces, that has commanded finance via initiative. Black theatre practitioners are not exempt from creating this sub-standard theatre in their desperation to see their work on a recognised stage; they should be aware of misleading an audience by perpetuating narratives that only concern stagnant motive. Teaching us nothing new, looking no further beyond narratives with pitiful constraint to new and established audience. Often theatre managers in the regions are noticed sneaking out the back door saying we've done what they asked now lets get on with some real theatre, we can't fill the seats anyway. The work has done this by way of forcing its way through the door via an argument for equality. Force should not be the issue, however often it has to be, positive integration wherein the theatre managers look again at their own programming and look again at the audience, look at your board members and look at yourselves. You can achieve a more natural progression this way. Do it honestly, before your audiences die. Since progress with no desire or passion or supposed progress without responsibility, void of real intention, will have no sustainability.

I am sometimes encouraged by the US, and the African American claim on their flag, the organization of their initiatives and institutions including theatre. This is not to say they don't have their own diversity issues. But they have a certain realization of the aesthetic, marketing and economic/cultural viability. A main house theatre in England is more likely to take on a piece considered as an African American classic than any would-be British equivalent, and then they cry 'Where are the writers?' The last two plays I witnessed (in the same week) which could be accredited to $1^{st}/2^{nd}$ generation Black-British, African-British, Afro-Caribbean (whatever the latest description is) concerned gun crime. Why are we so bad at looking into the future and taking note, while consulting the past.

We look on in the direction of the progression of the African American, but it is worth considering that they are older than us and that the West Indian in Britain has twice moved, once from Africa and then again from the West Indies. But much is to be learned from their education and their experience of civil rights, a struggle that created a fusion, an understanding and a programme of self-realization from which they have segregated and integrated, but above all have created opportunity to progress. They have been assertive.

Race is not the only prejudice, but in the continuing charge for equality by under-represented and disadvantaged groups, race, civil rights movements and individuals of note are very much the yardstick by which equality is measured. It is misguided to confuse race with any other prejudice or scheme of equality. The only thing that has placed me in such a position to comment so frequently on the subject of race, is my existence in this place.

Theatre is a massive team effort, the various individuals that come together to be involved in the creation of a work are invaluable. But before that, one should take some time to remember the writer and his thought, to remember the writer and the blank screen or page.

I have known many writers, writers that have shook more hands than written words, writers who believe the network is the most important thing - it's who you know isn't it?

But I try to remember my purpose. The purpose is to examine the stage, examine the moral integrity within one's self. Examine the social comment but listen to one conversation at a time. After that lay down your life for the audience. I wish I could say that a life is a life but some seem to be worth less than others. It is important then to breathe reality into any time. I create for the stage and through that hope that you, the audience, are captivated, that you are taken to a place that will remain in memory and remind your subconscious. That way I will have contributed to the wealthier existence of life which is born through understanding.

Sol B. River
2005

www.solbriver.com

Bapsi Sidhwa

Notes on a London Production of *Sock 'em With Honey*

Biographical Note

I was born in Karachi and grew up in Lahore. I began writing in my twenties after the birth of two children. In 1978, when publishing in English was non-existent in Pakistan, I self-published my novel *The Crow Eaters*. Jonathan Cape published *The Crow Eaters* in England in 1980. While *The Bride* was the first novel I wrote, it was the second to be published by Cape in 1982.

Ice-Candy-Man, my third novel, was published in the UK by Heinemann and by Milkweed in USA. It was a New York Times Notable Book for1991 and was listed among the best books in English by The Modern Library (Picador, June 1999, London). *Ice-Candy-Man*, [*Cracking India* in US] was made into the film *Earth* by Canadian director Deepa Mehta in 1999.

An American Brat, my latest book, was published by Milkweed in USA in 1994.

My novels have been translated into several European languages, Russian and Hindi. I held a Bunting Fellowship at Harvard in 1987. In 1991 I received the Sitara-i-Imtiaz, Pakistan's highest national honor in the arts, and the Lila Wallace-Reader's Digest Writer's Award In 1994. I was inducted into the Zoroastrian Hall of Fame in 2000.

In Lahore I did voluntary work in destitute women's and children's centres and orphanages. I worked on grassroots women's issues for years, including protesting – utilizing community mobilization and the media – against repressive measures aimed at women and minority communities. I served on Prime Minister Benazir Bhutto's advisory committee on Women's Development. I taught at Columbia University in New York, Mount Holyoke College, Brandeis among others.

My experience as a rookie playwright

In fact I was teaching at Southampton University in 2001 when Kali Theatre Company chanced to bring Rukhsana Ahmed's riveting play: *River Of Fire* to the university. I knew Rukhsana slightly. As I was talking to her after the performance, I mentioned that I had written a play loosely based on my novel *An American Brat*. Rukhsana, in her unassuming and direct way, asked me to mail it to her, explaining that Kali Theatre in London was always on the look out for plays written by Asian Women. I sent it to her with some trepidation – it was my first attempt at playwriting and I knew next to nothing about the genre. I was taken aback when I received a letter from Kali Theatre saying that they would like to option *Feroza Among the Farangees*, provided I was willing to make changes to it under their direction. Of course I was willing – I was euphoric! And elated by the offer of skilled guidance; I was aware of my clumsy attempts to navigate in uncharted terrain.

I received the first of a series of letters I was to receive from Penny Gold and Rukhsana Ahmed. I was told to reduce the 25 characters in my play to about eight, and later steered to amalgamate them and to further reduce them to five. I had characters who appeared only in a scene or two, and, of course, actors cost money. Step by step, under their tactful and skillful direction, I jettisoned some scenes, merged others and reduced the script from 125 pages to 85. I saw a clearer plotline emerge.

At the end of 6 months I was requested to travel to London for a reading of the play with actors. It was to be directed by Turan Ali.

Just before this another fortuitous event occurred; Kitu Gidwani came to say 'hello' after a reading I gave in New York. She had played the role of the Parsi mother in Deepa Mehta's film *Earth*, - based on my novel *Cracking India*. She is breathtakingly beautiful and with her hair cut she looked about nineteen. My heart skipped a beat - she would make a perfect Feroza. I told her about the reading in London and wistfully asked if she'd play the young heroine. To my amazement she agreed readily – it would coincide with her planned visit to London.

I arrived at the theater in London and met Penny Gold, my guiding angel, for the first time. My other guiding angel Rukhsana introduced me to the Turan Ali. He was a confident and affable young man of Turkish origins. The actors were going over their scripts; I was relieved to see Kitu. After discussing their roles with Turan Ali the actors huddled in small groups to practice, and then they arranged themselves on chairs as for the reading.

The earlier scenes in Lahore were as hilarious as I had expected and then some. The wonderful actors revealed aspects of their roles I hadn't even imagined. Later, when the location shifted to London, Kitu, as Feroza, was disappointing. But the actress who read the pivotal part of her mother, Zareen, was so frightfully miscast she sent shivers down my spine. During the interval Rukhsana walked me up and down and explained they couldn't get the actress they wanted and had to, at the last minute, recruit the poor woman. After the interval, when her role became more demanding, I was reduced to tears. I was a novice; it was the first time I was seeing my favourite character embodied and my reaction was extreme. Almost three years have passed since then and I now feel like an old hand. I've learnt to keep my expectations realistic and my emotions in check; I know everything can be taken care of. In fact I have learned to sit back and enjoy the experience.

Early in the play Cyrus, agitated by Feroza's decision to marry a non-Parsee, says to Zareen: 'We'll buy him off. I will give you the money.' Turan Ali thought it was a great line that needed to be developed. He made me hastily write a scene in which Zareen, in London, actually offers the shocked suitor money. This scene was eventually fleshed out to wonderful effect.

Brooding over Zareen on the flight back to Houston I hit upon a solution. Kitu, I realized was miscast as Feroza, but she would make a wonderful Zareen. A flurry of emails were exchanged. 'Isn't Kitu too young to play Zareen?' an email from London asked. I suggested they see the film Earth in which Kitu plays 8-year-old Lenny's mother to perfection. It was also revealed that Kitu was older than she looked; at 38, she was the right age play Zareen.

And she did. Spectacularly!

The script was, of course, under constant revision.

A month later I was faced with a huge disappointment; Rukhsana Ahmed had decided to leave Kali. I felt my play was being orphaned at a crucial juncture, but she assured me that Janet Steel, her replacement, loved the play and would also direct it.

I went to London again for the rehearsals and became acquainted with the cast. The actors we wanted for the roles of Cyrus and Mumma were not available but their replacements, Rohit Gokani and Norma Dixit were adequate. I had reservations about Sumitra Bhagat, cast as Feroza, but in the end she delivered magnificently. I was amazed how disciplined the actors were and how hard they and the rest of the crew worked. The script was fine-tuned and Janet Steel added a sensational tableau in which Feroza wears a sari. They had only one month of rehearsals.

I could not go for the opening at Leicester Haymarket Studio 20th – 29th Mar. It was just as well because the car loads of friends from London and Switzerland who went for the opening told me the actors fluffed their lines.

In April I flew for the London opening at Cockpit Theater. It was preceded by a wonderful event organized around it by the renowned Indian playwright Girish Karnad, at the Nehru Center. The Pakistan Ambassador gave a reception for the team at his home, attended, among others, by [late] Ismail Merchant.

I was enchanted to see the play performed on stage. Thankfully by now the actors knew their lines. There is a scene in which an actor smashes a glass underfoot. When the lights dimmed between scenes not only did I pick up some shards I thought the actors had overlooked, but I even directed a young man sitting closer to some other shards to do so. After the play the actors gathered around me and told me to never ever do that. I could tell they were quite aghast. There was a certain space at the edge of the stage no one in the audience was to ever cross. I was suitably abashed.

I attended the play several times with friends as it played to full houses. Vikram Seth called back with a superb analysis and I kept his suggestions in mind when I was writing later drafts. My friends Antonia Byatt and Aamer Hussein had valuable comments.

I discovered the elation a playwright goes through with each successful performance, and the dismay when the actors are not at their best. The reviewer from Time Out attended the play on a day when Kitu Gidwani, disturbed by some rowdy elements in the audience, gave what I thought was a flat performance. She got special mention in a rave review nevertheless!

But the most important bit of knowledge I imbibed was that a play is endlessly a work in progress. Since the London production the play has had two dramatized readings in New York under the able direction of Madhur Jaffery, and three in Houston. The setting of the play has reverted to Houston – where it was originally located. The Jewish grandmother Esther, who was only mentioned in the earlier avatars of the play was brought on stage for the last reading on May 14th 05. The reading received a standing ovation from an audience 250 people.

The Stages Repertory Theater of Houston plans a production of the play in fall of 2006. It will be titled *An American Brat.*

Bapsi Sidhwa
New York 2005

EDITOR AND CONTRIBUTOR BIOGRAPHIES

Elizabeth Barry is a Lecturer in English at the University of Warwick. She is completing a monograph on Samuel Beckett, language and authority. She works in the fields of British and European theatre, modernism and stylistics, and has published on modernism and cliché, Samuel Beckett, Jean Genet, James Joyce and J.M. Coetzee.

William Boles is an Associate Professor of English and Director of Film Studies at Rollins College in Winter Park, Florida. He is also Artistic Director of Darkness Visible Radio Theatre.

Claire Cochrane is Senior Lecturer in Drama and Performance Studies at University College Worcester. She is the author of *Birmingham Rep: A City's Theatre 1962-2002* (Sir Barry Jackson Trust: 2003). Birmingham born and bred, she currently serves as a director on the Boards of MAC (Midlands Arts Centre) and ArtSites, Birmingham.

Anthony Frost is a Lecturer in Drama and Director of the UEA Studio Theatre at the University of East Anglia. He was educated at RADA and the University of Birmingham, before helping to found the drama degree programmes at UEA. Frost is the co-author of *Improvisation in Drama* (Basingstoke: Macmillan 1990) and has edited *Theatre Theories: From Plato to Virtual Reality* (Norwich: Pen & Inc, 2000).

Dimple Godiwala has taught at various American and British Universities in England. Until recently, she was Senior Lecturer at York St John College (University of Leeds) where she taught drama and postcolonial theory. She writes mainly about twentieth century British culture viewing it through the lens of feminist, black and queer theatre. She is the author of the monographs *Breaking the Bounds: British Feminist Dramatists Writing in the Mainstream since c. 1980* (New York & Oxford: Peter Lang, 2003) and *Queer Mythologies: The Original Stageplays of Pam Gems* (Bristol & Portland: Intellect, 2005). Godiwala is currently compiling a critical anthology *Alternatives Within the Mainstream II: Postwar British Queer Theatres* for Cambridge Scholars Press.

AACIONEAlternatives within the Mainstream

Dominic Hingorani trained as an actor at The Royal Scottish Academy of Music and Drama and worked extensively in theatre, radio, television and film. Hingorani is a professional theatre director and Associate Director of Conspirators' Kitchen Theatre Company. He is a freelance lecturer/director in contemporary drama theory and practice. Hingorani has published articles on British Asian Theatre include 'Binglishing Britain' for *Contemporary Theatre Review*.

Samuel Kasule is Senior Lecturer and Programme Leader (English) at the University of Derby. He teaches African and South Asian literatures and drama. Kasule's research is in the field of East African oral music performance and drama. His publications on Black performance include: 'Climates of Performance: Ethnicity, Folk, Performance, Language and Theatre in a Post-authoritarian state' in E. Wamala et al (eds.), *Africa in World Affairs: Challenges to Humanities*, Kampala, Faculty of Arts (2004); 'Nze Bwemba Nnyimba Saagala Anyumya : Savouring Activity and Diversity in Uganda Today', written in collaboration with Peter Cooke, in *Cahiers de Musiques Traditionelles: Nouveaux Enjeux*, Geneva. Switzerland (1998)

Valerie Kaneko Lucas is Assistant Professor in Theatre at the Ohio State University, where she also develops outreach and diversity initiatives as OSU Extension State Specialist in the Arts. Her current research interests are in the areas of hybridity, British Asian and Black British writers from the post-Empire diaspora, and a comparative study of British-Asian and Asian American theatres. Lucas's articles and conference presentations have discussed the work of Tara Arts, Tadashi Suzuki, and most recently, the creation of *Hidden Voices*, a docudrama on the Japanese American internment.

Zodwa Motsa is an Associate Professor in the Department of English Studies, University of South Africa. She is a critic, translator and dramatist who has published widely in both English and SiSwati, her mother-tongue. Her works in drama include the plays: *Of Heroes and Man* (1985), *Lahloma Ladvumà* (1992) and *'Dladla Sembube* (1998) as well as the article, 'The Missing Link in SiSwati Drama' in *Pre-colonial and Post-colonial Drama and Theatre in Africa*, ed. Losambe Lokangaka, 2001. Motsa's latest contribution is the revival of Wole Soyinka's 1950s anti-apartheid play *The Invention* which she has edited (Unisa Press 2005).

Deirdre Osborne is a Lecturer at Goldsmiths College, University of London. Her publications in Black British Drama and Theatre are: 'A Recent Look at Black Women Playwrights' in Kadija George ed. *Six Black and Asian Women Playwrights* (London: Aurora Metro, 1993. Reprinted 2005); 'Judging a Book by Its Cover: Race, Reading and the Search for Identity in Kwame Kwei-Armah's *Fix Up*' in Susanne Peters, Klaus Stierstorfer, Laurenz Volkmann eds. *Teaching Contemporary Literature and Culture Vol.1* (Verlag: Wissenschaftlicher Verlag Trier 2005), and 'In Celebration of Dona Daley' *Sable: Black Lit Mag* Autumn/Fall 2004 Issue 5.

Kathleen Starck holds a post-doctoral position in British literature at Bremen University. Previously, she has taught British and American literature and cultural studies at Leipzig University. Her research interests include contemporary British and American drama, postcolonial/transcultural studies, feminist and masculinity studies, men's lifestyle magazines, and gender in British and American literature and film. She is the author of *'I Believe in the Power of Theatre.' British Women's Drama of the 1980s and 1990s* (Trier: WVT, 2005). Currently she is co-editing (with Cecile Sandten and Martina Schrader-Kniffki) *Transkulturelle Begegnungen.* (Trier: WVT, 2005).

Ashley Tellis is Assistant Professor in British and Anglophone Literatures and Women's Studies at Eastern Illinois University. He writes on gay and lesbian theory, South Asian literature and contemporary women's poetry. He is the author of 'The Well of Homeliness: South Asian Queers in Britain' in Kate Chedgzoy, Emma Francis, Murray Pratt, eds. *In A Queer Place: Sexuality and Belonging in British and European Contexts* (London: Ashgate, 2002).

Alda Terracciano has extensively researched intercultural and black British theatre and contributed to academic publications and conferences in the UK and internationally. She was consultant to the Arts Council and Heritage Lottery Fund on Cultural Diversity and researched the Theatre Museum Archive Collections for the publication on *Black and Asian Performance at the Theatre Museum: A Users' Guide.* She is Co-founder and Director of 'Future Histories', the first national repository for African, Asian and Caribbean performing arts in the UK. She is currently a Visiting Academic at Middlesex University.

Victor Ukaegbu is Senior Lecturer in Drama and Performance at University College Northampton. Recent publications include 'Femi Osofisan's *Once Upon Four Robbers* : Continuing the Intercultural Debate' in *African Theatre*

2: Playwrights and Politics; (2001); 'The Problem with Definitions: An Examination of Applied Theatre in Traditional African Context(s)' in *National Drama*; Volume 3, June 2004; 'Performing Postcolonially: Contextual Changes in the Adaptations of Wole Soyinka's *Death and the King's Horseman* and Femi Osofisan's *Once Upon Four Robbers'*, in *World Literature Written in English* Volume 40, No. 1.